All the Way with LBJ

The 1964 Presidential Election

All the Way with LBJ mines an extraordinarily rich but underused source – the full range of LBJ tapes – to analyze the 1964 presidential campaign and the political culture of the mid-1960s.

The president achieved a smashing victory over a divided Republican party, which initially considered Henry Cabot Lodge II, then U.S. ambassador to South Vietnam, before nominating Barry Goldwater, who used many of the themes that later worked for Republicans – a Southern strategy, portraying the Democrats as soft on defense, raising issues such as crime and personal ethics. Johnson countered with what he called a "frontlash" strategy, appealing to moderate GOP suburbanites, but he failed to create a new, permanent Democratic majority for the post–civil rights era.

The work's themes – the impact of race on the political process, the question of politicians' personal and political ethics, and the tensions between politics and public policy – continue to resonate.

Robert David Johnson is currently a Professor in the Department of History at Brooklyn College and the CUNY Graduate Center. He held the Fulbright Distinguished Chair in the Humanities at Tel Aviv University for the 2007–8 academic year. He is author of *Congress and the Cold War* (Cambridge, 2005), *20 January 1961: The American Dream* (1999), *Ernest Gruening and the American Dissenting Tradition* (1998), and *The Peace Progressives and American Foreign Relations* (1995); coauthor of *Until Proven Innocent: Political Correctness and the Shameful Injustices of the Duke Lacross Rape Case* (2007); and coeditor of volumes 2, 3, 4, and 5 of *The Presidential Recordings: Lyndon Johnson* (2007). For audio excerpts of many conversations cited in this book, see http://allthewaywithlbj.com.

All the Way with LBJ

The 1964 Presidential Election

ROBERT DAVID JOHNSON
Brooklyn College, City University of New York

CAMBRIDGE UNIVERSITY PRESS
Cambridge, New York, Melbourne, Madrid, Cape Town, Singapore, São Paulo, Delhi

Cambridge University Press
32 Avenue of the Americas, New York, NY 10013–2473, USA

www.cambridge.org
Information on this title: www.cambridge.org/9780521737524

First published 2009

Printed in the United States of America

A catalog record for this publication is available from the British Library.

Library of Congress Cataloging in Publication data
Johnson, Robert David, 1967–
All the way with LBJ : the 1964 presidential election / Robert David Johnson.
p. cm.
ISBN 978-0-521-42595-7 (hardback) – ISBN 978-0-521-73752-4 (pbk.)
1. Presidents – United States – Election – 1964. 2. Johnson, Lyndon B. (Lyndon Baines), 1908–1973. 3. Goldwater, Barry M. (Barry Morris), 1909–1998. 4. Political campaigns – United States – History – 20th century. 5. United States – Politics and government – 1963–1969. I. Title.
E850.J64 2009
973.923092–dc22 2008030599

ISBN 978-0-521-42595-7 hardback
ISBN 978-0-521-73752-4 paperback

Contents

Acknowledgments

As with all of my scholarly work, I owe my greatest debt to my parents, J. Robert Johnson and Susan McNamara Johnson; and to my sister, Kathleen Johnson, brother-in-law, Mike Sardo, and nephew, Darrion Sardo.

This book developed out of my affiliation with the Presidential Recordings Project at the Miller Center for Public Affairs, University of Virginia. I am grateful to Ernest May and Philip Zelikow for inviting me to participate in the project (and for their consistent support of my overall scholarly endeavors); and to Tim Naftali, David Shreve, David Coleman, and Kent Germany for all their assistance during my time with the Miller Center. My graduate and undergraduate advisers, Akira Iriye and Tom Schwartz, always have helped me whenever I have asked.

I have been privileged to work with Lew Bateman at Cambridge University Press, which has provided a welcome home for those of us interested in the study of U.S. political and diplomatic history. Anonymous reviewers for the Press provided useful critiques of an earlier version of the book.

Dan Weininger tracked down some of the more obscure newspaper passages cited and offered helpful commentary on several drafts of the manuscript.

I completed this book during a year as a Fulbright professor at the S. Daniel Abraham Center at Tel Aviv University, and I thank Raanan Rein, Ehud Toledano, Neil Sherman, and Judy Stasky for making my year in Israel such a pleasant one.

This project also received assistance and support from Brooklyn colleagues Margaret King, David Berger, Phil Napoli, Steve Remy, Andy Meyer, Paula Fichtner, Lenny Gordon, and Jamie Sanders. My department chairman, David Troyansky, willingly structured my schedule to facilitate research needs. I am also fortunate to work at the City University of New York, where Chancellor Matthew Goldstein and the Board of Trustees have worked hard to create an environment of scholarly excellence.

Finally, this book would never have appeared without the timely and courageous efforts of a remarkable group of Brooklyn College students – Dan Weininger, Brad Appell, Michael Duchaine, Isaac Franco, George Ionnaidis, Bobby Hardamon, Martine Jean, Yehuda Katz, John Makaryus, Nick Paras, Samantha Rosenblum, Christine Sciascia, and Thomas Stoppini. The book is dedicated to each of them.

Prologue

In an October 1964 conversation with Lyndon Johnson, Alex Rose, vice chairman of New York's Liberal Party, gushed, "I've never seen a man running for public office so on top of everything that's going on in the campaign." The president was, Rose continued, his "own campaign manager" – the "star performer" of the election.[1]

Despite his penchant for flattery, Rose in this instance expressed conventional wisdom: ignoring political custom, Lyndon Johnson managed his own campaign. The president involved himself with decisions ranging from how best to trigger a political realignment to determining the size and quantity of the campaign's bumper stickers.

Johnson's centrality to all aspects of his electoral effort might have posed a significant obstacle to examining how he achieved an overwhelming victory against Republican Barry Goldwater. Johnson rarely set his thoughts to paper, and he mistrusted many of the political advisers he inherited from John Kennedy. As a result, the Johnson campaign had no central organization that left behind extensive staff memoranda to explain the campaign's grand strategy or the rationale for its tactical decisions.

In the early 1970s, however, Johnson hinted at the existence of a different type of documentary materials for his campaign. In a conversation with his former aide, Doris Kearns, he spoke of "transcripts" from which,

[1] President Johnson and Alex Rose, 2:22 P.M., 10 Oct. 1964, Tape WH6410.06, Citation #5860, Recordings of Telephone Conversations – White House Series, Recordings and Transcripts of Conversations and Meetings, Lyndon B. Johnson Library [hereafter LBJ Recordings].

he said, she would learn more about the inner workings of politics and government than from 100 political science textbooks.[2]

Johnson was referring to the more than 800 hours of conversations that he secretly recorded during the course of his presidency. For 1964 these tapes consisted almost exclusively of telephone calls. The president certainly was not hesitant about conducting political business over the phone. An aide described him as "on the phone morning, noon, and night – almost any hour. He phones from the dinner table, from the bed, from the swimming pool, from the automobile."[3] A story circulated that Johnson, after failing to reach an aide who was indisposed, had a telephone placed in the aide's bathroom.[4]

These recordings provide a behind-the-scenes narrative of a president and a Democratic partisan coming to grips with the monumental political changes that the Civil Rights Act would produce, with the intersection between international crises and his domestic political needs, with the effects of policy initiatives on his electoral standing, and with personal crises caused by his poisonous relationship with Attorney General Robert Kennedy and the arrest of his closest aide, Walter Jenkins.

This private Johnson demonstrated extraordinarily keen political insights, unmatched by anyone on either side of the campaign (with the possible exception of his wife, Lady Bird). He also possessed a remarkable ability to detect how he could achieve political benefit from public policy developments. But the tapes also reveal a politician willing to employ tactics – trying to smear Goldwater as a member of the Ku Klux Klan, instructing his legal counselor to remove potentially incriminating documents from a White House safe just before FBI agents were scheduled to arrive – that might have troubled even twenty-first-century win-at-any-cost political figures such as the Clintons or Karl Rove.

Francis Sayre, dean of Washington's Episcopal Cathedral (and grandson of perhaps the greatest idealist in twentieth-century American politics, Woodrow Wilson), testified to these contradictions in a widely publicized sermon, delivered in mid-September 1964. After dismissing Goldwater as "a man of dangerous ignorance and devastating uncertainty," Sayre lamented Johnson's dominance of the Democratic national convention, calling the president "a man whose public house is splendid in its every

[2] Doris Kearns, *Lyndon Johnson and the American Dream* (Boston: Houghton Mifflin, 1976), p. 412.

[3] *U.S. News & World Report,* 13 Jan. 1964.

[4] *New York Times,* 1 Feb. 1964.

appearance, but whose private lack of ethic must inevitably introduce termites at the very foundation."[5]

The tension between Johnson's willingness to cross ethical lines and his idealistic policy goals would not have surprised Russell Baker. The long-time *New York Times* columnist described Johnson as "a human puzzle so complicated nobody could ever understand it" – a "storm of human instincts: sinner and saint, buffoon and statesman, cynic and sentimentalist, a man torn between hungers for immortality and self-destruction."[6] Johnson balanced his crusade for civil rights with occasional racist comments. He used government both to improve the lot of the poor and to promote his financial self-interest. His obvious joy in the art of governing and political life coexisted with a self-pitying nature that magnified routine criticism to the level of attacks on his personal integrity. His ability to forge the legislative coalitions necessary to implement his agenda failed to temper an insecurity that sometimes fueled a sense of paranoia. As his onetime protégé – and later adversary – Joe Kilgore recalled, Johnson possessed an amazing capacity to "convince himself of anything, even something that wasn't true."[7] He was a candidate, and a political strategist, unlike anything before in American politics.

Born in 1908 to a strong-willed mother and a father whose reputation for integrity survived the tumultuous world of Texas politics, Lyndon Baines Johnson graduated from Southwest Texas State Teachers College. His first break came in late 1931, in a special election in Texas's 14th Congressional District. Although Johnson's father by that point had fallen on hard times, Richard Kleberg, a conservative Democrat from King County, sought out Sam Johnson's support. After he narrowly won the election, Kleberg named Lyndon as his secretary. In Washington Johnson distinguished himself with his ambition, work ethic, and political skills. He helped manage Kleberg's successful reelection campaign in 1932 and, like many young Texas politicians of the era, supported Franklin Roosevelt's New Deal. In mid-1935 he was rewarded with an appointment as Texas director of the National Youth Administration (NYA).[8]

The New Deal relied on bureaucracies like the NYA to interpret vaguely worded legislation, enhancing the administration's maneuverability.

[5] *Time*, 25 Sept. 1964.

[6] Russell Baker, *The Good Times* (New York: Plume, 1989), pp. 281–2.

[7] Robert Dallek, *Lone Star Rising: Lyndon Johnson and His Times, 1908–1960* (New York: Oxford University Press, 1991), p. 52.

[8] Dallek, *Lone Star Rising*, p. 77.

FDR assembled a talented staff, which bonded in what historian Alan Brinkley described as an "informal pattern of friendships and intellectual associations."[9] This network spread beyond the bounds of former Ivy Leaguers to include strong Roosevelt supporters in Congress, legislators like Claude Pepper of Florida and Maury Maverick of Texas. Johnson gradually entered this circle of New Dealers, coming into contact with figures such as James Rowe, Tommy Corcoran, Abe Fortas, and Ben Cohen. Ideologically, he never relinquished his faith in New Deal liberalism as the most appropriate expression of Democratic idealism.

Johnson, however, was not in Washington to partake in intellectual exchange among the capitol's elite. Throughout his career, he placed a premium on pragmatism, a pattern evident in his work with the NYA. For someone so young, Johnson demonstrated remarkable executive ability during his time with the organization. He also expanded his political contacts. In 1937, when a vacancy opened in the Texas 10th Congressional District, he made a bid for the seat. Employing a slogan of "Franklin D. and Lyndon B.," Johnson defended FDR at a time when the court-packing fight left the president on the political defensive. At the start of the campaign, few observers gave Johnson much of a chance: poorly known in Austin, the heart of the district, he registered only about 5 percent in polls. But by outworking his opposition, he rallied to defeat a field of eight candidates.[10]

For the next eight years Johnson was one of Roosevelt's few consistent backers in an increasingly conservative Texas delegation. The new congressman arrived in Washington as the New Deal was running out of steam; the court-packing scheme galvanized an opposition that eventually coalesced into an alliance between Southern Democrats and Republicans. This conservative coalition remained in place, in various manifestations, until the 1960s, when Johnson would confront it as president.

Blocked on the domestic front, Roosevelt turned his attention to the international situation. In East Asia Japanese expansionism spread beyond Manchuria into other parts of China. In Europe Hitler's German regime discarded the restrictions established by the Treaty of Versailles. Prospects for peace all but vanished in 1938 after Britain and France signed the Munich agreement, which turned over German-speaking areas of Czechoslovakia (along with the country's defenses) to the Third

[9] Alan Brinkley, *The End of Reform: New Deal Liberalism in Recession and War* (New York: Knopf, 1995), p. 52.

[10] Robert A. Caro, *The Years of Lyndon Johnson: Volume 1, The Path to Power* (New York: Knopf, 1982), pp. 185–270.

Reich. The concession failed to appease Hitler, and, when the Germans invaded Poland on September 1, 1939, England and France declared war. Roosevelt inched the United States closer to involvement in the conflict, persuading Congress to weaken the Neutrality Act, first by expanding the cash-and-carry policy, then by approving the Lend-Lease Act.

Johnson supported all of these initiatives, in the process learning the lessons of the era – the dangers of appeasing an expansionist tyrant, the need to prevent America's defenses from lapsing. A quarter century later, nearly every prominent figure in his administration would recall the 1930s in a similar fashion. But Johnson alone among them held public office during the period, and his reluctance to move beyond the lessons of Munich seemed just a touch stronger than for the rest.

Johnson's reputation during his House service came not from his national security activities but from his continuing ties to FDR, his close relationship with Speaker Sam Rayburn, and his effective work as chair of the Democratic Congressional Campaign Committee. As Johnson advanced nationally, though, Texas politics changed. In 1938 the reaction against Roosevelt cost pro–New Deal congressmen Maury Maverick and W. D. McFarlane their House seats. Texas voters also installed the reactionary W. Lee ("Pappy") O'Daniel as governor.[11]

Despite the state's rightward turn, Johnson launched a bid for the Senate after incumbent Morris Sheppard died in April 1941. The special election did not require him giving up his House seat, and so he had little to lose by running. He obtained support from FDR – the first time the president had made an endorsement in a Democratic primary since the unsuccessful attempt to purge conservative Democrats in 1938 – but still faced long odds. Johnson's House colleague, the ultra-conservative Martin Dies, state Attorney General Gerald Mann, and Governor O'Daniel all filed for the seat.

As in 1937, Johnson strongly identified himself with the president, though on this occasion largely on foreign policy matters. That approach netted him what appeared to be a stunning upset: with 96 percent of the vote counted, he led O'Daniel by more than 5,000 votes. But then O'Daniel allies in East Texas went to work, changing tallies that once had favored Dies to boost O'Daniel's total. By the time the counting was concluded, O'Daniel had squeaked out a 1,095-vote victory. As Robert Dallek, one of Johnson's biographers, has noted, the defeat convinced Johnson "as never

[11] George Norris Green, *The Establishment in Texas Politics: The Primitive Years, 1938–1957* (Westport, CT: Greenwood Press, 1979), pp. 20–8.

before that politics was a dirty business in which a willingness to be more unprincipled than your opponents was a requirement for success."[12]

The bitter loss did not temper Johnson's statewide ambitions. Once the United States entered World War II, he sensed that status as a veteran would form a precondition for postwar political success. The congressman used his influence with Roosevelt first to obtain a naval commission (he was sent to inspect the morale of U.S. forces in Australia) and then a presidential statement urging members of Congress to tend to their work in Washington rather than serve in the military.[13]

During the months that Representative Johnson was in the Pacific, he ceded responsibility for running his House office to his wife. Born in 1912 to an emotionally troubled mother and a wealthy merchant father, Claudia Taylor, nicknamed Lady Bird, had a hard childhood; her mother died when she was six and her father paid her little attention. Despite such trials, Lady Bird was a person of unusual gifts. Like her future husband, she was ambitious; she distinguished herself at the University of Texas in the early 1930s by obtaining both a B.A. and a Bachelor of Journalism degree. At the university she encountered Lyndon, who proposed to her only 24 hours after they met. They were married shortly thereafter. Observers in her husband's office would scarcely have known that she lacked a background in politics; after a few months, most believed that she would win the seat if Lyndon remained in the military.[14]

When the congressman returned from the Pacific, his priorities changed. Like most prominent figures in Texas politics, Johnson benefited from the blurry line between money and politics in his state's political culture. His assistance for prominent Texas businessmen, especially George and Herman Brown, co-owners of the Brown and Root construction firm, helped him not only to obtain campaign contributions but also to satisfy his expensive tastes. Meanwhile, after Lady Bird used money from an inheritance to purchase Austin radio station KTBC, Johnson's political influence ensured a series of favorable rulings from the Federal Communications Commission. By implying that those wanting his favor on government policy should advertise with the station, LBJ turned KTBC into a highly profitable venture.[15] In 1952 KTBC assumed control of an

[12] Dallek, *Lone Star Rising*, p. 224.

[13] Dallek, *Lone Star Rising*, pp. 182–8.

[14] Dallek, *Lone Star Rising*, pp. 153, 186, 234; Carl Anthony, *First Ladies: The Saga of Presidents' Wives and Their Power* (New York: Morrow, 1990), vol. 2, pp. 38–51.

[15] Robert A. Caro, *The Years of Lyndon Johnson: Volume 2, Means of Ascent* (New York: Knopf, 1989), pp. 80–118.

Austin television station, and FCC rulings ensured that it was the only station to carry network television programming in the Austin market. By the mid-1950s Lyndon Johnson was a multimillionaire, with a fortune accrued during his stint on the federal government payroll.

While he grew financially more secure, Johnson's influence lessened in the postwar political environment. The Republicans seized control of the House and Senate in 1946, consigning the congressman to minority status. Johnson thus became all the more determined to make another bid for the Senate. This time, however, he would have to risk his political career. O'Daniel's term expired in 1948, and the senator, whose support had dropped to 7 percent in one poll, retired.[16] Johnson entered the race as an underdog to Coke Stevenson, O'Daniel's successor as governor and a man whose vote-getting prowess was unmatched in modern Texas history. Later Texas governor John Connally recalled the contest as "the beginning of modern politics," as Johnson employed all of his political skills – and fundraising ability – to win an election that many considered unwinnable.[17]

In the primary Johnson finished a disappointing second, with 34 percent of the vote to Stevenson's 40 percent. The third-place finisher, Houston attorney George Peddy, was a strong conservative, and observers figured his runoff votes to go to the conservative Stevenson. But Johnson had other ideas. On the campaign trail he portrayed Stevenson as out of touch with the postwar world and contended that the former governor had obtained labor's support only by promising to vote to repeal the Taft-Hartley Act. (This charge was baseless: many Texas unions had endorsed Stevenson to punish Johnson for his rightward drift in the late 1940s.) Behind the scenes Johnson allies poured money into regions of the state – San Antonio and counties on the Mexican border – where large blocs of votes could be purchased.

On election night the race was too close to call, with Stevenson ahead by 854 votes out of nearly 1,000,000 cast. But then "corrected" votes started arriving, especially from the south Texas counties controlled by the "Duke of Duval," George Parr. In Duval County Parr claimed that 99.6 of the registered voters went to the polls, where they favored Johnson by a margin of 4,622 to 40. Six days after the election, however, Stevenson retained the lead – until the "corrected" returns from another Parr-controlled precinct arrived. In Box 13 in Alice, Texas, Johnson gained

[16] Green, *The Establishment in Texas Politics,* p. 56.
[17] Connally quoted in Caro, *Means of Ascent,* p. 193.

200 votes, including at least three from registered voters who had died but whose names remained on the rolls. With these 200 votes the final tally gave Johnson 494,191 votes to Stevenson's 494,104.[18]

With such blatant evidence of vote fraud, Stevenson challenged the results. He obtained an injunction preventing Johnson's name from being listed on the ballot as the Democratic nominee, and a federal judge ordered an inquiry into the Box 13 ballots. Johnson's national contacts then worked to his advantage. A team of high-profile attorneys headed by Abe Fortas, at the time a partner at an influential Washington law firm, successfully blocked the injunction, employing a high-risk legal strategy that involved a direct appeal to Supreme Court Justice Hugo Black. With his 87-vote margin of victory, "Landslide Lyndon" was headed to the Senate.[19]

In 1957 the political columnist, Washington insider, and Johnson admirer William S. White sympathetically portrayed the institution Johnson now would call home. *Citadel* described the upper chamber as dominated by tradition, mutual respect among its members, and a set of unwritten rules handed down by its Inner Club. In White's view a good senator lacked "petty exhibitionism," could concentrate on the "coherent and important" rather than the "diffuse and doubtful," possessed a "deep skill" at understanding what the body could realistically achieve, could understand others' points of view, and recognized the need to compromise. Indeed, "one of the ultimate truths of the Senate" was that "the art of high negotiation is an absolutely necessary part of senatorial equipment."[20]

These requirements perfectly suited Johnson's personal, political, and legislative skills. In 1953 Johnson took over as Senate Democratic leader, a post from which his two predecessors had failed to win reelection. He used the position to become the second most powerful man in government.[21] Between 1953 and 1959, as Johnson revolutionized the role of Senate party leader, he also transformed the Senate. He demonstrated an almost unparalleled parliamentary imaginativeness, mined his local contacts to raise funds for other Democratic candidates, worked with Republicans as comfortably as Senate liberals, and entered into a highly

[18] Caro, *Means of Ascent,* pp. 255–300.

[19] Caro, *Means of Ascent,* pp. 300–410.

[20] William S. White, *Citadel: The Story of the U.S. Senate* (New York: Houghton Mifflin, 1957), pp. 84, 107, 115–17.

[21] Robert A. Caro, *The Years of Lyndon Johnson: Volume 3, Master of the Senate* (New York: Knopf, 2002), p. 315.

profitable alliance with Bobby Baker, the aide whose fate would play an important role in the 1964 election. The heart of Johnson's power came from his ability to craft compromises, a task he accomplished through what some termed the "Johnson treatment" and what White more precisely described as "cajoling, entreating, flattering, blandly threatening, sometimes saying words and taking action that would have been forgiven in none other than a Senate type."[22] Asked later about his legislative philosophy, Johnson stated bluntly, "I'm more a compromiser and a maneuverer. I try to get something. That's the way our system works."[23]

In *Citadel* White observed that "the qualities that make a good senator are in no important way those that make a good President."[24] Or a good presidential candidate, as Johnson discovered in 1960. In a Democratic field that included Minnesota senator Hubert Humphrey, Massachusetts senator John Kennedy, Missouri senator Stuart Symington, and two-time presidential nominee Adlai Stevenson, Johnson's chances seemed reasonably strong. Yet he conducted his campaign in an uncharacteristically passive way, allowing Kennedy to garner momentum with a string of primary victories. Johnson's skills in cobbling together diverse coalitions in Congress translated poorly to national politics, and he could not prevent Kennedy's narrow victory at the national convention. Then, to almost everyone's surprise, he agreed to serve as Kennedy's running mate, where he critically assisted the ticket in several Southern states.

The vice presidency, however, did not suit this self-described "can-do man." Although Kennedy went out of his way to include Johnson in the decision-making process, by 1963 the vice president's importance had diminished to such an extent that rumors circulated of Kennedy choosing another running mate in 1964. And then, to the shock of the nation, Lyndon Johnson was president.

The new chief executive had a keen, if topically limited, understanding of history, and he eagerly applied what he considered the "lessons of the past" to his presidential bid in 1964. Indeed, Lyndon Johnson's knowledge of American politics probably surpassed that of any other president before or since. Beginning in 1932 Johnson, like every Democrat who followed FDR, reaped the benefits as well as the tensions of the New Deal

[22] White, *Citadel*, pp. 89, 105, 210.

[23] Robert Mann, *The Walls of Jericho: Lyndon Johnson, Hubert Humphrey, Richard Russell, and the Struggle for Civil Rights* (New York: Harcourt, Brace, 1996), p. 135.

[24] White, *Citadel*, p. 219.

coalition, which brought together liberals, labor, blacks, and the South in an uneasy but politically potent alliance. But the two contests that most affected Johnson's approach to the 1964 election were Roosevelt's successful reelection races in 1936 and 1940.

Roosevelt in 1936 perfected the strategy of running from ahead. He portrayed himself as the leader of "all the people," eschewing campaign appearances in favor of "nonpolitical" events that he understood were actually "the most effective political trips a President can make."[25] Even his overtly political addresses occurred on an "almost biblical plane" – he instructed his advisers to insert biblical passages dealing with themes of hope, faith, and charity into all his campaign speeches.[26] (Johnson would mimic the strategy 28 years later.) In 1940, despite pleas from Democrats, FDR resisted overt partisan appeals and instead praised Republicans who sympathized with his national security policies. The president also (in another tactic duplicated by Johnson) instructed his aides to avoid mentioning Republican Wendell Willkie's name – "call him our opponent. Call him anything, but never call him bad names."[27]

In 1948, meanwhile, as Johnson was winning election to the Senate, presidential politics featured the biggest upset in the twentieth century, as Harry Truman bested the heavily favored Republican nominee, New York governor Thomas Dewey. The lessons from the 1948 presidential contest were contradictory and thus much harder to interpret than those from 1936 or 1940. But the memories of Truman's performance nonetheless played a key role in 1964, especially for the Democratic operatives with whom Johnson dealt. The first, and most obvious, was for politicians to trust political instinct over polls, since every major pollster had predicted a comfortable Dewey triumph. Second, political observers detected dangers in waging a campaign based on generalities. As one wit observed, Dewey's proposals were so bland that "the next thing we know he'll be endorsing matrimony, the metal zipper, and the dial telephone."[28] Third, Truman proved that a Democratic victory did not require a solid South. After the Democratic convention passed a platform plank urging a renewed federal commitment to civil rights, South Carolina governor Strom Thurmond, running as a "States' Rights Democrat," captured the

[25] Frank Freidel, *Franklin D. Roosevelt: A Rendezvous with Destiny* (Boston: Little, Brown, 1990), p. 198.

[26] Gil Troy, *See How They Ran: The Changing Role of a Presidential Candidate* (New York: Free Press, 1991), pp. 169–72.

[27] Frances Perkins, *The Roosevelt I Knew* (New York: Viking Press, 1946), p. 115.

[28] Troy, *See How They Ran*, p. 195.

electoral votes of Alabama, Louisiana, Mississippi, and South Carolina. Truman compensated by winning traditionally Republican states in the Midwest.[29]

How to apply lessons of past presidential races to the 1964 contest would emerge as a subject of dispute between the president, who tended to look much more to 1936 and 1940 for guidance, and his political advisers, who drew more upon the lessons of 1948. Meanwhile, for Republicans the 1964 campaign would recall events from the 1940 and 1952 races, years in which the GOP had nominated moderates popular with the voters but viewed suspiciously by many party operatives.

This unusually rich set of historical legacies suggests continuity between 1964 and the eight presidential contests that preceded it. At the same time, however, the 1964 election also prefigured future presidential races. It featured the first extensive use of one-minute television commercials, often of the negative variety that would later become commonplace; indeed, with the "daisy ad," 1964 offered the most famous attack ad in American political history. The year marked the emergence of crime as a national issue, as right-wing candidates attempted, with varying success, to link crime and race. The transformation of the Republican Party into a more ideologically cohesive, conservative political organization traces its roots to the 1964 primary season, which witnessed the last time an ideological moderate – in this case Henry Cabot Lodge – had a legitimate chance of capturing the nomination. (That in 1980 George H. W. Bush, who as a Senate candidate had opposed passage of the Civil Rights Act, and in 2000 John McCain, whose lifetime ranking from the liberal Americans for Democratic Action was less than 20 percent, represented the preferred candidates of GOP "moderates" offered a sense of how far to the right the party had drifted.) Among Democrats the election generated a robust debate over the meaning of liberalism, an exchange in which the president himself participated and that would resonate for the next three decades. Finally, the 1964 campaign represented a watershed in the role that ethics played in American political culture. Republican attacks on Johnson changed how the political culture interpreted questions of personal morality, and Johnson's responses foreshadowed the partisan wrangling over real and alleged obstruction of justice that would characterize American politics for much of the late twentieth century.

[29] Zachary Karabell, *The Last Election: How Harry Truman Won the 1948 Election* (New York: Knopf, 2000), pp. 99–175.

The emergence of John Kennedy, the Kennedy-Nixon debates, and the ability of Kennedy Democrats to set the tone for the 1960s have brought students of American politics to the 1960 election.[30] The collapse of the New Deal coalition, the tactical brilliance of Richard Nixon's Southern strategy, and the third-party phenomenon of George Wallace explains the focus on 1968.[31] And so the contests of 1960 and 1968 have attracted considerably more popular and scholarly attention than the Johnson-Goldwater race. But 1964 contained elements of both the preceding and succeeding elections. The election also illuminated several important paths in American politics that, although ultimately not taken, would resurface in the generation after Lyndon Johnson bested Barry Goldwater on November 3, 1964.

Johnson, of course, assumed the presidency in the most trying of circumstances. The assassination of John Kennedy led both political parties to adjourn politics for a 30-day mourning period. Still, the new president never had respected a boundary between politics and policy, and Kennedy's death did not change this. In his first address before Congress, Johnson committed himself to passing Kennedy's program, fully aware that success in this effort also would allow him to stand as a "can-do" president in the fall. In the process Johnson not only established himself as chief executive in his own right: he redefined the nature of running for the presidency.

In the initial weeks of his tenure, Johnson challenged long-established tradition by making an ability to shepherd legislation through Congress a tangible political asset. In so doing he shifted the playing field to an area where he possessed an overwhelming advantage over any possible foe. In 1999 C-SPAN asked 60 historians, journalists, and presidential scholars to rate the presidents in 10 categories. In 9 of the 10 listings, George Washington, Abraham Lincoln, or Franklin Roosevelt unsurprisingly received the highest ranking. But in one category – relations with Congress – first place went to Johnson.[32] The intensity and productivity of his dealings with the institution the *Washington Star* considered his "first and lasting love" represented one of Johnson's sharpest breaks from

[30] Christopher Matthews, *Kennedy and Nixon: The Rivalry That Shaped Postwar America* (New York: Simon and Schuster, 1996).

[31] Dan Carter, *The Politics of Rage: George Wallace, the Origins of the New Conservatism, and the Transformation of American Politics* (New York: Simon and Schuster, 1995); E. J. Dionne, Jr., *Why Americans Hate Politics* (New York: Simon and Schuster, 1991).

[32] www.americanpresidents.org/survey/historians/35.asp, last accessed 2 Mar. 2008.

his predecessor.[33] Among twentieth-century chief executives, FDR might have pioneered the strategy of benefiting politically from performing presidential duties, but no previous president had established legislative success in and of itself as a political test.

Borrowing from FDR's strategy of shielding the presidency from the political arena, Johnson did not deliver his first overtly political speech as president until February 29, 1964. On the domestic front, he pushed through Kennedy's major legislative items even as he ostensibly remained above the political fray. In championing the administration's civil rights bill, Johnson proved that despite his Southern heritage he would be a national, not a regional, chief executive. Johnson's handling of his predecessor's tax bill accrued for him more political benefits than did civil rights: he willingly paid the price demanded by Senate conservatives – reducing the federal budget to below $100 billion – to fortify his reputation as a Democrat capable of appealing to both business and labor. And on no legislative measure did Johnson's political motives appear more clearly than in his handling of Kennedy's farm bill, which presented a chance first to keep together the New Deal Democratic coalition and then to woo Midwestern Republicans beyond the reach of the Democratic Party since 1936.[34]

That political concerns affected public policy decisions in the Johnson administration (or that of any other president) comes as no great insight. But this study illuminates how and in what specific ways politics shaped policy. A fusion of politics and policy extended to the international arena as well. Johnson has been portrayed – both at the time and by many historians thereafter – as a somewhat passive president on international matters, at least in the initial period of his presidency. "The frivolous answer here," newspaper columnist Max Frankel mocked in early February 1964, "to inquiries from abroad about President Johnson's inclinations in foreign policy has been: 'Haven't you heard? There isn't going to be any foreign policy in the next year.' " Frankel feared that the president had ignored the truism "often proclaimed by President Kennedy [that] the line between domestic and foreign affairs has become almost nonexistent."[35]

[33] *Washington Star*, 3 Dec. 1963.

[34] Robert David Johnson, "Politics, Policy, and Presidential Power: Lyndon Johnson and the 1964 Farm Bill," in Mitchell Lerner, ed., *Looking Back at LBJ: White House Politics in a New Light* (Lawrence: University Press of Kansas, 2005), pp. 153–80.

[35] *New York Times*, 3 Feb. 1964.

In fact, Johnson fully understood how domestic politics and foreign policy intersected. But unlike Kennedy, who frequently worried about domestic forces constraining his international agenda, Johnson tailored his foreign policies to advance his perceived political needs. In the process he assumed an active – indeed, decisive – role on a host of international issues. This pattern emerged most clearly in the administration's response to Latin America, but recent interpretations of Johnson's early Vietnam and European policies also show a decisiveness on international matters almost from the start of his presidency.[36] Unfortunately for the president, he lacked the magical touch internationally that he displayed with Congress. By the early summer of 1964, his handling of foreign policy matters seemed to provide an opening for a strong Republican candidate. That this ultimately did not occur represented one of the great surprises of the 1964 campaign.

As the 1964 election began to take form, it remained unclear whether the GOP would nominate a viable challenger. Johnson's elevation to the presidency transformed the Republican contest. By late 1963 Arizona senator Barry Goldwater had assumed a healthy lead in Republican polls – due to the weakness of his principal opponent, New York governor Nelson Rockefeller, party leaders' excitement at Goldwater's ability to outpoll John Kennedy in the South, the senator's grassroots support from conservatives, and the fact that few prominent Republicans wanted to challenge Kennedy. But few political observers, at least in early 1964, believed that even Goldwater, despite his criticism of civil rights legislation, could best Johnson in the South. Accordingly, several Republicans – Richard Nixon, William Scranton, and Henry Cabot Lodge chief among them – seriously considered entering the race. Lodge ultimately emerged as the most potent of these challengers, thanks to his upset victory in the New Hampshire primary and his strength in subsequent public opinion polls. Goldwater and Lodge not only differed ideologically but also tactically. While Goldwater focused on winning delegates through state conventions, Lodge embraced what had been dubbed "Kennedy's Law," after the Massachusetts Democrat's success in 1960: political professionals would nominate the candidate who demonstrated the greatest popular appeal.

[36] See especially Fredrik Logevall, *Choosing War: The Lost Chance for Peace and the Escalation of the War in Vietnam* (Berkeley: University of California Press, 1999), and Thomas Alan Schwartz, *Lyndon Johnson and Europe: In the Shadow of Vietnam* (Cambridge, MA: Harvard University Press, 2003).

Lodge ultimately failed to sustain his public backing. Perhaps, as Rick Perlstein has most persuasively argued, the Massachusetts Republican never threatened Goldwater's status as the frontrunner.[37] But the Lodge candidacy nonetheless requires students of 1964 to entertain some counterfactual considerations. The thrust of recent scholarship has portrayed the right's capture of the Republican Party as a linear process, caused by the decline of the liberal Republicans, the emergence of a new suburban base for the GOP, or the creation of a powerful base of conservative grassroots activists.[38] But what if Lodge had prevailed in the Oregon primary, as he was favored to do, and a Lodge-Rockefeller coalition had then defeated Goldwater in California? Such victories would have given Lodge a realistic chance at the nomination. And had the GOP selected this ardent champion of civil rights as its nominee, Alabama governor George Wallace almost certainly would have proceeded with a third-party presidential bid. An election with Wallace threatening Johnson's hold over the South and urban ethnic voters while Lodge challenged the president for predominance in the suburbs and among Cold War liberals would have yielded a different result on November 3 – and possibly altered subsequent political history.

Although it was not entirely clear to many observers at the time, the collapse of the Lodge candidacy all but ensured Goldwater's nomination. Meanwhile, passage of the Civil Rights Act, which Johnson signed into law on July 2, 1964, revived suspicions that a white backlash could determine the November outcome. In many ways, however, the most interesting question regarding the civil rights issue focuses on why the backlash failed to substantially assist the Republicans in 1964 – in contrast to the 1968, 1980, and 1988 presidential races, in which backlash sentiment peeled off enough Democrats to ensure GOP triumphs. Shortcomings in Goldwater's strategy alone do not provide a sufficient explanation. Although the 1964 San Francisco convention is generally remembered as an example of how political parties should not conduct national gatherings, commentary at the time viewed the affair differently. Many in the media argued that Goldwater had mobilized a conservative base that, when joined with a "silent" backlash vote, could propel the senator to at least an unexpectedly close finish.

[37] Rick Perlstein, *Before the Storm: Barry Goldwater and the Unmaking of the American Consensus* (New York: Hill and Wang, 2001).

[38] Perlstein, *Before the Storm;* Nicol Rae, *The Decline and Fall of the Liberal Republicans: From 1952 to the Present* (New York: Oxford University Press, 1989); Mary Brennan, *Turning Right in the Sixties: The Conservative Capture of the GOP* (Chapel Hill: University of North Carolina Press, 1995).

The 1964 contest distinguished itself from its successors by featuring an issue to trump the backlash – national security policy. In October 1964 Richard Reston of the *Los Angeles Times* discussed how Johnson had used foreign policy "in a conscious political effort to isolate the more aggressive stand" of Goldwater. Democrats' celebration of a bipartisan foreign policy linked Dwight Eisenhower, John Foster Dulles, and Henry Cabot Lodge with Johnson's portrayal of the mainstream foreign policy against which Goldwater was rebelling. Moreover, Goldwater's positions against the nuclear test-ban treaty and in favor of granting NATO commanders more discretion to use nuclear weapons allowed Johnson to portray the Arizonan as someone who would create "fear instead of confidence, division instead of unity, and controversy in times that demand a common front." In this sense, foreign policy emerged as the president's most potent political weapon.[39]

The end of the Republican convention in late July returned the political focus to Johnson, where it would remain for the rest of the year. At the time the most significant undecided issue in the Democratic campaign was the identity of the president's running mate. Minnesota senator Hubert Humphrey recalled Johnson's attitude: "It was the kind of situation he delighted in: floating a trial balloon, deflating it, suggesting different names. He held all the cards and played them as the whim struck."[40]

Until the end of July the central figure in this drama was Attorney General Robert Kennedy. One author has termed the battle between Johnson and Kennedy the "feud that defined a decade," and, if it was not quite that, it certainly played a critical political role in the early months of the Johnson presidency. The two men first came into regular contact in 1960, when Robert managed his brother's campaign and fumed at Johnson's desperate tactics in the weeks before the convention. On the other side, the convention instilled in Johnson a deep dislike for Kennedy, whom Johnson believed wanted to eliminate him from national politics. Relations between the two deteriorated during John Kennedy's presidency. In 1964, although the Attorney General made sporadic gestures of trying to force Johnson to nominate him, the president was not intimidated. In late July he announced that Kennedy, along with all other members of the Cabinet, would not be considered for the vice-presidential slot.[41]

[39] *Los Angeles Times*, 14 Oct. 1964.

[40] Hubert Humphrey, *Education of a Public Man: My Life and Politics* (New York: Doubleday, 1976), p. 289.

[41] Jeff Shesol, *Mutual Contempt: Lyndon Johnson, Robert Kennedy, and the Feud That Defined a Decade* (New York: W. W. Norton, 1997).

Kennedy's elimination made Humphrey, the Senate majority whip, the frontrunner for the nomination. Humphrey and Johnson had a long-standing, mutually profitable relationship. The Minnesotan won election to the Senate in 1948 after electrifying that year's Democratic convention with a speech endorsing a strong civil rights platform plank – the same plank that produced Strom Thurmond's brief departure from the party. The upper chamber, however, was far less receptive to his oratorical capabilities. He owed his political rehabilitation to Johnson, who saw in Humphrey a potential ally among Senate liberals skeptical of Johnson's commitment to traditional Democratic programs.[42]

Over the course of 1964, in a revealing commentary on their future relationship, Johnson and Humphrey never had a conversation between equals. Humphrey neither challenged nor chastised the president, while Johnson disparaged Humphrey's political and intellectual skills, sometimes directly, more usually behind the senator's back. The president, who obsessed over press leaks, frequently complained about Humphrey's loquaciousness with journalists.

This hesitancy led Johnson to search for an alternative to Humphrey as the 1964 Democratic convention in – of all places – Atlantic City drew near. This quest eventually focused on Montana senator Mike Mansfield, the Senate majority leader. Humphrey salvaged his nomination only thanks to Mansfield's obvious reluctance for the post and Humphrey's work in resolving a key convention controversy. After Mississippi's segregated Democratic Party sent an all-white, pro-Goldwater delegation to the convention, civil rights activists from the state countered with a mixed-race delegation calling itself the Mississippi Freedom Democratic Party. The president harbored little sympathy for the Mississippi party establishment but recognized that denying them their seats would cause other Southern delegations to bolt the convention. Johnson eventually defused the crisis with a compromise that many liberals considered unsatisfactory and that generated surprisingly strong opposition in the other direction from a significant supporting player in the 1964 contest, Georgia governor Carl Sanders.

With even the moderate Sanders dubious about the president's political approach to civil rights, Johnson entered the fall campaign fully understanding that he lacked a secure base of Southern support. Both publicly and privately, however, the president expressed little concern: while commentators anticipated a backlash vote, he introduced a new word to the

[42] Mann, *The Walls of Jericho*, pp. 100–4.

political lexicon. For several weeks following the convention, Johnson aggressively cultivated what he termed the "frontlash" – independents and Republicans uncomfortable with Goldwater's positions on national security issues and civil rights. The fiscal conservatism of these voters had made them the core supporters of the GOP in many Northern and Eastern states after World War II, since the New Deal economic agenda made them suspicious of the Democrats.

In 1964 Johnson not only wanted their votes – he wanted their permanent allegiance for his party. He used the fall campaign's early weeks to outline a program based on peace, prosperity, and social justice that seemed tailor-made to persuade frontlash voters to switch to the Democratic Party. That process, however, proved much more difficult than Johnson, in his campaign manager persona, had anticipated. The effort ultimately was undone by the difficulty of balancing the economic agenda demanded by frontlash voters with domestic policies preferred by traditional Democratic constituencies, such as labor unions, liberals, and, ultimately, the president himself. By the end of September, under criticism for offering only the blandest of economic proposals, even Johnson concluded that the frontlash approach would not produce a permanent realignment.

Just as the Lodge campaign compels a closer look at alternative paths for the GOP, the frontlash effort forces us to reconsider the foundations of 1960s liberalism. Serious scholarship on the issue dates from Allen Matusow's magisterial *Unraveling of America,* which posited an ideological continuity between the Kennedy and Johnson administrations based on what Matusow termed "corporate liberalism."[43] On the surface Johnson's advocacy of a fiscally responsible, pro-business, pro-growth agenda would suggest a similarity between his economic approach and that of Kennedy, as would the retention of Kennedy's key economic advisers. But Johnson's economic program also included antipoverty initiatives and a strongly favorable attitude toward labor, items that Kennedy had struggled to translate into public policy.

In this sense Johnson's frontlash agenda represented much more a political than an economic program, a general approach that would resurface in the 1990s under the monikers "the Third Way" in Europe and "New Democrat" in the United States. Like Tony Blair and Bill Clinton, Lyndon Johnson wanted to make liberalism acceptable to upper-middle-class and

[43] Allen Matusow, *The Unraveling of America: A History of Liberalism in the 1960s* (New York: Harper and Row, 1984).

middle-class voters by deemphasizing calls for expanding the welfare state and income redistribution, while stressing instead aspects of rights-related liberalism where the frontlash voters and traditional Democratic constituencies could make common cause. In the end, of course, Johnson would not be able to anticipate the successes of Clinton or Blair in this endeavor. But it is testimony to his political acumen that, recognizing how the Civil Rights Act would shatter the New Deal coalition, he made the attempt at all.

Johnson shared with Clinton one other important trait – a tendency toward blowing small scandals out of proportion by responding to them inappropriately. In 1964 Johnson's ethical difficulties originated in an influence-peddling investigation involving his former aide and protégé, Bobby Baker. The inquiry revealed what Cabell Phillips of the *New York Times* termed a "moral climate where the habitual wheeling and dealing in the coin of politics, privilege, and the reciprocal good turn tends to dull the sensibilities."[44] If leveled at John Kennedy or Dwight Eisenhower, allegations of rampant ethical improprieties would have been dismissed out of hand. But when it came to "Landslide Lyndon," the man who became a multimillionaire while serving exclusively on the government payroll, such charges seemed entirely plausible.

Months of investigation uncovered only two specific – and very minor – links between Johnson and improprieties by Baker. Had the president been immediately forthcoming, the matter might have caused little political damage. Instead, Johnson's conduct magnified the problem. He first offered legalistic responses that sounded evasive. He then dismissed the charges as irrelevant to a political campaign, since they involved private morality rather than public policy, and he pressured Senate Democrats to close down the inquiry. He urged the FBI to investigate Baker's accusers and turned a blind eye to the leaking of confidential personnel information designed to discredit Baker's attackers. Finally, when the investigation began examining possible campaign finance law violations, the president authorized his lawyer and friend Abe Fortas, the man whose legal strategizing had saved his political career in 1948, to obstruct justice.

His having already gone to such extremes makes understandable Johnson's response to the biggest scandal of the fall campaign – the arrest of his closest aide, Walter Jenkins, on what was delicately termed a "morals" charge. With virtually no other line of attack, Goldwater had made restoring "morality" in Washington the centerpiece of his campaign.

[44] *New York Times*, 7 Nov. 1963.

To provide himself with political cover from additional criticism, Johnson responded to Jenkins's arrest by ordering a full-scale FBI inquiry into the affair, only to realize that Jenkins's office safe contained damaging files, including, among other things, evidence of campaign finance irregularities. Accordingly, the president, at the time in New York for a campaign address, ordered Fortas to remove the files from the office, calling his legal counselor three times to confirm his instructions.

The Jenkins affair and Johnson's difficulties in articulating a frontlash agenda ensured that the 1964 campaign would not produce a permanent realignment. Instead, the contest's closing weeks featured the president trying to solidify his historical legacy, chiefly by outperforming the 1936 showing of his mentor, Franklin Roosevelt, and by using his margin of victory to ensure the defeat of his most vituperative congressional foes. Johnson achieved mixed success, and the strategy – an approach he chose over the advice of most of his political counselors – paved the way for the quick collapse of his 1964 coalition when economic and international conditions subsequently deteriorated. In this sense 1964 represented something of a hollow victory, since the president failed to create a new coalition that would ensure a Democratic majority over the long term.

1

Establishing an Image

Lyndon Johnson assumed the presidency at a transformational moment in American political culture. The civil rights movement threatened generations of Democratic dominance of the South. A grassroots conservative movement exposed a yawning gap between Republican activists and much of the party's elite. The growth of the federal government had outpaced Congress' ethics laws, creating an opening for both parties to seize upon ethics as a political issue. The expansion of the national media and the development of television news provided new avenues for reporters to cover politics and for politicians to reach the masses.

After the assassination of President Kennedy, Johnson maintained a frenetic schedule, and his ability to usher a stunned nation and Capitol through this chaotic period represented a high point of his career.[1] The new chief executive's first formal address, before a joint session of Congress on November 27, was one of Johnson's most striking rhetorical performances. Beginning somberly – "All I have I would have given gladly not to be standing here today" – Johnson urged translating "into effective action" Kennedy's "ideas and ideals" by passing the late president's civil rights, tax, and education bills.[2]

The month-long "adjournment" of politicking following the assassination allowed Johnson to shape his own agenda – and his own image to the nation – free from partisan attacks. He needed the opportunity. Despite his long career in politics, a Republican poll conducted in late 1963 showed that only 5 percent of the respondents knew a "great deal" about

[1] *U.S. News & World Report*, 2 Mar. 1964.

[2] *Congressional Quarterly Weekly Report*, 29 Nov. 1963, p. 2089.

Johnson; 67 percent, on the other hand, knew little or nothing about him.[3] A weak performance as vice president explained these figures; by 1963 Johnson was the subject of speculation that Kennedy would drop him from the ticket. "Where's Lyndon?" his detractors mocked. Johnson later admitted that he "detested every minute" as vice president.[4]

Johnson's behavior immediately after the assassination established his image as a healer, guiding the country through a turbulent emotional period. But he still had the business of the state to which to attend. Johnson biographer Robert Caro has observed that Johnson was at his best when the national interest complemented his political self-interest.[5] Such was the case following the assassination, when Johnson used his skills as a legislative leader and his status as a Southerner to advance Kennedy's bill to desegregate public accommodations.

Johnson was also well suited to promote Kennedy's major piece of economic legislation, a bill to stimulate economic growth by lowering corporate and personal income taxes. As with the civil rights bill, this measure was stalled in Congress; Senate conservatives led by Harry Byrd (D-Virginia) pressed for budget reductions before they would agree to cuts in revenue. Where the nexus between budget, tax, and congressional policy had stymied Kennedy, Johnson detected an opportunity for enhancing his pro-business image. Unlike Kennedy (or, for that matter, most Democrats), the new president had extensive personal connections to buttress such an image. Johnson's relationship with Brown and Root, whose government contracts had made it one of the country's largest construction companies, was well known.[6] Furthermore, throughout the 1950s then-Senator Johnson championed legislation favorable to Texas oil, gas, and railroad interests, while few surpassed Johnson's insistence on frugality and efficiency. As George Brown, co-owner of the construction firm of Brown & Root, once remarked, "Basically, Lyndon was more conservative, more practical than people understood."[7] Sometimes Johnson's efforts to economize federal spending were purely symbolic, as when he ordered the White House staff to turn off the lights in all vacant

[3] Republican National Committee, "Some Indications of Public Opinion at the Close of 1963," n.d., Box 9, Barry Goldwater Papers, Hayden Library, Arizona State University.

[4] Robert Dallek, *Flawed Giant: Lyndon Johnson and His Times, 1961–1973* (New York: Oxford University Press, 1998), pp. 8–48.

[5] Robert A. Caro, *The Years of Lyndon Johnson: Volume 3, Master of the Senate* (New York: Knopf, 2002), pp. 832–6.

[6] Robert Dallek, *Lone Star Rising: Lyndon Johnson and His Times, 1908–1960* (New York: Oxford University Press, 1991), pp. 175–6.

[7] George Brown oral history, Lyndon B. Johnson Presidential Library.

FIGURE 1-1. Lyndon Johnson on the telephone, in the Oval Office. © Courtesy of the Lyndon Baines Johnson Presidential Library. Photo by Yoichi Okamoto.

rooms.[8] (Phil Potter, the White House correspondent for the *Baltimore Sun*, jibed that any savings would go for naught, since "the telephone bill is surely up.")[9] More often, however, Johnson was serious, focusing on the

[8] *New Republic*, 7 Mar. 1964; Dallek, *Flawed Giant*, p. 15.
[9] *Baltimore Sun*, 4 Feb. 1964.

Pentagon budget, which consumed roughly 50 percent of federal spending.[10] As the president explained to Georgia senator Richard Russell, unless the budget was reduced, "the Republicans are going to be tearing me up for being a failure."[11]

Johnson's economic agenda attracted praise from executives like Fred Kappel, the chief executive officer of AT&T, who announced that business leaders possessed "undiminished confidence in the economic and moral strength of our country" under Johnson's leadership.[12] Syndicated columnists Rowland Evans and Robert Novak struggled to describe Johnson's economic ideology: perhaps it was "right-wing liberalism," or maybe "New Frontier conservatism."[13] But at the same time he was assuring Harry Byrd of his frugality, the president told United Auto Workers chief Walter Reuther to dismiss "about all this crap about economy" in spending, because he did not really mean what he had said to conservatives.[14]

In the end Johnson's chief goal seemed to be to get a bill of any sort. When word reached him that the tax bill might collapse in the Finance Committee, he promptly phoned three wavering Democrats – Chairman Byrd and two freshmen, Vance Hartke (D-Indiana) and Abraham Ribicoff (D-Connecticut). To Hartke, whose career Johnson had helped launch by funneling donations to Hoosier State Democrats in 1958, the president was blunt: "We've got in a big screwed-up mess, and we – all of us – are going down in defeat if we can't operate any better than that." The Indiana senator's protest that he wanted a deal to protect the musical instrument industry (a major employer in Elkhart, Indiana) drew a savage retort. "What's important is the big credit to the Democratic Party," Johnson replied. "The goddamned band and musical instruments – they won't be talking about it next November."[15] As the president desired, the three senators voted his way: the committee killed a crippling amendment by a 9-to-8 vote, setting up passage of the bill. The president would use the measure to fortify his credentials as an economic moderate in the fall campaign.

[10] Kermit Gordon oral history, Lyndon B. Johnson Presidential Library.

[11] President Johnson and Richard Russell, 5:00 P.M., 7 Dec. 1963, Tape K6312.05, PNO #2, LBJ Recordings.

[12] *Wall Street Journal*, 5 Dec. 1963; *New York Times*, 5 Dec. 1963; *U.S. News & World Report*, 13 Dec. 1963.

[13] *New York Herald Tribune*, 6 Dec. 1963.

[14] President Johnson and Walter Reuther, 9:18 P.M., 23 Dec. 1963, Tape K6312.16, PNO #6, LBJ Recordings.

[15] President Johnson and Vance Hartke, 1:11 P.M., 23 Jan. 1964, Tape WH6401.19, Citation #1492, LBJ Recordings.

Johnson's fusion of politics and policy appeared most prominently when he rehabilitated a piece of Kennedy's domestic program that had collapsed in Congress: the farm bill. In January 1963 Harold Cooley (D-North Carolina), chairman of the House Agriculture Committee, introduced a bill to establish a "one-price cotton" system through payments to domestic mills. The measure, which promised a more costly and confusing cotton policy, became caught in a bind common to agriculture legislation, then and now: it could not obtain sufficient votes from nonfarm representatives without reducing subsidy levels, but the very act of cutting subsidies would render it useless to its advocates.[16]

The administration's wheat policy also was in disarray. In May 1963 nearly 600,000 farmers, making up 52.2 percent of the total vote, cast ballots against Kennedy's proposal to couple a mandatory acreage control program for wheat with higher subsidy rates. After the vote *Fortune* termed the "farm mess" a political threat to Kennedy in 1964: Republicans using "the wheat vote as the start of a campaign for gradual reversal of federal intervention in farm economics" would ensure that the Democrats did not penetrate the Farm Belt.[17]

On agricultural issues, the change from Kennedy to Johnson was sharp and immediate. As *U.S. News & World Report* observed, "Mr. Johnson has taken personal charge of administration farm policy."[18] He did so on behalf of the Cooley bill, guided by politics, not public policy concerns. First, the measure offered a chance to reach out to Southerners alienated by the party's stance on civil rights. The New Dealer in Johnson believed, as had Franklin Roosevelt a generation before him, that addressing the region's economic needs would keep the South loyal to the Democrats. In addition, the Cooley bill enjoyed strong support from House Speaker John McCormack (D-Massachusetts), who had ties to textile interests once powerful in the Bay State. With an opportunity to pacify both Southerners and McCormack, Johnson correctly gambled that "the nature and geography of the doubtful Democrats" would ultimately win their votes.[19]

Johnson's ability to establish the image from which he would run from ahead in the 1964 presidential election – that of a healer, a compromiser, a figure of accomplishment – soon was reflected in the polls. Only one

[16] Willard Cochrane to Orville Freeman, 5 Nov. 1963, Box 10, Orville Freeman Papers, Lyndon B. Johnson Presidential Library.

[17] *Fortune,* July 1963.

[18] *U.S. News & World Report,* 30 Dec. 1963.

[19] Larry O'Brien, "Memorandum for the President," 2 Dec. 1963, Box 2, Henry Wilson Papers, Lyndon B. Johnson Presidential Library.

state survey was taken in the immediate aftermath of the assassination. In California, though Johnson enjoyed a healthy margin over both Barry Goldwater and New York governor Nelson Rockefeller, he led former vice president Richard Nixon by an unimpressive 49 to 44 percent.[20] By the middle of December, however, Johnson had assumed margins of greater than 30 points over all potential Republican candidates, including Nixon.[21]

Despite this demonstration of political strength, Johnson had to confront the less flattering elements of his past as he introduced himself to the American public. Bobby Baker had performed an invaluable political role for Johnson in the 1950s, but his position as the "101st senator" also brought him considerable personal gain. In 1961 Baker fell deep into debt financing a resort hotel on Maryland's Eastern Shore. To assist his former aide, Johnson arranged for Oklahoma senator Robert Kerr to provide a $300,000 line of credit.[22] The funds allowed Baker to open the resort. Visitors to "The Carousel" were promised an experience "where every minute is an adventure" – a locale "where you glimpse Washington big-wigs at play, as well as Hollywood and Broadway stars in town for a few days of play, play, play."[23] The opening night celebration's honored guest, arriving by limousine from Washington, was Vice President Lyndon Johnson.

In mid-1963, however, a business competitor filed a lawsuit charging that Baker had demanded a $5,600 kickback for a Defense Department contract.[24] Word of the suit piqued the interest of a key figure in the political history of the subsequent twelve months, Delaware senator John Williams. A native of Millsboro, Delaware (population 536), Williams made his living selling chicken feed. His political activism dated from World War II, fueled by resentment against the Office of Price Administration's regulation of the poultry business. He made his first bid for public office in 1946, when no prominent Republican challenged Democratic senator John Tunnell. Williams, despite low name recognition, prevailed in the year's general Republican sweep.[25]

[20] *U.S. News & World Report,* 10 Feb. 1964.

[21] *The Gallup Poll: Public Opinion, 1935–1997* (Wilmington: Scholarly Resources, 2000), CD-ROM.

[22] Bobby Baker, *Wheeling and Dealing: Confessions of a Capitol Hill Insider* (New York: W. W. Norton, 1978), pp. 82–4.

[23] "Carousel" brochure, n.d., Box 30, John Williams Papers, University of Delaware.

[24] *Congressional Quarterly Weekly Report,* 20 Dec. 1963, p. 2214.

[25] Carol Hoffecker, *Honest John Williams* (Newark: University of Delaware Press, 2000), pp. 53–62.

FIGURE 1-2. John Williams (left) with Senator Jacob Javits (R-NY). The Delaware Republican, hailed by his admirers as the "Conscience of the Senate," emerged in 1964 as Johnson's most vitriolic Senate critic. © Courtesy of the U.S. Senate Historical Office.

The Republican senator devoted considerable effort to investigating low-level government corruption; *Reader's Digest* hailed him as "Delaware's one-man FBI."[26] His investigations, carried on with the support of his secretary, Eleanor Lenhart, helped produce 169 indictments and 125 convictions, mostly for minor fraud in tax-related cases. Williams's work proved politically popular: he was the only member of the Republican class of 1946 to secure a third term in 1958. In Washington, though, he had a "tiresome Johnny One-Note" reputation

[26] Hoffecker, *Honest John Williams*, p. 107.

for tackling petty cases but avoiding major ones.[27] The Baker inquiry gave him a chance to establish a national profile.

After Williams approached Majority Leader Mike Mansfield with his preliminary evidence against Baker, Mansfield summoned the Senate secretary to defend himself against the charges. Instead, on October 8, 1963, Baker resigned his position. This tactic backfired. Two days later, the Senate unanimously authorized the Rules Committee to investigate the financial and business interests of current or former Senate employees.[28] While Lady Bird Johnson called to offer her sympathies at Baker's plight, the vice president arranged for his longtime associate, Abe Fortas, to serve as counsel for the man *Newsweek* dubbed "Lyndon's boy."[29]

Democrats did their best to squelch the inquiry. For committee counsel, Rules Committee chair B. Everett Jordan (D-North Carolina) hired perhaps the least vigorous lawyer he could find, the 74-year-old former mayor of Chapel Hill, L. P. McLendon. (*New York Times* reporter Cabell Phillips described McLendon as displaying "the benign face and warm-hearted disposition of a Mr. Tutt or a Foxy Grandpa.")[30] Meanwhile, Attorney General Kennedy met privately with Mansfield and Minority Leader Everett Dirksen (R-Illinois) to share FBI reports that Baker had secured female companionship for a host of senators, including black mistresses for several Southerners. The international damage that would come from such revelations, Kennedy argued, justified suppressing the material.[31]

On November 21, 1963, Everett Jordan convened a press conference to announce that he saw "no significant political implications" in the case.[32] The next day, Lyndon Johnson became President of the United States. On the evening of December 6, Jordan telephoned the White House to say that Clark Mollenhoff, the Washington bureau chief for the *Des Moines Register* and a close ally of Williams, was "*really* bearing down." The North Carolina senator conceded it "certainly looks like an awful lot of influence peddling," but promised "to keep the Bobby thing from spreading."[33]

[27] Frederic Collier, "Senator Williams – Public Eye," *New York Times Magazine*, 9 Feb. 1964.

[28] Baker, *Wheeling and Dealing*, p. 180.

[29] *Newsweek* quoted in *Honest John Williams*, p. 191; Baker, *Wheeling and Dealing*, p. 182.

[30] Cabell Phillips, "The Senate Shocks a Senate Prober," *New York Times Magazine*, 15 Aug. 1964; New *York Times*, 18 Dec. 1963.

[31] *Washington Star*, 11 Jan. 1964.

[32] *Washington Star*, 21 Nov. 1963.

[33] President Johnson, Walter Jenkins, and B. Everett Jordan, 5:34 P.M., 6 Dec. 1963, Tape K6312.04, PNO #28, LBJ Recordings.

Through mid-December it remained unclear exactly how badly the Baker inquiry would damage the president. The issue's mere existence disrupted Johnson's introduction to the American public, but the initial hearings established no direct link between Baker's misdeeds and Johnson, much less any wrongdoing by the president. In mid-December Representative H. R. Gross (R-Iowa) urged broadening the inquiry to include Johnson's own business holdings, especially KTBC.[34] Gross's call went unheeded, but nonetheless most observers agreed with the *Washington Star:* "The unfortunate truth seems to be that what is called 'private morality' will turn out to have been intimately tied up with public impropriety."[35]

The snowballing of the Baker affair was not the only trouble spot for the new president. Defying expectations, Johnson showed no greater electoral strength than had Kennedy in the South. Intraparty rivalries further threatened Johnson's standing in several key Southern states. Richard Russell complained when the First Lady invited Georgia governor Carl Sanders to sit in her box to hear Johnson's November 27 address; Sanders, a moderate, was considering challenging Russell in the 1966 Democratic primary. North Carolina featured a nasty gubernatorial primary between moderate L. Richardson Preyer and two conservatives vying for segregationist support, Dan Moore and I. Beverly Lake. In Tennessee Democratic congressman Ross Bass and Governor Frank Clement both entered the primary to complete the late Estes Kefauver's Senate term. In Louisiana a wild race for governor featured two pro-Johnson candidates and two bitter opponents of the administration; an administration critic, John McKeithen, was elected in February 1964. And Texas governor John Connally blasted the White House for reaching out to Senator Ralph Yarborough, leader of the Lone Star State's liberal Democrats and a longtime rival of both Johnson and Connally.[36]

Johnson's elevation to the presidency did challenge the conventional wisdom that the GOP nomination itself was of little value. While few observers went as far as Warren Weaver of the *New York Times,* who predicted in early December that the Republicans had "an even chance" of defeating Johnson, it remained uncertain whether a native Southerner could appeal to Democratic constituencies in key Northern states.[37]

[34] Congressional Record, 88th Cong., 1st sess., p. 24560 (13 Dec. 1963).

[35] *Washington Star,* 17 Dec. 1963.

[36] President Johnson, Walter Jenkins, and John Connally, 11:21 A.M., 18 Dec. 1963, Tape K6312.09, Citation #27, LBJ Recordings.

[37] *New York Times,* 1 Dec. 1963.

Johnson, moreover, had not previously demonstrated an aptitude for handling national politics. As veteran political observer Richard Rovere noted in 1956, "Lyndon Johnson's reputation as an uncommonly astute Senate leader remains unimpaired, but the fact has been established – as it was not before – that in the jungle of a national convention he cannot employ the gifts he uses in the Senate."[38]

At the time of Kennedy's death, the GOP frontrunner, Barry Goldwater, was concluding his second term in the U.S. Senate. The son of a Jewish department store magnate who converted to Episcopalianism, Goldwater was a native Arizonan who inherited the family business in the 1930s. His first political tract, an open letter to Franklin Roosevelt published in the *Phoenix Gazette*, criticized the New Deal's Fair Labor Standards Act. An accomplished pilot, Goldwater obtained a World War II commission; upon his return home, he intensified his political activity and eventually declared for the Senate seat held by Democrat Ernest McFarland.[39] Though before 1952, Arizona had elected only one Republican senator in its history, Goldwater edged McFarland by 6,725 votes – just over 2 percent of the total vote.[40]

Goldwater was not a powerful legislator during the eight years of Eisenhower's presidency and Johnson's Senate leadership. (His most famous line came when he dismissed the president's domestic agenda as a "dime store New Deal.") In international affairs he advocated a hard-line anti-communism and strongly supported the Air Force. As chair of the Republican Senate Campaign Committee, he built a grassroots network of supporters. His ability to articulate a conservative agenda distinguished him from most national Republicans, who, cognizant of their minority status, blurred the ideological boundaries between the parties. His 1960 book *Conscience of a Conservative* emphasized the role of morality in American political discourse and established Goldwater as a leading conservative thinker.

In 1960 Goldwater made a token bid for the Republican presidential nomination, offering this advice to the national convention: "Let's grow up, conservatives. If we want to take this party back, and I think we can someday, let's get to work."[41] When Goldwater uttered those words, he

[38] Richard Rovere, "The Last Hurrah," *The New Yorker*, 25 Aug. 1956.

[39] Lee Edwards, *Goldwater: The Man Who Made a Revolution* (Washington, DC: Regnery, 1995), pp. 14–100.

[40] Robert Alan Goldberg, *Barry Goldwater* (New Haven, CT: Yale University Press, 1995), pp. 94–9.

[41] *Congressional Quarterly Weekly Report*, 29 July 1960, p. 1339.

was speaking to an audience far greater than even he knew: one of the most important changes in American political culture during the 1960s came in the expansion of grassroots right-wing political activism. Many of these movements stood very far to the right indeed. For instance, the John Birch Society, founded in 1958, contended that communists had secretly infiltrated the American government; by the spring of 1961 the society had at least 20,000 members. Demographic changes helped explain the rise of the right – mostly white suburban areas such as Orange County (California) frequently dependent upon military-related jobs, provided fertile ground for an ultra-conservative message. Finally, the civil rights movement stimulated a backlash. The line between the "extremist" and a conservative activist, however, was very hard to draw – either in the early 1960s, when these groups hovered on the fringe of American politics, or in late 1963 and 1964, when they attracted much more attention.[42]

The iconoclastic journalist I. F. Stone described the Goldwater coalition as a group "which likes to think of itself as rugged and frontier because [it is] Western and Southwestern. But the covered wagons in which it travels are Cadillacs and its wide open spaces have been air-conditioned."[43] Grassroots members of the coalition were led by a brilliant political tactician, F. Clifton White, who sought to accumulate support for the senator at state conventions. With 715 of the 1,308 GOP delegates not elected – and with Goldwater on record as wanting to avoid primaries – this strategy seemed sound.[44] White focused on the South, where the identification of the national party with civil rights had eroded the Democrats' predominance. In the 1962 midterm elections, GOP Senate candidates had almost defeated moderates Lister Hill (Alabama) and Olin Johnston (South Carolina), while Texas and Florida elected freshmen Republicans to the House.

Nonetheless, throughout 1963 Goldwater continued to express ambivalence about a possible candidacy. In January the Arizona senator bluntly told White, "Clif, I'm not a candidate. And I'm not going to be. I have no intention of running for the presidency." When White suggested that activists could nonetheless organize a draft, Goldwater was dismissive: "I'm telling you now, don't paint me into a corner. It's my political neck and I intend to have something to say about what happens to it...My

[42] Rick Perlstein, *Before the Storm: Barry Goldwater and the Unmaking of the American Consensus* (New York: Hill and Wang, 2001), pp. 114–57.

[43] Stone quoted in Matusow, *The Unraveling of America*, p. 137.

[44] John Kessel, *The Goldwater Coalition: Republican Strategies in 1964* (Indianapolis: Bobbs-Merrill, 1968), p. 69.

wife loves me, but she'd leave me if I ran for this thing."[45] The senator was equally blunt in public, stating in a March appearance on the *Jack Paar Show* that "I have said hundreds of times that I am not" going to run.[46]

Despite these expressions of disinterest, Goldwater increasingly seemed like the GOP's strongest potential challenger to Kennedy. His criticism of a federal civil rights measure made him the candidate to beat in the South.[47] Polls showed Goldwater leading Kennedy in the region by 20 percent, with only 12 percent undecided. The Arizona senator even possessed a small advantage in Johnson's home state of Texas.[48] By the fall of 1963, a Gallup poll found Goldwater the choice of 42 percent of Republicans, to Nelson Rockefeller's 26 percent and Michigan governor George Romney's 15 percent.[49] *Newsweek* claimed that Goldwater had 500 committed delegates and another 82 leaning to his side – nearly 90 percent of the total needed for the nomination.[50] The Arizona senator seemed well suited to exploit what GOP polling had identified as Kennedy's vulnerabilities – racial problems, government finance and the economy, and relations with Cuba.[51] According to William Loeb, the ultraconservative publisher of the *Manchester* (New Hampshire) *Union-Leader*, a Goldwater victory would allow the GOP to say "to hell with...the 'salt water bastards'" of the two coasts.[52]

Then came the assassination. Goldwater himself was stunned by the event. While Johnson dominated the news scene in the weeks following Kennedy's death, Goldwater was described by the *Wall Street Journal* as "practically incommunicado"; the only public statement that he issued hinted at a "major reassessment" of his political plans.[53] When the *Journal* broke the news that Goldwater operatives had withdrawn advertising buys in New Hampshire, it looked as if the Arizona senator might bypass the presidential contest altogether. But the senator's supporters retained the faith. To Senator John Tower (R-Texas), "The basic issues remain the

[45] F. Clifton White with William Gill, *Suite 3505: The Story of the Draft Goldwater Movement* (New Rochelle, NY: Arlington House, 1967), pp. 115–18.
[46] Perlstein, *Before the Storm*, p. 191.
[47] Bill Rusher, "Crossroads for the GOP," *National Review*, 12 Feb. 1963.
[48] Goldberg, *Barry Goldwater*, p. 176.
[49] *New York Times*, 7 Oct. 1963.
[50] *Newsweek*, 7 Oct. 1963.
[51] Republican National Committee, "Some Indications of Public Opinion at the Close of 1963," Box 9, Goldwater Papers, Arizona State University.
[52] William Loeb to John Tower, 10 July 1963, Box 442, John Tower Papers, Southwestern University.
[53] *Wall Street Journal*, 6 Dec. 1963.

same, the new Administration will cleave to the policies of the old, and Barry Goldwater can still inspire more precinct workers and doorbell ringers to get out the maximum Republican vote."[54] In early December, when the leaders of the Draft Goldwater effort joined Senators Carl Curtis (R-Nebraska) and Norris Cotton (R-New Hampshire) to urge him to carry forward, Goldwater agreed. (His wife, Peggy, greeted the decision tepidly: "If that's what you want to do, go ahead and do it. I don't particularly want you to run, but I'm not going to stand in your way.")[55] Though his candidacy remained alive, in the first Gallup poll taken after the assassination, Goldwater's support slipped to 26 percent of Republican voters. While conservative grassroots activists might have grown more powerful between 1961 and 1963, they were hardly a majority of the Republican Party as the presidential campaign got underway.[56]

The assassination's aftermath left three other campaigns stalled in their previous, weak positions. The most aggressive belonged to Nelson Rockefeller. In 1954 party leaders spurned his efforts to run for governor: as one noted, "For the Republican Party to nominate a Rockefeller would be *suicidal*."[57] Perhaps they misjudged the electorate: that year's winner was a figure of similar background, Democrat Averell Harriman. In 1958 Rockefeller easily received the nomination and surprised friend and foe alike with his skill at personal campaigning. He also spent whatever was necessary from his personal fortune to win. Along with Goldwater's triumph in the Arizona Senate race, Rockefeller's ouster of Harriman was one of the few bright spots for the GOP in 1958.

Rockefeller was the frontrunner for the 1964 nomination until March 1962, when he divorced his wife, Mary Todhunter Clark. Then, on May 4, 1963, Rockefeller unexpectedly remarried, to a woman 20 years his junior, Margarita ("Happy") Murphy, who four weeks earlier had divorced her husband and had signed away custody of the couple's four children. For many, such behavior seemed beyond the pale. In a June 1963 address, Connecticut senator Prescott Bush asked, "Have we come to the point in our life as a nation where the governor of a great state can desert a good wife, mother of his grown children, divorce her, then

[54] John Tower to Raymond Moley, 30 Nov. 1963, Box 442, John Tower Papers, Southwestern University.

[55] Harold Faber, ed., *The Road to the White House: The Story of the 1964 Election by the Staff of the New York Times* (New York: McGraw-Hill, 1965), p. 15.

[56] Perlstein, *Before the Storm*, p. 257.

[57] Cary Reich, *The Life of Nelson A. Rockefeller: Worlds to Conquer, 1908–1958* (New York: Doubleday, 1996), p. 538.

persuade a young mother of youngsters to abandon her husband and their four children and marry the governor?"[58]

Rockefeller's standing in polls plummeted, his 17-point lead replaced by a 5-point deficit.[59] As the remarriage sacrificed his foremost asset – electability – the New York governor tried to reframe his candidacy as an attempt to save the Republican Party from itself. The party, he declared in a June 1963 address, "is in real danger of subversion by a radical, well-financed, and highly disciplined minority…The transparent purpose behind this plan is to erect political power on the outlawed and immoral base of segregation and to transform the Republican party from a national party of all the people to a sectional party for some of the people…A program based on racism or sectionalism would in and of itself not only defeat the Republican party in 1964, but would destroy it altogether."[60] This message, however, showed little indication of reviving the New York governor's candidacy. At a Rockefeller campaign stop in Illinois shortly after his remarriage, columnist Robert Novak wrote, "It was like observing a political corpse who did not realize that he was dead."[61]

Lacking a clear ideological agenda, Rockefeller fell back on his campaigning ability and his money. If party operatives believed that his personal problems rendered him unelectable, he would disprove the theory by winning primaries. He focused on two contests – New Hampshire, with its first-in-the-nation status, and California, with its 86 delegates. In New Hampshire he staffed an elaborate operation largely through contacts from his alma mater, Dartmouth College. In California he offered a blank check to the state's foremost political consulting firm, Spencer-Roberts. In a stunning admission of Rockefeller's weakness as a candidate, the firm detected "problems for a Rockefeller campaign such as lack of volunteers, the necessity of a new type of scheduling for the candidate, and recruitment to obtain a brand new organization."[62] Testimony from Rockefeller's chief political adviser, George Hinman, confirmed the point, and so Rockefeller went negative. He hired Graham Molitor, a self-described "Goldwater's assassin," whose staff sifted through everything Goldwater had written since the 1930s and

[58] *Time*, 14 June 1963.

[59] Kessel, *The Goldwater Coalition*, p. 50.

[60] Perlstein, *Before the Storm*, p. 224.

[61] Robert Novak, *The Agony of the G.O.P., 1964* (New York: Macmillan, 1965), p. 224.

[62] Spencer-Roberts and Associates Survey, Oct. 1963, Box 23, George Hinman Papers, Rockefeller Archives.

secretly recorded Goldwater speeches. Soon the campaign had a file of Goldwater's most extreme statements for Rockefeller to use on the hustings.[63] Spencer-Roberts' Stu Spencer bluntly articulated the goal: the Rockefeller campaign aimed at "destroying Barry Goldwater as a member of the human race."[64]

Goldwater's decline and Rockefeller's weakness raised the possibility of a brokered convention, an idea that appealed to Pennsylvania governor William Scranton, whom Goldwater's forces considered their strongest potential opponent.[65] Scranton had enjoyed a meteoric rise in politics, going from Eisenhower's State Department to upsetting a Democratic incumbent in a 1960 House contest to besting former Philadelphia mayor Richardson Dilworth in the 1962 gubernatorial race. In the House, Scranton supported both civil rights and federal aid to underdeveloped areas, two issues of critical importance to moderates. In his victory against Dilworth, meanwhile, he earned a reputation as a ferocious, and effective, campaigner: one Pennsylvania newspaperman said that the Scranton-Dilworth contest "came close to being the dirtiest personally in Pennsylvania history, and it takes some doing to get that close."[66] Johnson agreed, terming the governor "a real character assassin" who "does it in a Brooks-Brothers style."[67]

While Scranton's gubernatorial accomplishments earned him the label the "first of the Kennedy Republicans," he publicly denied interest in a presidential bid.[68] Privately, though, he received attention from key players in Republican circles, such as Dwight Eisenhower, who spent five hours with him discussing political matters in mid-December. On December 23 the *New York Herald Tribune* described Scranton as "a man who is of presidential caliber, who has proven himself as a campaigner, who has no visible political liabilities, who may be the one person who could unite the party's diverse and divergent factions."[69] But Scranton's refusal to assert himself publicly kept his name recognition low, and his standing in GOP polls hovered in the single digits.

[63] Perlstein, *Before the Storm*, pp. 262–3.
[64] Perlstein, *Before the Storm*, pp. 262–3, 337.
[65] Campaign outline, 31 Oct. 1963, Box 442, John Tower Papers, Southwestern University.
[66] George Wolf, *William Warren Scranton: Pennsylvania Statesman* (University Park: Pennsylvania State University Press, 1981), p. 61.
[67] President Johnson and John Connally, 11:38 A.M., 3 July 1964, Tape WH6407.03, Citation #4145, LBJ Recordings.
[68] Wolf, *William Warren Scranton*, p. 72.
[69] *New York Herald Tribune*, 23 Dec. 1963.

Name recognition was not a problem for another potential compromise candidate – the party's 1960 nominee, Richard Nixon. Nixon first came to national prominence in the late 1940s as a member of the House Un-American Activities Committee. His 1950 election to the upper chamber was among the dirtiest Senate races ever, best captured by Nixon's famous line that his opponent, Representative Helen Gahagan Douglas, was "pink down to her underwear."[70] He cemented his reputation as a party hatchet man as Eisenhower's running mate in 1952, a race that also exposed him to charges of lax ethics after revelations that California businessmen had secretly subsidized his living expenses. When Eisenhower considered removing him from the ticket, Nixon responded with the first effective use of television in a national campaign. He denied wrongdoing and added that he would never ask his daughters to part with their dog, "Checkers," even if the pooch had been acquired through the slush fund.

After eight years as the most powerful vice president in history to that time, Nixon's 1960 campaign started with a good deal of promise, but he faltered after the GOP convention. His chief asset – his experience, especially in the international realm – was undercut after a reporter asked Eisenhower to name an important decision Nixon had made as vice president. The president responded, "If you give me a week, I might think of one." Nixon also came across poorly in the four presidential debates. Still, the final result was agonizingly close – Kennedy prevailed by only 112,803 votes, and a shift of fewer than 28,000 voters in Illinois and Texas would have given Nixon a majority in the Electoral College.[71]

After his loss, Nixon returned to his home state to challenge Governor Pat Brown in the 1962 election. But in an outcome few dared to predict at the start of the campaign, Brown prevailed easily. Addressing the press after his defeat, the candidate scowled, "You won't have Nixon to kick around any more."[72] In 1963 he moved to New York to join a Wall Street law firm, but Kennedy's assassination rekindled Nixon's presidential ambitions. In turbulent times voters would want familiarity, a trend reflected when the former vice president seized the lead in the first poll of GOP contenders taken after Kennedy's death. Johnson himself viewed Nixon as his most likely challenger, regularly tracked the Republican's

[70] George Mitchell, *Tricky Dick and the Pink Lady: Richard Nixon vs. Helen Gahagan Douglas – Sexual Politics and the Red Scare, 1950* (New York: Random House, 1998).

[71] Christopher Matthews, *Kennedy and Nixon: The Rivalry That Shaped Postwar America* (New York: Simon and Schuster, 1996), pp. 134–65.

[72] *Congressional Quarterly Weekly Report*, 16 Nov. 1962, p. 2162.

public statements, and ordered the Democratic National Committee to tally up issues on which Nixon had reversed his position.[73]

Still, as with Rockefeller and Scranton, Nixon had more than his share of vulnerabilities. He remained saddled with the image of "Tricky Dick." The memory of his last press conference was particularly vivid. In mid-December, when John Steele of *Time* told the president that Nixon "*really* is desperately interested," Johnson chuckled, "I hope they still got a copy of his news conference film."[74]

While Nixon, Rockefeller, and Scranton held steady and Goldwater's support declined, a very different kind of Republican emerged as a contender. At the time of the assassination, Henry Cabot Lodge II was serving as U.S. ambassador to South Vietnam, in what figured to be the final public post of his career. Raised by his grandfather and namesake after his father died young, Lodge's career as a moderate Republican began after he won election to the Senate in 1936. He generally supported Roosevelt's foreign policy, often backed the president on domestic matters, and coasted to reelection in 1942. Shortly thereafter, he resigned his seat to enter the U.S. Army (the first member of the Senate to do so since the Civil War) and saw service in North Africa and Italy. After the war he was elected back to the Senate, providing crucial Republican backing for the Truman administration's approach to European affairs. In 1952 he played a key role in Eisenhower's securing of the GOP presidential nomination, but had the bad luck to be challenged at home by the ambitious congressman from Massachusetts' 8th District, John Kennedy.[75] In November, even though Eisenhower carried the Bay State by 208,000 votes, Lodge fell short. After the results were official, General George Marshall wrote that he was "terribly sorry" at the "great error" committed by Massachusetts voters.[76]

After eight years as U.S. ambassador to the United Nations – Lodge's debates with Soviet ambassador Andrei Vishinsky made him a master of what the *New York Times* called the "Back Bay, or codfish, deep freeze" – Lodge was selected by Nixon as his running mate in 1960.[77]

[73] Perlstein, *Before the Storm*, p. 289.

[74] President Johnson and John Steele, 7:59 A.M., 20 Dec. 1963, Tape K6312.12, PNO #17, LBJ Recordings.

[75] Kessel, *The Goldwater Coalition*, p. 36.

[76] Marshall quoted in Thomas Whalen, *Kennedy versus Lodge* (Boston: Northeastern University Press, 2000), p. 157.

[77] Stanley Karnow, "The Quandary of Henry Cabot Lodge," *Saturday Evening Post*, 7 Feb. 1964.

Polling suggested the wisdom of the selection: of those with opinions about Lodge, an amazing 96 percent viewed him favorably.[78] But Nixon came to regret his choice. Lodge's father's premature death had given him a lifelong concern with his health, and he kept to a leisurely campaign schedule that included sufficient time for daily rest.[79] He also proved less than stellar on the campaign trail; as journalist Stanley Karnow observed, while "it is all very well to be cold and arrogant with Soviet delegates, one of Lodge's most serious shortcomings is his tendency to treat other people the same way."[80]

Lodge's defeat in 1960 seemed to mark the end of his public career. After the election, he quipped, "I may be too old to play touch football, but I'm too young to retire."[81] He joined *Time/Life* as a consultant and headed up the Atlantic Institute, a think tank focused on improving U.S.-European relations. His opportunity to return to public service came in mid-1963. Upon coming to the presidency in 1961, Kennedy had inherited a substantial commitment in South Vietnam, where the U.S.-backed regime of Ngo Dinh Diem faced external opposition from Ho Chi Minh's North Vietnamese government and internal rebellion from the National Liberation Front. Seeing South Vietnam as a testing ground for its national security doctrine – called flexible response – the administration escalated U.S. involvement. In May 1963 widespread Buddhist protests prompted a government crackdown, sowing doubts in Washington that Diem would ever win the hearts and minds of his people. Kennedy, disenchanted with his representation in Saigon, subsequently offered Lodge the ambassador's position.[82]

The administration hoped the move would communicate that the United States expected Diem to enact more comprehensive political and social reforms. The State Department also wanted a representative with political skills to temper press criticism of the war, while Kennedy himself envisioned a type of intellectual diplomat who could "pull together"

[78] Kessel, *The Goldwater Coalition,* p. 52.

[79] Theodore H. White, *The Making of the President 1960* (New York: Atheneum, 1961), pp. 206–30.

[80] Stanley Karnow, "The Quandary of Henry Cabot Lodge," *Saturday Evening Post,* 7 Feb. 1964.

[81] Stanley Karnow, "The Quandary of Henry Cabot Lodge," *Saturday Evening Post,* 7 Feb. 1964.

[82] Fredrik Logevall, *Choosing War: The Lost Chance for Peace and the Escalation of the War in Vietnam* (Berkeley: University of California Press, 1999), pp. 3–25; Robert Schulzinger, *A Time for War: The United States and Vietnam, 1945–1975* (New York: Oxford University Press, 1997), pp. 16–88.

the various reports from Vietnam.[83] Lodge seemed appropriate on all three counts. But Lodge's chief qualification was his party affiliation. With the hawkish Goldwater as his likely opponent, Kennedy wanted to neutralize Vietnam as a political issue. As one Democrat stated bluntly, "If we're going to lose a country, we may as well have a Republican there."[84]

Initially, the appointment fulfilled Kennedy's expectations – the new ambassador certainly proved to Diem that unconditional U.S. support had ended. But Lodge went well beyond his stated orders and concluded that salvaging the war effort required removing Diem. The senator who had played a key role in building bipartisan support for the Truman Doctrine and Marshall Plan proved out of his intellectual depth in Southeast Asia. Behaving as almost the caricature of a Western imperialist, Lodge maneuvered among the various Vietnamese factions and encouraged generals to oust Diem. When the coup occurred, on the morning of November 1, 1963, the ambassador coldly received a phone call from the beleaguered Diem requesting a clarification of the U.S. position. Less than 24 hours later, Diem and his brother were dead.[85]

Lodge was on his way back to the United States to consult with Kennedy when he learned of the assassination. Continuing on to Washington to brief the new president, the ambassador discovered a man with a very different approach to foreign policy than that of his predecessor. Although he had addressed many national security matters during his tenure as majority leader, Johnson lacked intellectual interest in international matters and seemed overly deferential to the advisers that Kennedy had assembled. These characteristics triggered a subtle but significant change among top administration policymakers. By March 1964 most prominent supporters of the coup against Diem had either lost influence or left government service altogether.[86] One figure, however, defied the new bureaucratic calculus. On several occasions in December 1963 and January 1964, Johnson

[83] Lodge confidential journal, entries for 12 June 1963, 17 June 1963, Reel 17, Henry Cabot Lodge II Papers, Massachusetts Historical Society. (The Society refers to the collection as the "Henry Cabot Lodge Jr." Papers, but these notes will use "Henry Cabot Lodge II," which is the correct form of his name.)

[84] Stanley Karnow, "The Quandary of Henry Cabot Lodge," *Saturday Evening Post,* 7 Feb. 1964.

[85] Lodge to President Kennedy, 6 Nov. 1963, *Foreign Relations of the United States 1963, vol. IV,* pp. 575–8; "Memorandum for the Record," 22 Nov. 1963, *Foreign Relations of the United States 1963, vol. IV,* pp. 625–6.

[86] President Johnson and McGeorge Bundy, 5:55 P.M., 9 Dec. 1963, Tape K6312.06, PNO #12, LBJ Recordings.

speculated on the possibility of replacing Lodge, whom the president (not incorrectly) felt had "got things screwed up good" in Saigon.[87] But each time Johnson considered a change, he backed off. He had good reason for doing so. For in one of its most unanticipated consequences, the assassination of Kennedy had made Henry Cabot Lodge a contender for the Republican presidential nomination.

Before Kennedy's death, few considered Lodge a serious candidate. Since he could not "imagine anyone could possibly be interested in Lodge," pollster George Gallup did not even include him in surveys.[88] On December 5, however, syndicated columnist Cornelius Dalton detected an increasing perception among Republicans that the "political upheaval" made Lodge "the logical candidate" for 1964.[89] Three days later, *New York Times* columnist Felix Belair reported that Eisenhower privately favored the ambassador's nomination.[90] That evening in the *New York Herald Tribune,* Roscoe Drummond predicted that Lodge would not only run, but would win, due to his strength in foreign policy, his national exposure from the 1960 race, his experience in both the executive and legislative branches, and his position at the GOP's ideological center.[91] In the next day's *Christian Science Monitor,* Richard Strout also predicted a Lodge nomination. He conceded that Lodge was "not the warmest personality in American politics, but he is knowledgeable in the field of foreign affairs and has a good record on civil rights."[92]

The boomlet generated an immediate response from Lodge's critics. Evans and Novak reported that party leaders considered the former senator "poison" who had committed "political treason" by working in the Kennedy administration.[93] A few days later, Eisenhower claimed that his comments to Belair signaled only that he wanted all qualified candidates to consider running for the party's nomination. Columnists close to Johnson attacked from a different angle. Gerald Griffin of the *Baltimore Sun* reasoned that Lodge lacked "either the spark of personal appeal or the intense ambition usually associated with a winning presidential

[87] President Johnson and J. William Fulbright, 2 Dec. 1963, 7:01 P.M., Tape K6312.02, PNO #9, LBJ Recordings.

[88] Gallup quoted in William Miller, *Henry Cabot Lodge: A Biography* (New York: James Heineman, 1967), p. 358.

[89] Dalton, "Political Pulse," 5 Dec. 1963, copy in Box 32, Henry Cabot Lodge II Papers, Massachusetts Historical Society.

[90] *New York Times*, 8 Dec. 1963.

[91] *New York Herald Tribune*, 8 Dec. 1963.

[92] *Christian Science Monitor*, 9 Dec. 1963.

[93] *New York Herald Tribune*, 11 Dec. 1963.

candidate."[94] Meanwhile, political columnist William S. White condemned Lodge's "wholly unexpected injection of himself into partisan politics in an area of hot war with communist invaders."[95]

White also conceded, however, that the prospect of a Lodge candidacy troubled his administration sources. In light of the press reports, Johnson asked National Security Adviser McGeorge Bundy to examine rumors of an Eisenhower-sponsored Lodge candidacy. Bundy reported back that Belair "swears up and down that General Eisenhower told him personally of his interest in the race, and specifically said that he had let Lodge know of his intent." Further, Bundy received word from Vietnam that "Cabot has indeed begun to think in terms of political responsibilities"; as he "would very much like to be honorably free of his responsibilities in Saigon," he hoped to report within two months that "the situation is now so much better that he can now fairly ask for relief."[96]

From Saigon, Lodge himself publicly denied any interest in a presidential bid, citing the Hatch Act, which prohibited federal employees from engaging in political campaigns. In fact, Lodge was very much interested in making the race and worked secretly through his son, George, to coordinate "phase one" of his campaign. Harking back to his role in the 1952 Draft Eisenhower effort, he noted the "importance which Senators can have on a situation like this," namely, by presenting the absent candidate's point of view on news and interview programs.[97] Lodge first advised his son to find a key money man to finance the skeleton operation. The ambassador then laid down two ground rules for his candidacy. The effort "must *not,* in any degree, injure Rockefeller."[98] And under no circumstances would he return from Saigon to campaign for the nomination.[99] He would stand, like Eisenhower in 1952, as the citizen-patriot, willing to accept a draft; in the meantime he would remain on the front lines in the battle against communism.

The first of these conditions was inherently implausible, as Lodge certainly knew: with his record as a moderate Republican, his support for

[94] *Baltimore Sun,* 11 Dec. 1963.

[95] *Washington Star,* 11 Dec. 1963; *Time,* 16 Dec. 1963.

[96] McGeorge Bundy, "Memorandum for the President," 9 Dec. 1963, Box 1, Bundy memos, NSF File, Lyndon Johnson Presidential Library.

[97] Henry Cabot Lodge to George Cabot Lodge, 16 Dec. 1963, Box 33, Henry Cabot Lodge II Papers, Massachusetts Historical Society.

[98] Henry Cabot Lodge to George Cabot Lodge, 31 Dec. 1963, Box 32, Henry Cabot Lodge II Papers, Massachusetts Historical Society.

[99] Henry Cabot Lodge to George Cabot Lodge, 23 Dec. 1963, Box 32, Henry Cabot Lodge II Papers, Massachusetts Historical Society.

civil rights, and his Establishment credentials, a viable Lodge candidacy had to threaten Rockefeller's natural base. Lodge's second condition required a bit of revisionist history: though Eisenhower had remained above the fray for most of the 1952 campaign, he did come back to the United States for several crucial weeks of politicking before the GOP convention started.[100] Lodge calculated, however, that his doing so in the context of 1964 – while perhaps increasing the likelihood of his winning the nomination – would sufficiently tarnish his luster as to render a victory against Johnson unlikely.

In this respect the closest historical parallel for the Lodge effort was not Eisenhower's 1952 bid but that of Wendell Willkie in 1940. A former Democrat and utilities executive, Willkie presented himself as a political outsider. He showed a surprising amount of popular appeal, especially among the party's more liberal, internationalist wing. At the convention, one source estimated that a million telegrams were sent to GOP delegates urging Willkie's selection. On the sixth ballot, Willkie captured the nomination, an apparent lesson that convention delegates would not ignore a candidate who had demonstrated deep voter appeal.[101] Lodge could only hope that political conditions 24 years later remained the same.

In the abstract, Lodge was the most dangerous foe for Johnson in the fall election. Unlike the ultraconservative Goldwater or the unelectable Rockefeller, Lodge sported an impeccable record on civil rights, possessed the national security credentials that even Johnson's supporters admitted the president lacked, and enjoyed extensive contacts within the same Eastern Establishment of which Johnson was both jealous and distrustful. His unannounced candidacy confronted Johnson with an unprecedented situation of a sitting ambassador – in a war zone, no less – actively seeking the opposing party's presidential nomination.[102]

Events in the first two months of 1964 unintentionally highlighted Lodge's two areas of strength: foreign policy and personal ethics. On January 9 anti-American riots in the Panama Canal Zone left 20 Panamanians and four Americans dead. On January 11 Panamanian president Roberto Chiari announced that diplomatic ties with the United States would resume only when Washington agreed to renegotiate the Panama Canal Treaties. The developments generated criticism from

[100] Kessel, *The Goldwater Coalition*, p. 38.

[101] Gil Troy, *See How They Ran: The Changing Role of the Presidential Candidate* (Cambridge, MA: Harvard University Press, 1996), pp. 175–80.

[102] President Johnson to Henry Cabot Lodge, 30 Dec. 1963, *Foreign Relations of the United States 1961–1963*, vol. 4, p. 744.

several GOP presidential candidates, most notably Nixon, for whom the crisis symbolized "a general sickness in our Latin American policy."[103] Neutralizing such attacks gave Johnson a good reason for exercising a decisive role as the crisis developed: he worried how a policy perceived as soft would affect his political standing, lest he "be accused of knowing exactly what was going to happen and not doing anything."[104]

After Johnson appointed a team to travel to Panama for discussions, signs of a resolution emerged. Having taken a firm line that satisfied his own domestic constituency, Chiari welcomed the creation of a five-member Inter-American Peace Committee (IAPC). Most in the administration similarly saw the IAPC approach as a good way to produce a face-saving outcome.[105] But on the (absurd) grounds that the dispute was primarily "Communist-inspired," the president questioned the need for any dialogue at all.[106]

Johnson's chief interest came in how foreign policy would affect politics. When Assistant Secretary of State Thomas Mann asked the president to evaluate the long-term ramifications of his acts, Johnson retorted that the administration "may not be around to judge" if the American public "think we're sitting down to revise some treaties.[107] When pressed further to make concessions, Johnson exploded, "I am not about – not one *goddamned bit* – as long as I'm President, which is going to be for 11 months, gentlemen, I'm not about to get on my knees and go crawling to him and say I want to apologize to you for you shooting my soldiers. By God, I ain't going to do it."[108]

In the end Johnson's actions, as the *New York Times* pointedly noted, left him "fiddling while Panama burns."[109] He performed similarly in the next Latin American crisis, about a month later. After Cuban fishermen accidentally strayed into U.S. territorial waters, the Coast Guard,

[103] *Congressional Quarterly Weekly Report*, 17 Jan. 1964, p. 133.

[104] Bromley Smith, "Memorandum of Conference with the President," 13 Jan. 1964, Box 38, Schoenbaum Files, Dean Rusk Papers, Series IV, Russell Library, University of Georgia.

[105] State Department, "Memorandum of Conversation: Panama Situation," 22 Jan. 1964, Box 2652, State Department Decimal Files, 1964–1966, Record Group 59, National Archives.

[106] President Johnson and Richard Russell, 1:05 P.M., 11 Jan. 1964, Tape WH6401.12, Citation #1321, LBJ Recordings.

[107] President Johnson and Thomas Mann, with Bill Moyers and Ralph Dungan, 1:03 P.M., 14 Jan. 1964, Tape WH6401.14, Citation #1360, LBJ Recordings.

[108] Johnson quoted himself in President Johnson and Richard Russell, 1:05 P.M., 11 Jan. 1964, Tape WH6401.12, Citation #1321, LBJ Recordings.

[109] *New York Times*, 6 Feb. 1964.

ignoring procedure, turned them over to Florida authorities.[110] Fidel Castro's government retaliated by cutting off the water supply to the U.S. naval base at Guantánamo.[111]

As with the outbreak of the Panamanian crisis, the president instantly sensed the domestic implications of Castro's actions.[112] So too did Secretary of Defense Robert McNamara, who recommended firing all Cuban workers on the base.[113] But as time went on, a difference of opinion emerged within the administration. Director of Central Intelligence John McCone – hardly known as a figure soft on communism – speculated that as the Cuban fishermen had not been intentionally sent into American waters, the United States should fine the ship captains and release the fishermen. McGeorge Bundy and Robert Kennedy likewise preferred a mild public statement on the matter.[114] To the question of issuing "a little statement" and doing nothing else, Johnson had a straightforward response: "To hell with that."[115]

Perhaps because of the prominence that political concerns played in his own decision-making process, Johnson assumed that his rivals approached foreign policy disputes as he did. In this instance the president believed that Kennedy disingenuously proposed negotiations so that he could subsequently claim that Johnson was undermining his brother's hard-line Cuban policy.[116] For Johnson, then, both his broader requirements of not appearing soft on communism and his more personal desire to outmaneuver the attorney general dictated a firm approach to Castro. As a result, the confrontation escalated: after Castro accused the United States of stealing Cuban water, Rear Admiral John Bulkley, commander of the U.S. base at Guantánamo, cut the lines bringing water into the installation, symbolically confirming the base's independence from Castro's pressure.

[110] Gordon Chase, "Memorandum for Mr. Bundy," 3 Feb. 1964, Box 23, NSF Country File, Lyndon B. Johnson Presidential Library.

[111] "Facts Relating to Base Water Supply," 6 Feb. 1964, Box 23, NSF Country File, Lyndon B. Johnson Presidential Library.

[112] "Memorandum of Conference with the President, February 7, 1964, 9:00 A.M. – Subject: Cuba," Box 1, Bromley Smith Files, NSF Files, Lyndon B. Johnson Presidential Library.

[113] Lyndon Johnson and Robert McNamara, 9:00 A.M., 7 Feb. 1964, Tape WH6402.08, Citation #1917, LBJ Recordings.

[114] "Memorandum of Conference with the President, February 7, 1964, 4:45 P.M. – Subject: Cuba," Box 1, Bromley Smith Files, NSF Files, Lyndon B. Johnson Presidential Library.

[115] Lyndon Johnson and Richard Russell, 4:30 P.M., 7 Feb. 1964, Tape WH6402.09, Citation #1932, LBJ Recordings.

[116] Lyndon Johnson and Bill Moyers, 11:25 A.M., 8 Feb. 1964, Tape WH6402.11, Citation #1961, LBJ Recordings.

Regarding both Cuba and Panama, Johnson overruled advice from a majority of his counselors in large part to forestall anticipated domestic criticism. It was ironic, then, that the resulting developments only exposed him to strong partisan attacks.[117] Nixon addressed the question in the greatest detail, recognizing that a campaign centered on foreign policy issues would improve his chances. He informed a group of Republican activists that "the new international dart game is to hang a world's map on the wall and try to hit a spot where the United States is not being kicked around, blackmailed, or threatened."[118] The former vice president claimed that while Johnson "seems to be more effective as a political manipulator in getting legislation through Congress, he lacks the idealism and sense of purpose which the world expects from the President of the United States."[119]

The president struggled to respond coherently to the GOP charges. Before astounded employees at the Internal Revenue Service, Johnson branded his Republican foes "bellyachers" and "alarmists" whose actions helped "our other enemies."[120] Privately, though, the criticism did not surprise him. He informed his aide Walter Jenkins, "Of course they're going to make foreign policy the issue. If we could find out how to handle Vietnam or what to do about Cuba…maybe we'd know how to answer it."[121]

In late January and into February, the president suffered political reverses on another front – the question of ethics in government. Two months into the Bobby Baker inquiry, connections to the White House were finally established when GOP senators charged that Walter Jenkins had committed perjury in a deposition for the Rules Committee. They further contended that Johnson himself, during his time in the Senate, had received a kickback arranged by Baker. But as with foreign policy, the president suffered mostly from self-inflicted damage.

In early January Maryland insurance agent Don Reynolds twice told his tale to an executive session of the Rules Committee. In late 1956 or early 1957, in a deal brokered by Baker, Reynolds sold Johnson $100,000 of life insurance, paid for by KTBC, for which Reynolds received a commission of $2,500. Shortly thereafter, he claimed, Jenkins called to say that it was expected that Reynolds should purchase $1,208 in advertising from

[117] *Wall Street Journal*, 14 Feb. 1964.

[118] *Philadelphia Inquirer*, 15 Feb. 1964.

[119] *Wall Street Journal*, 12 Feb. 1964.

[120] *New York Herald Tribune*, 12 Feb. 1964.

[121] President Johnson and Walter Jenkins, 10:55 A.M., 10 Feb. 1964, Tape WH6402.13, Citation #1995, LBJ Recordings.

KTBC. Two years later, according to Reynolds, Baker said that it would be appropriate for him to give Johnson a hi-fi set. Baker forwarded a catalog, saying that Lady Bird had indicated her preference, and Reynolds made the purchase, for $542.[122] For each of these allegations, Reynolds supplied cancelled checks or other forms of receipts.

In light of Reynolds's testimony, the *Washington Post* reported that prominent Republicans were considering reviving their 1952 anti-corruption campaign.[123] The gift of the hi-fi set raised questions about Johnson's ethics. (Barry Goldwater stated that when Baker presented him with the gift, Johnson should have asked, "Where did you get this, buster?")[124] But the advertising time charge was even more serious. Not only did it sound as if Johnson demanded a kickback, but also Reynolds's version of events directly contradicted a Jenkins affidavit of January 11, 1964.[125]

Few people had played a more central role in Johnson's political career than Walter Jenkins. A native of rural Texas, Jenkins finished high school at age fifteen, junior college at age seventeen, and attended the University of Texas before joining Johnson's staff in 1939. He remained on Johnson's payroll – except for a four-year stint in the Army and an unsuccessful bid for the House of Representatives in 1951 – for the next quarter century. Throughout the 1950s, he served Johnson politically as his administrative assistant and personally as treasurer of the LBJ Corporation; Jenkins then was Johnson's chief aide as vice president. *Time* described him as "so reticent" about "public exposure" that "he is almost a recluse."[126]

Reynolds came to the Rules Committee's attention through the efforts not of the inert committee counsel, L. P. McLendon, but of John Williams, who by this time was devoting almost all of his efforts to tracking down leads – legitimate and otherwise – in the Baker inquiry. The Delaware senator criticized Johnson on the hi-fi and insurance issues, but he also wanted to move beyond the particulars of the Reynolds charges.[127] Williams displayed particular interest in two matters that would become

[122] U.S. Senate, Rules Committee, *Hearings, Financial or Business Interests of Officers or Employees of the Senate*, 88th Cong., 2nd sess., p. 81 (9 Jan. 1964).

[123] *Washington Post*, 26 Jan. 1964.

[124] *New York Times*, 25 Jan. 1964.

[125] Walter Jenkins affidavit, 11 Jan. 1964, Box 32, John Williams Papers, University of Delaware, University of Delaware.

[126] *Time*, 3 Apr. 1964.

[127] *U.S. News&World Report*, 3 Feb. 1964.

familiar to students of later American political scandals: campaign finance and sex.

On March 29, 1962, Billy Sol Estes, a 37-year-old financier from Pecos, Texas, was arrested for fraud and theft after a complicated scheme designed to monopolize the West Texas fertilizer market. The case became politically explosive after revelations that Estes had placed nearly 60 calls to the office of the leader of the Texas Democratic liberals, Ralph Yarborough, and had contributed to the campaign of Representative J. T. (Slick) Rutherford, a prominent West Texas liberal. Although rumors existed of a tie between Johnson and Estes, Senate investigators never uncovered evidence. Estes went to jail, Rutherford lost his seat in 1962 to Republican Ed Foreman, and talk in Washington persisted that Estes, through the vice president's longtime associate Cliff Carter, had funneled contributions to Johnson.[128]

Another high-profile inquiry more directly implicated Johnson. In February 1963 the Senate Permanent Investigations Subcommittee looked into the Pentagon's decision to overrule military review panels and award the TFX fighter aircraft to a General Dynamics/Grunman consortium, based in Fort Worth and Long Island. The Defense Department estimated that the program would generate 20,000 jobs, making it the largest tactical airplane contract in American history.[129] While chairman John McClellan (D-Arkansas) strongly questioned Pentagon denials that the decision was not based on political influence, Representative William Stinson (R-Washington) more bluntly termed the TFX "the LBJ aircraft."[130]

McClellan's investigation intensified rumors about Johnson's corruption, and now Reynolds offered testimony from someone previously inside Johnson's camp seemingly confirming the suspicions. The insurance agent claimed that Baker had shown him a sack containing $200,000 in cash, allegedly Johnson's payoff for the TFX contract, which Baker said had come from Fred Black of General Dynamics and Roy Evans of Grunman.[131] The Rules Committee, citing inaccuracies in Reynolds's account, refused to investigate. Williams, desperate, contended that even if Reynolds himself were "inaccurate or confused," the awarding of the

[128] *Congressional Quarterly Weekly Report*, 20 Apr. 1962, p. 638.

[129] *Congressional Quarterly Weekly Report*, 15 Mar. 1963, p. 328.

[130] 109 *Congressional Record*, 88th Cong. 1st sess., pp. 3407 (4 Mar. 1963), 4693 (21 Mar. 1963).

[131] Eleanor Lenhart memorandum, 11 Feb. 1964, Box 30, John Williams Papers, University of Delaware.

TFX contract was "so irregular" that a payoff must have occurred.[132] That line of thinking unsurprisingly failed to persuade committee Democrats.

Just as Williams was convinced of Johnson's involvement in a campaign finance scandal, so too did he want the Rules Committee to expand its inquiry to the "call girls" question. He played off the Profumo scandal in Britain from the previous year, in which the British defense minister had been forced to resign after discovery of his involvement with a model/showgirl who was also having an affair with the Soviet naval attaché. The Delaware senator revealed that one of the women allegedly in Baker's employ, Ellen Romestch (whom journalist Clark Mollenhoff breathlessly described as a "lesbian-prostitute"), had been deported to her native East Germany.[133] Williams wondered whether she had carried any U.S. government secrets with her.

Everett Dirksen blocked this line of inquiry, informing his Delaware colleague that FBI director J. Edgar Hoover had reported that a Senate inquiry "would disclose such a large percentage of the Senate as being of such low morals it could undermine the confidence of the people in the integrity of our Government and may even prove disastrous to our country."[134] Frustrated on this angle, Williams was reduced to dealing in unsubstantiated gossip about Johnson's sex life.[135] Baker responded in kind, passing word covertly that he had a call girl willing to testify to having had sex with (the notoriously Puritan) Williams.[136]

Despite his reckless charges, Williams kept the Baker inquiry alive; unless the Rules Committee made a pretense of a good-faith investigation, the Delaware senator possessed enough information to prove a whitewash. (Williams deliberately left the impression that he had not turned over all his files to the committee.) With Williams pressuring them from one direction and many of their colleagues doing so from the other side, committee Democrats stumbled awkwardly along. Writing in *The New Republic,* Richard Strout compared the case to "an electric rod building up potential until finally the spark jumped from the Senate committee

[132] Eleanor Lenhart memorandum, n.d., Box 34, John Williams Papers, University of Delaware.

[133] Clark Mollenhoff to John Williams, 28 Oct. 1963, Box 30, John Williams Papers, University of Delaware.

[134] Eleanor Lenhart memorandum, 10 Jan. 1964, Box 30, John Williams Papers, University of Delaware.

[135] Eleanor Lenhart memorandum, n.d., Box 30, John Williams Papers, University of Delaware.

[136] Eleanor Lenhart memorandum, 10 Jan. 1964, Box 30, John Williams Papers, University of Delaware.

to the White House."[137] As with foreign policy, Johnson's own actions provided the spark.

Livid at his critics – especially Williams, "a mean, bitter, dirty Republican that will do anything to try to win a seat for any Republican" – Johnson claimed to have no knowledge of who purchased the hi-fi. He wondered what why it mattered anyway: "I paid $88,000 worth of premiums, and, by God, they could afford to give me a Cadillac if they wanted to and there wouldn't have been a goddamned thing wrong with it."[138] After unsuccessfully pressing Senate allies such as Richard Russell and George Smathers (D-Florida) to squelch the inquiry, the president seized the offensive himself. He unexpectedly appeared before reporters to issue a meaningless statement on Panama, and then asked for questions, having received Abe Fortas's poorly considered assurance that his addressing the Reynolds affair in this fashion would make it "a one-day play."[139] A reporter asked Johnson about relations with Congress. Although the query had nothing to do with Baker, Johnson supplied his prearranged answer. He termed the hi-fi set nothing more than a gift from "the Baker family," denied receiving any kickbacks, and commented that he had obtained the life insurance policy "so Mrs. Johnson and the children wouldn't have to sell their stock on the open market and lose control of the company" if he died.[140]

The president then hurriedly retreated from the room, prompting portrayals of his having fled from reporters' questions. Capturing the journalistic consensus, the *New York Times*' Cabell Phillips foresaw the Baker affair "rapidly developing into *the* political scandal of the mid-sixties," since the case symbolized "a chronic amorality that has been eroding the public conscience."[141] One Johnson associate lamented, "Everyone says the Baker dirt is just beginning to spill out."[142]

Conceding the problem – "we're blowing it up ourselves" – Johnson searched for a solution. His advisers provided little help. In yet another similarity with more modern political scandals, Fortas failed to recognize the political fallout that his legalistic recommendations would produce.

137 *The New Republic,* 25 Jan. 1964.

138 President Johnson and George Smathers, 9:01 P.M., 10 Jan. 1964, Tape WH6401.11, Citation #1312, LBJ Recordings.

139 President Johnson, Abe Fortas, and Walter Jenkins, 7:40 P.M., 17 Jan. 1964, Tape WH6401.16, Citation #1410, LBJ Recordings.

140 *Congressional Quarterly Weekly Report*, 31 Jan. 1964, p. 214.

141 *New York Times*, 25 Jan. 1964, 26 Jan. 1964; see also *Newsweek*, 3 Feb. 1964; *Washington Star*, 25 Jan. 1964; *New York Herald Tribune*, 26 Jan. 1964.

142 Katie Louchheim journal, 26 Jan. 1964, Box 79, Katie Louchheim Papers, Library of Congress. My thanks to Bill Leuchtenburg for this citation.

FIGURE 1-3. President Johnson with Abe Fortas. Johnson followed Fortas's legalistic guidance in responding to the Bobby Baker affair—inadvertently intensifying impressions that the president had something to hide. © Courtesy of the Lyndon Baines Johnson Presidential Library. Photo by Yoichi Okamoto.

Johnson's aide George Reedy, soon to take over as press secretary, proposed issuing late-night statements countering Republican attacks. (An amazed Johnson wondered whether Reedy would wander up and down Pennsylvania Avenue to track down the press after they had left the White House for the day.) Johnson's special assistant Jack Valenti, a former advertising executive and later president of the Motion Picture Association of America, recommended employing "the basic principle of public relations or whatever you want to call it: just keep your name out of the paper."[143] Jenkins, reflecting his preference for operating covertly, advocated leaking material from Reynolds's Air Force file or memoranda that offered "considerably more detail on Reynolds' love life."[144] Longtime Washington insider and lawyer Clark Clifford, who Johnson regularly consulted on such matters, wanted the Rules Committee to announce that "they're not going to go into things that don't have anything to do with the government."[145] Meanwhile, from Senate allies implicated in the scandal, the response was panic: in Senator Smathers's words, "This whole thing is going to come down on all of our heads. We might as well forget about the election."[146]

The president's strategy patched together aspects of the recommendations from Jenkins, Fortas, and Clifford (and Smathers, to an increasing degree) as well as his own partisan instincts. He wanted to get the Rules Committee's six Democrats "to tell the Republicans to go straight to hell." Unfortunately, two members of the majority, Joe Clark of Pennsylvania and Claiborne Pell of Rhode Island, would not accommodate such a request. Nor could the president rely on Jordan's skills in leading the committee; as Senator Richard Russell dryly explained, the North Carolina Democrat "labors *very* earnestly to understand that two and two is four. He's not a very smart fellow."[147]

Frustrated in his attempt to bully the Rules Committee, Johnson tried to persuade Democratic senators of the merits of his case. He

[143] President Johnson, Bill Moyers, George Reedy, Abe Fortas, Walter Jenkins, and Jack Valenti, 8:55 P.M., 27 Jan. 1964, Tape WH6401.23, Citation #1593, LBJ Recordings.

[144] President Johnson and Walter Jenkins, no time reported, 28 Jan. 1964, Tape WH6401.24, Citation #1606, LBJ Recordings.

[145] Clifford as reported in President Johnson and Walter Jenkins, 11:45 A.M., 29 Jan. 1964, Tape WH6401.24, Citation #1618, LBJ Recordings.

[146] President Johnson and George Smathers, 6:20 P.M., 29 Jan. 1964, Tape WH6401.25, Citation #1642, LBJ Recordings.

[147] President Johnson and Richard Russell, 10:30 A.M., 29 Jan. 1964, Tape WH6401.24, Citation #1612, LBJ Recordings.

contended that even if everything Reynolds said were true, the charges were irrelevant, since they involved private morality, not public conduct.[148] Moreover, the Reynolds testimony involved alleged improprieties committed before he entered the White House. "It's almost," the president disingenuously reasoned, "like talking about what I did in high school."[149]

In addition to trying to minimize the charges, the president worked to discredit Reynolds. Johnson spoke on several occasions about leaking Reynolds's Air Force file to a friendly journalist or senator but never could find an appropriate time to act. Then someone from the Air Force, no doubt believing he was assisting the president's cause, leaked the file to *Washington Merry-Go-Round* reporter Drew Pearson, one of Johnson's closest journalistic confidants. Reaction was swift and harsh. John Barron of the *Washington Star* termed the inquiry "completely out of control," with "sensational new charges" expected; "no one," he reported, "knows when it will end."[150]

The leak of personnel material, obviously, was a serious event. But broader concerns explained the reaction to the Pearson article. As Barron's editors at the *Star* realized, the smear "threatens these days to overshadow the Baker case itself."[151] Richard Strout believed that "there is hardly a reporter in Washington who doesn't think the leak was arranged by the administration." The affair only confirmed his suspicion that "the only man who can beat Lyndon Johnson is Lyndon Johnson." The Republicans had no real issue – their foreign policy criticisms smacked of desperation – but "maybe they can work up a personality attack," betting that the president's "heavy-handedness in dealing with critics" would cause him to abuse the power of his office.[152]

The turn of events left the president shell-shocked. He tried to explain away the problem on the preposterous grounds that the *New York Times* and *Washington Post* "must have a conspiracy to wreck us."[153] But Johnson also understood that the affair gave the Republicans a "little hope and

[148] President Johnson and Mike Mansfield, 11:11 A.M., 29 Jan. 1964, Tape WH6401.24, Citation #1615, LBJ Recordings.

[149] President Johnson and William S. White, 9:40 A.M., 12 Feb. 1964, Tape WH6402.15, Citation #2055, LBJ Recordings.

[150] *Washington Star*, 9 Feb. 1964; see also *New York Times*, 6 Feb. 1964, *New York Times*, 8 Feb. 1964.

[151] *Washington Star*, 17 Feb. 1964.

[152] *The New Republic*, 22 Feb. 1964.

[153] President Johnson, Walter Jenkins, and Bill Moyers, 11:25 A.M., 8 Feb. 1964, Tape WH6402.11, Citation #1971, LBJ Recordings.

little life."[154] The president's predicament grew worse as February drew to a close: the long-awaited appearance of Baker before the committee lasted two-and-a-half hours and featured the former aide pleading the Fifth Amendment 121 times. Johnson's only solace came when Baker's attorney, Edward Bennett Williams, prevented the proceedings from being televised.[155]

Wall Street Journal correspondent Henry Gemmill most perceptively analyzed the danger that Johnson faced on the matter. To Gemmill, "Lyndon Johnson's greatest political problem is that he is a man with two very different images." In the image dominant after the assassination, "he is the President who lifts mastery of politics to the level of uncommonly skilled statesmanship," rallying support from a cross section of the American public. But Johnson also was viewed as "an opportunist whose mastery of pure politics is devoted not to principle but to personal ambition or even profit," an image that had cost him in the race for the 1960 Democratic nomination. The possibility of this image reviving explained "why some politicians sense real danger…in the Bobby Baker scandal." In the end, how the public viewed Johnson's political strategy depended on its personal opinion of the president. In this respect, "current economic and social problems which obviously have no direct connection with such a thing as the 'Bobby Baker scandal' could yet by chain reaction completely alter their appearance." In a worst-case scenario, Gemmill predicted that "the psychology of politics could indeed convert them into fuel for further 'scandal.' "[156]

Johnson did not need Gemmill to tell him the Baker affair could harm his chances of winning in November. Entering office a relatively unknown figure, he had only one chance to define himself to the American public. The Republicans' ability to sustain the Baker inquiry – aided, as the *Los Angeles Times*' Richard Wilson observed, by the impression that "what is seen in the Baker case is only the tip of the iceberg" – ensured that the issues of personal morality and ethics in government represented a real threat to the president's political standing.[157]

Johnson fought back with one tool that all presidents possess: changing the focus of the national debate. The farm bill presented a golden opportunity. Though the administration had initially planned to press the

[154] President Johnson and George Brown, 12:20 P.M., 14 Feb. 1964, Tape WH6402.16, Citation #2082, LBJ Recordings.

[155] *Washington Star*, 25 Feb. 1964.

[156] *Wall Street Journal*, 30 Jan. 1964.

[157] *Los Angeles Times*, 19 Feb. 1964.

Senate to abandon the House's textile subsidy scheme, Johnson reversed course after hearing from Everett Jordan, who adopted a straightforward mantra: "Get relief for the textile mills."[158] Jordan was not a subtle man, and he made clear that his continued cooperation in curtailing the Baker inquiry depended on the administration's approach to the farm bill.[159] Meanwhile, with the civil rights bill working its way through the House, the farm bill represented an opportunity for Johnson to soothe his relations with anti–civil rights Southern Democrats. As he bluntly explained to Allen Ellender (D-Louisiana), chair of the Senate Agriculture Committee, "This is an election year. Democrats are up. If we don't have that farm bill, they're going to catch hell."[160]

Senate consideration of the bill marked the high point of Johnson's strategy of using economic issues to appeal to his party's disaffected Southern base. As the *New Republic* noted, "Seldom have so many people been offered such a variety of things as in the Administration's wheat-cotton legislation." Indeed, the whole scheme "perfectly fit the requirements of an election year," since it gave Johnson some "footing in the South, the Midwest, and the West – much of it Goldwater country not long ago."[161] With this multiregional, bipartisan coalition, the measure passed the Senate by a vote of 55 to 35. Richard Russell pointed to Johnson's legislative acumen to explain passage of a measure that a month before he thought needed a "miracle" to prevail.[162]

The farm bill was not Johnson's only significant legislative triumph in the upper chamber. *Newsweek*'s Kenneth Crawford, normally a critic of Democratic presidents, noted with awe Johnson's ability "to disarm foes of government spending without dismaying liberals."[163] Privately, Johnson chortled, "The Republican community got hit awfully hard by the budget, and they don't know what the hell to do. They've got no positive, affirmative program: they're not *for* anything."[164] The president

[158] U.S. Senate, Common Agriculture and Forestry, *Hearings, Cotton Programs*, 88th Cong., 1st sess., p. 45 (20 May 1963).

[159] President Johnson, B. Everett Jordan, and Walter Jenkins, 5:34 P.M., 6 Dec. 1963, Tape K6312.04, PNO #28, Recordings of Telephone Conversations – White House Series, Recordings and Transcripts of Conversations and Meetings, Lyndon B. Johnson Presidential Library.

[160] President Johnson and Allen Ellender, 5:04 P.M., 15 Feb. 1964, Tape WH6402.17, Citation #2094, LBJ Recordings.

[161] *The New Republic*, 28 Mar. 1964.

[162] Richard Russell to R. F. Burch, 30 Jan. 1964, Richard Russell Papers, Series IX, Box 19, University of Georgia.

[163] *Newsweek*, 20 Jan. 1964.

[164] President Johnson and Frank Stanton, 12:30 P.M., 6 Feb. 1964, Tape WH6402.07, Citation #1907, LBJ Recordings.

reached out to liberals, meanwhile, by supporting civil rights and launching a war on poverty. The latter program was stalled by bureaucratic infighting until February 1, when the president made a surprise move. One Johnson innovation was regular Saturday press conferences – so as to ensure maximum coverage in the widely read Sunday newspapers. With the Baker story the week's hottest news, he needed "something to say to the press."[165] So Johnson decided to announce that Peace Corps director Sargent Shriver, a Midwestern Catholic who had married into the Kennedy family, would coordinate the administration's anti-poverty initiative.

There was only one problem with this plan: Shriver himself did not "know what the hell they're doing."[166] Johnson's concerns, however, were practical: "I've got an election ahead of me," he told Shriver, and he needed Shriver "to get all the damn publicity you can."[167] As the president desired, poverty rather than corruption was the top story in most Sunday newspapers the next day. For such reasons, said Scotty Reston of the *New York Times,* Johnson was "playing the political game with a skill and persistence that has not been seen here since the days of Roosevelt."[168]

The more time that passed, of course, the more difficult it became for Johnson to mimic the political tactic pioneered by FDR in the 1936 and 1940 elections – claiming to ignore political matters while making policy decisions in such a way to maximize political benefit. Try as he might, he could not avoid formal politics altogether. Indeed, the Shriver announcement in part attracted attention because of its potential effect on the vice-presidential race.[169] Johnson would quickly sour on Shriver, but he did find himself spending more and more time addressing the vice-presidential issue – or what columnist Richard Wilson described as "the Bobby Kennedy problem."[170] Jeff Shesol, who has studied the Johnson-Kennedy relationship in the greatest detail, has described Kennedy's thinking on the vice-presidential issue as "incoherent and often downright

[165] President Johnson and Sargent Shriver, 1:02 P.M., 1 Feb. 1964, Tape WH6402.01, Citation #1804, LBJ Recordings.

[166] President Johnson and Sargent Shriver, 1:02 P.M., 1 Feb. 1964, Tape WH6402.01, Citation #1804, LBJ Recordings; President Johnson and Sargent Shriver, 2:25 P.M., 1 Feb. 1964, Tape WH6402.01, Citation #1807, LBJ Recordings.

[167] President Johnson and Sargent Shriver, 1:02 P P.M., 1 Feb. 1964, Tape WH6402.01, Citation #1804, LBJ Recordings; President Johnson and Sargent Shriver, 6:28 P.M., 1 Feb. 1964, Tape WH6402.02, Citation #1815, LBJ Recordings.

[168] *New York Times*, 26 Jan. 1964.

[169] *Wall Street Journal*, 14 Jan. 1964; see also *Newsday*, 1 Jan. 1964; *New York Herald Tribune*, 14 Jan. 1964.

[170] *Los Angeles Times*, 23 Mar. 1964.

irrational."[171] In early 1964 Kennedy started attempting to force his way onto the ticket, rationalizing that his name and background would give him an unusual degree of independence as vice president. If nothing else, the effort provided a way to strike back at Johnson personally.[172] As Kennedy's goal became more widely known, he attracted strong support from Democratic activists: in a January poll he comfortably led former nominee Adlai Stevenson and Minnesota senator Hubert Humphrey. Articulating the conventional wisdom, *Saturday Evening Post* journalist Stewart Alsop wrote in February that it would "be remarkably hard for President Johnson to turn him [Kennedy] down if wanted the vice presidency."[173]

Johnson responded predictably. He told his aide Ken O'Donnell, "I don't want to go down in history as the guy to have the dog wagged by the tail and have the Vice President elect me, because that's what they're going to write."[174] The president's paranoia about Kennedy's intentions increasingly affected his approach to governing. Johnson wildly claimed to have "found out pretty definitely" that Kennedy had started the Bobby Baker investigation as part of a plot to drive him off the ticket in 1964; he further asserted that the attorney general had leaked damaging information to (of all people) the ultra-conservative Clark Mollenhoff so as to embarrass Johnson.[175] To those who pointed to popular surveys showing a Kennedy preference for the number-two slot, Johnson turned to polls of Democratic county leaders, which showed Humphrey ahead.[176]

The relationship between the two men deteriorated further in early February, after word reached the White House that a Kennedy aide then working for the Democratic National Committee, Paul Corbin, was in New Hampshire organizing a Kennedy write-in campaign. Of Corbin, few had anything positive to say. O'Donnell referred to him as the "Rasputin of our administration," Kennedy's assistant deputy attorney general Joe Dolan termed him "the dark side of Bobby Kennedy," and to *Newsweek* bureau chief Ben Bradlee, Corbin was "really a terrible

[171] Jeff Shesol, *Mutual Contempt: Lyndon Johnson, Robert Kennedy, and the Feud That Defined a Decade* (New York: W. W. Norton, 1997), p. 178.

[172] Ken O'Donnell oral history, Lyndon B. Johnson Library.

[173] Stewart Alsop, "LBJ and RFK," *Saturday Evening Post*, 22 Feb. 1964.

[174] Ken O'Donnell oral history, Lyndon B. Johnson Library.

[175] President Johnson and Edwin Weisl, 4:15 P.M., 9 Mar. 1964, Tape WH6403.06, Citation #2417, LBJ Recordings.

[176] *New York Times*, 3 Jan. 1964.

little guy."[177] Johnson told O'Donnell that he wanted Corbin fired; he suggested that O'Donnell ask the attorney general to perform the task. O'Donnell did as ordered, and Kennedy had a straightforward response: "Tell him to go to hell."[178] Later that afternoon Kennedy arrived at the Oval Office for a meeting to discuss strategy on the civil rights bill. The president informed the attorney general that he considered Corbin's behavior inappropriate. Kennedy defended his protégé and noted that President Kennedy had supported Corbin's efforts to root out corruption in the DNC. The recollections of the two men differed as to exactly how Johnson replied, but Johnson clearly said something to the effect that he was president now, not John Kennedy.[179] The attorney general coldly responded, "I know you're President, and don't you ever talk to me like that again." He later described the conversation as "the meanest one that I've ever heard."[180]

Kennedy was not the only figure campaigning for the vice presidency. Immediately after the assassination, Hubert Humphrey's top advisers convened a strategy session to plot the senator's bid for the post. The Minnesotan first had attracted national attention in 1948, when, as mayor of Minneapolis, he delivered a brilliant address favoring a strong civil rights plank in the Democratic platform.[181] The speech established a reputation for political oratory to which Humphrey would struggle to live up. For 1964 Max Kampelman, one of Humphrey's intimates, recalled that "our goal was not so much to win a competition with other people, but to elevate Humphrey beyond competition," thereby making the senator "the only possible choice for Johnson."[182] Humphrey backers believed that the senator had two important assets, beyond the president's dislike of Robert Kennedy. First, they suspected that the battleground in 1964 House elections would be in the Midwest, home to 29 of the 77 seats Democratic party operatives considered marginal.[183]

[177] Shesol, *Mutual Contempt*, p. 183; President Johnson, Jack Valenti, and Ben Bradlee, 11:30 A.M., 7 Mar. 1964, Tape WH6403.04, Citation #2380, LBJ Recordings.

[178] Kennedy quoted in Dallek, *Flawed Giant*, p. 58.

[179] Shesol, *Mutual Contempt,* p. 186.

[180] Dallek, *Flawed Giant*, p. 135.

[181] Steven Gillon, *Politics and Vision: The ADA and American Liberalism, 1947–1985* (New York: Oxford University Press, 1987), pp. 43–62.

[182] Kampelman quoted in Robert Mann, *The Walls of Jericho: Lyndon Johnson, Hubert Humphrey, Richard Russell, and the Struggle for Civil Rights* (New York: Harcourt Brace, 1996), p. 433.

[183] Bill Connell, memo to the Senator, 29 Jan. 1964, Box 56, Hubert Humphrey Papers, Minnesota State Historical Society, St. Paul.

Humphrey, as the region's most prominent Democrat, would help the party's efforts more than any other vice-presidential candidate. Second, Johnson wanted to select someone clearly qualified to step in as chief executive. "The beauty" of this requirement, the Senate whip's staffers believed, "is that we can be almost completely objective and yet be certain that our man would come out on top."[184]

Humphrey, however, had serious weaknesses. His own staff conceded that his speeches were often long, uninspiring, and stale; one Humphrey performance recalled for Norman Thomas remarks that the former Socialist presidential nominee had delivered in 1932.[185] On the religious issue, the Humphrey team searched in vain for ways of "diluting the pressure for a Catholic on the ticket."[186] Many in the senator's natural constituency, liberal activists, backed Stevenson; in addition, as a longtime champion of civil rights, Humphrey had to overcome the suspicion of some Democrats that he would hurt the ticket in the South.

Humphrey possessed one other liability: the president himself. Johnson once told his special assistant Bill Moyers, "I would have lots of problems with him. He's so exuberant, so enthusiastic; he'd get off the reservation all the time."[187] Moyers was known to favor his former boss, Shriver, for the vice-presidential nod, but Johnson repeated similar sentiments to others. In one way, the lack of a clear vice-presidential frontrunner helped Johnson because it generated public interest and made putative nominees more likely to assist him in his legislative agenda. But it also created an awkward, semi-open campaign that could embarrass the president, if only by taking the focus away from Johnson's own accomplishments.

If Johnson wanted to avoid speculation about the vice presidency, he looked to eschew state political squabbles even more. Nonetheless, as with the vice-presidential contest, he discovered that as president sometimes he could not control political events. After New Hampshire, the next Democratic primary was held in Wisconsin, where Johnson had unintentionally waded into an intraparty fight. Among the items he inherited from Kennedy was the judicial nomination of David Rabinowitz, a

[184] Marvin Rosenberg to Bill Connell, 18 Feb. 1964, Box 76, Humphrey Papers, Minnesota State Historical Society.

[185] Marvin Rosenberg to Bill Connell, 3 Feb. 1964, Box 76, Humphrey Papers, Minnesota State Historical Society.

[186] Marvin Rosenberg to Bill Connell, 18 Feb. 1964, Box 76, Humphrey Papers, Minnesota State Historical Society.

[187] Johnson quoted in Dallek, *Flawed Giant*, p. 137.

Wisconsin labor lawyer who had earned the enmity of business leaders after he represented the United Auto Workers in a bitter dispute between the union and the Kohler Company.[188] Conservatives were not the only critics of Rabinowitz: the *Washington Post* charged that Kennedy had nominated Rabinowitz only to bypass James Doyle, a prominent Badger State attorney and friend of Wisconsin senator Gaylord Nelson. Doyle's sin: he had backed Stevenson over Kennedy in 1960.[189]

The situation within the Wisconsin Democratic Party was complicated. Nelson, previously Wisconsin's governor, had a cool relationship with his successor in Madison, John Reynolds, who coincidentally was Rabinowitz's most enthusiastic political supporter. Johnson failed to explore the politics of the issue: national liberals who had his ear, notably Joseph Rauh of the Americans for Democratic Action and Walter Reuther of the United Auto Workers, favored Rabinowitz. So, less than an hour before the 1964 congressional session opened, the president gave Rabinowitz a recess appointment, allowing him to serve until the end of the year.[190]

The decision unsurprisingly antagonized the Nelson wing of the state party. Meanwhile, since Wisconsin law did not allow write-in candidacies and Johnson's political operatives had determined that the president would not enter any primaries (so as to maintain his nonpolitical aura), the White House needed to find a Wisconsin Democrat to run as a favorite son. The choices were not appealing: apart from Nelson or Reynolds, the only viable option was the state's senior senator, William Proxmire, a strong critic of Johnson's performance as Senate majority leader. The president wanted to stay as far away from Wisconsin as he could, because "they're going to fight among themselves out there all the time."[191] Unfortunately, Reynolds was also very close to Robert Kennedy, and Johnson worried that, if spurned by the White House, the governor might embrace the attorney general's vice-presidential bid. Accordingly, the president persuaded Nelson to allow Reynolds to run as a favorite-son candidate – a choice that would have important consequences.[192]

[188] President Johnson to Mrs. David Rabinowitz, 17 May 1965; Bill Moyers to President Johnson, 19 Nov. 1964; both in Box 471, John Macy files, Lyndon B. Johnson Presidential Library.

[189] *Washington Post*, 3 Jan. 1964.

[190] Bill Moyers to President Johnson, 19 Nov. 1964, Box 471, John Macy files, Lyndon B. Johnson Presidential Library.

[191] President Johnson and Cliff Carter, 1:00 P.M., 11 Mar. 1964, Tape WH6403.09, Citation #2474, LBJ Recordings.

[192] *New York Times*, 9 Feb. 1964.

Johnson's unwillingness to place his name on primary ballots also drew him into state party battles in California and Ohio. As one observer noted, "The politics of California sometimes embarrasses even Californians." In 1958 Democrats made their best showing in the history of the Golden State, electing Pat Brown governor and an obscure congressman, Clair Engle, senator. Democrats also seized control of both houses of the state legislature, elevating Jesse Unruh to the post of Assembly Speaker. The relationship between Unruh and Brown quickly deteriorated, and Kennedy turned to Unruh, a more competent politician than the governor, as his chief California ally.[193]

Kennedy's death gave Brown an opportunity to reestablish his primacy. He embraced the idea of running as a favorite son in 1964 but first wanted a firm statement of support from the White House. Johnson's chief California political operative, Lloyd Hand, pleaded with the president to express his confidence in Brown, but, as in Wisconsin, Johnson was reluctant to intervene; he had more than enough to do without "playing with every city councilman that wants to come and see me." And the frequent conversations he had with "that son of a bitch" Brown were not pleasant: "each time he has to tell me what a great man he is, and how he defeated Nixon."[194]

Upon reflection, however, Johnson made the phone call.[195] Unfortunately, while this move soothed Brown, it enraged Los Angeles mayor Sam Yorty, a maverick who had supported Nixon in 1960 and who now filed his own slate of delegates geared toward "independent minded Democrats." The mayor informed Johnson that while he "would like to be helpful," he had "reached the point of being insulted."[196]

Similar intraparty divisiveness confronted in Johnson in Ohio. The state party chair, Bill Coleman, wanted to head a favorite-son delegation, but Coleman's leadership was opposed by Representative Wayne Hays, a hard-nosed pragmatist later known for his tyrannical chairmanship of the House Administration Committee. The Buckeye State also featured what Stewart Alsop predicted would be "the most exciting and significant

[193] Bill Stout, "California Democrats: Battle Royale for the Senate," *The Reporter*, 7 May 1964.

[194] President Johnson and Lloyd Hand, 9:33 P.M., 9 Feb. 1964, Tape WH6402.13, Citation #1990, LBJ Recordings.

[195] President Johnson, Ken O'Donnell, Sam Yorty, and Lloyd Hand, 11:30 A.M., 14 Feb. 1964, Tape WH6402.15, Citation #2076, LBJ Recordings.

[196] Sam Yorty to President Johnson, 8 June 1964, Box 32, WHCF-PL, Lyndon B. Johnson Presidential Library.

political race this year" outside of the presidential contest.[197] The incumbent senator, Stephen Young, was described by the *Washington Star* as endowed with "the tongue and the vocabulary of a drill sergeant."[198] (Young was famous for his combative letters to hostile constituents, which began with phrases such as "Dear Sir: You are a liar.") The 75-year-old Young was an accidental senator. In 1958 he upset incumbent John Bricker after organized labor boosted voter turnout to defeat a right-to-work referendum. For the 1964 contest, polls showed Young, a Coleman ally, badly trailing his likely Republican opponent, Representative Robert Taft, Jr. And so Hays, searching for someone to challenge the incumbent in the primary, turned to former astronaut John Glenn, who resigned his commission in the Marine Corps to make the race.[199]

Like Brown in California, Hays intended to use Johnson to gain control of the state party apparatus. When Coleman signaled his desire to include Young in his slate, the congressman protested to the White House. Glenn, he predicted, "will beat the hell out of Young, and I wouldn't think that you fellows would be wanting your cart tied to Young." Walter Jenkins repeated the administration's mantra – "we have very little, if anything, to gain, and a good deal to lose by going into primaries."[200] In this case the choices were even less appealing than in California: Young was an unreliable maverick, while Glenn frequently dined at Robert Kennedy's Hickory Hill home. Fate then intervened in Johnson's favor. Glenn slipped in his bathtub and hit his head, suffered health complications, and had to withdraw from the race.

The difficulties Johnson experienced in Wisconsin, California, and Ohio paled in comparison to the challenge presented by the internal dissension of the Texas Democratic Party. The first few days of February featured a confrontation few would forget, involving the three towering personalities of the 1960s Texas Democrats – Governor John Connally, Senator Ralph Yarborough, and Johnson himself.

Connally was an early member of Johnson's inner circle who carved out his own political identity after World War II. He managed Johnson's campaign in 1948 and briefly worked for the senator, but then returned home to become counsel for oilman Sid Richardson, one of the richest people in Texas. (He owned his own island.) During the 1950s Connally

197 Stewart Alsop, "Rough Ride for a Hero," 12 May 1964, *Saturday Evening Post*.
198 *Washington Star*, 18 Jan. 1964; Alsop, "Rough Ride for a Hero."
199 *Time*, 24 Jan. 1964.
200 President Johnson, Walter Jenkins, Bill Moyers, and Wayne Hays, 7:05 P.M., 14 Jan. 1964, Tape WH6401.14, Citation #1378, LBJ Recordings.

aligned with Johnson and Sam Rayburn in their battle against former governor Allan Shivers and the "Shivercrats." But as the Shivers threat receded in the late 1950s, the Texas party became polarized along more strictly ideological lines. Both Johnson and Connally affiliated with the state's political, financial, and social elite, although for personal reasons their relationship had grown more distant. Of the duo, one observer wrote, "You could take either of their egos, slice it up, and have healthy portions for any ordinary six men."[201]

The liberals' leader was Ralph Yarborough, who first entered state government in 1931. He soon demonstrated his legal expertise – and his ideological credentials – by successfully suing several oil companies to establish the right of public schools and universities to oil-fund revenues. Yarborough twice, unsuccessfully, challenged Shivers for the gubernatorial nomination, beaten back by conservative Red-baiting tactics. His loss for governor in 1956, ironically, paved his way for his accession to the Senate; the winner of the gubernatorial race, Price Daniel, had to vacate his Senate seat. Texas law at the time required all special election candidates to run on the same ballot, with – crucially – no runoff if the leading candidate did not receive 50 percent. When 22 candidates declared for the seat, Yarborough prevailed with 38 percent; he then surprised observers by winning renomination against a wealthy conservative, "Dollar Bill" Blakley, in 1958. By 1960 ideological and temperamental differences had created a personal rift between Johnson and Yarborough.[202]

Meanwhile, after a brief stint as Kennedy's secretary of the navy, Connally returned to Texas to run for governor after Daniel declared for a fourth two-year term in 1962. On primary day Connally finished first, and Daniel failed to even make the runoff. The governor was bested by Don Yarborough, who, though not related to the senator, drew support from the same labor and liberal groups that had propelled Ralph Yarborough to victory in 1957 and 1958. Connally began the runoff with a large lead, but Don Yarborough closed fast and lost by only 2 percent.

Relations between Connally and Johnson on the one hand and Yarborough on the other deteriorated in 1963 as both Connally and Yarborough prepared to stand for reelection. The vice president actively encouraged the Connally faction to find a challenger for Yarborough;

[201] Richard Morehead, *50 Years in Texas Politics* (Austin, TX: Eakin Press, 1982), p. 116.

[202] Walter S. Gray, "John Bowden Connally, Jr.," *Handbook of Texas Online*, http://www.tsha.utexas.edu/handbook/online/articles/print/CC/fcosf.html, last accessed 16 Dec. 2007; James Reston, Jr., *The Lone Star: The Life of John Connally* (New York: Harper and Row, 1989).

Bobby Baker claimed that Johnson even toyed with the idea of resigning as vice president and opposing Yarborough himself.[203] The need to paper over this feud – which threatened not only his ticket's political standing but also the supply of Democratic money from the Lone Star State – was one reason John Kennedy traveled to Texas in November 1963. Neither Connally nor Yarborough distinguished himself at the time. Yarborough refused to ride in the same car with the governor; after the assassination, Connally, who was hit by one of the bullets that killed the president, speculated that he too might have been an assassination target.[204]

In December Connally, still convalescing, expressed concern about rumors that Johnson and Yarborough had reconciled – reports reinforced by the president's decision to visit Yarborough's residence in early January. The governor, now teamed with his former adversary Allan Shivers, accordingly searched for a challenger to Yarborough. (Shivers himself considered the race until a poll showed him losing to Yarborough by a 2-to-1 margin.) Connally and Shivers settled on Representative Joe Kilgore, a conservative congressman who, ironically, had entered politics as a volunteer for Johnson's 1941 Senate bid. Meanwhile, Don Yarborough did nothing to discourage speculation that he would make another run for governor.[205]

Surveying matters a few days before the February 3 filing deadline, the president observed that "everybody's just as nervous as a whore in church."[206] National labor groups, who saw Ralph Yarborough as an important ally, pressured Johnson to ensure the senator's renomination. But Connally was convinced that unless Senator Yarborough had opposition, Texas labor would concentrate on Don Yarborough's effort. If the White House forced Kilgore out of the race, he threatened, he would not run for reelection.[207]

With Connally uncooperative, the president swung into action. Working through Ken O'Donnell, he obtained a commitment from Hank Brown, head of the Texas AFL-CIO, that labor would not endorse Don Yarborough's gubernatorial bid. Teaming with Houston congressman

[203] Baker, *Wheeling and Dealing*, p. 144.

[204] "Yarborough, Ralph Webster," *Handbook of Texas Online*, http://www.tsha.utexas.edu/handbook/online/articles/print/YY/fyags.html, last accessed 10 Jan. 2008.

[205] Patrick Cox, *Ralph W. Yarborough: The People's Senator* (Austin: University of Texas Press, 2001), pp. 203–8.

[206] President Johnson and Houston Harte, 12:10 P.M., 29 Jan. 1964, Tape WH6401.24, Citation #1623, LBJ Recordings.

[207] President Johnson, Walter Jenkins, and Jack Valenti, 5:55 P.M., 31 Jan. 1964, Tape WH6401.27, Citation #1696, LBJ Recordings.

Albert Thomas, he then cut off Kilgore's financial support.[208] At 2:00 P.M. on February 3, after a long discussion with Walter Jenkins in which his pleas for presidential neutrality were rejected, Kilgore announced that he would not run, citing family concerns.[209] One Texas Democrat joked, "His family? Well, I guess that's true in a way; Lyndon talked to him like a Dutch uncle."[210]

But then, a few hours later, Don Yarborough, joined by several labor leaders, filed papers to run for governor. A furious Connally called Washington to relay the news – adding, for good measure, "I hope Mr. Ralph Yarborough just opens his mouth one time, because I'd like to run against him at the same time."[211] (Reciprocating the sentiment, the senator told an aide, "I want those sons of bitches to run somebody against me because I want to beat the hell out of them.")[212] The president, double-crossed, now searched for someone to run against Senator Yarborough.[213] He eventually turned to Fort Worth congressman Jim Wright, the future Speaker of the House, but Wright, despite considering the offer "tempting as hell," declined.[214] Just before midnight a right-wing radio station host and owner, Gordon McLendon, filed against Yarborough, but few considered him a serious threat.

The *Washington Star* marveled at "an amazing demonstration of power politics." But, the paper noted presciently, "only time will tell how much strain the tug of war put on the friendship between Governor Connally and President Johnson."[215] With Connally, as the *Houston Post* reported, "seething," the president returned to the Lone Star State the following weekend for the funeral of Louise Kellam, wife of KTBC's general manager. Connally also attended the funeral, at which the duo "showed little more than a nodding acquaintance"; as the doors opened for the procession, the president and Connally stood side by side, each waiting

[208] President Johnson and Jack Brooks, 6:26 P.M., 1 Feb. 1964, Tape WH6402.02, Citation #1814, LBJ Recordings.

[209] Walter Jenkins and Joe Kilgore, 1:20 P.M., 3 Feb. 1964, Tape WH6402.02, Citation #1828, LBJ Recordings.

[210] *New York Times,* 5 Feb. 1964.

[211] John Connally and Jack Valenti, 8:25 P.M., 3 Feb. 1964, Tape WH6402.04, Citation #1861, LBJ Recordings.

[212] Cox, *Ralph W. Yarborough*, p. 207.

[213] President Johnson, Jack Brooks, and Jack Valenti, 8:35 P.M., 3 Feb. 1964, Tape WH6402.04, Citation #1863, LBJ Recordings.

[214] President Johnson and Jim Wright, 9:15 P.M., 3 Feb. 1964, Tape WH6402.04, Citation #1867, LBJ Recordings.

[215] *Washington Star*, 4 Feb. 1964.

for the other to depart first.[216] (Johnson eventually did.) After Connally publicly stated that he had no future plans to speak to Johnson, the president responded in kind: "Damn if I believe that John got shot in the shoulder – I believe he got shot in the head, giving out these interviews every day."[217]

Of all state developments, those in Texas most threatened the president's political standing. The one clear advantage that Johnson possessed over any Democrat was an ability to take the Lone Star State out of play in the fall election. But if Connally threw the state party apparatus behind the Shivercrats, there was no reason to believe that Republicans could not carry the state in 1964 as they had in 1952 and 1956. And if Texas fell even before the Senate passed the Civil Rights Act, could Johnson rely on any Southern state?

The first two months of 1964 revealed the strengths and limitations of Lyndon Johnson's strategy of fusing politics and policy. In the arena of public policy, the president continued to dominate, his mastery of Congress unchallenged and his ability to frame legislative debates to maximize political benefits awe-inspiring. But Johnson also discovered that even presidents could not always control the agenda. Seemingly insignificant events could trigger international crises in which both his policy making and political skills failed him. His continuing tendency to explain away his dealings with Baker in narrowly legalistic terms only magnified the issue, bringing his "alter-image" back into the public perception. Finally, since his status as president made him national party leader, avoiding internal fights among state parties proved difficult.

As Johnson established himself in the White House, broader changes in American political culture were beginning to emerge. Lodge's unconventional strategy challenged the Republican consensus even as most in the party elite seemed unaware of the revolutionary developments among the conservative grassroots. The media, which generally had ignored the personal lives of presidents from FDR to Kennedy, showed an inclination to ask hard questions about Johnson's personal ethics and business practices. And the president himself demonstrated how the growth of the federal government provided myriad opportunities for a talented commander-in-chief to utilize the public policy process for political ends.

[216] *Houston Post*, 9 Feb. 1964.

[217] President Johnson and George Brown, 12:20 P.M., 14 Feb. 1964, Tape WH6402.16, Citation #2082, LBJ Recordings; *Houston Post*, 10 Feb. 1964.

2

The Rise and Fall of Henry Cabot Lodge

While the president dealt with the Bobby Baker scandal and his foreign policy difficulties, the Republican race began in earnest. On the surface, the GOP battle was two contests – one between the announced candidates (Rockefeller and Goldwater), the second featuring the three major unannounced contenders (Lodge, Nixon, and Scranton). But when Lodge and Nixon launched write-in efforts in the March 10 New Hampshire primary, the two races merged. Moreover, because of his position in the Johnson administration, Lodge's effort triggered an unusual fusion of politics and policy, this time with regards to the U.S. conduct of the Vietnam War. The New Hampshire result set off a two-month scramble in which the ambassador emerged as the frontrunner in Republican national polls, threatening to transform the race in wholly unexpected ways.

Barry Goldwater began the new year with perhaps the least productive opening of a presidential candidacy in modern American history. He formally launched his campaign at his home in Paradise City, an exclusive suburb of Phoenix, on Friday, January 3 – rejecting counsel that, as Saturday papers had the lowest circulation figures, he should delay his announcement a day or two. Standing on crutches (after surgery to remove a bone spur on his heel), Goldwater promised not to change his beliefs to win votes. Instead, he would present "a choice, not an echo."[1]

Signs of the difficulties that would plague his candidacy immediately emerged. Goldwater's staff consisted almost entirely of Arizonans lacking in national experience: he had to spell the names of two of his key figures, Richard Kleindienst and Dean Burch, since most of the assembled

[1] *Congressional Quarterly Weekly Report*, 10 Jan. 1964, p. 42.

reporters had heard of neither man. In an impolitic attempt at humor, the senator quipped that Burch was "not related to John Birch."[2] Reaction to the announcement was tepid, from both the press and moderate Republicans.[3]

Goldwater then returned to Washington to appear on *Meet the Press*. On the nationally televised program, in the words of the *New York Times,* he "unsmilingly gave his views" and "fully lived up to expectations that he would campaign as a champion of unbending conservatism."[4] Accustomed to the critic's role, the senator struggled to outline a positive program. Goldwater opened the interview by noting that "it would be worthwhile to explore what we might accomplish with the Soviet in threatening to withdraw recognition." He promised to renounce the 1963 Limited Test-Ban Treaty, a point of view, he claimed, seconded by "Dr. Hans Morganthau, one of the great physicists in the world." (Morganthau, who did not share Goldwater's opposition to the treaty, was a political scientist.) On the domestic front, Goldwater was hardly less conciliatory: he suggested that Mississippi and Alabama could end segregation through "moral persuasion."[5] David Broder, just beginning a career that would establish him as the dean of the Washington press corps, dryly observed that Goldwater seemed to be suffering from an "information gap."[6]

The Arizonan then headed off for his first campaign swing through New Hampshire, where he continued to come across as extreme. The government, he stated, should consider making Social Security voluntary. When asked to defend his comments about the unreliability of U.S. ICBMs, he admitted, "It's classified, and I'll probably catch hell for saying it, but our long-range missiles are not dependable at all."[7] Secretary of Defense Robert McNamara termed the senator's charges "completely misleading, politically irresponsible, and damaging to the national security."[8] (*New York Times* journalist Scotty Reston later commented that Goldwater offered Granite State voters "rugged individualism, jungle economics, and gunboat diplomacy.")[9] A few days later Goldwater

[2] *Congressional Quarterly Weekly Report*, 10 Jan. 1964, p. 43.
[3] *Washington Post*, 4 Jan. 1964; *Detroit News*, 4 Jan. 1964; *Washington Star*, 4 Jan. 1964.
[4] *New York Times,* 6 Jan. 1964.
[5] *Congressional Quarterly Weekly Report*, 10 Jan. 1964, pp. 43–5.
[6] *New York Times*, 6 Jan. 1964; *Washington Star*, 7 Jan. 1964.
[7] *Newsweek*, 20 Jan. 1964.
[8] McNamara quoted in Rick Perlstein, *Before the Storm: Barry Goldwater and the Unmaking of the American Consensus* (New York: Hill and Wang), p. 271.
[9] *New York Times*, 12 Mar. 1964.

attacked Johnson's decision to declare war on poverty, since the "attitude or the actions" of the poor caused their plight.[10] In a sign of how the political climate of the mid-1960s differed from that of a generation later, even syndicated columnist Joseph Alsop, hardly a flaming liberal, expressed "horror" at Goldwater's remarks.[11]

Despite its iconic status in the twenty-first-century political environment, in 1964 the New Hampshire primary had been significant for scarcely a decade. It first affected the nominating process in 1952, when Tennessee senator Estes Kefauver campaigned in his coonskin cap and scored an upset victory, ending any thoughts President Harry Truman had of extending his stay in the White House. The Kefauver win established a precedent of New Hampshire voters expecting a personal, freewheeling style of campaigning from presidential candidate. Goldwater had no enthusiasm for this approach. He complained that his state manager, Norris Cotton, had overscheduled him; Cotton blandly responded, "That's the way we campaign in New Hampshire." When a large crowd greeted the candidate after a night-time landing at the Concord airport, Goldwater asked Cotton, "Don't you New Hampshire people believe in going to bed?"[12] After an awkward coffee hour in Hanover, on the Vermont border, the Arizona senator admitted, "I'm not one of those baby-kissing, handshaking, blintz-eating candidates."[13]

The *New York Times*' Charles Mohr described Goldwater as a "mercurial candidate" whose performance fluctuated depending on his mood.[14] In off-the-cuff discussions, the senator tended to say things that, in Mohr's words, sounded "more strident in the columns of tomorrow's newspaper than he does in today's speech on a New Hampshire street corner."[15] One editor in Portsmouth summed up the problem: "If Goldwater would shut himself in a closet, he'd do better."[16]

Goldwater thus compiled a record of extreme statements that both the Rockefeller and Johnson campaigns catalogued to exploit. Johnson's staff focused on the Arizonan's civil rights commentary, such as Goldwater's assertion that "after the first ten [constitutional amendments], we have

[10] *New York Times*, 16 Jan. 1964.
[11] *Washington Post*, 24 Jan. 1964.
[12] Perlstein, *Before the Storm*, pp. 268, 282.
[13] F. Clifton White with William Gill, *Suite 3505: The Story of the Draft Goldwater Movement* (New Rochelle, NY: Arlington House, 1967), p. 294.
[14] *New York Times*, 10 Feb. 1964.
[15] *New York Times*, 27 Jan. 1964.
[16] *New York Times*, 12 Feb. 1964.

generally been wrong."[17] The Rockefeller staff detected Goldwater's chief vulnerability in the recklessness of his foreign policy statements.[18] Both campaigns accumulated material on the almost casual way Goldwater discussed nuclear weapons and on his ties to extremist groups, particularly the John Birch Society (he said he was "impressed by the type of people" it attracted).[19] Bluntly, Johnson described the Arizonan's difficulties: Goldwater was "just nutty as a fruitcake."[20]

By late January Goldwater was unsurprisingly downplaying New Hampshire's importance – while Rockefeller started calling the primary a significant test.[21] Rockefeller's state campaign chair, former governor Hugh Gregg, pushed him to stress his hard-line foreign policy views, his support for federal aid to education, and his fidelity to U.S. membership in the United Nations.[22] But, as he had before the assassination, Rockefeller largely stayed away from issues. Instead he focused on his electability – claiming that the Republicans needed to nominate a candidate capable of winning Northern industrial states – and wooed New Hampshire's 90,000 Republicans through an aggressive campaign of personal appearances.[23] But Rockefeller still had much to overcome. In addition to almost nonexistent grassroots support, he encountered vitriolic opposition from William Loeb of the *Union-Leader,* who suggested for him a campaign slogan of "Deception, Deceit, and Divorce." It was not for nothing that John Kennedy had once said, "I believe that there is a publisher who has less regard for the truth than William Loeb, but I can't think of his name."[24]

Rockefeller's standing was little better in his other key state, California. In a late January survey of conditions, the Goldwater forces rejoiced that their opposition consisted of "most of the second-string and,

[17] "Glossary of Goldwater Opinionata," Box 87, Office Files of Bill Moyers, Lyndon B. Johnson Library.

[18] Roswell Perkins to Nelson Rockefeller, 6 Apr. 1964, Box 8, Graham Molitor Papers, Rockefeller Archives.

[19] "Glossary of Goldwater Opinionata," Box 87, Office Files of Bill Moyers, Lyndon B. Johnson Library.

[20] President Johnson and John Connally, 9:03 A.M., 8 Feb. 1964, Tape WH6402.10, Citation #1966, LBJ Recordings.

[21] *New York Times,* 29 Jan. 1964, 12 Feb. 1964.

[22] "Notes on Telephone Conversation with Hugh Gregg," 14 Oct. 1963, Box 79, George Hinman Papers, Rockefeller Archives.

[23] Hugh Gregg memo, 28 Feb. 1964, Box 79, George Hinman Papers, Rockefeller Archives.

[24] Loeb and Kennedy quoted in Daniel Ford, "The Nation's Primary Primary," *The Reporter*, 27 Feb. 1964.

frankly, has-been fraternity." California conservatives understood that Rockefeller was on the wrong side of the state's most important state issue in 1964: Proposition 14, which called for repealing the state's open housing law. While the Goldwater forces did worry that some "politically potent Jewish names" had signed on for Rockefeller, they believed that the governor's campaigners were out of their league in vote-rich southern California. In this one-time home of Richard Nixon, the Goldwater team observed, "many political practitioners seem to feel campaigns need a certain amount of trickery to succeed."[25]

In the end, though, tactical decisions one way or the other could only do so much for Rockefeller. As he had with Goldwater, the president pithily summed up the governor's dilemma: "Rockefeller's wife ain't going to let him get off the ground."[26] With the approach the two major candidates adopted, it was no wonder the *New York Times*' Warren Weaver described the Goldwater-Rockefeller contest as "a return to the bare-knuckle boxing days of the 1860s."[27] In the process the appeal of both candidates plummeted. Public opinion data, which fluctuated wildly, showed a growing number of undecided voters, with Nixon opening up a solid national lead over both announced candidates.[28]

In the Granite State an opening existed for an alternative choice, and one other intriguing candidate announced a bid. Maine senator Margaret Chase Smith already had a career of distinction before becoming the first woman to enter a major-party presidential primary. After her husband, Representative Clyde Smith, died in 1940, she ran in his stead and was elected to the first of four terms in the House of Representatives. In 1948 she succeeded Senate Majority Leader Wallace White to become only the second woman to win election to the Senate. Smith distinguished herself in the upper chamber almost immediately: with her "Declaration of Conscience" in 1950, she was the first GOP senator to publicly rebuke Joseph McCarthy. Smith easily won reelection in 1954 and 1960 even as Democrats gained strength in the state; her moderate voting record and personal campaigning style wore well.[29]

[25] "Memo for week ending Jan. 26, 1964," Box 12, Barry Goldwater Papers, Arizona State University.

[26] President Johnson and John Connally, 9:03 A.M., 8 Feb. 1964, Tape WH6402.10, Citation #1966, LBJ Recordings.

[27] *New York Times*, 12 Jan. 1964.

[28] George Gallup, *The Gallup Poll, 1935–1971*, vol. 3, poll for 10 Jan. 1964, p. 1864; *Wall Street Journal*, 11 Jan. 1964.

[29] Janann Sherman, *No Place for a Woman: A Life of Senator Margaret Chase Smith* (New Brunswick, NJ: Rutgers University Press, 2000).

Despite her credentials and impressive political career, Smith seemed to confirm the worst of stereotypes about women in politics. She greeted the Washington press corps on the morning of January 27 with two announcements, one declaring her candidacy, the other stating that she would not run. Smith began by reviewing the reasons both for and against her making the race. "As gratifying are the reasons urging me to run," the Maine senator stated, "I find the reasons not to run to be far more compelling"; therefore, "I have decided I shall."[30] Afterwards, the *Wall Street Journal*'s Henry Gemmill declared that Smith had made "a powerful bid…for the nation's illogical vote."[31]

Smith outlined only a bare agenda in her announcement address; instead, she focused on her intention to run a different kind of campaign, based on unpaid volunteers. She promised not to purchase television or radio time for advertisements and to stand on her "record rather than on promises."[32] She fulfilled her pledge – the campaign's budget in New Hampshire totaled $250.[33]

On the campaign trail in New Hampshire, Smith covered 1,000 miles in six days. At Plymouth State College she tackled her biggest handicap immediately, asserting that her gender would not prevent her from authorizing a nuclear strike if necessary. With no campaign organization, Smith chatted with women about fabrics, men about foxes, and the press about anything. She put in long days – she once surprised a group of loggers at 5:30 A.M. Much like Rockefeller, the Maine senator focused her criticism on Goldwater, targeting his positions on Social Security and civil rights and his opposition to federal aid for education. But also much like Rockefeller, she seemed to lack a positive agenda. When pressed by one reporter as to why she was running, she offered only, "I have some ideas I would like to put into action."[34] It was perhaps for that reason that most observers, in the words of David Broder, "seemed to be struggling to grasp the idea that this charming gentlewoman was truly running for President."[35] To a certain extent, Smith herself seemed unable to grasp the idea: after her initial foray into New Hampshire, she did not again campaign there, nor did she open a campaign office. Broder sensed that

[30] *Congressional Quarterly Weekly Report*, 31 Jan. 1964, p. 223.
[31] *Wall Street Journal*, 28 Jan. 1964.
[32] *Washington Star*, 28 Jan. 1964.
[33] Herbert Alexander, *Financing the 1964 Election* (Princeton, NJ: Citizens Research Foundation, 1966), p. 29.
[34] *Washington Star*, 12 Feb. 1964.
[35] *Washington Star*, 11 Feb. 1964.

her support might be greater than political professionals suggested, but Smith's own conduct prevented testing the hypothesis.[36]

With the announced candidates all demonstrating such weaknesses, focus turned to those who had not formally declared their intentions. Scranton, the "Harrisburg Hamlet," continued to attract attention, though he never polled above 7 percent, either in New Hampshire or nationally.[37] Though a more serious candidate, Nixon began the race with serious drawbacks: a Harris survey of late January found Nixon's "pleasant, attractive, and well-known personality" to be his chief asset – hardly an encouraging sign for those with any personal experience with the former vice president.[38]

Unlike Scranton, however, Nixon very much wanted the nomination, and in early February he jumpstarted his campaign by delivering a "non-political" address in Cincinnati. Nixon condemned the "irresponsible tactics of some of the extreme civil rights leaders" for creating "an atmosphere of hate and distrust which, if it continues to grow, will make the new [civil rights] law a law in name only."[39] The speech, which foreshadowed Nixon's "Southern Strategy" of 1968, attracted immediate comment. This "new Nixon," Evans and Novak declared, would appeal to suburbanites disturbed by the civil rights movement – the type of people backing Proposition 14 in California.[40] One "cynical" Nixon backer doubted the former vice president believed a word of what he said: "Dick figures that Goldwater is going to have the biggest bloc of votes at the convention" and wanted to position himself when the Arizonan's bid fell short.[41]

The difficulty of ascertaining the true strength of candidates like Scranton and Nixon compounded the uncertainty of the Republican race.[42] It also remained unclear whether the nomination would even be worth having. A late January Harris poll showed all Republican candidates – announced and unannounced – faring poorly against the president. Rockefeller and Goldwater trailed by 61 and 58 points, respectively; Nixon was down by 47.[43] Scranton ran 60 points behind Johnson

[36] *Washington Star*, 14 Feb. 1964.
[37] *Washington Post*, 12 Jan. 1964.
[38] *Washington Post*, 21 Jan. 1964.
[39] *Washington Star*, 14 Feb. 1964.
[40] *New York Herald Tribune*, 20 Feb. 1964.
[41] *Wall Street Journal*, 14 Feb. 1964.
[42] *Wall Street Journal*, 7 Jan. 1964.
[43] *Washington Post*, 25 Jan. 1964.

in his own state of Pennsylvania.[44] Despite such figures, a sense existed of the president's potential vulnerability. As Richard Strout noted in the *Christian Science Monitor,* Johnson had never before faced a partisan campaign, his bids for the Democratic presidential nomination in 1956 and 1960 were unimpressive, and the "uncertainty" he demonstrated in the Bobby Baker matter raised doubts about the president's ability to handle ethical scandals.[45]

The *Wall Street Journal*'s Al Otten addressed Johnson's potential difficulties in the greatest detail. He attributed the wild swings in the public portrayal of Johnson – from "a Texan ten feet tall" to "the other extreme" of a foreign policy incompetent – to the fact that "Washington 'insiders' really do not yet know just what kind of President Mr. Johnson will be." Tentative signs, however, had emerged. Otten detected "subsurface evidence" that Johnson could not focus on more than one major problem at a time. He also doubted that the president was getting the best service possible from the White House staff – Johnson loyalists were too loyal, Kennedy holdovers had other agendas. The response to the Baker affair suggested that "Mr. Johnson's over-sensitivity to criticism could prove an Achilles heel." And Otten questioned Johnson's tendency to delay major changes until after the election: if these problems remained through November, Johnson "may never become President in his own right."[46]

The late winter polls reflected one other unusual sign: the candidate who consistently ran best against Johnson was not even in the country. After the boomlet on his behalf in December, Henry Cabot Lodge had seemed to do little during the following month. Nonetheless, among Republican voters, he fared better than any possible GOP candidate, besting Johnson by a 61–31 margin (this at a time when Johnson outpolled Rockefeller among Republicans and trailed Goldwater by only four points). Lodge ran strongest against Johnson among independents, and he scored the best overall against the president – although even he trailed by 30 points.[47] In addition, as February proceeded, Lodge appeared, against all odds, to be picking up strength in New Hampshire.

Though he said the proper things about the Hatch Act precluding his candidacy, the ambassador was very much involved with mapping out his campaign. He urged his son to create the appearance of spontaneous

[44] *Washington Post*, 24 Jan. 1964.
[45] *Christian Science Monitor*, 3 Mar. 1964.
[46] *Wall Street Journal*, 17 Mar. 1964.
[47] *Washington Post*, 24 Jan. 1964.

grassroots support, an idea the campaign quickly embraced.[48] (He then told his son to be sure to destroy all letters he sent from Saigon, lest his involvement in the effort be accidentally revealed.) "Surprised" to hear from Sherman Adams, formerly the Granite State's governor and Eisenhower's chief of staff, that he had "considerable latent support" in New Hampshire, Lodge ridiculed those who argued that he refused to work hard; indeed, "if a man were thinking primarily of his health and comfort, he would prefer campaigning in New Hampshire to serving in Saigon."[49]

Lodge also benefited from a remarkably capable campaign staff, which operated on three levels. Nationally, the key figure was Robert Mullen, a Washington publicist who had joined Lodge in the Draft Eisenhower movement of 1952. Mullen communicated the message of an absent candidate, a goal that he accomplished through lengthy press releases and coordinating the burgeoning Draft Lodge state organizations. (Twenty-four existed by late January.)[50] While Mullen operated nationally, a small Draft Lodge movement appeared on the ground in New Hampshire. Its coordinator, a business executive and former journalist named Paul Grindle, was looking for "something exciting to do."[51] Reporting back after a brief visit to New Hampshire, Mullen believed that the Lodge effort "has zeal and drive, and some excellent people."[52]

With both Mullen and the New Hampshire volunteers technically operating independently, the task of acting as a liaison between their efforts and the ambassador fell to Lodge's son, George. In a backhanded compliment, the Rockefeller staff described George Lodge as "by far the most attractive of his line which is inclined to arrogance and mistakes in judgment."[53] The younger Lodge had political experience; he had drawn a respectable 36 percent against Ted Kennedy in the 1962 Massachusetts Senate race. George Lodge's role in the campaign proved critical: he

[48] Perlstein, *Before the Storm*, p. 291.

[49] Henry Cabot Lodge to George Lodge, 3 Jan. 1964, Box 32, Henry Cabot Lodge II Papers, Massachusetts Historical Society.

[50] Robert Mullen, "For President: Henry Cabot Lodge," enclosed in Mullen to Henry Cabot Lodge, 16 Jan. 1964, Box 32, Henry Cabot Lodge II Papers, Massachusetts Historical Society.

[51] Charles Brereton, *First in the Nation: New Hampshire and the Premier Presidential Primary* (Portsmouth, NH: P. E. Randall, 1987), p. 77.

[52] Robert Mullen to Henry Cabot Lodge, 16 Jan. 1964, Box 32, Henry Cabot Lodge II Papers, Massachusetts Historical Society.

[53] George Hinman, memorandum for the files, 26 Sept. 1962, Box 64, George Hinman Papers, Rockefeller Archives.

consistently, if subtly, persuaded his father that the effort had a chance not only to affect internal GOP debates but also to capture the nomination. In his trips to New Hampshire, Lodge discovered that his father's reputation "as a Commie fighter" had given the ambassador surprising grassroots strength.[54] Though the Vietnam War was a problem for the president, for one figure, it served as a political asset.

Ambassador Lodge was adamant on one issue: under no circumstances would he return to the United States and campaign for the nomination.[55] Demonstrating the inflated sense of self-worth that had marred his performance as ambassador from the start, he insisted that "this extraordinarily subtle and complicated situation" required his continued presence in South Vietnam.[56] But such an approach also benefited him politically. First, running as a write-in offered his only chance of victory in the fall. By deciding to return only if drafted by the convention, he could pose as the citizen-patriot, the figure above politics.[57] Second, remaining in Saigon allowed Lodge to conceal the weaknesses inherent in his campaign. He had, after all, lost his previous two bids for elected office and certainly was not known for his warm personality. Scotty Reston once remarked, "There is something slightly sniffish about Henry Cabot Lodge, as if he were vaguely annoyed with the human race."[58]

Finally, Lodge lacked the detailed knowledge expected of a presidential candidate. In late January the ambassador asked his son for briefing papers on "the things which I haven't had time to follow lately" – aid to parochial schools (a key dispute in congressional debate about Kennedy's education proposals), farm policy, labor, tax policy, and – incredibly – civil rights. In short, by his own admission, Lodge was ignorant about the entire domestic agenda that Johnson was pushing through Congress. Though "my own ideas on the broad issues are all clear in my head," he lacked a sense of "the precise bone of contention at the moment."[59]

[54] George Lodge to Henry Cabot Lodge, 6 Feb. 1964, Box 35, Henry Cabot Lodge II Papers, Massachusetts Historical Society.

[55] Henry Cabot Lodge to George Lodge, 6 Jan. 1964, Box 35, Henry Cabot Lodge II Papers, Massachusetts Historical Society.

[56] Henry Cabot Lodge to Robert Mullen, 12 Feb. 1964, Box 35, Henry Cabot Lodge II Papers, Massachusetts Historical Society.

[57] Lodge to Earl Newsom, 24 Dec. 1963, Box 35, Henry Cabot Lodge II Papers, Massachusetts Historical Society; Lodge to George Cabot Lodge, 10 Jan. 1964, Box 32, Henry Cabot Lodge II Papers, Massachusetts Historical Society.

[58] *New York Times*, 12 Mar. 1964.

[59] Henry Cabot Lodge to George Lodge, 27 Jan. 1964, Box 32, Henry Cabot Lodge II Papers, Massachusetts Historical Society.

The candidate's distance and silence forced the Lodge team to employ unconventional methods. At the end of January, the campaign sent a brochure to each of New Hampshire's Republican voters, with an eye-catching motto: "Select the best."[60] The brochure contained three smart photos of Lodge, one in military garb beside an anti-aircraft gun ("this military service now stands him well in Saigon"); a second with Eisenhower (to illustrate the ambassador's "intimate, cherished, and enduring" relationship with the former president); and a third of Lodge at the United Nations (where he helped "halt" Communist expansion worldwide).[61] The brochure asked the recipient to send back an enclosed postcard to Lodge in Saigon as an expression of support. Over 10,000 people did so; the campaign entered each name in a database and then forwarded the missives to Saigon. The Lodge forces also charged both Goldwater and Rockefeller with evading New Hampshire laws restricting primary expenditures, in the process making a virtue of their own meager treasury.[62]

The *Baltimore Sun*'s Gerry Griffin described Lodge as a candidate "following his own rules"; Illinois Democratic senator Paul Douglas considered the ambassador "the hardest man to beat they have."[63] At Rockefeller headquarters, staffers took to calling him "Henry Sabotage."[64] Loeb's *Union-Leader,* in a front-page editorial, denounced Lodge as "an appeaser" who was "partially responsible for the cynical betrayal of our missing fighting men" in Korea.[65] Goldwater, more credibly, commented that the ambassador had "kind of balled up" in Vietnam.[66]

Seeking to contain the Lodge surge, Rockefeller phoned his rival to urge him to withdraw from the race.[67] When Lodge refused, the New York governor, in the midst of a 13-hour campaign swing, blamed the ambassador for conditions in Vietnam. Rockefeller argued that if Lodge did not support Johnson's policies, he should resign, to "come back and tell us what he thinks is wrong."[68] The next day, recognizing that his

[60] Brereton, *First in the Nation*, p. 87.

[61] Perlstein, *Before the Storm*, p. 293.

[62] Robert Mullen to Henry Cabot Lodge, 10 Feb. 1964, Box 32, Henry Cabot Lodge II Papers, Massachusetts Historical Society.

[63] *Baltimore Sun*, 22 Mar. 1964; *Christian Science Monitor*, 2 Mar. 1964.

[64] Arthur Schlesinger, Jr., *History of American Presidential Elections, 1798–1968*, vol. 4 (New York: Chelsea House, 1971), p. 3015.

[65] Perlstein, *Before the Storm*, p. 294.

[66] Perlstein, *Before the Storm*, p. 294.

[67] Henry Cabot Lodge to George Lodge, 22 Feb. 1964, Box 35, Henry Cabot Lodge II Papers, Massachusetts Historical Society.

[68] *New York Times*, 21 Feb. 1964.

words had only attracted attention to the Lodge write-in bid, Rockefeller called to apologize.[69] Lodge himself considered Rockefeller's attack "very stupid and counterproductive," since it demonstrated the write-in effort's potency.[70]

Fresh off the fight with Rockefeller, the Lodge campaign launched the next stage of its impressive strategy, a five-minute advertisement shown on the state's only VHF station, Manchester's Channel 9. Belying the campaign's public denunciations of negative campaigning, the advertisement employed some trickery of its own. The commercial contained voice-overs from Eisenhower praising Lodge in 1960, but a blast of trumpets obscured the sound when Eisenhower said "vice" before his endorsement of Lodge for vice president, thereby implying that the backing applied to 1964.[71]

The impact of the Lodge surge extended beyond the Republican race. One of the deans of the Washington press corps, Marquis Childs of the *Washington Post,* realized that regardless of the ultimate effect of a Lodge candidacy, "the presence in Saigon of an ambassador whose presidential candidacy is already a sizable cloud on the political horizon" complicated Johnson's foreign policy.[72] Throughout early 1964, the president worried that Lodge could use Vietnam as a springboard from which to criticize him, as Douglas MacArthur had tried to do in 1951 after Harry Truman dismissed him for insubordination. Accordingly, Johnson reasoned, the administration needed to accede to Lodge's requests whenever possible, at least until the political situation clarified. Once again, as in the postwar years, partisan politics had aligned in such as a way as to grant Henry Cabot Lodge influence far disproportionate to the position he occupied.

Johnson devoted little attention to Vietnam between mid-December 1963 and mid-February 1964. What public comments he did make revealed indecisiveness: Scotty Reston described the administration's approach as "awkward, contradictory, and even dangerous," characterized by "blabbermouth" leaking from sources trying to protect the president's political flank.[73] This clumsiness reached its height in a February 21 speech at UCLA, where Johnson – without seeming to recognize the

[69] *New York Times*, 23 Feb. 1964.

[70] Henry Cabot Lodge to George Lodge, 22 Feb. 1964, Box 35, Henry Cabot Lodge II Papers, Massachusetts Historical Society.

[71] Stephen Shadegg, *What Happened to Goldwater? The Inside Story of the 1964 Republican Campaign* (New York: Holt, Rinehart and Winston, 1965), p. 99.

[72] *Washington Post*, 27 Jan. 1964.

[73] *New York Times*, 18 Feb. 1964.

ramifications of his remarks – hinted at American military escalation when he accused Hanoi of waging a "deeply dangerous game" by supporting the southern insurgents.[74]

The UCLA speech sparked a sudden surge of presidential interest in Vietnam. Action might have been expected in late January, when a coup headed by General Nguyen Khanh had toppled the increasingly neutralist government of General Duong Van Minh. Late February, on the other hand, featured few significant international developments. Domestically, however, the period saw Vietnam emerge as a political issue. From the left, Senator Mike Mansfield endorsed French president Charles de Gaulle's call for neutralizing Southeast Asia. From the right, Goldwater urged carrying the war to North Vietnam. Criticism also expanded into the press, with a cover story in *Newsweek* and two articles by syndicated columnist Joseph Alsop.[75]

The most spectacular evidence of Vietnam's political importance, however, resulted from the impression that Lodge's New Hampshire candidacy would do better than expected. Like Goldwater and Rockefeller, Johnson had noticed Lodge's growing political strength – and feared that the ambassador's political ambitions and professional responsibilities might intersect. Lodge, the president mused to Secretary of State Dean Rusk in early March, "is a long ways from here, and he's thinking of New Hampshire, and he's thinking of his defeats in the Republican Party, and he's feeling sorry for himself, and he's naturally a martyr." Johnson guessed that Lodge expected the administration to rebuff his requests. Instead, the president told his secretary of state, "Every time he sends us a cable, I'd like to get one right back to him, complimenting him and agreeing with him, if it's in the national interest, if it's at all possible," so as "to build that [documentary] record."[76] To Robert McNamara, he added, "As long as we've got [Lodge] there, and he makes recommendations, and we act on them, particularly if we act favorably, then we're not in too bad a condition politically."[77]

The degree to which Johnson's fear of the ambassador affected his perspective became clear at a March 7 National Security Council meeting

[74] *Washington Post*, 22 Feb. 1964.

[75] Joseph Alsop, "The Test in Vietnam," *Washington Post*, 26 Feb. 1964; Alsop, "Matter of Fact," *Washington Post*, 24 Feb. 1964.

[76] President Johnson and Dean Rusk, 11:35 A.M., 2 Mar. 1964, Tape WH6403.01, Citation #2305, LBJ Recordings.

[77] President Johnson and Robert McNamara, 11:00 A.M., 2 Mar. 1964, Tape WH6403.01, Citation #2301, LBJ Recordings.

to finalize the agenda for McNamara's latest Vietnam study mission. The president wanted to ensure that "all recommendations made by Ambassador Lodge had been dealt with without exception – promptly and generally favorably."[78] He followed up with two private letters to McNamara, informing the defense secretary that "one of the most important things you can do for me in South Vietnam is to talk privately on my behalf with Cabot Lodge" and "make it clear that we mean to continue to be responsive to his needs."[79] As Primary Day drew near, NSC staffer Mike Forrestal prepared a memorandum assessing "the extent to which we have responded to Lodge's requests,"[80] and McGeorge Bundy passed the document on to the president.

In his desire to appease Lodge, Johnson focused most on building a record to rebuff future political attacks.[81] At the very least, as Fredrik Logevall has observed, this reaction reinforced Johnson's disinclination to scale back the U.S. commitment in Vietnam.[82] At the most, the Lodge candidacy caused the president to endorse a bolder U.S. course in Southeast Asia, in both economic and military terms, than he otherwise would have pursued at the time. Johnson asserted that he "sure as hell don't want to get in the position of Lodge recommending" a specific policy "and we turned him down."[83]

Ironically, despite the president's sensitivity to the political implications of his Vietnam actions, it was the administration that suffered political fallout from the developments in Southeast Asia – while Lodge continued to benefit from his situation. In a March 3 editorial, the *Washington Post* ranked Vietnam "foremost" among American foreign policy priorities and said that the president needed a "reexamination" of his policies.[84] By contrast, in that evening's *Herald Tribune,* Roscoe Drummond placed Lodge in a perfect political situation. If the write-in effort fell short, Lodge could simply say that he never desired to run; if he won, he would become a

[78] NSC Meetings, vol. 1, tab 4, National Security Files, Lyndon B. Johnson Presidential Library.

[79] President Johnson to Robert McNamara, 5 Mar. 1964, *Foreign Relations of the United States 1964–1968*, vol. 1, pp. 132–3.

[80] National Security File, Vietnam Country File, vol. V, Memos, published in *Declassified Documents, 1978*, 128C.

[81] Johnson to Lodge, 19 Feb. 1964, quoted in Lodge, "Confidential Journal," vol. 3, p. 9, Reel 17, Henry Cabot Lodge II Papers, Massachusetts Historical Society.

[82] Fredrik Logevall, *Choosing War: The Lost Chance for Peace and the Escalation of the War in Vietnam* (Berkeley: University of California Press, 1999), p. 50.

[83] President Johnson and Robert McNamara, 11:00 A.M., 2 Mar. 1964, Tape WH6403.01, Citation #2301, LBJ Recordings.

[84] *Washington Post*, 3 Mar. 1964.

serious contender. And Drummond, who had traveled to Saigon to interview Lodge, had no doubt that the ambassador "is willing, even eager, to be nominated."[85]

Uncertainty as to the final outcome dominated the final days before the March 10 primary. In his last campaign appearance in the Granite State, Goldwater forecast a victory with 40 percent of the vote. "I've got it made," he asserted.[86] Joe Alsop predicted a Rockefeller win.[87] Arthur Krock anticipated the primary's key theme as "Nixon's resurrection."[88] The *Washington Post*'s Julius Duscha forecast a narrow Lodge victory, but speculated the result would benefit Scranton.[89] Last-minute polling data, meanwhile, showed "spectacular gains" for Lodge, who was tied with Rockefeller and only two points behind Goldwater.[90]

Primary Day featured a heavy snowfall – 10 to 14 inches throughout most of the state. Dixville Notch, whose voters, per tradition, cast their ballots just after midnight, reported its results first and offered the initial sign of an upset – Lodge and Nixon each attracted three write-in votes, Rockefeller secured two votes, Goldwater only one.[91] Early returns showed Lodge with a small lead. In a remarkably heavy turnout (around 94,000 people voted), the ambassador's margin widened to impressive proportions. In the final tally Lodge received 33,521 votes, or 35.3 percent, easily besting Goldwater, whose 21,775 votes gave him 23 percent. Rockefeller came third with 19,496 votes (20.6 percent); Nixon occupied fourth, with 15,752 votes (16.6 percent); and Smith finished fifth, with 2,812 votes (3 percent).[92] Lodge backers secured all 14 of the state's delegate slots, defeating such better-known names as Senator Norris Cotton, former governor Hugh Gregg, and former senator Doloris Bridges.

From Saigon, Lodge hailed the result as "a great honor and a great commitment" but reaffirmed that he would not return to campaign.[93] Goldwater admitted that he "goofed up somewhere."[94] His staffers

[85] *New York Herald Tribune*, 3 Mar. 1964.
[86] *New York Times*, 7 Mar. 1964.
[87] *Washington Post*, 6 Mar. 1964.
[88] *New York Times*, 8 Mar. 1964.
[89] *Washington Post*, 8 Mar. 1964.
[90] *Washington Post*, 9 Mar. 1964.
[91] *Washington Post*, 11 Mar. 1964.
[92] Goldwater quoted in unidentified clipping, Box 8, Graham Molitor Papers, Rockefeller Archives; *Congressional Quarterly Weekly Report*, 13 Mar. 1964, p. 500.
[93] *New York Times*, 12 Mar. 1964.
[94] *Congressional Quarterly Weekly Report*, 13 Mar. 1964, p. 500.

FIGURE 2-1. Henry Cabot Lodge II. The surprise of the 1964 presidential election, the former Massachusetts senator, ambassador to the United Nations, and sitting U.S. ambassador in South Vietnam led in Republican polls for most of the spring. Lodge "is a long ways from here…and he's feeling sorry for himself," complained Johnson. © Courtesy of the U.S. Senate Historical Office.

downplayed the significance of New Hampshire's tally by noting that state conventions in Oklahoma (22 delegates) and North Carolina (26 delegates) had elected slates pledged to the Arizona senator.[95] Rockefeller's state leader, Hugh Gregg, candidly termed the governor's finish "miserable," but, moving on to the next fight, breezily commented, "This is the adventure that is politics."[96] The sourest reaction came from William

[95] *Congressional Quarterly Weekly Report*, 6 Mar. 1964, p. 472.
[96] Hugh Gregg to George Hinman, 13 Mar. 1964, Box 94, George Hinman Papers, Rockefeller Archives; *New York Herald Tribune*, 11 Mar. 1964.

Loeb, who ran a front-page editorial denouncing the state voters' "temporary political lunacy."[97] One way or the other, however, Lodge had become, in the words of the *Los Angeles Times'* Richard Wilson, "the hottest article in the Republican showcase."[98] A California Republican proposed a new slogan: "Make Cabot a Habit."[99]

The Lodge surge had two unintended effects for the president – one positive, the other negative. On the positive side, the Lodge victory turned attention away from Robert Kennedy's vice-presidential write-in bid. By a narrow margin, Johnson, whose backers hastily organized to maximize his write-in vote, tallied more votes for president than Kennedy did for vice president (29,317 to 25,094). This small difference, *Time* noted, "drew a sigh of relief that could be heard right in the White House Oval Office.[100] On the negative side, Lodge's victory ensured that public attention would remain focused on Vietnam. In early March McNamara had cautioned the president "to say as little as possible" about events in Southeast Asia, because "the frank answer is we don't know what's going on out there."[101] Such advice was no longer politically feasible: according to Takashi Oka, who covered Asia for the *Christian Science Monitor,* Lodge's triumph meant that the "tropical capitol of Saigon is inextricably involved in domestic American politics."[102]

A few days after the primary, the ambassador reflected on the "extraordinary" turn of events in a confidential letter to his son. "Quite astounded" at his victory, he wondered if he was "right in thinking that there is a very different attitude toward me than there has ever been in the past." "Is it," he mused, "because people like the idea of my being out here?" The result was "truly constructive" from all angles: Goldwater's loss eliminated any chance that the Arizonan would receive the nomination, his own victory ensured him a position of influence at the GOP convention, and his new prestige enhanced his standing in Vietnam. Lodge dismissed reports suggesting that opposition from party leaders would block his nomination. Recalling his experience with the Draft Eisenhower movement, he believed that Republican operatives "never like to support a candidate

[97] *Manchester Union-Leader*, 12 Mar. 1964.

[98] *Los Angeles Times*, 17 Mar. 1964.

[99] *Washington Star*, 14 Mar. 1964.

[100] *Time*, 20 Mar. 1964.

[101] President Johnson and Robert McNamara, 11:00 A.M., 2 Mar. 1964, Tape WH6403.01, Citation #2301, LBJ Recordings.

[102] *Christian Science Monitor*, 13 Mar. 1964.

who is popular." Still, he wondered whether he had the drive to mount a full-fledged campaign.[103]

Lodge's team in the United States harbored no such doubts. George Lodge told his father that he had a patriotic duty to run, given the alternatives. In the Republican race, Rockefeller was "stupid," Nixon "sullied," and Goldwater "ignorant to the point of being dangerous." And Johnson was a "sleazy, hard-drinking, immoral, superficial, and insensitive politician."[104] (The ambassador agreed with all descriptions but the last, which he considered too harsh.) Robert Mullen, flooded with phone calls, analyzed the problems ahead. "Like it or not," he mused, "we have projected him into the stance of a leading contender for the nomination." Mullen did worry, though, about the campaign's meager financial base (the Lodge forces had spent only $25,000 to win New Hampshire). A "desperate need" for "Eastern money" existed in the next key battleground primary, Oregon. The New Hampshire victory also triggered the formation of Draft Lodge organizations in nine more states, upping the total to 33. "You know," Mullen confided to George Lodge, "I think we can bring this off."[105]

In Saigon the ambassador reached a similar conclusion. He understood that if he lost in Oregon, "that ends the matter." But, if he won, he would start taking a more overt political role. Lodge planned to begin by issuing a statement confirming that he would accept a draft. He did not worry about "my relations with what in the U.S.A. Government is called the 'highest levels' "; he, and not Johnson, had the leverage in their relationship. And, at a "*deeply confidential*" level, he stated that if a draft developed, he would fly home directly to San Francisco, "acceptance speech in hand," to achieve the maximum dramatic and political effect.[106]

In late March, Henry Cabot Lodge was a long way from delivering an acceptance speech. But his victory did shake up a Republican race that Marquis Childs had taken to describing – borrowing Winston Churchill's phrase about the Soviet Union – as "a mystery wrapped in an enigma surrounded by a riddle."[107] As Mullen had noted, the next key contest came

[103] Henry Cabot Lodge to George Lodge, 16 Mar. 1964, Box 35, Henry Cabot Lodge II Papers, Massachusetts Historical Society.

[104] George Lodge to Henry Cabot Lodge, 24 Mar. 1964, Box 35, Henry Cabot Lodge II Papers, Massachusetts Historical Society.

[105] Robert Mullen to George Lodge, 15 Mar. 1964, Box 35, Henry Cabot Lodge II Papers, Massachusetts Historical Society.

[106] Henry Cabot Lodge to George Lodge, 27 Mar. 1964, Box 35, Henry Cabot Lodge II Papers, Massachusetts Historical Society.

[107] *Washington Post*, 13 Apr. 1964.

in Oregon, whose primary, scheduled for May 15, allowed the secretary of state to place on the ballot all candidates that he considered viable unless they filed an unequivocal statement of withdrawal.[108] Michigan governor George Romney filed such a statement; Lodge, Nixon, and Scranton did not. So, for the first and only time in the 1964 primary season, all five serious candidates for the GOP nomination would face each other on the same ballot.

In a perceptive column, the *Washington Star*'s Gould Lincoln described the Republican race as "two separate kinds of conflict." The first was the customary battle for the nomination. But the second, and in many ways more interesting, fight came between "newer techniques of popularity polls and primaries against an old-fashioned political professionalism which relies on back-room party organizational activity." Lodge "typifies and leads the moderns – those who believe that a man can and should be nominated by the people over the heads of the orthodox pros." Goldwater, on the other hand, was pursuing the "exact opposite" strategy, building up a delegate lead by dominating conventions and caucuses.[109]

Throughout April and early May, Goldwater had some concrete demonstrations of the merit of his tactics. In Southern states Goldwater grassroots forces ousted the traditional "black and tan" coalitions; for the first time in the history of the party, Tennessee and Georgia sent all-white delegations to the national convention. In the Mountain West, the Arizona senator fared similarly well: in Utah, Montana, Washington, Wyoming, and Nevada, the Rockefeller forces conceded that the best they could hope for was uncommitted delegations.[110]

Lodge, meanwhile, vigorously pursued his preferred course. In early April a Harris poll showed the ambassador with a "clear and decisive lead" over his rivals, backed by 41 percent of Republicans (as opposed to 14 percent on February 1).[111] Richard Nixon came second, with 28 percent, down from 44 percent in early February; Goldwater, Rockefeller, and Scranton trailed badly. As significant was Lodge's standing against Johnson. The president led Lodge by 19 points, a margin of 52 to

[108] Lodge, to fulfill his obligations under the Hatch Act, did send a telegram disavowing his candidacy, but did so after the stated deadline and failed to use the language required by the Oregon law. As Evans and Novak observed, "any last doubt" about the ambassador's intent to run "was wiped away" by the gambit. *Washington Post*, 22 Mar. 1964.

[109] *Washington Star*, 1 May 1964.

[110] Mort Frayn to George Hinman, "Western States Meeting," 16 Apr. 1964, Box 94, George Hinman Papers, Rockefeller Archives; *Washington Post*, 7 May 1964.

[111] *Washington Post*, 2 Apr. 1964.

33 percent, with 15 percent undecided. Outside of the South, Lodge trailed only by single digits. All other GOP candidates, meanwhile, ran behind the president by 30 points or more.[112] Walter Straley, president of Pacific Northwest Bell Telephone, reflected on the appeal: "People are looking for a kind of impeccable background that represents a sort of dignity and solid, stable reputation that they can count on – and I think Lodge epitomizes that."[113]

In early April Richard Nixon toured East Asia and stopped by the Saigon embassy for a long, frank conversation with Lodge. The former vice president reported that, in his mind, Rockefeller was finished, and that Scranton, while likeable, could not be nominated. Goldwater, on the other hand, could still prevail, by employing a "rotten boroughs" strategy of sweeping the South. If the Arizona senator received the nomination, Nixon predicted, "it would be another disaster for the party." He correctly anticipated that Goldwater would not soften his positions to appeal to moderate Republicans – "we could all go straight to hell as far as he is concerned."[114]

Nixon then moved on to matters of more pressing interest. A Lodge victory in Oregon would end the possibility of anyone receiving a first-ballot nomination and thus doom Goldwater's campaign. Given that Nixon had already expressed his belief that neither Rockefeller nor Scranton could receive the nomination, this analysis left only two possible nominees – and both were, at that moment, in the same room in Saigon. Expressing his admiration for Lodge's strategy, the former vice president agreed that making a "breathless" campaign before the convention would demean the ambassador; Lodge needed to rely on the power of his image. In the general election, Nixon recommended conceding the South to Johnson and instead focusing on battleground states elsewhere – Connecticut, New York, New Jersey, Ohio, Michigan, Illinois, Missouri, and California. With Lodge as the GOP nominee, he contended, the Republicans could sweep all eight states – and with them the election.[115]

As for the issues, Nixon forecast a backlash among "low income urban white groups," especially Italian-Americans, Hispanics, and Jews. The former vice president, Lodge relayed, also "spoke of the practice known

[112] *Washington Post*, 2 Apr. 1964.

[113] Miller, *Henry Cabot Lodge*, p. 361; see also *Washington Post*, 16 Apr. 1964.

[114] Henry Cabot Lodge to George Lodge, 2 Apr. 1964, Box 32, Henry Cabot Lodge II Papers, Massachusetts Historical Society.

[115] Henry Cabot Lodge to George Lodge, 2 Apr. 1964, Box 32, Henry Cabot Lodge II Papers, Massachusetts Historical Society.

as 'bussing' [*sic*] whereby the white child is transported by bus from his suburban home into the slums to go to the slum school, and the Negro is transported by bus from his home in the slums to the school in the suburbs." Betraying again his appalling ignorance about contemporary domestic issues, Lodge confessed to his son, "I haven't read much about this in the papers."[116]

By early April, at least, Lodge considered himself sufficiently schooled in the affairs of the moment to outline a skeletal agenda, one typical of the eclectic ideological approach that had characterized his public career. On the domestic front, the ambassador called for a strong civil rights program, more aggressive even than Johnson's. He intended to "vigorously enforce" the legal right to vote for blacks, as well as whatever civil rights bill emerged from the Senate. Lodge also promised to use his powers as president to urge the Senate to change its rules regarding the imposition of cloture (to a majority vote, as part of a more general program of reforming Congress). He also wanted to appoint more blacks in government service and to use federal power "to erase the last vestiges of segregation and discrimination wherever these may exist." Lodge provided much less detail on other domestic programs.[117]

In international affairs Lodge was on surer footing. He proposed a three-pronged policy based on honoring international agreements, ensuring that all potential foes knew of the U.S. commitment to resist aggression with force, and taking the propaganda offensive in world affairs. On the first issue, Lodge faulted Johnson for the Panama crisis, not from the typical Republican perspective (the dangers of negotiation), but for failing to take action against the Canal Zone residents – who had, after all, violated an agreement between the United States and Panama concerning the flying of the U.S. flag in the Zone. On the second issue, Lodge argued that the United States could have minimized its risks in the Cuban Missile Crisis had Kennedy not left doubts about U.S. firmness. And on the third question, Lodge lamented that under Johnson the United States too often had seemed to react to the proposals of others – de Gaulle, Ho Chi Minh, Prince Sihanouk of Cambodia. What he had in mind, of course, required developing practical initiatives, "lest they be adopted."[118]

[116] Henry Cabot Lodge to George Lodge, 2 Apr. 1964, Box 32, Henry Cabot Lodge II Papers, Massachusetts Historical Society.

[117] Henry Cabot Lodge, "Confidential: Working Paper – Unfinished," 2 Apr. 1964, Box 32, Henry Cabot Lodge II Papers, Massachusetts Historical Society.

[118] Henry Cabot Lodge, "Confidential: Working Paper – Unfinished," 2 Apr. 1964, Box 32, Henry Cabot Lodge II Papers, Massachusetts Historical Society.

This combination of proposals dramatically contrasted to the Goldwater agenda, but it also revealed a different approach to the presidency than Johnson's. Lodge sought to concentrate on a small number of domestic issues and provide a much more engaged international program.

Back in the United States, the Lodge campaign bet on a simple maxim of politics: in the words of the campaign's new national coordinator, veteran party official Maxwell Rabb, "When all is said and done, the pros will back a winner."[119] In California's Field Poll, Lodge led all Republican candidates and held Johnson to 58 percent in the state (the president tallied at least 70 percent against all other prospective GOP nominees, including Nixon).[120] In polls leading up to the Oregon primary Lodge had grabbed a 29-point margin over his nearest rival, prompting the *Washington Star*'s Gould Lincoln to term the ambassador "a serious and perhaps winning candidate for the Republican presidential nomination."[121] Even some of Lodge's earlier critics gave him a second look. Political columnist William S. White confessed that immediately after New Hampshire he, along with most others in the political commentariat, had doubted that Lodge would play well nationally. Now, though, it seemed clear that for "whatever the reason" – and no one ever seemed to be able to identify it – "it is no longer possible to dismiss Mr. Lodge's candidacy out of hand." To White, "nothing in political history quite parallels the strange case of Henry Cabot Lodge."[122]

The Lodge phenomenon was the central topic at the year's Gridiron Club dinner, which brought together Washington's political and journalistic elite. A George Romney impersonator crooned the following words to the melody of the song "Won't You Come Home, Bill Bailey:

Won't you come home now, Cabot?
Won't you come home?
You've been away too long.
Excepting in New Hampshire,
Things don't look good.
But you are going strong!
How can we fight old Lyndon about Vietnam?
Why can't you get it through your dome?
You're spoiling our aim, and it's just a shame!
Oh, Cabot, won't you please come home?[123]

[119] *New York Times*, 22 Apr. 1964.
[120] *Washington Post*, 10 Apr. 1964; *Washington Post*, 15 Apr. 1964.
[121] *Washington Star*, 24 Apr. 1964.
[122] *Washington Star*, 4 Apr. 1964.
[123] *Washington Star*, 28 Apr. 1964.

As in the run-up to the New Hampshire primary, not only Republicans addressed the effects of Lodge's political strength. The day after Lodge's victory in New Hampshire, Dean Rusk admitted that he had "better knuckle down as to what can be said about Lodge."[124] The president himself instructed his National Security Adviser McGeorge Bundy to "be damn sure this guy's [Lodge's] recommendations are either carried out or that I know about it."[125] Administration officials also leaked word – in this case, to Marquis Childs – that Johnson had issued a standing order to respond promptly to all Lodge requests, "and obviously those telegrams are the official record of how the Administration has bent over backward to give the Ambassador shaping policy on the spot everything he asks for."[126]

Despite these precautions, Johnson remained obsessed with the MacArthur analogy, so much so that as April proceeded he all but turned over the framing of Vietnam policy to the whims of Henry Cabot Lodge. Having conceded that "Lodge is coming home," Johnson predicted that the ambassador would "fall out with us about something." But the president would outsmart his foe: "I'm not going to let him have any differences." If Lodge wanted to manufacture a break with the administration, "he's going to have to run and catch me before he does. I'm going to approve every damn thing he does."[127] To inoculate himself further, Johnson leaked to columnist Drew Pearson – whose most recent role in the campaign had come in his attempt to discredit Don Reynolds – word that Lodge was "preparing to disassociate himself from the South Vietnamese policies of the Johnson Administration."[128] If Lodge nonetheless acted, Johnson hoped, the ambassador would sacrifice his image as a citizen-patriot.

Whatever his shortcomings as ambassador, however, Lodge proved equal to the task of matching Johnson's political maneuverings. In mid-April Dean Rusk led a State Department delegation to Saigon for intensive discussions with Lodge. On his way to South Vietnam, the secretary of state was reminded by Bundy that

> the President sets the highest possible importance on maintaining the effective understanding with Ambassador Lodge which has been established ever since

[124] President Johnson and Dean Rusk, 1:05 P.M., 11 Mar. 1964, Tape WH6403.09, Citation #2476, LBJ Recordings.

[125] President Johnson and McGeorge Bundy, 1:31 P.M., 20 Mar. 1964, Tape WH6403.12, Citation #2574, LBJ Recordings.

[126] *Washington Post*, 24 Apr. 1964.

[127] President Johnson and McGeorge Bundy, 1:08 P.M., 14 Apr. 1964, Tape WH6404.09, Citation #3025, LBJ Recordings.

[128] *Washington Post*, 21 Apr. 1964.

November, and he thinks it of the greatest importance that this cooperation should be sustained, especially in the light of the possibility that others may try to inject partisan politics into the matter...The President will wish to give the most sympathetic and careful study to any specific recommendation which the Ambassador makes, and will go to very considerable lengths to assure full harmony.[129]

Once Rusk arrived, he discovered the ambassador urging a hard-line approach. Lodge wanted to give Hanoi an "ultimatum": North Vietnam needed to cease all support for the National Liberation Front. The United States could accompany its demand with an element of "fear, to be produced by bombing some target" in North Vietnam. He conceded that carrying the war to the North in this fashion might entail risks, including the possibility that the North's forces, "perhaps followed by the Chinese Communist Army," would invade South Vietnam. Since the United States could never match the manpower of the Chinese army, "would the defense of the South," Lodge mused, "necessarily involve U.S. use of nuclear weapons?"[130]

In the weeks before the Oregon primary, Lodge proposed a variety of other measures to intensify the conflict – well beyond anything he had endorsed before he became a serious presidential candidate. He urged the Khanh regime to sever relations with France to protest de Gaulle's call for a neutralized Vietnam.[131] He increasingly inserted himself into military matters, calling on U.S. forces to pursue communist guerrillas across the Cambodian border and to launch preemptive strikes into Laos to block possible infiltration routes. He endorsed the idea of "tit-for-tat raids on North Vietnamese targets in the event of terror against Americans."[132] And he complained that "the Ambassador, contrary to the understanding in very high quarters, has not got authority over all military activities of the U.S. Government in Viet-Nam," with the military's "special status" frustrating his efforts to create the "proper political atmosphere"

[129] "Memorandum from the President's Special Assistant for National Security Affairs (Bundy) to the Secretary of State, at Taipei," 16 Apr. 1964, www.state.gov/www/about_state/history/vol_i/108_145.html, accessed 12 Mar. 2007.

[130] "Memorandum of a Conversation, U.S. Embassy, Saigon, Apr. 19, 1964, 10 a.m.," 19 Apr. 1964, www.state.gov/www/about_state/history/vol_i/108_145.html, accessed 12 Mar. 2007.

[131] "Memorandum from Michael V. Forrestal of the National Security Council Staff to the President," 10 Apr. 1964, www.state.gov/www/about_state/history/vol_i/108_145.html, accessed 12 Mar. 2007.

[132] "Memorandum by the Secretary of State's Special Assistant for Vietnam (Sullivan)," 27 Apr. 1964, www.state.gov/www/about_state/history/vol_i/108_145.html, accessed 12 Mar. 2007.

to achieve victory.[133] The clear implication: Lodge envisioned himself as a de facto consul general of Vietnam, with authority over U.S. civil and military policy.

The State Department delicately observed that "Lodge's plan runs counter to realities."[134] NSC staffer Mike Forrestal was blunter: "Almost any of the actions suggested by Lodge, but not yet implemented, could start a chain of escalation for which we are not yet prepared."[135] Johnson, however, was clear: political realities dictated that Lodge's proposals, no matter how dangerous, could not be summarily rejected. With the ambassador in effect holding Vietnam policy hostage, he remained a political threat.

In mid-April Richard Wilson imagined how a Lodge-Johnson race would unfold. "In various subtle ways," the *Los Angeles Times* columnist asserted, "the Lodge campaigners direct attention to the resemblances between Henry Cabot Lodge and John Fitzgerald Kennedy." That approach, Wilson speculated, would make "the personality issue" the key question in a Lodge-Johnson contest. In the television age, personality was important anyway, and people saw in Lodge not only someone of "presidential stature" but also a figure with "the same meticulous attention to casual dress, the brisk tones of speech, and other hallmarks of the Northeastern, Harvard-bred patrician" that had made Kennedy so appealing. For those who doubted Lodge's ability to campaign effectively, Wilson recalled the Draft Eisenhower effort, where Lodge had performed the role of substitute candidate while Eisenhower remained in Europe. The professionals still said Lodge could not win, and perhaps they were right. But if so, "there will be a lot of disappointed – and vocal – people watching the Republican National Convention in July."[136]

The combination of his experience, personality, eclectic ideology, and position in Saigon made Lodge's challenge to the president unique. Beyond the Lodge issue, though, Johnson remained vulnerable on the two issues that had tested him earlier in 1964: foreign policy and ethics

[133] "Letter From the Ambassador in Vietnam (Lodge) to the Secretary of State," 30 Apr. 1964, www.state.gov/www/about_state/history/vol_i/108_145.html, accessed 12 Mar. 2007.

[134] "Memorandum from the Deputy Assistant Secretary of State for Far Eastern Affairs (Green) to the Assistant Secretary of State for Far Eastern Affairs (Bundy)," 9 Apr. 1964, www.state.gov/www/about_state/history/vol_i/108_145.html, accessed 12 Mar. 2007.

[135] "Memorandum From Michael V. Forrestal of the National Security Council Staff to the President's Special Assistant for National Security Affairs (Bundy)," 28 Apr. 1964, www.state.gov/www/about_state/history/vol_i/108_145.html, accessed 12 Mar. 2007.

[136] *Los Angeles Times*, 17 Apr. 1964.

in government. The relative importance of the two, however, had changed from earlier in the year. In international affairs, apart from Vietnam, the situation turned more placid in April than it had been in February and March. The crises with Panama and Cuba subsided without requiring any U.S. concessions, and flare-ups in Zanzibar and Cyprus eased without the United States sending troops. And the president's efforts to create "a little peace demagoguery for the mothers" made the Democrats appear the party more committed to achieving peace with the Soviet Union.[137]

While the foreign policy issue (apart from Lodge and Vietnam) receded in importance, questions about the president's ethics assumed new forms. The Baker case, much to the president's chagrin, lurched forward with no end in sight. On March 13 the Rules Committee held a stormy meeting to consider Deleware senator John Williams's latest charges – that Baker's accountant had committed perjury and that another kickback to Johnson had occurred.[138] Two days later Senators Hugh Scott and Carl Curtis castigated the Democratic performance throughout the inquiry. For over three hours Williams, Curtis, and Scott accused committee Democrats of wanting to "cut and run." Joe Clark, Scott's colleague from Pennsylvania and the only Rules Committee Democrat on the Senate floor at the time, seemed unprepared for the assault.[139]

On March 17 Everett Jordan responded, thus keeping the inquiry in the papers, exactly what the president wanted to avoid. Terming the Republican speeches "a brass-knuckled political attack" reflective of "back-alley politics," the North Carolina senator announced that he would no longer be "intimidated, sidetracked, or abused."[140] (Bizarrely, in private he praised his ability to "not let myself lose my temper because of the harsh and unfair political comments that have been made.")[141] Hugh Scott hit back, ridiculing Jordan for overseeing an investigation that "proceeded in a zigzag fashion" due to White House pressure.[142] As had been the case throughout the inquiry, editorial boards – regardless of ideological inclination – seconded the criticism.[143]

[137] President Johnson and McGeorge Bundy, 10:16 A.M., 24 Mar. 1964, Tape WH6403.15, Citation #2630, LBJ Recordings.

[138] *Congressional Quarterly Weekly Report*, 20 Mar. 1964, p. 566.

[139] *New York Times*, 17 Mar. 1964.

[140] 110 *Congressional Record*, 88th Cong., 2nd sess., pp. 5616–18 (18 Mar. 1964).

[141] B. Everett Jordan to Carson Bain, 25 Mar. 1964, Box 37, B. Everett Jordan Papers, Duke University Library.

[142] 110 *Congressional Record*, 88th Cong., 2nd sess., pp. 5626–7 (18 Mar. 1964).

[143] *Newsday*, 13 Mar. 1964; *Washington Post*, 21 Mar. 1964; *Christian Science Monitor*, 27 Mar. 1964; *Baltimore Sun*, 13 Mar. 1964.

Johnson, meanwhile, complained privately that "all we've done on this one is just absorb it."[144] But the president's preference for responding to the affair legalistically was worse than no response at all. He termed GOP accusations that he was close to Baker during the aide's period of unethical behavior "slander," outrageously suggesting that "all of [Baker's] business ventures were after I left the leadership. He worked for Mansfield, but they want to hook it on me."[145] The president also continued to distinguish between private and public morality. "What damned difference does it make," Johnson complained, "whether Baker gave a hi-fi or this fellow [Reynolds] gave a hi-fi," since neither man was attempting to influence government policy? The issue was solely "a matter between individuals."[146] This distinction proved no more persuasive than when first raised earlier in the year.

The Baker case was not terribly damaging in and of itself, but other issues reinforced the impression the affair had made. The most serious of these involved how the president obtained his wealth. In late March Louis Kohlmeier of the *Wall Street Journal* explored how KTBC had evolved into an Austin broadcasting behemoth. "It would take," the reporter concluded, "a subtle scientist to measure precisely how Lady Bird's broadcasting business may have benefited from Lyndon's political prominence," but the "practical effect" of Johnson's influence appeared in a string of FCC rulings making Austin the most populous market in the country with only one VHF station.[147] (Topeka was the next largest.) In one of the campaign's better lines, the Texas Republican Party joked, "LBJ thinks an extremist is anybody who believes Austin ought to have two TV stations."[148]

The White House responded frostily to questions about the story; Johnson's legal adviser Abe Fortas considered it "essential that everybody be buttoned up absolutely." The president fantastically reasoned that, since his holdings had been placed in trusteeship, he could not ethically comment on the report.[149] As with Fortas's counsel on the Baker affair,

[144] President Johnson and Walter Jenkins, 11:20 A.M., 16 Mar. 1964, Tape WH6403.10, Citation #2511, LBJ Recordings.

[145] President Johnson and John McCormack, 12:30 P.M., 7 Mar. 1964, Tape WH6403.04, Citation #2385, LBJ Recordings.

[146] President Johnson and Deke DeLoach, 1:26 P.M., 12 Mar. 1964, Tape WH6403.12, Citation #2561, LBJ Recordings.

[147] *Wall Street Journal*, 23 Mar. 1964.

[148] John Knaggs, *Two-Party Texas: The John Tower Era, 1961–1984* (Austin, TX: Eakin Press, 1985), p. 51.

[149] President Johnson and Abe Fortas, 6:05 P.M., 24 Mar. 1964, Tape WH6403.15, Citation #2639, LBJ Recordings.

this legalistic approach only inflamed the matter, prompting charges that the president was stonewalling on whether KTBC had received sweetheart rulings from federal regulators. The Kohlmeier story also refocused attention on Texas, where the *Wall Street Journal*'s "Washington Wire" detected a GOP plan "to picture LBJ as a wheeler-dealer."[150]

The most explosive allegation of corruption, however, came not from a Republican but from events associated with the Democratic Senate primary in Texas. For his first two months as a candidate, right-wing radio station owner Gordon McLendon – boosted by occasional appearances from movie star John Wayne – focused on attacking Ralph Yarborough as a "left-wing lizard" and a "spineless jellyfish."[151] The McLendon effort suddenly gained traction on April 12, when the *Dallas Morning News* published convicted financier Billy Sol Estes's claim that, in 1960, he had given Yarborough $50,000 in a brown paper bag.[152] Yarborough denied the allegation and demanded an FBI investigation. McLendon then produced two men who claimed to have witnessed the event and demanded that Yarborough withdraw from the race. Yarborough responded by going on statewide television with two men charging that McLendon's witnesses were lying. *He* demanded that *McLendon* pull out of the race. Three days later, under pressure from Yarborough allies in the Justice Department, the FBI issued a report stating that one of McLendon's witnesses lied. Johnson (probably correctly) guessed that Yarborough did take the money – "as all of us do." Yet he had no reason to believe that the senator acted for corrupt purposes. As he later noted, "My own judgment is that Yarborough's a damn fool, but he's the last man in the world I'd think would be a crook."[153]

The *Washington Star* termed the contest the "toughest political fight in recent Texas history" – quite an assertion, given the competition.[154] Yarborough wound up winning the primary, though by an unimpressive margin of 57 to 43 percent. The big loser in the affair was the president. Reports from Texas indicated that a surprising number of Democrats considered Johnson vulnerable in the state, partly because many conservatives believed that the president's actions had denied them the chance to oust Yarborough.

[150] *Wall Street Journal*, 24 Apr. 1964.

[151] *Congressional Quarterly Weekly Report*, 17 Apr. 1964, p. 723.

[152] *Dallas Morning News*, 12 Apr. 1964.

[153] President Johnson and Nicholas Katzenbach, 7:56 A.M., 15 Oct. 1964, Tape WH6410.11, Citation #5891, LBJ Recordings.

[154] *Washington Star*, 2 May 1964.

The president suffered a series of additional minor blows throughout late March and April. When he returned to Texas for Easter, news reports described him as putting "a heavy foot on the accelerator," pulling away from a press automobile that was itself going 70 miles per hour, and tossing a beer can out of the window.[155] Later in the month, Johnson's two beagles, Him and Her, yelped after he picked them up by their ears; a spokesman for the Society for the Prevention of Cruelty to Animals denounced the action.[156] The accumulation of such events prompted public opinion analyst Samuel Lubell to detect "image trouble" for the president. Lubell asserted that Johnson's "popularity ratings in the polls are deceiving. Relatively few voters have identified personally with the President and his hold on their loyalty is thin."[157]

Johnson responded to the portrayals with a mixture of mockery, defiance, and anger. Still, despite a concern that he too often had acted in a reactive fashion, his most consistent response to the issue was defensive. Pointing to polls showing half of those surveyed doubted that he could keep corruption out of government, he bent over backwards to avoid the appearance of impropriety. He candidly admitted to his special assistant Larry O'Brien, "I'm afraid of this corruption issue." At the same time he appeared baffled as to why the media was interested in his personal ethics, or in any aspect of his personal life. Such questions had been considered mostly out of bounds for Franklin Roosevelt or John Kennedy: why, Johnson felt, should journalists treat him any differently?[158]

As he had throughout the start of the year, Johnson responded to political difficulties by turning to his public policy agenda. The fusion of the two concepts was, by this point, undeniable: one White House aide confessed, "The President believes that the best politics is not to talk about politics."[159] For March and the first week of April, Johnson spent more time on the farm bill, then making its final push through the House of Representatives, than on any other measure. With continuing signs of backlash over civil rights, it seemed possible – or even likely – that the issue would paralyze Johnson in the South. Indeed, the president recognized, to a much greater extent than did his advisers, how significantly civil rights

[155] *Washington Star*, 1 Apr. 1964.
[156] *Washington Star*, 28 Apr. 1964.
[157] *Congressional Quarterly Weekly Report*, 24 Apr. 1964, p. 772.
[158] President Johnson and Larry O'Brien, 12:45 P.M., 23 Apr. 1964, Tape WH64.11, Citation #3116, LBJ Recordings.
[159] *New York Times*, 19 Apr. 1964.

would realign Southern politics. He also was ahead of his advisers in recognizing that the Democratic Party would need traditionally Republican votes to retain its majority status. He developed this theme in more detail later in 1964, when he began speaking of the "frontlash" – the prospect of Republicans changing parties because of GOP positions on social and national security issues.

The farm bill's final stages represented the first step in Johnson's frontlash campaign. Johnson initially had backed the cotton measure as a payoff to Southern supporters. He then abruptly shifted course, and the bill's purpose became almost exclusively to appease Everett Jordan. But, with the continuing resistance to civil rights among Southern senators, it seemed doubtful that the New Deal strategy utilized by Johnson – using federal generosity to appeal to the South – would succeed. This political reality increased the significance of wheat-growing areas. The farm belt, including Wisconsin, Minnesota, the Dakotas, and parts of Montana, Wyoming, Missouri, Illinois, and Nebraska, had been mostly Republican territory since 1938. But between 1957 and 1959 Democrats captured Senate seats in Wisconsin, Wyoming, Minnesota, and North Dakota. In 1960 despite the presence of a Catholic heading the ticket, Democratic challengers in this predominantly Protestant region almost won Senate races in Iowa and South Dakota, while the party reelected incumbents in Montana, Illinois, and Missouri. Then, in 1962, Democrats George McGovern and Gaylord Nelson took seats in South Dakota and Wisconsin, respectively.

Tantalizing signs existed that Johnson could duplicate the success of figures like McGovern and Nelson. In early March polls showed the president running ahead of all potential GOP opponents in Iowa, which only one Democrat had carried in the previous six presidential elections, and in North Dakota, which had last gone Democratic in 1936.[160] Johnson exulted, "We've got a chance – not much – but a *little* chance to hold a few farm states," if he could provide some concrete benefits for affiliating with the Democratic Party. The bill itself, the president still believed, "won't make a damn" difference in terms of public policy. But the political benefits were enormous: in addition to denying the GOP nominee traditionally Republican electoral votes, ending the "all-Republican delegations from

[160] President Johnson and John McCormack, 12:30 P.M., 7 Mar. 1964, Tape WH64.04, Citation #2385, Recordings of Telephone Conversations – White House Series, Recordings and Transcripts of Conversations and Meetings, Lyndon B. Johnson Presidential Library.

the Midwest" would "let us control this Congress."[161] Massive presidential pressure in what Larry O'Brien termed "the hard nut-cutting" period resulted in the House narrowly passing the bill.[162] The *Wall Street Journal* correctly interpreted the result as an example of the "growing presidential intervention in legislative strategy" – and intervention for political gain.[163] The struggle was worth it: as would emerge over the next several months, the farm bill played a key role in election contests in both the South and the Midwest.

Johnson also continued to present himself as acceptable to Republicans by stressing his fiscal responsibility.[164] In late April the president addressed the U.S. Chamber of Commerce; after joking that "I suppose it might not be entirely accurate to greet you as 'my fellow Democrats'," he stressed his record of budget cutting to warm applause.[165] Syndicated columnist Walter Lippmann, in a typical glowing tribute, attributed the president's political strength to his having "quite deliberately and very skillfully raised a standard to which the prudent majority can repair."[166] One sign of Johnson's success came in the rhetoric of the two GOP candidates who most strongly criticized him, Nixon and Goldwater. Though the two attacked the president on issues relating to ethics and to foreign policy, they shied away from most economic questions, beyond generalized assertions of hostility to government spending.

With his economic agenda in place, Johnson faced two challenges to his hold over the Democratic Party apparatus – one entirely predictable, the other most unexpected. Throughout March and April public opinion polls on the vice-presidential race showed Robert Kennedy's lead expanding. In the first such measurement, taken in January, Kennedy enjoyed an eight-point margin over Adlai Stevenson (34 to 26 percent), with Hubert Humphrey third at 14 percent.[167] By March a Harris survey

[161] President Johnson and Larry O'Brien, 4:15 P.M., 7 Mar. 1964, Tape WH6403.05, Citation #2397, Recordings of Telephone Conversations – White House Series, Recordings and Transcripts of Conversations and Meetings, Lyndon B. Johnson Presidential Library.

[162] President Johnson and Larry O'Brien, 4:06 P.M., 2 Apr. 1964, Tape WH6404.02, Citation #2835, LBJ Recordings.

[163] *Wall Street Journal*, 10 Apr. 1964.

[164] President Johnson and John McCormack, 12:30 P.M., 7 Mar. 1964, Tape WH64.04, Citation #2385, Recordings of Telephone Conversations – White House Series, Recordings and Transcripts of Conversations and Meetings, Lyndon B. Johnson Presidential Library.

[165] *Washington Post*, 28 Apr. 1964.

[166] *Washington Post*, 23 Apr. 1964.

[167] Jeff Shesol, *Mutual Contempt: Lyndon Johnson, Robert Kennedy, and the Feud That Defined a Decade* (New York: W. W. Norton, 1997), p. 193.

showed Kennedy ahead of Stevenson by 14 points (38 to 24 percent), with Humphrey still third at 13 percent.[168] Privately Johnson tried to sell the argument that this result meant that Kennedy and Humphrey were actually tied, because all of Stevenson's supporters would favor Humphrey. In April, though, Kennedy's lead had grown to overwhelming proportions, with 47 percent of Democratic voters supporting him, as compared to 18 percent for Stevenson and 10 percent for Humphrey.[169]

Kennedy, meanwhile, was "acting more and more like a candidate," according to the *Wall Street Journal.* His disavowals of interest in the position were "conducted in terms likely to discourage only the most naïve voter."[170] Indications also existed of a Kennedy contingent emerging in the Senate. In Massachusetts Ted Kennedy was running for his first full term. In Maryland Joseph Tydings, a close friend of the Kennedys, was heavily favored to oust first-term Republican J. Glenn Beall. For Johnson the most alarming situation came in California, where the Democratic incumbent, Clair Engle, was ill with brain cancer. The first candidate to jump into the race was State Comptroller Alan Cranston. At this point only midway through a career that would culminate in a 24-year tenure in the upper chamber of Congress, Cranston earned the backing of the California Democratic Council, a group of liberal activists vital to Pat Brown's battle for control of the state party. Brown reciprocated by pressuring Attorney General Stanley Mosk not to run; when Representative James Roosevelt, the late president's son, deferred to Cranston, the state comptroller was Engle's only primary challenger and thus seemingly assured of winning.[171]

Worried that a Cranston victory would benefit Brown, Assembly Speaker Jesse Unruh searched for another candidate. On March 20, just before the filing deadline, an unexpected entrant jumped into the race. Though a California native, Pierre Salinger had moved East even before coming to national prominence as John Kennedy's press secretary. But by March, with Salinger eager to depart the Johnson White House, Unruh desperate for a candidate, and Mosk acting as a facilitator, Salinger declared his candidacy.[172] Brown privately denounced the "selfish" act

[168] *Washington Post*, 5 Mar. 1964.
[169] Shesol, *Mutual Contempt*, p. 193.
[170] *Wall Street Journal*, 13 Mar. 1964.
[171] Bill Stout, "California Democrats: Battle Royale for the Senate," *The Reporter*, 7 May 1964.
[172] Bill Stout, "California Democrats: Battle Royale for the Senate," *The Reporter*, 7 May 1964.

that made it look "like the Kennedys are opposing the governor of the State of California."[173] The former press secretary established a lead in polls over both Cranston and Engle, who refused to withdraw although he could not campaign. After the three leading Republican candidates – Nixon's 1962 primary challenger Joe Shell, former senator William Knowland, and state party chair Caspar Weinberger – all declined to make the race, it appeared as if the Democratic nominee was certain to capture the seat.[174]

At the national level, the press – and the president himself – continued to float names other than Kennedy as vice-presidential possibilities. Kennedy's main challenger, Humphrey, maintained his outreach program to businessmen and Southerners. Sargent Shriver's entirely predictable struggles to develop a coherent anti-poverty program dimmed his luster; by the end of March a consensus developed that the Shriver "trial balloon" had burst.[175] As Shriver's position deteriorated, William S. White – known for his close ties to the White House – detected growing support for Robert McNamara. If the president had "a single overmastering political instinct it is to broaden the base of the Democratic Party wherever he can," and McNamara, as a registered Republican and former business executive, fit the bill.[176] Meanwhile, at one White House dinner, Johnson told Humphrey that he would "drop Mike Mansfield's name into the hopper," a seemingly casual move that actually initiated an important development in the race.[177]

The president's other intraparty threat could not have come from a more different source. Alabama governor George Wallace had earned a national reputation for his implacable hostility to civil rights, as expressed through grandiose gestures – such as his standing at the door to figuratively block the integration of the University of Alabama – or through the extremist policies of his state, such as Bull Connor's turning fire hoses and police dogs on Birmingham's unarmed civil rights protesters. But Wallace was also a politician of enormous ambition and talent. Convinced that he had been singled out unfairly for prejudicial beliefs that existed far beyond Alabama, the governor launched a national speaking tour that

[173] President Johnson and Pat Brown, 3:31 P.M., 6 Apr. 1964, Tape WH6404.03, Citation #2860, LBJ Recordings.

[174] *Congressional Quarterly Weekly Report*, 12 Apr. 1964, pp. 1021–3.

[175] *Washington Star*, 26 Mar. 1964.

[176] *Washington Star*, 27 Apr. 1964.

[177] Robert Mann, *The Walls of Jericho: Lyndon Johnson, Hubert Humphrey, Richard Russell, and the Struggle for Civil Rights* (New York: Harcourt, Brace, 1996), p. 436.

brought him to more than 20 top universities. His unflappability in the face of hecklers and his ability to frame his case in legalistic rather than racial terms impressed many listeners.[178]

Wallace stopped at the University of Wisconsin on February 19, where he attracted the attention of Lloyd and Dolores Herbstreith. These veteran right-wing activists urged him to file in the Wisconsin presidential primary. Johnson, of course, would not be on the ballot, and the president's designated stand-in, Governor John Reynolds, had seen his popularity plummet after he abandoned a campaign promise to repeal the state's sales tax and supported an open housing law. Wallace, intrigued, decided not only to enter the Badger State contest but also primaries in Indiana and Maryland.[179]

Early polls in Wisconsin showed Wallace receiving about 5 percent of the vote, but his right-wing populism struck a chord, especially in ethnic areas of Milwaukee. Sensing a threat, Reynolds and his allies demonized Wallace, stating that for the Alabama governor to receive 100,000 votes in a state like Wisconsin would be a catastrophe.[180] In a nod to the new political climate, the White House sent Postmaster General John Gronouski, a native of the Badger State, home to campaign. A few days before the primary, Salinger's successor as press secretary, George Reedy, reported that the situation "looks very bad"; Wallace had succeeded in getting Johnson's "prestige too much into the thing."[181] The outcome confirmed Reedy's fears – Wallace polled 264,000 votes, more than 30 percent of the total. In the aftermath, Marquis Childs wondered how "profoundly" patterns of prejudice "will alter the familiar pattern of American political life."[182]

The Alabama governor then carried his campaign on to Indiana. The Democratic National Committee funneled money in to assist Johnson's stand-in, Governor Matthew Welsh, and the president flew to Indiana to be photographed with the governor.[183] But Wallace possessed a built-in advantage: Gary, the state's largest Democratic city, was also a center of backlash sentiment. When Wallace took 33 percent of the

[178] Dan Carter, *Politics of Rage: George Wallace, the New Conservatism, and the Transformation of American Politics* (New York: Simon and Schuster, 1996), pp. 200–1.
[179] Carter, *Politics of Rage*, pp. 201–4.
[180] *Congressional Quarterly Weekly Report*, 3 Apr. 1964, p. 168.
[181] President Johnson and George Reedy, 4:50 P.M., 6 Apr. 1964, Tape WH6404.03, Citation #2863, LBJ Recordings.
[182] *Washington Post*, 13 Apr. 1964.
[183] Carter, *Politics of Rage*, pp. 207–10.

Indiana vote, national Democrats portrayed the result as repudiation, but, as the *Indianapolis Star* observed, "If any responsible official had suggested six months ago that a segregationist from the Deep South could poll such a vote in Indiana, he would have been hooted into silence and shuffled quietly into obscurity."[184] Wallace carried Gary with 53 percent of the vote; Welsh did not win a single white-majority precinct in the city.[185]

Surveying the Democratic race shortly thereafter, journalist Richard Rovere commented that despite "the current efforts of liberals to discount the Wallace showing, the fact is that there are few, if any, of them who have not been astonished and dismayed" at the governor's performance.[186] The Wallace threat manifested the strength of backlash sentiment. The president could only hope that his domestic agenda would bring him sufficient political benefits to either neutralize the backlash or compensate for its effects by attracting normally Republican votes.

In early May political attention returned to the Republican Party, for the crucial West Coast primary contests in Oregon and California. Lodge was so confident about winning in Oregon that he started planning for the post-primary effort.[187] Rebuffing pleas from Draft Lodge activists in the United States, he reiterated his refusal to return home before the convention. Any other course, he believed, "would largely destroy something which I think I really have built here: an example to the other side that it *is* good to risk reputation, being maimed or sick or dead, in a hot, dangerous place for the sake of the country."[188] The ambassador had tried, he said, "to conduct myself so that people like Walter Lippmann would say that I am not open to criticism on the grounds that I am playing politics from an embassy abroad" – especially since "he has never in more than thirty years said anything like this about me."[189] (The Lippmann article began by asserting, "Whatever the reasons for Ambassador Lodge's increasing strength among Republican voters, he is not open to criticism on the ground that he is playing politics from an embassy abroad."

[184] *Indianapolis Star*, 6 May 1964.

[185] *New York Times*, 10 May 1964.

[186] Richard Rovere, "Letter from Washington," *The New Yorker*, 16 May 1964.

[187] Lodge actually prepared a draft victory statement for the primary. "Statement by H.C. Lodge," enclosed in Henry Cabot Lodge to George Lodge, 14 Apr. 1964, Box 32, Henry Cabot Lodge II Papers, Massachusetts Historical Society.

[188] Henry Cabot Lodge to George Lodge, 31 Mar. 1964, Box 32, Henry Cabot Lodge II Papers, Massachusetts Historical Society.

[189] Henry Cabot Lodge to George Lodge, 14 Apr. 1964, Box 32, Henry Cabot Lodge II Papers, Massachusetts Historical Society.

By accepting the ambassadorship, Lodge had "proved beyond all cavil his stout-heartedness and the sincerity of his public spirit.")[190] Lodge saw only three ways for him to return home: to resign in protest, to complete his job, or to receive a draft for president. "Only No. 3 is even theoretically possible."[191]

Of course, Lodge continued to believe that this strategy best served his political interests as well. If he left Saigon prematurely to "connive with the delegates, I would never pull up even with Johnson in the public opinion polls."[192] He could win only by appearing as "a non-politician who tries to be a good citizen, who tries to do his duty, who does not scheme, connive, talk himself to death with fulsome praise." Lodge understood that "the way in which the Republican nomination is obtained can have a tremendously helpful effect in bringing about victory in November if it is something new and fresh." Those to whom he presented his ideas agreed. He reported back a "most interesting" conversation he had with syndicated columnist Charles Bartlett, who visited Saigon in mid-April to predict that Lodge could "perpetrate a coup of the first magnitude this November."[193] Lyndon Johnson was not the only 1964 candidate who fused politics and policy when approaching his public duties.

Lodge urged his son to think about what to "look for if there is a big victory in Oregon." He hoped for endorsements from Nixon, Scranton, and Rockefeller; he also stressed the need for support from GOP governors and members of Congress. He did not underestimate the difficulty of a draft, but, showing his own belief in "Kennedy's Law," noted that both parties "have always nominated the man who is the high man in the public opinion polls."[194] And if he were wrong and Goldwater did receive the nomination, he would not vote for the GOP ticket. "Doesn't it," Lodge mused, "boil down to this: at a rock-bottom minimum, both parties must nominate *prudent* men in terms of the atomic bomb, use of which the President must decide?" Therefore, "regardless of how you feel about civil rights, Social Security, Vietnam, you must oppose a man who

[190] *Washington Post*, 7 Apr. 1964.

[191] Henry Cabot Lodge to George Lodge, n.d., Apr. 1964, Box 32, Henry Cabot Lodge II Papers, Massachusetts Historical Society.

[192] Henry Cabot Lodge to George Lodge, 14 Apr. 1964, Box 32, Henry Cabot Lodge II Papers, Massachusetts Historical Society.

[193] Henry Cabot Lodge to George Lodge, 27 Apr. 1964, Box 32, Henry Cabot Lodge II Papers, Massachusetts Historical Society.

[194] Henry Cabot Lodge to George Lodge, 23 Apr. 1964, Box 32, Henry Cabot Lodge II Papers, Massachusetts Historical Society.

has responsibility for the atomic bomb and who is *impulsive* – which Barry, unfortunately, is."[195]

Lodge, indeed, was beginning to think very much like a nominee. He seconded suggestions from his campaign team that Massachusetts Attorney General Edward Brooke (later the first black senator since Reconstruction) nominate him at the convention.[196] At his father's behest, George Lodge lobbied Kentucky senator John Sherman Cooper, a prominent Republican moderate, to head the Draft Lodge movement.[197] Ruminating about possible running mates, Lodge ruled out Goldwater, Nixon, Rockefeller, and Romney. Scranton, he felt, was the obvious choice, but House Minority Whip Gerald Ford, Kentucky senator Thruston Morton, and California senator Thomas Kuchel also deserved consideration. And then, in his most daring idea, he wondered, "How about McNamara?"[198]

Lodge also prepared a draft acceptance speech, although "unsure of how far to go, underconcentrated on domestic questions, overconcentrated on foreign affairs."[199] The address actually featured the ambassador at his most impressive. In it he presented himself "as a progressive Republican convinced we must rediscover and conserve the true meaning and tradition of the Republican Party."[200] Arguing that the GOP had not done enough for urban areas and the unemployed, Lodge called for a new program for American cities modeled on the Marshall Plan. Taking a different approach to the Bobby Baker affair, the ambassador argued that the United States could not succeed at home or abroad if there were anything questionable about the nation's moral tone, and the "deeply serious" signs of conflict of interest in Washington had shaken public confidence.[201] But handling world affairs, Lodge claimed, represented

[195] Henry Cabot Lodge to George Lodge, n.d., Box 33, Henry Cabot Lodge, II Papers Massachusetts Historical Society.

[196] Paul Grindle to Henry Cabot Lodge, 6 May 1964, Box 33, Henry Cabot Lodge II Papers, Massachusetts Historical Society.

[197] George Lodge to Henry Cabot Lodge, 28 Apr. 1964, Box 35, Henry Cabot Lodge II Papers, Massachusetts Historical Society.

[198] Henry Cabot Lodge to George Lodge, 27 Apr. 1964, Box 32, Henry Cabot Lodge II Papers, Massachusetts Historical Society.

[199] Henry Cabot Lodge to George Lodge, 6 May 1964, Box 35, Henry Cabot Lodge II Papers, Massachusetts Historical Society.

[200] Henry Cabot Lodge, draft acceptance speech, enclosed in Henry Cabot Lodge to George Lodge, 12 June, Box 34, Henry Cabot Lodge II Papers, Massachusetts Historical Society. Although sent in June, Lodge said that he had written the address in April. Henry Cabot Lodge to George Lodge, 23 Apr. 1964, Box 32, Henry Cabot Lodge II Papers, Massachusetts Historical Society.

[201] Henry Cabot Lodge, draft acceptance speech, enclosed in Henry Cabot Lodge to George Lodge, 12 June, Box 34, Henry Cabot Lodge II Papers, Massachusetts Historical Society.

the most important function of the presidency. In an unsafe world the United States needed to maintain its strength and recognize change – as the Truman administration had done in formulating the Marshall Plan. To achieve this purpose, Lodge advocated creating an international organization going beyond NATO to include all noncommunist states, even those professing neutrality in the Cold War.

Lodge had good reason for his confidence. Throughout April, in primary after primary, he fared surprisingly well, Goldwater finished below expectations, and GOP voters supported moderate nominees in down-the-ticket races. In the April 14 Illinois race, with only Goldwater and Margaret Chase Smith on the ballot, the Arizona senator captured just 64.5 percent of the vote, obtaining nearly 400,000 voters less than Robert Taft received in the 1952 primary. Smith traveled only once to the state and spent a grand total of $85 on her effort, the cost of a plane ticket from Washington to O'Hare Airport.[202] Moreover, despite the technical difficulties under Illinois law in casting a write-in vote, 6 percent of the electorate did so for Lodge.[203] One veteran Republican leader openly wondered after the vote if Goldwater was "spinning his wheels."[204]

The next week Lodge easily captured the New Jersey primary, where all of the candidates ran as write-ins; the uncommitted slate of delegates elected had a moderate bent, led by state party chair Webster Todd. Then, on April 28, Lodge crushed Goldwater in Massachusetts, taking 80 percent of the vote to Goldwater's 10 percent and winning all of the delegates – in a state where Taft had received one-third of the votes in 1952 and where the Rockefeller campaign seriously contested several delegate contests. When Goldwater claimed that he did "very well" in the primary, Democratic National Committee chair John Bailey quipped, "With victories like that, who needs defeat?"[205]

More impressive was Lodge's showing in Pennsylvania, where the campaign put in no effort, deferring to Scranton and to political realities. The governor won, but with an unimpressive 58 percent of the vote; Lodge came second with 21 percent, with 79,781 votes. (Scranton supporters had stated that anything less than 300,000 votes would be a setback;

Although sent in June, Lodge said that he had written the address in April. Henry Cabot Lodge to George Lodge, 23 Apr. 1964, Box 32, Henry Cabot Lodge II Papers, Massachusetts Historical Society.

[202] Alexander, *Financing the 1964 Election*, p. 29.

[203] *Congressional Quarterly Weekly Report*, 17 Apr. 1964, p. 723.

[204] *Washington Star*, 15 Apr. 1964.

[205] *Washington Post*, 30 Apr. 1964.

the governor received just over 220,000.)[206] Evans and Novak agreed that Lodge had shown "his phenomenal grass-roots strength again"; to Joseph Loftus, writing in the *Washington Post,* Lodge "looks more and more like the principal challenger of Senator Barry Goldwater."[207]

A few days later, in a Texas primary established for the sole purpose of demonstrating Goldwater's monolithic support in the South, what the *New York Times* dubbed Lodge's "phantom candidacy" again appeared.[208] Goldwater won, of course, with 99,143 votes, but Lodge, with no establishment backing, outpolled Smith and Rockefeller, both of whom were on the ballot. He took 11,222 total votes, a stunning total given his presumed nonexistent strength in the South. (In that same GOP primary, Republican voters nominated for senator a first-time candidate named George Herbert Walker Bush, who refuted the insinuations of his opponent, Jack Cox, that liberal leanings existed "behind the Bushes.")[209] Even the May 5 contests in Indiana and Ohio, neither of which allowed write-in votes, offered some encouragement for Lodge. In Indiana, despite outspoken support from the state party organization and newspaper magnate Eugene Pulliam, Goldwater received only 67 percent of the vote, with perennial candidate Harold Stassen attracting an embarrassingly high 26 percent. And in Ohio's hotly contested Republican Senate primary, Ohio Secretary of State Ted Brown, after mounting a vigorous challenge to Representative Robert A. Taft, Jr., from the right, lost by nearly 50 points.[210]

News from outside the primary states also looked good for Lodge. In an early May survey by the *Minneapolis Tribune,* Lodge rated the first choice of Minnesota Republicans, with 36 percent, up from just 9 percent in a January poll.[211] Just to the south, in the Iowa caucuses (then held in early May), Lodge and Rockefeller backers cooperated in an effort brokered by Robert Mullen to elect an uninstructed slate. The Rockefeller campaign considered it likely that Lodge would claim every Hawkeye State delegate at the convention.[212] The Kansas caucuses, expected to select 20 delegates committed to Goldwater, instead chose only eight pledged to the Arizona senator and 12 uninstructed delegates, who Mullen pre-

[206] *Congressional Quarterly Weekly Report*, 1 May 1964, p. 877.
[207] *Washington Post*, 3 May 1964.
[208] *Washington Post*, 4 May 1964; *New York Times*, 4 May 1964.
[209] Knaggs, *Two-Party Texas*, p. 45.
[210] *Washington Post*, 12 Apr. 1964.
[211] *Minneapolis Tribune*, 3 May 1964.
[212] "Minutes of the Operation Committee," 5 May 1964, Box 16, Nelson Rockefeller Papers, Politics Series, Rockefeller Archives; *New York Times*, 24 Apr. 1964.

dicted ultimately would vote for Lodge.[213] In the North Dakota caucuses, an expected Goldwater victory failed to materialize, and instead another Midwestern state selected an uninstructed delegation.[214] Maxwell Rabb took the fight to Goldwater's home turf in early May, touring six states in the Mountain West to describe Lodge "as a hard-working statesman whose interests lie far above partisan politics."[215] Finally, in California, though state election law did not permit write-ins, Lodge easily bested both Goldwater and Rockefeller in public opinion polls.[216]

Lodge's national standing increasingly complicated his position as ambassador. During the early months of his stint in Saigon, Lodge had strongly pushed for Diem's removal. But he had just as equally opposed Americanizing the conflict, citing fears that the United States would be perceived as a colonial power. Now, however, with his political fortunes linked to deteriorating conditions in South Vietnam, the ambassador reversed course. On April 30 he requested from Johnson authority over all military activities in Vietnam, so as to produce the "proper political atmosphere."[217] (Lodge was not on speaking terms with MACV commander Paul Harkins.) In early May the ambassador called for escalating clandestine operations against North Vietnam, to include air strikes by American pilots in unmarked planes. He offered railroad bridges as an example target.[218] Washington denied both proposals. Though Lodge consistently denied any political influence on his Vietnam recommendations, it seems hard to imagine he was unaware of the political benefits of propping up the Saigon regime, if only until he left Southeast Asia.

Appraisals of Lodge's performance remained unchanged at the White House. The NSC's Mike Forrestal dryly noted that Lodge's inability to offer consistent advice on Vietnam "is partly because management is not one of his talents."[219] Johnson put matters more bluntly, terming Lodge

[213] Robert Mullen memorandum, 4 May 1964, Box 94, George Hinman Papers, Rockefeller Archives; White, *Suite 3505*, pp. 308–11.

[214] *Washington Star*, 15 Apr. 1964.

[215] *New York Times*, 8 May 1964.

[216] *Washington Star*, 28 Apr. 1964.

[217] Lodge to President Johnson, 30 Apr. 1964, *Foreign Relations of the United States, 1964–1968*, Document 133, vol. I, www.state.gov/www/about_state/history/vol_i/index.html, accessed 10 Jan. 2008.

[218] William Sullivan memorandum, 4 May 1964, *Foreign Relations of the United States, 1964–1968*, Document 148, vol. I, www.state.gov/www/about_state/history/vol_i/index.html, accessed 10 Jan. 2008.

[219] Michael Forrestal to McGeorge Bundy, 26 May 1964, *Foreign Relations of the United States, 1964–1968*, Document 116, vol. I, www.state.gov/www/about_state/history/vol_i/index.html, accessed 10 Jan. 2008.

"one of our biggest problems there" who just "ain't worth a damn."[220] Georgia senator Richard Russell agreed, noting that while Lodge was "bright" and "intelligent," he was "not a man that persists."[221] Moreover, Russell feared, Lodge "thinks he is dealing with barbarian tribes out there, and that he's the emperor, and he is going to tell them what to do."[222]

Journalist Drew Pearson, known as always for his link to the Oval Office, wrote in early May that among the Republicans, only Lodge "would give Johnson a run for his money."[223] In early May, *Time,* the *New York Times Magazine,* and *Saturday Evening Post* all placed Lodge on their covers. *Saturday Evening Post* delivered a virtual endorsement, arguing that the Republicans could defeat Johnson only with the right kind of candidate, someone who embodied the basic principles of "modern, progressive Republicanism." Lodge's "cold-war experience," the magazine added, "has given him a realistic grasp of the Communist threat."[224]

The *Post* considered Lodge the GOP frontrunner, thanks to supporters filled with "gutsy enthusiasm."[225] In the *New York Times,* Peter Grose cast Lodge "as a leading player in the politics of two countries," someone who was "quiet and almost Orientally devious" in his approach to both his job and his presidential bid.[226] Joe Alsop discovered in Saigon that the resident American community had "developed a new spare-time sport: Lodge-watching." In words that Lodge could have written himself, Alsop wondered, "What could give the campaign a better or more striking send-off than the newly chosen candidate flying home from a war zone, to pick up the gauge of political battle at home?"[227]

[220] Telephone Conversation between President Johnson and Senator Richard Russell, Washington, 27 May 1964, 10:55 P.M., *Foreign Relations of the United States, 1964–1968*, Document 53, vol. XXVII, www.mtholyoke.edu/acad/intrel/vietnam/lbjrr.htm, accessed 10 Jan. 2008.

[221] Telephone Conversation between President Johnson and Senator Richard Russell, Washington, 27 May 1964, 10:55 P.M., *Foreign Relations of the United States, 1964–1968*, Document 53, vol. XXVII, www.mtholyoke.edu/acad/intrel/vietnam/lbjrr.htm, accessed 10 Jan. 2008.

[222] Telephone Conversation between President Johnson and Senator Richard Russell, Washington, 27 May 1964, 10:55 P.M., *Foreign Relations of the United States, 1964–1968*, Document 53, vol. XXVII, www.mtholyoke.edu/acad/intrel/vietnam/lbjrr.htm, accessed 10 Jan. 2008.

[223] *Washington Post*, 12 May 1964.

[224] "Don't Overlook Henry Cabot Lodge," *Saturday Evening Post*, 9 May 1964.

[225] John Skow, "Lodge Faces His Biggest Test in Oregon," *Saturday Evening Post*, 16 May 1964.

[226] Peter Grose, "Portrait of a Distant Candidate," *New York Times Magazine*, 10 May 1964.

[227] *Washington Post*, 12 May 1964.

New York Times columnist Tom Wicker compared Lodge to the ghost of Hamlet's father. As a "resurrected figure from the bygone days of Eisenhower, Taft, and the Great Crusade," his presence in the campaign seemed "ghostly." Lodge's spectacular rise in Republican polls prompted a question of whether he was popular or simply the symbol of GOP indecision. Almost all professionals initially had thought the latter, but now they were uncertain. They did realize, however, harking back to the Wendell Willkie phenomenon in 1940, that Lodge "is just ghostly enough and just real enough to scare the pants off everybody who is for anybody else."[228]

Of course, Wicker realized, if Lodge lost Oregon, the former senator "might as well follow Hamlet's father's ghost off to the 'sulphurous and tormenting flames' wherein dwell the also-rans."[229] This fact, as the *New York Times* pointed out, gave the Beaver State's primary an "importance far beyond the 18 committed delegates at stake."[230]

Oregon had played a decisive role once before in the Republican presidential process, in 1948, when Harold Stassen's loss to Thomas Dewey destroyed the insurgent governor's candidacy.[231] Sixteen years later the state exemplified the tradition of moderate Republicanism. Its governor, progressive Republican Mark Hatfield, would later gain fame as the first governor to oppose Johnson's policy in Vietnam. On the questions critical to the Goldwater campaign, Oregon voters favored the test ban treaty (73 to 18 percent), opposed terminating diplomatic relations with the Soviet Union (84 to 9 percent), and supported compulsory rather than voluntary Social Security (75 to 19 percent). They differed from the national norm, though, in one respect: only 22 percent supported the Johnson administration's approach to Vietnam, as opposed to 46 percent nationally. Twenty-six percent wanted a more aggressive policy, 17 percent desired a less aggressive policy, and 35 percent were unsure.[232] Moreover, in a Harris poll, 84 percent of voters in Oregon said that Lodge had some responsibility for the U.S. situation in Vietnam.[233]

The first comprehensive survey taken in Oregon, from mid-April, showed Lodge with an astonishing 29-point lead over Nixon, who came

[228] *New York Times*, 12 Apr. 1964.
[229] *New York Times*, 12 Apr. 1964.
[230] *New York Times*, 4 Apr. 1964.
[231] Zachary Karabell, *The Last Campaign: How Harry Truman Won the 1948 Election* (New York: Knopf, 2000), pp. 96–106.
[232] "Issue Polls," Box 35, Graham Molitor Papers, Rockefeller Archives. The poll was taken in March 1964.
[233] *Washington Post*, 13 Apr. 1964.

in second.[234] Less than one in five voters said that Lodge's absence from the state affected their view of him. On the issues before Oregon voters, Lodge scored equally impressively, taking the top spot on six of the nine specific questions in the Harris survey – such as which candidate would do a better job of winning against Johnson, which candidate would most capably lead the free world, and which candidate would best maintain American strength.[235]

In discussions with Oregon voters, journalist Roscoe Drummond discovered that Lodge had three assets: a positive image from his tenure as ambassador to the United Nations, his willingness to take on a difficult assignment in Vietnam, and his personal similarities with John Kennedy.[236] Stephen Shadegg, Goldwater's Oregon campaign manager, lamented, "The guy's not here. What can you do?"[237] The best that Rockefeller hoped for was a second-place finish; the campaign leadership struggled in vain to find a "catch phrase" for their Oregon effort.[238] Less than a month before the primary, then, the ambassador's lead seemed both wide and deep, with his opposition in disarray. An enthusiastic, early endorsement from the state's most powerful paper, *The Oregonian,* prompted the Lodge campaign's Robert Mullen to boast that "Oregon is in the bag."[239] And from there, anything was possible. As one Lodge organizer commented, "The professionals may be slow, but they're not completely moronic. They want to win, and Oregon will prove Lodge is the one most likely to do that."[240]

Between April 20 and April 25, however, three unrelated events conspired to blunt the Lodge momentum. First, Goldwater all but abandoned the state, canceling his scheduled appearances and reducing his advertising buys. The decision eliminated the Goldwater-Rockefeller crossfire that had provided a useful foil for Lodge in New Hampshire.[241] Second, in response to Goldwater's decision, the Rockefeller forces chose "He Cares Enough to Come" as their new Oregon slogan – hoping that an appeal to local pride might at least clinch second place. Rockefeller committed to several additional visits to the state, while his campaign

[234] *Washington Post*, 13 Apr. 1964.
[235] *Washington Post*, 14 Apr. 1964.
[236] *Washington Post*, 4 Apr. 1964.
[237] *Washington Post*, 7 May 1964.
[238] Minutes of the Operations Committee, 20 Apr. 1964, Box 16, Nelson Rockefeller Papers, Politics Series, Rockefeller Archives.
[239] John Skow, "Lodge Faces His Biggest Test in Oregon," *Saturday Evening Post*, 16 May 1964.
[240] *Wall Street Journal*, 6 May 1964.
[241] *New York Times*, 21 Apr. 1964.

increased its purchases of half-hour television advertisements, started running radio spot announcements mimicking newscasts, and purchased billboards announcing the new slogan.[242] Third, upon his return from Southeast Asia, Nixon authorized a $50,000 covert effort targeted at Lodge, making the ambassador the subject of sustained negative attacks for the first time in the campaign. Before May 15 Nixon personnel would reach 125,000 Oregon Republicans by phone, casting aspersions on Lodge's fitness for the nomination.[243]

This combination of events changed the campaign's momentum. The Rockefeller office reported that the "Nixon people are apparently doing a good hatchet job on Lodge," describing the ambassador as a lazy campaigner who was responsible for the difficulties in Vietnam.[244] (Nixon forces also circulated an anti-Lodge broadside asking, "How Soft on Communism Is Henry Cabot Lodge?")[245] As the local Rockefeller workers called for their campaign to join in the anti-Lodge barrage, the governor monopolized Oregon news coverage, asking, "What do the absent advocate? Where do the silent stand?"[246] The Eugene *Register-Guard,* the state's largest paper outside of Portland, endorsed Rockefeller, as did former governor Charles Sprague, publisher of the *Oregon Statesman.*

On May 8 Samuel Lubell detected an "outside chance that Lodge could be beaten."[247] Three days later a Harris survey showed Lodge's lead, while still healthy, had fallen to 18 points, 40 to 22 percent over Nixon, with Rockefeller gaining strength, at 19 percent. The attacks had some impact. Fourteen percent of Oregon voters now viewed Lodge as a lazy campaigner, as opposed to only 5 percent in mid-April; 27 percent said he should have returned to the state to campaign, up from 19 percent in mid-April; and support for the administration's policy in Vietnam dropped by four points, to 34 percent.[248]

Even at the height of Lodge's Oregon popularity, some had expressed skepticism about the ambassador's chances. In mid-April state GOP

[242] Minutes of the Operations Committee, 18 May 1964, Box 16, Nelson Rockefeller Papers, Politics Series, Rockefeller Archives.

[243] John Kessel, *The Goldwater Coalition: Republican Strategies in 1964* (Indianapolis: Bobbs-Merrill, 1968), p. 66.

[244] Minutes of the Operations Committee, 8 May 1964, Box 16, Nelson Rockefeller Papers, Politics Series, Rockefeller Archives; *Washington Star*, 28 Apr. 1964.

[245] *New York Times*, 3 Apr. 1964.

[246] *New York Times*, 12 May 1964; *Washington Post*, 15 May 1964.

[247] Minutes of the Operations Committee, 8 May 1964, Box 16, Nelson Rockefeller Papers, Politics Series, Rockefeller Archives.

[248] *Washington Post*, 11 May 1964.

chair Elmo Smith, who was neutral in the primary, speculated that "Lodge's strength is a shadowy thing that could change very rapidly."[249] The *Washington Post*'s Julius Duscha noted that most local Republicans did not "sense any depth of commitment to Lodge," although they still expected the ambassador to win. One suburban housewife, Jennie Dawson of Menlo Park, typified the voters with whom Duscha spoke. Somewhat unenthusiastically, she said, "I suppose I'll still vote for Lodge, but I'm beginning to get a little shaky," largely due to negative reports of Lodge's campaigning style in 1960.[250] Other voters expressed uncertainty about what Lodge believed.

The Lodge team struggled to respond. They planned to air their "Meet Mr. Lodge" commercial from New Hampshire, but Goldwater forces persuaded Eisenhower to deny any implication that he had endorsed anyone in the 1964 campaign. (In an ironic line, given the candidate's later behavior as president, the Nixon state chair termed the aborted Lodge plan characteristic of a campaign using "fancy tricks" from "the East.") George Lodge traveled to the state to denounce the "misrepresentations" and "inferences" that the ambassador was not serious about his campaign or that he had appeased communist expansionism during his time at the United Nations.[251] The day before the primary, Lodge's lead had dropped to 11 points, 35 to 24 percent, with Rockefeller surging to second and Nixon holding steady. "There's something sleepy going on," one Oregon GOP leader remarked, regarding these "second thoughts about the Lodge candidacy."[252]

On Primary Day those second thoughts appeared with cascading force. In a shocking result, Rockefeller captured first place, winning 93,032 votes, or 33 percent. Lodge finished second, with 28 percent, and Goldwater edged Nixon for third, 18 percent to 17 percent. Smith and Scranton trailed far behind, each with less than 3 percent of the vote. Rockefeller's chief political adviser, George Hinman, considered the result "too good to be true."[253] To Al Otten of the *Wall Street Journal*, the result most pleased the party professionals, who were now "off the hook" from the dilemma of deciding whether to stomach a Lodge nomination.[254]

[249] *Los Angeles Times*, 12 Apr. 1964; see also *Washington Star*, 15 May 1964.
[250] *Washington Post*, 11 May 1964.
[251] *New York Times*, 14 May 1964.
[252] *New York Times*, 15 May 1964.
[253] George Hinman to Donald DuShane, 1 June 1964, Box 82, George Hinman Papers, Rockefeller Archives.
[254] *Wall Street Journal*, 18 May 1964.

Reflecting on the primary, the Rockefeller staff believed that the Lodge campaign simply "fell apart."[255] Lodge's support collapsed among businessmen and white-collar workers, paving the way for the upset – and, essentially, for the end of his campaign. The *New York Times* announced that the results showed the "flash-and-fade experience" of Lodge; the *Washington Post* indicated that the defeat "appears to have shot down his political balloon just as quickly as it was inflated"; the *Los Angeles Times* noted that the vote "punctured the myth of Henry Cabot Lodge's party popularity."[256] Goldwater dismissed the result as a victory for the "radical left," but still found some room to rejoice; at the very least, "under no circumstances" would Lodge get the nomination.[257] Lodge himself admitted as much, conceding that his chances had "disappeared entirely."[258]

From the start, Lodge had pursued a high-risk, high-reward strategy. He insisted on a low-budget, mostly volunteer effort. He refused to issue position papers to clarify his stances on key issues. He would not return to the United States to campaign and would accept the nomination only through a draft that did not require his lobbying the delegates. The reward, of course, would be that, having received the nomination in this fashion, he could campaign in the fall as the citizen-patriot, which he – probably correctly – considered the only way that a Republican could defeat Johnson. But the strategy carried with it risks: to have any chance of success, Lodge had to abide by "Kennedy's Law," winning or running better than expected in all contested primaries and maintaining a healthy lead in national polls. His strategy worked until three weeks before the Oregon primary, but an absent candidate and an amateur campaign staff could not rebut what were, in many ways, eminently refutable criticisms. With the myth of his electoral invincibility shattered, Lodge's candidacy collapsed – and so too did the most promising chance for the Republicans to defeat Johnson in 1964.

The Lodge candidacy described itself as a grassroots effort. Yet, of course, grassroots activists of a different sort spent early 1964 seeking to move the party to the right. That they ultimately succeeded while

[255] Minutes of the Operations Committee, 18 May 1964, Box 16, Nelson Rockefeller Papers, Politics Series, Rockefeller Archives.

[256] *New York Times*, 17 May 1964; *Washington Post*, 17 May 1964; *Los Angeles Times*, 17 May 1964.

[257] *Washington Post*, 17 May 1964.

[258] Henry Cabot Lodge to Milton Katz, 19 May 1964, Box 35, Henry Cabot Lodge II Papers, Massachusetts Historical Society.

Lodge's group failed should not obscure how close to success Lodge's bid came, nor how fragile the conservatives' hold on the GOP actually was in early 1964.

For Johnson, Lodge's demise ended the power that the ambassador held over the administration's Vietnam policy; no longer did the president have to fear that refusing a Lodge request could produce a campaign issue. Yet Johnson's handling of Lodge and Vietnam mirrored his tactics in earlier foreign policy crises in Panama and Cuba. In each instance the president eschewed negotiations lest they expose him to domestic attacks. This approach to managing foreign policy would serve Johnson well in 1964, but as a long-term strategy, it would prove disastrous.

3

The Politics of Backlash

After the Oregon shocker, political attention was focused on the two coasts. On the Pacific Coast, California hosted the GOP's final presidential primary, where a Goldwater win would eliminate any doubt of the nomination. On the Atlantic, the Senate debated the administration's civil rights bill as voters in the Maryland primary tested the appeal of George Wallace's backlash message. By the end of June, the backlash and the GOP race would become intertwined, setting up the foundation for the remainder of the 1964 campaign.

The Oregon result eliminated Lodge as a viable candidate – and thus blocked the only realistic chance for Republican moderates to prevent a Goldwater nomination. Rockefeller, however, interpreted the outcome as a sign that he had put behind him his candidacy's basic problems – electability, his personal life, lack of party support for many of his key positions – and had a realistic chance at the nomination. (This even though he had almost no delegates and could go to the convention with, at best, two primary wins outside of his home state.) Campaign workers reported that the governor was now "supremely confident, eager to work even harder" as he traveled on to California, site of the nation's final primary, scheduled three weeks after the Oregon vote.[1]

The rejuvenated Rockefeller entered a state with a badly fractured Republican Party. As late as 1958 the California GOP had held both Senate seats and the governorship, but that year Senator William Knowland, angling for a run at the White House and eager for some

[1] Graham Molitor, "Summary of May 21 Staff Conference," Box 35, Graham Molitor Papers, Rockefeller Archives.

executive experience, decided to run for governor against the moderate incumbent, Goodwin Knight. After his funding sources dried up, Knight dropped out of the gubernatorial race and declared for the Senate. The moves had disastrous repercussions for the state party: Democrats Pat Brown and Clair Engle swept both contests, while Knight refused to even endorse his ticket-mate.[2]

California's political tradition seemed hospitable to Rockefeller's brand of Republicanism. In the early 1900s progressives led by Governor Hiram Johnson had seized control of the state GOP. Though Johnson himself veered toward the right later in his career, the ideological tradition he bequeathed lived on in figures such as Earl Warren and Thomas Kuchel, whom Warren named to the Senate seat vacated by Nixon in 1953. In the upper chamber, Kuchel developed a reputation as an effective partisan (hence his election as minority whip) whose liberal Republicanism more resembled that of GOP senators from New York or Vermont than from the West. Kuchel's brand of politics, however, was anathema to conservative grassroots activists in Southern California, especially in fast-growing Orange County. In early 1964 the right took control of the California Republican Assembly; by the time of the presidential primary, Kuchel and his allies had seen their power gradually eroded. (Kuchel himself would fall in the GOP primary four years later to conservative Max Rafferty.) But it was not clear which ideological group had predominance – the Rockefeller-Goldwater primary would decide. And there would be no division of delegates: California's primary was winner-take-all.[3]

As Goldwater's political tactician Clifton White argued at the time, "No one has ever been able to quite fathom the depths of the intricate whirlpools that spin and churn across California's changing political landscape."[4] The Rockefeller campaign certainly struggled with the process. Citing the state's grassroots right-wing strength, Rockefeller pollsters cautioned the governor against mentioning his support for public power, his vision of urban renewal, his desire for increased funds for public housing, and his backing for mass transit. They also urged him not to

[2] Gayle Montgomery and James Johnson, *One Step from the White House: The Rise and Fall of Senator William F. Knowland* (Berkeley: University of California Press, 1998), pp. 232–50.

[3] Rick Perlstein, *Before the Storm: Barry Goldwater and the Unmaking of the American Consensus* (New York: Hill and Wang, 2001), , pp. 334–7.

[4] F. Clifton White with William Gill, *Suite 3505: The Story of the Draft Goldwater Movement* (New Rochelle, NY: Arlington House, 1967), p. 334.

speak out on Proposition 14, advice that he refused to heed: Rockefeller consistently and vociferously denounced the measure.[5]

Before his victory in Oregon, Rockefeller and his staff harbored no illusions about their chances in California. In mid-April the campaign's California consultants proposed developing two strategies for the primary, depending on the Oregon outcome. The Rockefeller staff concluded that "really only one plan was needed," since they had no chance of winning in Oregon.[6] Accordingly, Rockefeller planned to campaign in California on a theme of saving "the party from the right wing," stressing Goldwater's ties to extremist groups, especially the John Birch Society.[7] As late as the day before the Oregon primary, the Rockefeller forces were resigned to basing their California effort on an implication that the governor would "step aside" for a more electable moderate.[8] Accordingly, the Lodge and Rockefeller campaigns discussed cooperating in California, with the Draft Lodge movement planning to inform its supporters that a vote for Rockefeller was really a vote for Lodge.[9] Indeed, a good portion of those slated as Rockefeller delegates actually favored Lodge over the New York governor, and all could be expected to vote for the ambassador at the convention.[10]

Then came Oregon – and with it, a temporary boost in Rockefeller's standing.[11] On the eve of the Oregon primary, Rockefeller had trailed Goldwater by 16 points in the Field Poll, 43 to 27 percent.[12] After Oregon, Rockefeller surged to a near-tie and by the end of May had grabbed a nine-point lead. Running on his (poll-tested) theme of "responsible Republicanism," Rockefeller painted Goldwater as an extremist; one campaign adviser boasted, "We're going to make Goldwater live with every crazy statement he's ever made."[13] Three days after Oregon, the Draft Lodge forces formally endorsed Rockefeller, adding to his momentum.

[5] Issue Poll, 21 Mar. 1964, Box 73, George Hinman Papers, Rockefeller Archives.
[6] Minutes of the Operations Committee, 16 Apr. 1964, Box 16, Nelson Rockefeller Papers, Politics Series, Rockefeller Archives.
[7] Minutes of the Operations Committee, 16 Apr. 1964, Box 16, Nelson Rockefeller Papers, Politics Series, Rockefeller Archives; *Washington Post*, 22 Apr. 1964.
[8] John Wall to George Hinman, 14 May 1964, Box 94, George Hinman Papers, Rockefeller Archives.
[9] *Washington Post*, 6 May 1964; *New York Times*, 10 May 1964.
[10] White, *Suite 3505*, p. 335.
[11] *Washington Post*, 24 May 1964.
[12] *New York Times*, 14 May 1964.
[13] *Washington Post*, 18 May 1964.

For the first time in the campaign, the New York governor seemed to receive some lucky breaks. On May 24 a Goldwater appearance on ABC's *Issues and Answers* revived the extremist image. When asked how the United States could stop Ho Chi Minh, the Arizona senator responded, "Defoliation of the forests by low-yield atomic weapons could well be done." When pressed on whether such a policy could bring China into the Vietnam conflict, Goldwater seemed blasé: "You might have to." The comments attracted widespread ridicule: Robert Kennedy announced that Goldwater had discovered a "solution for crime in Central Park. He would use conventional nuclear weapons and defoliate it."[14]

In the next day's newspapers, shortly after maintaining that any campaign to "stop" a particular candidate would be "divisive," Eisenhower issued a statement implying that he was finally endorsing a stop-Goldwater movement.[15] Goldwater countered with a bizarre reply attributing the former president's statement to "this mysterious clique in the East that nobody seems to know anything about...the nebulous mysterious wing of the party that I've never been able to figure out who they are."[16]

Caught up in the surge of momentum, Rockefeller's campaign deluded itself into thinking that the nomination was within its grasp. With local supporters "assuring a victory," the staff envisioned a "massive reappraisal" of strategy to include joint appearances with Pennsylvania governor Scranton.[17] This process would begin with a high-minded victory statement, thus using the California campaign as a launching pad to project a new, positive Rockefeller image.[18] Rockefeller aide Graham Molitor worried about overconfidence, noting reports of a "substantial" Goldwater television buy, but he was assured that the campaign wanted to avoid any "mud-slinging."[19] Molitor's caution was well placed: through an impressive grassroots fundraising effort, the Goldwater campaign raised $2 million for the primary, matching Rockefeller's spending in the state.[20]

[14] Perlstein, *Before the Storm*, p. 347.

[15] *New York Times*, 25 May 1964.

[16] *Newsweek*, 8 June 1964.

[17] Minutes of the Operations Committee, 28 May 1964, 2 June 1964, Box 16, Nelson Rockefeller Papers, Politics Series, Rockefeller Archives.

[18] Minutes of the Operations Committee, 29 May 1964, Box 16, Nelson Rockefeller Papers, Politics Series, Rockefeller Archives.

[19] Graham Molitor to "List C," 28 May 1964, Box 8, Molitor Papers; Minutes of the Operations Committee, 29 May 1964, Box 16, Nelson Rockefeller Papers, Politics Series, Rockefeller Archives.

[20] Herbert Alexander, *Financing the 1964 Election* (Princeton, NJ: Citizens Research Foundation, 1966), p. 20.

But Rockefeller instead focused on the size of his triumph; he worried that a narrow win could allow the Draft Lodge forces to claim that they provided the margin of victory.[21] With a decisive outcome in California, the governor anticipated a showdown with Nixon for the nomination. The Rockefeller staff looked for Nixon to emphasize his foreign policy experience, his coded attacks on civil rights, and his ability to portray Johnson as a "wheeler-dealer."[22] Nixon, however, was also vulnerable on several counts. His campaign had very little money (it had struggled even to raise the $50,000 required for its Oregon effort) and suffered under the legacy of defeats in 1960 and 1962.[23] Moreover, the former vice president had a reputation of campaigning poorly under pressure, and his shifting positions on civil rights left him exposed in key Northern states.[24]

Rockefeller aides harbored few illusions about the nature of a contest with Nixon: both sides, because of the candidates' weaknesses, would confine themselves to vapid pronouncements on the public policy issues of the day. George Gilder, a young staffer who joined the campaign after *Advance,* a liberal Republican magazine, folded, analyzed Nixon's strategy perceptively – as well as sarcastically. Gilder argued that Nixon's strength came in inverse proportion to Goldwater's, since the former vice president had adopted an approach of "tough demagogic speeches on civil rights and foreign policy." In general, though, Gilder considered Nixon a "weak candidate who would have to depend upon foreign reverses to hope for victory, and for a white revulsion against the Negro revolution." Of the states he lost to Kennedy in 1960, Nixon perhaps could take Illinois from Johnson, but that gain would be offset by an almost certain defeat in California. Accordingly, Gilder believed, the Nixon campaign was really about the former vice president's ego. Unlike Rockefeller, Nixon would not use the run-up to the convention to position himself for victory against Johnson, but merely to obtain the nomination. Gilder predicted that Nixon "will try to play the role of a toned down Goldwater, more politically astute, but appealing to the same general groups in the country." Beyond civil rights and foreign policy, Nixon

[21] Minutes of the Operations Committee, 1 June 1964, Box 16, Nelson Rockefeller Papers, Politics Series, Rockefeller Archives.

[22] Minutes of the Operations Committee, 27 May 1964, Box 16, Nelson Rockefeller Papers, Politics Series, Rockefeller Archives.

[23] Evans and Novak noted that Nixon raising the 12 to 15 million dollars necessary to run a fall campaign "would be as easy as paving gold in a swimming pool." *Washington Post,* 1 June 1964.

[24] Roswell Perkins to George Hinman, 29 May 1964, Box 15, Nelson Rockefeller Papers, Politics Series, Rockefeller Archives.

would confine himself to bland pronouncements. For instance, on health: "In general, Nixon is for it." Or on aging: "Generally Nixon believes that aging is an inevitable aspect of the human condition."[25]

Despite the campaign's confidence, favorable opinion toward the New York governor actually began to tail off in the days before the primary.[26] Meanwhile, Rockefeller's bad luck returned. Eisenhower issued a statement denying that his earlier, anti-Goldwater remarks constituted an attack on any particular candidate.[27] Back in New York, Happy Rockefeller gave birth to the couple's first son, Nelson Rockefeller, Jr., unintentionally reminding voters of the governor's divorce and remarriage.[28] The Goldwater campaign responded with a none-too-subtle ad featuring a child asking his mother why she favored Goldwater. The reply: "If all children are to grow up respecting truth, morality, courage, and justice, we must show them that we too respect these principles."[29]

Primary Day featured a heavy turnout – 72 percent – and an extremely close tally. The wire services called the race for Rockefeller, but, testimony to their organizational strength, conservatives had voted heavily by absentee. When all the ballots were counted, Goldwater won with 51 percent, taking 1,120,403 votes to Rockefeller's 1,052,053 – and all of California's 86 delegates.[30]

The California results, as syndicated journalists Evans and Novak reported, left the stop-Goldwater leadership "in a state of shock."[31] *The Times* of London typified international sentiment, opining that "even the faintest chance" of a Goldwater victory in November "would be enough to shake faith in the maturity and stability of American politics."[32] Back at home, the state of concern spread beyond partisans of Rockefeller, Lodge, and Scranton. A survey by the Republican National Committee predicted that with Goldwater heading the ticket, the Democratic House majority would increase by anywhere from 30 to 47 seats, and five Republican governors most likely would not win reelection. In addition, the party would lose five Senate seats – those

[25] George Gilder memo, enclosed in Roswell Perkins to George Hinman, 29 May 1964, Box 15, Nelson Rockefeller Papers, Politics Series, Rockefeller Archives.
[26] *Washington Post*, 8 June 1964.
[27] *Washington Post*, 5 June 1964.
[28] *Los Angeles Times*, 29 May 1964.
[29] *Los Angeles Times*, 1 June 1964.
[30] *Washington Post*, 3 June 1964.
[31] *Washington Post*, 4 June 1964.
[32] *The Times* (London), 4 June 1964.

of Edwin Mechem in New Mexico, Hiram Fong in Hawaii, J. Glenn Beall in Maryland, Kenneth Keating in New York, and Hugh Scott in Pennsylvania.[33]

Privately, however, even Democrats considered this estimate overly pessimistic. A review by one Democratic operative predicted that a Goldwater nomination might even bolster the Republicans in marginal House races, by increasing turnout among disaffected conservatives. The Arizonan's effect on Senate contests, moreover, would largely be a wash: Goldwater would probably help GOP candidates in California, Indiana, Montana, North Dakota, Oklahoma, Utah, and Wyoming, and hurt the GOP in New Jersey, Maine, Maryland, New York, Pennsylvania, Ohio, and Michigan.[34] For much of the campaign, this viewpoint more reflected the political consensus than did the RNC survey.

Goldwater's victory was not the only sign of an ascendant right wing. A few days before the California vote, Maryland Democrats went to the polls in the final primary contested by George Wallace. As in Wisconsin, the president had a weak stand-in, Senator Daniel Brewster. And as in Indiana, the state had a pocket of backlash strength, in this case Maryland's Eastern Shore, whose nominally Democratic voters resembled rural Southern Democrats. Johnson wanted to "take up the cudgels" against Wallace by leaking word that the FBI was investigating the governor for fraud regarding highway contractors. But, recalling his last experience with a politically motivated leak, he admitted his fears of "another Don Reynolds thing" and backed off.[35]

Wallace displayed the same gifts as a campaigner he had shown in Wisconsin and Indiana. When hecklers in Baltimore asked him what philosophers he had studied, he had a quick retort: "Well, I've read Socrates and Plato and Aristotle and all those fellows. I've even read Machiavelli."[36] One Maryland merchant described the problem for Brewster's campaign: voters saw "Governor Wallace on TV and they can't believe the mild man they see is the bad man they keep reading about. What he says makes a lot of sense down here." On primary day, Wallace captured 46 percent of the vote, winning 16 of Maryland's 23 counties; only overwhelming

[33] *Washington Post*, 11 June 1964.

[34] Ross Strinett to Cliff Carter and Walter Jenkins, 16 June 1964, Box 56, Hubert Humphrey Papers, Minnesota State Historical Society.

[35] President Johnson and George Reedy, 7:35 P.M., 13 May 1964, Tape WH6405.07, Citation #3451, LBJ Recordings.

[36] *Washington Post*, 1 May 1964.

losses in Montgomery and Baltimore Counties prevented Wallace from carrying the state.[37]

Still, despite what one reporter termed a "fascinating" ability to claim "victory after defeat," a close finish netted the governor no delegates, and Wallace had no more primaries to enter.[38] And so he began talking of a third-party run for the presidency. He outlined an endeavor more ambitious than Strom Thurmond's in 1948 in that it would target not only the South but also selected Northern states. By the early summer, Wallace was on the ballot in 16 states.

A Wallace candidacy would cripple Goldwater's chances in the fall campaign. But the Arizona senator still needed to reach that stage, since his rivals refused to concede defeat. With Rockefeller and Lodge eliminated, the attention of Goldwater's party critics turned to Scranton. The 56th annual Governors' Conference was scheduled for Cleveland, from June 8 through 10; in addition to Scranton, Rockefeller, and Romney, who represented their states, the Republican governors invited Eisenhower, Nixon, and Goldwater to attend.

Scranton charted a typically inconsistent course. He began, two days after the California primary, by separating himself from Rockefeller's attacks against Goldwater, announcing that he did not "know of any extremely basic difference" between Goldwater and himself.[39] The next day, however, Scranton conferred for 85 minutes with Eisenhower to discuss a possible presidential bid.[40] Two moderate Republican governors, John Chafee of Rhode Island and John Anderson of Kansas, publicly urged their colleague to enter the race.[41] Meanwhile, Pennsylvania senator Hugh Scott and representative Robert Corbett announced the establishment of a Congressional Scranton-for-President Committee, on the grounds that a Goldwater nomination would produce disastrous House losses.[42]

Then, on June 7, the anti-Goldwater momentum sputtered when Scranton appeared on CBS's *Face the Nation*. The Pennsylvania governor had planned to use the nationally televised event to announce his candidacy. But, just before his departure to the studio, he received a call from

[37] Dan Carter, *The Politics of Rage: George Wallace, the Origins of the New Conservatism, and the Transformation of American Politics* (New York: Simon and Schuster, 1995), p. 215.

[38] *Washington Post*, 3 May 1964.

[39] *Washington Star*, 5 June 1964.

[40] *New York Times*, 7 June 1964.

[41] *New York Herald-Tribune*, 7 June 1964.

[42] *Washington Post*, 7 June 1964.

Eisenhower. Reversing course from the previous day, the former president now said that he would not be a party to any stop-Goldwater movement. He urged Scranton similarly to avoid involvement in such a "cabal."[43]

Scranton backed down, and in the process came across as almost dazed. When asked if he would run, he replied that he would accept a draft but was not a candidate. When pressed specifically on whether Goldwater fit the ideological tradition of Lincoln, Theodore Roosevelt, and Eisenhower, Scranton offered an extraordinary response: "I don't know yet." He suggested that he needed a private conference with Goldwater to discuss the Arizonan's viewpoints. The governor reaffirmed his support for the administration's civil rights bill, but added that it was "not necessarily" true that Goldwater would be an unacceptable nominee if, as expected, he wound up opposing the legislation. "There are a great many people," Scranton mused, who did not support the measure but nonetheless "stand strongly for equal rights for all persons."[44] Rockefeller used an afternoon press conference to denounce Eisenhower for ineffective leadership and Scranton for intellectual incoherence.

From Kansas the party's 1936 nominee, Alf Landon, took a different view. The patron of the moderate Republicans termed himself "thoroughly disgusted" with the party's leadership. Even if Scranton had declared his candidacy, Landon realized, the Pennsylvania governor had no chance at the nomination. Rockefeller, he thought, should not even have run: "If he wanted to play Anthony and Cleopatra, he should have quit public life." The mistake Republican moderates had made, Landon understood, came in their failure to build up Lodge. Now that the ambassador was eliminated, Landon saw no chance to stop Goldwater.[45]

To the *Washington Post,* "The Republican floundering continues without any indication that it is retarding the pace of the Goldwater bandwagon."[46] With Scranton evidently out of the running, attention shifted to Nixon, who announced, "It would be a tragedy for the Republican Party in the event that Senator Goldwater's views, as he previously stated, were not challenged and repudiated."[47] Nixon, however, lacked the credibility to lead any broad movement in the party. When asked about the comments, Goldwater replied simply: "I guess he doesn't

[43] *Washington Post,* 8 June 1964.

[44] *Congressional Quarterly Weekly Report*, 12 June 1964, p. 1184.

[45] Alf Landon, notes of conversation with Maurice Rosenblatt, 6 June 1964, Box 83, WHCF-PL, Lyndon B. Johnson Presidential Library.

[46] *Washington Post,* 9 June 1964.

[47] Perlstein, *Before the Storm*, p. 358.

know my views very well; I got most of them from him."[48] (The next day, the Arizonan was more caustic: Nixon "is sounding more and more like Harold Stassen every day.")[49] By the end of the day, Nixon, in Baltimore for a fundraiser, clarified his remarks, commenting, "I'm not opposing Goldwater."[50] For journalist Richard Strout, this maneuver provided the highlight of the conference, since it revived the "devious Dick Nixon, trying to push everybody else into the fray from which he could snatch the chestnuts."[51] The Nixon campaign, though ending in an unspectacular fashion, could claim one accomplishment: the *Baltimore Sun*'s Price Day tartly observed that it brought into political "speech the term 'kook.'"[52]

Then, to complete the farce, Scranton changed his mind again. On June 12, before the Maryland Republican convention, he declared, "I reject the echo we have thus far been handed – the echo of fear and reaction, the echo from the never-never land that puts our nation on the road backward to a lesser place in the world of free men." Goldwater scowled, "It's just like Nixon to set this up and then run off to London."[53] (The former vice president had flown to England for a brief business trip.) Later in the day the Draft Lodge movement endorsed Scranton, and Rockefeller offered his campaign staff to the Scranton effort. Goldwater contended that Scranton's supporters were confined to the "radical columnists" and the "radical newspapers," such as the *New York Times*, the *Washington Post*, and – *Izvestia!*[54]

Former Rockefeller staffers lamented that Scranton's team seemed "almost completely unorganized,"[55] and the race thus stalled for most of June. In Washington for final debate over the civil rights bill, and running what the *Washington Post*'s Joe Alsop described as a "front-porch campaign," Scranton veered toward gratuitous personal attacks.[56] Polls did show Scranton the more popular of the two among Republicans nationwide, but only marginally so, while doubts emerged about Scranton's chief argument – that he was more electable than Goldwater.[57]

[48] *New York Times*, 10 June 1964.
[49] *Washington Post*, 11 June 1964.
[50] *New York Times*, 10 June 1964.
[51] *The New Republic*, 20 June 1964.
[52] *Baltimore Sun*, 7 July 1964.
[53] Perlstein, *Before the Storm*, p. 227.
[54] *Washington Post*, 17 June 1964.
[55] Minutes of the Operations Committee, 17 June 1964, Box 16, Nelson Rockefeller Papers, Politics Series, Rockefeller Archives.
[56] *Washington Post*, 6 July 1964; *New York Herald Tribune*, 27 June 1964.
[57] *Washington Post*, 30 June 1964.

Indeed, the politics of race gave Goldwater an opening, even though many in the mainstream media and the GOP establishment failed to recognize the change. Walter Lippmann, for instance, who penned some of the most outlandish columns, contended that a Goldwater candidacy "presents a grave threat not only to the regular Republicans but to the whole nation."[58] Rockefeller claimed that Goldwater's opposition to the Civil Rights Act made "crystal clear the fact that the mainstream of Republican thought and action today remains true to our party's heritage and faithful to its deep conviction of the worth and dignity of each individual."[59]

On the surface, Goldwater's decision to vote against the Civil Rights Act did seem to place him badly out of step with the mainstream. During the Senate floor debate, GOP minority leader Everett Dirksen, jerking his arm in Goldwater's direction, proclaimed, "Utter all the extreme opinions that you will, it will carry forward. You can go ahead and talk about conscience! It is *man's* conscience that speaks in every generation." Goldwater responded with constitutional dogma. He deemed unconstitutional the bill's sections prohibiting racial discrimination in employment and public accommodations; "I can," Goldwater warned, "see a police state coming out of that without any problem at all." He also appealed to regional pride, denying that it was his "right as an Arizonan to come in and tell a Southerner what to do about this thing." Moral suasion, not federal legislation, could best ensure equal rights for all.[60]

While Goldwater reached his position for legalistic, not crass political, reasons, a reverence for "strict constructionists" was a hallmark of segregationist rhetoric in 1964. But Rockefeller, Lippmann, and likeminded figures badly underestimated how the passage of the Civil Rights Act would revolutionize American politics, allowing Republicans to exploit the backlash vote.[61] A Harris poll from July revealed that 58 percent of white Americans feared that blacks wanted to "take over" their jobs, 43 percent worried that blacks wanted to move into their neighborhoods, and 35 percent claimed that blacks wanted to take over their schools.[62] Scranton, certainly, could not tap this sentiment.[63] Two weeks into his campaign, he

[58] *Washington Post*, 1 July 1964.

[59] Nelson Rockefeller press release, 19 June 1964, Box 94, George Hinman Papers, Rockefeller Archives.

[60] Perlstein, *Before the Storm*, pp. 334, 365.

[61] *New York Herald Tribune*, 23 June 1964.

[62] *Newsweek*, 13 July 1964.

[63] *Washington Post*, 30 June 1964.

could not name even five Goldwater delegates that had switched to him.[64] It seemed, one Rockefeller staffer noted, as if Scranton, lacking any grand plan, formed his strategy "minute-by-minute."[65]

For the most part, Johnson watched the opposition's collapse with bemusement. Privately he considered Goldwater the easiest candidate to beat and was relieved to discover that Eisenhower was not planning active involvement in the campaign.[66] The president's "nonpolitical" national appearances continued, such as a four-state anti-poverty tour he coordinated with secretary of labor Willard Wirtz. After the swing, Jerry Landauer of the *Wall Street Journal* marveled, "Lyndon Johnson seems as adept on the stump as he was agile in the jungle of congressional politics."[67]

The development of the Republican race did, however, have one concrete effect on the president: he needed to replace Henry Cabot Lodge. Confirming once and for all that his reluctance to return to the United States was primarily a political gambit, the ambassador informed the State Department in mid-June that he would come back home to campaign on Scranton's behalf. As he departed Saigon, Lodge termed the situation in South Vietnam "fragile and unstable" and wondered if the "advocacy phase is about to be played out and the time is approaching for U.S. control."[68] Still, he believed that Vietnam could not "possibly be a partisan issue unless the U.S. should get pushed out."[69]

The president was not so certain. As Johnson predicted, Republican attacks on his handling of the situation in Vietnam increased. In late June House Minority Whip Gerald Ford (R-Michigan) called for the United States to assume operational military command in Southeast Asia.[70] Everett Dirksen and House Minority Leader Charles Halleck (R-Indiana) jointly attributed the Vietnam mess to Johnson's "indecision."[71] But as the critique picked up steam, Lodge gave an interview to the *New York Times*

[64] *Washington Star*, 1 July 1964.

[65] Minutes of the Operations Committee, 2 July 1964, Box 16, Nelson Rockefeller Papers, Politics Series, Rockefeller Archives.

[66] President Johnson and Robert Anderson, 11:16 A.M., 18 June 1964, Tape WH6406.10, Citation #3768, LBJ Recordings.

[67] *Wall Street Journal*, 1 May 1964.

[68] Henry Cabot Lodge, Confidential Journal, p. 15, 22 May 1964, Reel 17, Henry Cabot Lodge II Papers, Massachusetts Historical Society.

[69] Henry Cabot Lodge to Robert Mullen, 14 Apr. 1964, Box 35, Henry Cabot Lodge II Papers, Massachusetts Historical Society.

[70] *New York Times*, 29 June 1964.

[71] *New York Times*, 3 July 1964.

arguing that Ford's proposal would make the United States "a colonial power."[72] The conflict could be won without the United States turning it into a major war: more efficient interdiction of the outside arms flow, intensified special operations, increased air support, and improved political and civil action would eventually produce a U.S. victory. As Thomas O'Neill of the *Baltimore Sun* recognized, the GOP could not politically profit from Vietnam as long as Lodge remained "vinegary and blunt in condemnation of a trigger-happy approach to a delicate problem."[73]

As he sought to protect his right flank on foreign policy, the president continued to worry about liberal enthusiasm for his campaign. *Los Angeles Times* writer Richard Wilson traced Johnson's quest for as broad an ideological coalition as possible as rooted in his recognition that, in their hearts, many liberals distrusted him. Much of this sentiment was rooted in suspicion "of the kind of political power complex which Mr. Johnson considers normal, the interplay of the privileged interests so common in Texas."[74] Viewed through this ideological lens, the TFX, Billy Sol Estes, and Bobby Baker scandals, which Johnson considered minor incidents, proved the president's ideological infidelity.

On that point Johnson at least seemed to have squelched, once and for all, the Baker inquiry. In early May in the *Washington Post* Roscoe Drummond sarcastically praised Rules Committee Democrats for "showing positive genius" in "thinking up ways not to do their work."[75] Then, on May 12, Clifford Case made the Democrats work a little harder. The New Jersey Republican urged broadening the inquiry to have each senator describe what interaction, if any, he or she had with Baker. When Committee Counsel L. P. McLendon, as expected, ruled Case's proposal out of order, Hugh Scott announced that "McLendon's opinion isn't worth a tinker's damn in the Senate."[76]

In response, the next day John Williams introduced a resolution to continue the investigation until September 1 to explore the issues that Case had detailed. The proposal met with fierce opposition: Everett Jordan charged Case with scaling "the height of demagoguery."[77] Privately, Richard Russell discovered his North Carolina colleague "sweating blood

[72] *New York Times*, 1 July 1964.
[73] *Baltimore Sun*, 11 July 1964.
[74] *Los Angeles Times*, 4 May 1964.
[75] *Washington Post*, 4 May 1964.
[76] *Washington Star*, 12 May 1964.
[77] 110 *Congressional Record*, 88th Cong., 2nd sess., p. 10789 (13 May 1964).

about this dang Bobby Baker thing" and "about to throw up his hands and just say, 'Well, you-all can have it.' "[78]

Fully aware of Jordan's incapacity to squelch the inquiry, Johnson set to work himself. "Between you and me and God," he told Hubert Humphrey, Everett Dirksen needed to know that if the inquiry went forward, "we can authorize the FBI to go into all the Republican ones that have ever been made." Ending the Baker affair promptly, the president insisted, was "more important than anything."[79] Johnson complained to Montana's Mike Mansfield about Williams's playing "pure cheap politics and using the Senate as a forum."[80] Jordan certainly could not handle the matter – indeed, it was about time that someone told the North Carolina Democrat that he needed to "quit getting into debate if he doesn't want to get cut up."[81] Only one solution existed to this problem: "We'll just have to go after Mr. Williams" in the fall election.[82]

In the meantime Johnson's lobbying – and threats against Dirksen, who himself had received $5,000 from Baker in his successful 1962 reelection bid – helped beat back the Case-Williams resolution on a 42–33 vote. Nine Democrats, eight of them good-government liberals (Bob Bartlett, Frank Church, Paul Douglas, Ernest Gruening, Phil Hart, Gaylord Nelson, William Proxmire, and Harrison Williams), voted against the president.[83]

The Baker flare-up, ironically, displaced Senate consideration of the civil rights bill. The expected Southern filibuster lasted throughout the spring, but, by a 71 to 29 tally, the Senate finally imposed cloture. On June 19, after 106 roll call votes defeating Southern amendments, the upper chamber approved the measure, by a vote of 73 to 27.[84] Goldwater and Texas Republican John Tower cast the only two GOP votes against it. On July 2, 1964, at the White House, the president staged a signing ceremony for the bill. Johnson fully understood the political ramifications; at the

[78] President Johnson, Richard Russell and B. Everett Jordan, 5:17 P.M., 13 May 1964, Tape WH6405.06, Citation #3443 and Citation #3444, LBJ Recordings.

[79] President Johnson and Hubert Humphrey, 5:10 P.M., 13 May 1964, Tape WH6405.06, Citation #3445, LBJ Recordings.

[80] President Johnson and Mike Mansfield, 5:17 P.M., 13 May 1964, Tape WH6405.06, Citation #3443, LBJ Recordings.

[81] President Johnson and George Reedy, 7:35 P.M. 13 May 1964, Tape WH6405.07, Citation #3451, LBJ Recordings.

[82] President Johnson and Mike Mansfield, 8:38 P.M., 14 May 1964, Tape WH6405.07, Citation #3457, LBJ Recordings.

[83] *Washington Post*, 15 May 1964.

[84] Mann, *The Walls of Jericho*, pp. 406–32.

FIGURE 3-1. President Johnson signs the Civil Rights Act, July 2, 1964. Race would play a key role in the campaign, but the president successfully managed the "backlash" effect. © Courtesy of the Lyndon Baines Johnson Presidential Library. Photo by Cecil Stoughton.

event he told his 30-year-old special assistant Bill Moyers, "I think we just gave the South to the Republicans for your lifetime and mine."[85]

Meanwhile, as the Republican convention in San Francisco drew near, all signs pointed to a first-ballot Goldwater victory, even though the senator's national polling numbers remained weak. "Rarely," pollster Lou Harris observed, "has a man in such a commanding position for a major party presidential nomination found his political position as understood by the public to be so diametrically opposed by the voters themselves."[86]

Looking ahead to the fall campaign, Johnson anticipated giving Goldwater "a lot of rope," in the hopes that the senator would make the same kinds of mistakes he made while campaigning in New Hampshire.[87] As for the Republicans as a whole, "we'll let them show all their hold cards and then we'll come in and trump them."[88] Scranton, alas, had no trump cards to play. Desperate for a breakthrough, he purchased a major advertising buy in Illinois and then traveled to the state to meet with its nominally uncommitted delegation.[89] Not only did he fail to receive the group's backing, but the state's top GOP officeholder, Everett Dirksen, agreed to nominate Goldwater. In a surprisingly strong blast at the Eastern Establishment of his own party, the Illinois senator declared, "Too long have we ridden the grey ghost of me-tooism."[90]

Desperate for a miracle, the anti-Goldwater forces turned, once again, to Eisenhower. On June 30 Lodge visited the former president for forty-five minutes and, over the next several days, conveyed his "impression" that Eisenhower would soon endorse the Pennsylvania governor.[91] But, once again, Eisenhower disappointed. On July 10, as one who abhorred the politics of "string-pulling, back-scratching, and log-rolling," he stated that he would not be a "kingmaker" at the convention."[92] The Scranton effort shortly thereafter ended with a letter sent out over the candidate's signature but without his having checked its contents. The missive told

[85] Joseph Califano quoted in Taylor Branch, *Pillar of Fire: America in the King Years, 1963–1965* (New York: Simon and Schuster, 1998), p. 404.

[86] Robert Dallek, *Flawed Giant: Lyndon Johnson and His Times, 1961–1973* (New York: Oxford University Press, 1998), p. 132.

[87] President Johnson and Ernest McFarland, 8:20 P.M., 16 July 1964, Tape WH6407.09, Citation #4255, LBJ Recordings.

[88] President Johnson and John McCormack, 1:20 P.M., 23 June 1964, Tape WH6403.13, Citation #3824, LBJ Recordings.

[89] Alexander, *Financing the 1964 Election*, p. 26.

[90] *Time*, 10 July 1964.

[91] *New York Times*, 2 July 1964, 6 July 1964.

[92] *New York Times*, 11 July 1964.

Goldwater that "with open contempt for the dignity, integrity, and common sense of the convention, your managers say in effect that *the delegates are little more than a flock of chickens whose necks will be wrung at will.*"[93] In journalist Mary McGrory's words, "the moderates of the Republican Party died easy."[94]

The 28th Republican National Convention opened on Monday, July 13, with civil rights demonstrators outside of the Cow Palace. Inside the hall the convention rejected a resolution to bar seating delegations that had denied anyone a spot on racial grounds. Speaking on behalf of an amendment condemning extremist groups of both the right and left, Nelson Rockefeller did not reach the speaker's podium until nearly midnight Eastern time. He began with a familiar line, criticizing the radical minority "wholly alien to the broad middle course that accommodates the mainstream of Republican principles."[95] As he recounted his experiences with right-wing groups in the primary season, he was met with boos and catcalls, so deafening as to drown out his voice. The New York governor persevered, delighting in agitating the crowd, but his address did not affect the fate of the amendment, which was defeated by a voice vote. (One speech against the amendment came from Colorado senator Peter Dominick, who unknowingly quoted a spoof put out by Goldwater backers. He asserted that in the 1770s the *New York Times* had denounced Patrick Henry as "a spokesman of that small but vocal minority who seek to undermine confidence in the Crown.")[96] A Scranton-backed amendment to strengthen the civil rights plank of the platform lost by an 897 to 409 margin; one Texas Republican rejoiced, "The South took the Mason-Dixon Line and shoved it right up to Canada."[97]

Eisenhower addressed the convention on its second night; given the tense atmosphere, the former president might have been expected to deliver conciliatory remarks. But, in keeping with his consistent pattern of inconsistency, Eisenhower instead blasted the "sensation-looking columnists and commentators," the "people who couldn't care less about the good of our party."[98] A roar greeted these words, followed by many delegates turning around and shaking their fists at the media in glass-enclosed

[93] John Kessel, *The Goldwater Coalition: Republican Strategies in 1964* (Indianapolis: Bobbs-Merrill, 1968), p. 116.
[94] *Washington Star*, 16 July 1964.
[95] Perlstein, *Before the Storm*, p. 383.
[96] Kessel, *The Goldwater Coalition*, p. 112.
[97] *Newsweek*, 26 July 1964.
[98] *Washington Post*, 15 July 1964.

sets above the fray. On the convention floor, police seized John Chancellor after the NBC reporter refused a request from GOP operatives to stop interviewing delegates. "Am I going to be carried out?" Chancellor asked on live television. He signed off, "This is John Chancellor, somewhere in custody."[99]

The speech's most controversial line came when Eisenhower urged his fellow Republicans to avoid "maudlin sympathy for the criminal... roaming the streets with switchblade knife."[100] An appalled Roy Wilkins of the NAACP responded, "The phrase 'switchblade knife' means 'Negro' to the average American." Indeed, as *Time* noted, crime "makes sense as a national issue only if considered in conjunction with the 'white backlash.'"[101]

The vote on the civil rights amendment confirmed that Goldwater had considerably more than the 655 votes necessary to secure the nomination. The roll call for the presidential nomination was a foregone conclusion: Goldwater prevailed with 883 votes, followed by Scranton with 214 and Rockefeller with 114. Fittingly, the votes from South Carolina put the Arizona senator over the top.[102]

Since Scranton's bitter letter had eliminated him as a vice-presidential possibility, Goldwater turned to the chair of the Republican National Committee, upstate New York congressman William Miller. The *New York Times* described Miller as best known "for a caustic tongue and a dedication to conservatism."[103] Privately, the nominee told state party chairs that he wanted Miller on the ticket because "he drives Lyndon nuts."[104]

In the House Miller had earned little distinction; in 1962 he squeaked by in a Republican district with a mere 52 percent and shortly thereafter announced that he would not stand for reelection in 1964. But the congressman was an effective party chair, funneling money into the states of the old Confederacy to build up the Southern GOP; this initiative was partly why one analyst noted that the RNC "acquired a distinct Goldwater coloration since Miller took over."[105] If nothing else, the Miller selection confirmed Texas governor John Connally's earlier hunch

[99] Perlstein, *Before the Storm*, p. 382.
[100] *Washington Post*, 15 July 1964.
[101] *Time*, 24 July 1964.
[102] *Washington Star*, 15 July 1964.
[103] *New York Times*, 17 July 1964.
[104] *Baltimore Sun*, 17 July 1964.
[105] Paul Duke, "The GOP against Itself," *The Reporter*, 2 July 1964.

that "this is going to be the most personal, the most vicious campaign probably in this century."[106]

Miller had, in the words of Evans and Novak, waged "a campaign for Vice President that was a model of subtlety and efficiency."[107] These political skills were not evident in his acceptance speech, which was perfunctory, or in his first news conference as the nominee, which was worse. When asked about Johnson's War on Poverty, for instance, Miller chortled, "Bobby Baker is the chief expert on poverty in Washington."[108] In light of the remarks, *Time* dryly commented, "Some voters might wonder if a gift for vitriol is a sufficient qualification for Vice President."[109] Eisenhower counted himself among that number, admitting, "My own particular choice might have been some other person."[110]

The convention concluded with Goldwater's acceptance speech. Lodge refused to stay for the address; the day after his arrival in California, the former senator asked *Newsweek*'s Osborne Elliot, "What in God's name has happened to the Republican Party?"[111] Though still in San Francisco, Rockefeller did not attend. In the midst of the remarks, New York senator Kenneth Keating led over 40 Empire State delegates in walking out of the Cow Palace.[112]

The speech itself was organized around four central themes – freedom, liberty, order, and security – and dealt most impressively with international affairs. Goldwater promised to "restore a clear understanding of the tyranny of man over man in the world at large" by setting aside "the foggy thinking which avoids hard decisions in the delusion that a world of conflict will somehow resolve itself into a world of harmony, if we just don't rock the boat or irritate the forces of aggression." Looking back over twentieth-century American history, the GOP nominee detected a pattern. Twelve years before Bob Dole made the famous charge in a vice-presidential debate, Goldwater claimed that "it has been during Democratic years

[106] President Johnson and John Connally, 11:38 A.M., 3 July 1964, Tape WH6407.03, Citation #4145, LBJ Recordings.

[107] *Washington Post*, 8 July 1964.

[108] *New York Times*, 17 July 1964.

[109] *Time*, 24 July 1964; see also Richard Rovere, "Letter from San Francisco," *The New Yorker*, 25 July 1964.

[110] *Washington Post*, 17 July 1964.

[111] William Miller, *Henry Cabot Lodge: A Biography* (New York: James Heineman, 1967), p. 355.

[112] *New York Herald Tribune*, 17 July 1964.

FIGURE 3-2. Barry Goldwater. The Arizona senator's acceptance speech only strengthened perceptions that he was a radical. "He's just as nutty as fruitcake," joked Johnson. © Courtesy of the U.S. Senate Historical Office.

that we have weakly stumbled into conflicts," because the party failed to understand the need to achieve peace through strength.[113]

Goldwater offered a less coherent agenda for the home front. He mentioned typical conservative themes, endorsing "decentralized power" and opposing "centralized planning." Goldwater attacked the president's ethics and offered an extended call for increased governmental attention to crime. On this point he made the none-too-convincing link between crime and his desire for limited government by arguing that "nothing prepares the way for tyranny more than the failure of public officials to keep the streets safe from bullies and marauders."[114]

[113] *Congressional Quarterly Weekly Report*, 17 July 1964, pp. 1527–8.
[114] *Congressional Quarterly Weekly Report*, 17 July 1964, pp. 1527–8.

Of course, Barry Goldwater's 1964 acceptance address remains known for two sentences, interrupted by delirious applause, uttered near the end of his remarks: "*I would remind you that extremism in the defense of liberty is no vice. And let me remind you also that moderation in the pursuit of justice is no virtue!*"[115]

The immediate reaction to Goldwater's remarks was highly negative. Rockefeller termed the address "dangerous, irresponsible, and frightening."[116] Journalist Drew Pearson, Pat Brown, and Silvio Conte, a moderate Republican congressman from Massachusetts, each compared events in the Cow Palace to fascist movements in 1930s Europe. (When Brown announced that he detected the "stench of fascism" in the air, Goldwater retorted, "It's the stench of Brown – it's ignorance.")[117] Massachusetts Attorney General Edward Brooke, the GOP's highest-ranking black officeholder, said that the remark "came perilously close to a call to arms for both the radical left and right."[118] Eisenhower worried that the speech "would seem to say that the end always justifies the means."[119]

Walter Lippmann, for once avoiding overstatement, termed it "quite clear that Senator Goldwater does not understand the meaning of extremism." In the environment of 1964, "to be an extremist is to encourage and condone the taking of the law into unauthorized private hands."[120] Even the strongly Republican *New York Herald Tribune* worried that Goldwater's "first moves within 24 hours may come back to haunt him and plague him in the long months ahead." "The ebullience of victory," the paper feared, "led to unnecessarily abrasive decisions" – ones that would hurt the candidate himself, such as naming Goldwater aide Dean Burch rather than Ohio Republican leader Ray Bliss or mastermind of the Goldwater campaign Clifton White as chair of the RNC.[121]

The electricity of Goldwater's speech only highlighted the transformative effect of a convention *Newsweek* termed an "authentic party revolution."[122] The most obvious change came in the composition of the Southern delegations. For the first time since Reconstruction, every

[115] *Congressional Quarterly Weekly Report*, 17 July 1964, p. 1529. Emphasis in original.
[116] *Time*, 24 July 1964.
[117] *Time*, 24 July 1964.
[118] *Congressional Quarterly Weekly Report*, 24 July 1964, p. 1540.
[119] *Time*, 24 July 1964.
[120] *San Francisco Chronicle*, 21 July 1964.
[121] *New York Herald Tribune*, 21 July 1964.
[122] Carter, *The Politics of Rage*, p. 219.

Republican delegate from the South was white; 366 of the 375 voted for Goldwater. Eighty percent of these Southern delegates opposed any federal action on civil rights, even when blacks were denied the right to vote; 90 percent opposed federally funded medical care, unemployment insurance, education, or housing. All told, of the 1,308 delegates at the convention, only 14 were black.[123] As *Washington Post* correspondent Chalmers Roberts recognized, the 1964 Republican convention would go down as "one of those great turning points of party history."[124]

The San Francisco gathering is generally remembered as an example of a disastrous national convention. But in its immediate aftermath, columnists of all ideological persuasions agreed that Goldwater might just have a chance to score an upset, and that he certainly would run a much closer race than anyone had thought possible a month or two before.[125] The party platform deemphasized the importance of civil rights. The 1960 document contained 1,500 words on the issue; its 1964 counterpart had a mere 66.[126] Joe Alsop believed the "real guts" of the Goldwater campaign would be an appeal to the white backlash, a topic that Evans and Novak found omnipresent in San Francisco, even if "articulated only occasionally in soft whispers."[127] The rewards of cultivating the backlash clearly outweighed the risks: adding the Wallace Democrats to the Goldwater Republicans could bring the Arizonan close to a national majority.[128] Ohio governor Jim Rhodes certainly thought so. He decided to release his state delegation to Goldwater, he informed Scranton, after witnessing the power of the backlash in Youngstown, Cincinnati, and Cleveland.[129]

Writing in the *Saturday Evening Post,* Stewart Alsop seconded his brother's analysis, arguing that the "most important lesson" of San Francisco was not to "underestimate Barry Goldwater." On paper Alsop agreed that Johnson looked hard to beat. But Goldwater had a chance for three reasons: unlike Johnson, he was very likeable, a man with public and private charm; unlike Johnson, he had a significant band of die-hard, committed supporters; and unlike Johnson, he would benefit from the "X-factor" of race.[130]

[123] *Newsweek*, 27 July 1964.
[124] *Washington Post*, 12 July 1964.
[125] *Washington Star*, 14 July 1964.
[126] *The New Republic*, 25 July 1964.
[127] *Washington Post*, 15 July 1964; *New York Herald Tribune*, 15 July 1964.
[128] *Washington Star*, 20 July 1964; see also *San Francisco Examiner,* 21 July 1964.
[129] Perlstein, *Before the Storm*, p. 373.
[130] Stewart Alsop, "Can Goldwater Win?" *Saturday Evening Post*, 20 July 1964; see also *New York Times*, 19 July 1964; *Washington Star*, 24 July 1964, 6 Aug. 1964; *Los Angeles Times*, 31 July 1964.

In the days after San Francisco, many Democrats shared the Alsops' conclusion. White House aide Henry Wilson penned a jarring memo urging the campaign staff to tell "the President what apparently no one has yet said to him – that he could lose this election." Yes, Wilson noted, labor, minorities, virtually the entire media, and most business leaders backed the president, who also enjoyed de facto support from moderate Republicans like Rockefeller and Lodge. But "we're facing a situation brand new in American politics and that we're going to have to throw all the old rules out of the window and play it by ear."[131] Goldwater's ability to mine three "potent commodities" – racial prejudice, a chauvinistic nationalism, and a simplistic approach to complex problems – gave the Arizona senator a chance. David McDonald, president of the United Steelworkers of America, admitted that a majority of his union members in Indiana would vote for Goldwater.[132] Columnist Charles Bartlett found his Democratic contacts "uncomfortably aware" that Goldwater could "stir an avalanche of public outrage with his campaign complaint that law and order are breaking down in the big cities."[133]

Among the Democrats who shared this concern were the president and the attorney general. Two days after Goldwater's acceptance speech, Kennedy called Johnson to express his concern about the possibility of violence in Northern industrial centers. "It's a major mistake," the attorney general asserted, to "have the struggle in this election over the question of civil rights. Because if it comes down to the question of civil rights, Democrats are going to have a very tough time." Johnson agreed, but he had a response ready – "what we need to get it on is his impetuousness and his impulsiveness and his wanting to turn the bomb on somebody else." Kennedy conceded that scare tactics could work, yet wondered whether a more positive message might yield a better result. But the president had already made up his mind: "A mother is pretty worried if she thinks her child is drinking contaminated milk, or that maybe she's going to have a baby with two heads or things like that." The conversation offered an early glimpse at two of the lines of thought that would characterize the autumn debate over Democratic campaign strategy.[134]

The president addressed the matter in greater detail in a Cabinet meeting the next day. "Conscious of the drop in his position in the South," he

[131] Henry Wilson to Larry O'Brien, 8 July 1964, Box 1, Files of White House Aides – Henry Wilson, Lyndon B. Johnson Presidential Library.

[132] *Washington Star*, 7 Aug. 1964.

[133] *Washington Star*, 23 July 1964.

[134] President Johnson and Robert Kennedy, 8:00 P.M., 21 July 1964, Tape WH6407.12, Citation #4299, LBJ Recordings.

asserted that "Goldwater had more things going for him than we realized." Johnson predicted that the attacks on both civil rights and corruption would work well, and therefore foresaw a "tough, nasty, dirty campaign." Secretary of Agriculture Orville Freeman found the president "quite concerned, quite apprehensive, and quite tense." To neutralize the backlash, Johnson recommended the high road; offering a sense of how he used history, the president said that he had reviewed Roosevelt's four campaigns and found the 1940 version the most applicable to the current situation. Beyond that guidance, he wanted to force Goldwater to spell out exactly what kind of foreign policy he wanted.[135]

Freeman believed that Johnson "was definitely feeling his way along, that he was deeply worried about Goldwater." The agriculture secretary lacked a clear sense of what the president meant by taking the high road "outside of our sticking to the record and emphasizing accomplishments."[136] How that approach would push Goldwater to explicate his more extremist positions Johnson did not explain. In the corridor after the meeting, he expressed his concerns to his aide Jack Valenti and Johnson speechwriter Horace Busby. Valenti described the meeting as the clearest expression of the president's intentions to date, a remark that set Freeman to wondering what previous briefings had been like. Busby assured Freeman that the president was a "late starter" in campaigns and that he generally did not share with his advisers "what he was really going to do politically."[137]

The chances of the GOP successfully using the backlash received one immediate boost: Goldwater's nomination dried up support for Wallace's prospective third-party bid. In desperation, Wallace summoned Jim Martin, the Republican who had almost upset Lister Hill in the 1962 Senate race, to sound out Goldwater about his receiving the second spot on the Republican ticket. Martin did as told, but Goldwater had no interest. Within the week Wallace withdrew anyway. He correctly observed, "Today we hear more states' rights talk than we have heard in the last quarter-century."[138] The American people, the governor continued, "are sick and tired of columnists and TV dudes who...try to slant and distort

[135] Orville Freeman diary, 21 July 1964, Box 14, Orville Freeman Papers, Minnesota State Historical Society, St. Paul.

[136] Orville Freeman diary, 21 July 1964, Box 14, Orville Freeman Papers, Minnesota State Historical Society, St. Paul.

[137] Orville Freeman diary, 23 July 1964, Box 14, Orville Freeman Papers, Minnesota State Historical Society, St. Paul.

[138] Carter, *The Politics of Rage*, pp. 220–2.

and malign and brainwash this country."[139] Wallace left no doubt about his preference for Goldwater in the fall contest.

In the first public opinion survey after the convention, Goldwater gained 10 points nationally, although he still trailed Johnson by almost 30 percent.[140] The South witnessed the most dramatic shift. Before the convention, Johnson led Goldwater by a comfortable 61 to 39 percent margin. After San Francisco, Goldwater gained 16 points to take a 55–45 lead. And while the Arizona senator was strongest in Alabama and Mississippi, his support was widespread in the region. Operatives of both parties conceded that all 11 states of the Old Confederacy were in play, along with the border states of Oklahoma and Kentucky. A chance existed for Goldwater to sweep all 13 states, including Texas.[141]

With the Goldwater effort fully underway, Johnson began the transition into the fall campaign. In a perceptive article published after the Republican convention, Evans and Novak described the "transformation of the Democratic Party under the direction of Lyndon B. Johnson." The president had started to turn the Democrats "into a non-ideological broad-based 'consensus' party cleansed of over-partisanship," thus making it the "rallying point for all controllers of power in American today." No question existed, thus far in his administration, of Johnson's success in this regard. But the two columnists identified a key uncertainty: "whether these new Johnson voters, even if translated into a whopping majority in 1964, can be retained as Democrats in the future."[142]

Regardless of his strategy's long-term effects, the president certainly stepped up his short-term cultivation of the Establishment following the GOP convention. Chatting with Henry Ford II, Johnson stated that he needed to change business leaders' attitudes, since "Democrats have spent all their lives criticizing business, scaring them to death."[143] (Ford would reciprocate: after giving nearly $20,000 to Republicans in 1956 and sitting out the 1960 election, he donated $40,000 to the Democratic effort in 1964.)[144] To his long-time Texas supporter George Brown, the president boasted of creating a "little different atmosphere" for business. Indeed, he was moving beyond the New Deal mind-set regarding the proper rela-

[139] Branch, *Pillar of Fire*, p. 404.
[140] *Washington Post*, 22 July 1964.
[141] *Washington Post*, 22 July 1964; see also *Newsweek*, 31 Aug. 1964.
[142] *New York Herald Tribune*, 26 July 1964.
[143] President Johnson and Henry Ford II, during President Johnson and J. Edgar Hoover, 4:36 P.M., 5 Aug. 1964, Tape WH6408.08, Citation #4760, LBJ Recordings.
[144] Alexander, *Financing the 1964 Election*, p. 128.

tionship between the party and business. "Roosevelt was always talking about economic royalists. And they've been denounced by Truman and everybody else – Kennedy going in and waking them up with the FBI at night."[145] Under Johnson, as Mary McGrory observed, "businessmen have never been as welcomed by a Democratic President."[146]

The president devoured such articles; he complained about never reading "any columns or any editorials or anybody ever pointing up the Republican backlash."[147] Through his position at the Council of Economic Advisers, Walter Heller lobbied financial journalists, planting the idea of a financial backlash if Goldwater prevailed in the fall. Some in the business press needed no prodding. In mid-July, on the pages of *Forbes,* Bradbury Thurlow cautioned that the Goldwater candidacy threatened "a severe correction in prices" for the Stock Market, since the Arizonan's hostility to government spending would destabilize the Keynesian economic assumptions to which both investors and corporations had become accustomed. The financier's chief worry, though, resembled Henry Wilson's: Goldwater was "being too lightly dismissed by his opponents." In the end no one really knew "how widespread reaction against recent governmental policies and moral disapproval of aspects of our political system have become."[148]

Emphasizing the soundness of the administration's economic agenda – and, by implication, the unreliability of Goldwater's – formed one way to resolve what Orville Freeman had termed the incompatibility between taking the high road and exposing Goldwater's extremism. The president, at the same time, was not above personal attacks; when Goldwater's wife revealed in an interview for *Good Housekeeping* that the senator had twice experienced nervous breakdowns, Johnson responded gleefully.[149] The president also inoculated himself by claiming that criticism of his performance represented attacks on the government structure itself. When Goldwater dismissed him as a "faker" and a "phony" on civil rights, Johnson instructed his press secretary George Reedy to tell the press, "We've spent 100 years building the presidency up, and I'm not

[145] President Johnson and George Brown, 9:10 A.M., 29 July 1964, Tape WH6407.17, Citation #4378, LBJ Recordings.

[146] *Washington Star*, 9 Aug. 1964.

[147] President Johnson and Edwin Weisl, 1:35 P.M., 7 Aug. 1964, Tape WH6408.10, Citation #4791, LBJ Recordings.

[148] Bradbury Thurlow, "Politics and the Market," *Forbes*, 15 July 1964.

[149] President Johnson and Oveta Culp Hobby, 10:05 A.M., 29 July 1964, Tape WH6407.17, Citation #4379, LBJ Recordings.

going to try to tear it down."[150] Similarly, when the senator criticized the president's economic agenda, Johnson pointed to the healthy GNP figures and said, "In effect, you've got Goldwater out there who's getting all set to run against prosperity for the American people."[151]

More imaginatively, Johnson boasted of "the damndest record of any Congress since the Republic started."[152] He would favorably compare to the legislative performance of his first political idol, Franklin Delano Roosevelt. In that way he could avoid getting "into a defense argument with Goldwater" in which the Republicans could seize the initiative. Specifically, Johnson focused on his tax and budget cuts. Even though "that may start off all the liberals giving us hell," it would illustrate why "the backlash is against Goldwater and not against us."[153] At the most basic level, as Mary McGrory realized, Johnson wanted "to make it chic to be a Democrat," the first step in winning "back those suburbanites who have moved out of the city and out of the Democratic Party."[154]

From time to time Johnson liked to think that maybe the Civil Rights Act would not destroy Democratic dominance of the South.[155] But on most occasions he accepted political reality. Playing off Goldwater's embrace of extremism in his acceptance speech – and his refusal to denounce extremist groups before receiving the nomination – the president instructed Bill Moyers to formulate a statement in which he could denounce extremists on both sides, while focusing on the Ku Klux Klan.[156] In that way he could get at his real concern, the fear that civil rights protesters would damage him politically if he did not distance himself from them.[157] This initiative represented an early effort of what would emerge as an aggressive, and deeply unfair, attempt to link Goldwater to the Klan.

[150] President Johnson and George Reedy, 11:02 A.M., 16 July 1964, Tape WH6407.08, Citation #4245, LBJ Recordings.
[151] President Johnson and George Reedy, 7:03 P.M., 16 July 1964, Tape WH6407.09, Citation #4253, LBJ Recordings.
[152] President Johnson and Sargent Shriver, 9:23 A.M., 9 Aug. 1964, Tape WH6408.15, Citation #4843, LBJ Recordings.
[153] President Johnson and Horace Busby, 10:45 A.M., 11 Aug. 1964, Tape WH6408.17, Citation #4877, LBJ Recordings.
[154] *Washington Star*, 9 Aug. 1964.
[155] President Johnson and Larry O'Brien, 3:56 P.M., 8 July 1964, Tape WH6407.06, Citation #4187, LBJ Recordings.
[156] President Johnson and Bill Moyers, 6:20 P.M. 17 July 1964, Tape WH6407.09, Citation #4267, LBJ Recordings.
[157] President Johnson and Lee White, 6:50 P.M., 16 July 1964, Tape WH6407.09, Citation #4252, LBJ Recordings.

The president's concern about the backlash was intensified by the outbreak of riots in New York City. On July 16 an off-duty police lieutenant killed an unarmed 15-year-old black boy in Manhattan's Upper East Side. Two days later, a CORE rally in Harlem culminated in a march on a local police station and clashes between civilians and police. By July 20 widespread unrest in Harlem had left 15 people shot, 200 arrested, and more than 100 civilians injured. James Farmer, national director of CORE, termed the outburst a "bloody orgy of police violence." Over the next few weeks, similar riots occurred in Brooklyn's Bedford-Stuyvesant neighborhood, Newark, New Jersey, and Rochester, New York.[158]

Overlooking discrimination as a potential cause for this unrest, the president searched for a political motivation – namely, that blacks were the "tools of some of those right-wing cranks." It all started with Goldwater's acceptance speech, where, he alleged, the Arizonan said, "Extremism is a virtue." Such a line, Johnson mused, was "almost like advocating rioting."[159] Certainly the public's adopting such a view would neutralize the effects of the backlash issue.

This possibility concerned Goldwater, too, though for different reasons: he considered it anathema that his words could have triggered urban unrest. The day after the Harlem riots, Goldwater announced that he would withdraw from the race if he discovered that anyone fomented racial violence to assist his candidacy. The matter came up publicly on July 23, when a reporter asked him if he would issue a joint statement with the president urging urban peace. Goldwater went further, announcing that not only would he support such a statement but also that he wanted to meet with Johnson to discuss the question.[160]

The possible political effects of a meeting worried the president enormously. George Reedy told a press conference that the administration did not need a meeting to refrain from inflaming or inciting people, and if the senator felt the same way, there was no purpose in a parley. Privately, the president fretted that civil rights "is something around our neck" – an issue that was "*almost* beyond our reach." To Johnson, neutralizing the backlash required changing the campaign's focus to Goldwater's "impetuousness and his impulsiveness and his wanting to turn the bomb over

[158] Branch, *Pillar of Fire*, pp. 417–21; Michael Flamm, "'Law and Order': Street Crime, Civil Disorder, and the Crisis of Liberalism," Ph.D. diss., Columbia University, 1998, p. 86.

[159] President Johnson and Robert Wagner, Jr., 8:39 A.M., 22 July 1964, Tape WH6407.12, Citation #4304, LBJ Recordings.

[160] Perlstein, *Before the Storm*, pp. 396–7.

to somebody else." But Robert Kennedy, in a rare candid conversation between the two men, counseled otherwise. The attorney general likewise feared the political danger of a campaign geared around civil rights, but recommended a positive rather than a negative response, chiefly by proposing an economic policy geared toward "these Northern communities, and these industrial areas," thereby neutralizing the effects of a backlash. The president was not persuaded.[161]

In the short term Johnson had little choice but to accept Goldwater's offer and invited the Arizonan to the White House. Assuming as always the most cynical motives for actions of his political opponents, the president had no doubt about the senator's main goal in proposing the parley: "He wants to encourage a backlash. That's where *his* future is."[162] The day of the meeting, Johnson fretted that Goldwater would use the event to "get a little of this extremism off him." Like the civil rights issue in general, the conference "can't help *us*."[163] The White House staff expected Goldwater to try to maneuver Johnson into a position that would harm Democrats with either liberals or ethnic voters. Indeed, as Moyers and Valenti informed the president, in a worst-case scenario, the meeting might provide Goldwater with a "buffer against criticism that he is stirring up racism by claiming he is operating within the ground rules which you discussed."[164]

Such fears were entirely misplaced. Shortly after Goldwater left the Oval Office, Johnson described the 16 minutes as "the damndest experience I ever had in my life." The senator had no specific agenda. He just wanted to say "that 'I'm not going to get personal in this campaign, and that I don't want to talk about anything but the issues.'"[165] The president responded that he hoped to see the Civil Rights Act enforced, lest it become another Volstead Act, in which the failure of Prohibition destroyed respect for the legal system.[166] Then, incredibly, Goldwater

[161] President Johnson and Robert Kennedy, 8:00 P.M., 21 July 1964, Tape WH6407.12, Citation #4299, LBJ Recordings.

[162] President Johnson and John Connally, 5:31 P.M., 23 July 1964, Tape WH6407.13, Citation #4320, LBJ Recordings.

[163] President Johnson and Carl Sanders, 12:30 P.M., 24 July 1964, Tape WH6407.14, Citation #4328, LBJ Recordings.

[164] Memorandum, Bill Moyers, Dick Goodwin, and Jack Valenti to President Johnson, 21 July 1964, copy in "July 24, 1964," Box 7, Diary Backup, Lyndon B. Johnson Library.

[165] President Johnson and Robert McNamara, 5:56 P.M., 24 July 1964, Tape WH6407.14, Citation #4333, LBJ Recordings.

[166] President Johnson and Nicholas Katzenbach, 10:15 A.M., 25 July 1964, Tape WH6407.14, Citation #4337, LBJ Recordings.

started talking about the experimental A-11 plane, and how he would like to pilot a test model. Johnson joked that by the time the development phase was complete, Goldwater himself might be giving the orders.[167] The conference concluded with the two candidates issuing a joint statement that "the President met with Senator Goldwater and reviewed the steps he had taken to avoid the incitement of racial tension. Senator Goldwater expressed his position, which was that racial tensions should be avoided."[168]

Goldwater's failure to capitalize on the White House meeting exemplified his inability to sustain any momentum immediately following the GOP convention. In an era before the Christian Right had become a force in American politics, the Arizonan was badly hurt by postconvention attacks from religious leaders. *Christianity and Crisis,* a leading Protestant weekly, contended, "The mantle of religion is being used to support what we regard as an immoral nationalism, an immoral nuclear recklessness, an immoral racism...and an immoral economic individualism."[169] John Krumm, chaplain of Columbia University, denounced Goldwater as "a candidate who is so openly contemptuous of all the church has been saying and teaching for the last 30 years or so" that his election was morally unthinkable.[170] And the prominent theologian Reinhold Niebuhr termed Goldwater "diametrically opposed" to the positions of America's three major faiths on civil rights, international relations, and economic policy.[171]

More than anything else, though, the ticket's own conduct hurt its cause, particularly by strengthening the impression of extremism that Johnson eagerly cultivated. After the convention, Goldwater vacationed with retired general Albert Wedemeyer, a key figure in the China Lobby and a former official of the John Birch Society. (This move came at a time when one poll showed that only 8 percent had a favorable opinion of the far-right organization.)[172] William Miller, meanwhile, continued his abysmal performance as a vice-presidential candidate. After being asked if he would repudiate the KKK's backing, he responded that the ticket "would accept the support of any United States citizen who believed in

[167] Jack Valenti oral history, Lyndon B. Johnson Presidential Library.
[168] *Washington Post*, 26 July 1964.
[169] *Christianity and Crisis*, 30 July 1964.
[170] *Congressional Quarterly Weekly Report*, 7 Aug. 1964, p. 1701.
[171] *Time*, 7 Aug. 1964.
[172] George Gallup, *The Gallup Poll, 1935–1971*, vol. 3, poll for 5 Aug. 1964, p. 1900.

our principles, our posture, our platform."[173] Johnson started describing Miller as "a fellow that welcomes the Klan's support!"[174]

Goldwater struggled to neutralize the extremism issue. In early August Richard Nixon wrote the senator a "personal" letter asking that he clarify the meaning of the "extremism" clause in his acceptance speech. Goldwater responded three days later – "Dear Dick" – asking that the clause be viewed in the context of the remarks just before it in the speech, which had denounced Washington politicians as captives of "unthinkable labels." A few days later, on August 12, Goldwater met with virtually every key party leader (except Lodge) in a conference brokered by Eisenhower in Hershey, Pennsylvania. The resulting statement positioned Goldwater's foreign policy proposals as an extension of Eisenhower's approach to world affairs, promised a "faithful execution" of the Civil Rights Act, and asserted that Goldwater sought the support of "no extremist – of the left or of the right." Few came away from the affair convinced. Chatting with Nixon afterwards, Eisenhower commented, "You know, before we had this meeting, I thought that Goldwater was just stubborn. Now I am convinced that he is just plain dumb."[175]

By the end of July, Johnson had outlined the basics of his response to Goldwater: he would stress his administration's accomplishments and counteract the backlash by cultivating traditionally Republican constituencies through portraying Goldwater as an extremist. Even if successful, however, this strategy would still leave the two broad areas in which Johnson had shown vulnerability since early 1964 – ethics and foreign policy.

As had been the case since the start of his administration, Johnson's attempts to address the corruption issue only intensified the problem. The seemingly endless Bobby Baker inquiry officially closed in early July, when the Rules Committee issued a report castigating Baker but excluding any mention of public officials with whom Baker had done business. Privately, Everett Jordan conceded that he could have chaired the investigation more effectively, but blamed his failures on the "tremendous political pressures" he faced.[176] The committee's three GOP members,

[173] *Congressional Quarterly Weekly Report*, 31 July 1964, p. 1650.

[174] President Johnson and Edwin Weisl, 9:02 P.M., 30 July 1964, Tape WH6407.21, Citation #4453, LBJ Recordings.

[175] Kessel, *The Goldwater Coalition*, pp. 186–8; Eisenhower quoted in Richard Nixon, *RN: The Memoirs of Richard Nixon* (New York: Grosset and Dunlap, 1978), p. 262.

[176] B. Everett Jordan to L. P. McLendon, 14 Sept. 1965, Box 36, B. Everett Jordan Papers, Duke University.

in a blistering minority report, alleged "concealment and cover-up of evidence."[177] Summing matters up, writing in the *New Republic,* Murray Kempton termed the inquiry a "remarkably unproductive contribution to the Senate's conscience or the public's knowledge."[178]

For good measure, the committee Republicans praised the "fearless public service" of John Williams.[179] Johnson took notice of the Delaware senator as well but had a different response in mind. He commissioned a poll from Oliver Quayle to determine Williams's vulnerability to a challenge from Democratic governor Elbert Carvel, whom Williams had defeated in 1958. The survey suggested that while Williams would be tough to beat, a Democratic landslide could sweep him under.[180] Accordingly, Johnson asked the NAACP's Roy Wilkins to boost black voter registration in Delaware, which, as "a very small state...would be a good place for some of your surplus energy."[181] Fewer than half of the First State's eligible black voters (17 percent of the state's population) were registered; Carvel would need every vote to defeat the "mean" incumbent.[182] Wilkins promised to do his best.

Unfortunately for Johnson, the termination of the Baker inquiry did not end discussion about the issues the investigation raised. Instead, the focus returned to how the president had accumulated his personal wealth.[183] Johnson was particularly concerned when word reached him that *Life* planned a profile on the issue. Behind the scenes he tried to kill a story that he believed (yet again, and without foundation) that Robert Kennedy had planted.[184] When that effort failed, in late July, he volunteered himself as "primary source of information" to publisher Henry Luce. Johnson lobbied Luce to undertake a similar profile on Goldwater's fortune, and he "wondered how Kennedy stayed in four or five years" without any in-depth investigation of his family's shady finances. His

[177] U.S. Senate, Rules Committee, *Report, Financial or Business Interests of Officers or Employees of the Senate*, 88th Cong., 2nd sess., p. 81 (3 July 1964).

[178] Murray Kempton, "Bobby Baker Blossoms," *The New Republic*, 4 July 1964.

[179] U.S. Senate, Rules Committee, *Report, Financial or Business Interests of Officers or Employees of the Senate*, 88th Cong., 2nd sess., p. 81 (3 July 1964).

[180] Bruce E. Altschuler, *LBJ and the Polls* (Gainseville: University of Florida Press, 1990), p. 84.

[181] President Johnson and Roy Wilkins, 11:00 A.M., 28 July 1964, Tape WH6407.16, Citation #4361, LBJ Recordings.

[182] President Johnson and Roy Wilkins, 11:00 A.M., 28 July 1964, Tape WH6407.16, Citation #4361, LBJ Recordings.

[183] *Washington Star*, 9 June 1964.

[184] President Johnson and George Brown, 9:10 A.M., 29 July 1964, Tape WH6407.17, Citation #4378, LBJ Recordings.

enemies, the president complained, wanted "to make a very wealthy man out of a man that's 57 years old, that's done reasonably well all of his life and [is] worth between three and four hundred thousand [dollars]."[185]

How Johnson calculated his net worth only intensified the attacks. As so often occurred in 1964, legalistic advice from Abe Fortas backfired politically. In this instance Fortas hired an auditing firm that used the peculiar accounting technique of determining Johnson's net worth by measuring his property at its initial value, instead of estimating its current value. As a result, the audit showed a fortune of just under $4 million, the bulk of which fell under Lady Bird's control, since she nominally owned KTBC. Under this method Johnson himself claimed a net worth of only $400,000.[186]

In making the release, Johnson became the first chief executive in American history to provide a public accounting of his personal wealth, one of many ways in which the 1964 campaign ushered in a more modern conception of the relationship between ethics and public policy. Nonetheless, the reaction to the president's move showed that Johnson had not gone nearly far enough. Dean Burch, recently installed as the chair of the Republican National Committee, scoffed that, under Johnson's auditing techniques, the value of Manhattan Island would be $24.[187] By the middle of August, after several more stories had appeared on the matter, the president admitted to George Reedy, "We're getting a pretty big beating on the wealth thing." He predicted that it would "hurt us like hell"; indeed, "it will be a major issue, and corruption."[188] Johnson was right.

As the president dealt with continuing difficulties over personal and political ethics, he finally addressed another long-running problem: the Kennedy candidacy. In late June Kennedy gave a frank interview to *Newsweek*'s Ben Bradlee. "I'd be the last man in the world he would want because my name is Kennedy, because he wants a Johnson administration with no Kennedys in it." Nonetheless, "most of the major political leaders in the North want me. All of them, really." As vice president, he envisioned himself harnessing "all the energy and effort and incentive and

[185] President Johnson and Henry Luce, 5:15 P.M., 25 July 1964, Tape WH6407.15, Citation #4350, LBJ Recordings.
[186] President Johnson and Clark Clifford, 8:21 P.M., 29 July 1964, Tape WH6407.19, Citation #4409, LBJ Recordings.
[187] *Washington Star*, 20 Aug. 1964.
[188] President Johnson and George Reedy, 11:10 A.M., 20 Aug. 1964, Tape WH6408.29, Citation #5047, LBJ Recordings.

imagination that was attracted to government by President Kennedy," thus allowing "the striving for excellence [to] continue, that there be an end to mediocrity."[189]

The candor of Kennedy's remarks stunned political reporters and infuriated the White House.[190] Kennedy himself claimed to the president that he had just spoken "about all of these matters quite frankly and openly, as I always have." Johnson responded tartly: "I thought it was quite unfortunate." The interview, he complained, allowed the media to contend that Kennedy "extremists" were challenging the president.[191]

The next day Johnson revealed his fears to John Connally, with whom he had reconciled. He instructed the Texas governor to read the *Newsweek* story "*very* carefully." The President could see no way to avoid a "knock-down-drag-out" at the convention; he predicted that Jacqueline Kennedy would nominate the attorney general, and that fact alone, coupled with "*all* the emotions" associated with remembering the late president, could create a stampede for a Kennedy nomination.[192]

Johnson wildly overreacted to the threat from Kennedy. As early as May, Evans and Novak described the "unprecedented" pressure to commit Democratic delegates to support Johnson's vice-presidential selection as "a classic case of overkill."[193] But Johnson went forward. His stroking of Pat Brown's ego in California, for instance, produced the desired results. Obtaining a slot on Brown's slate required pledging support for the president's choice for a running mate.[194]

At times the president's view of the attorney general bordered on the paranoid. "When this fellow looks at me," Johnson remarked, "he looks like he's going to look a hole through me like I'm a spy or something." Philosophizing with Connally in late July, Johnson predicted that Kennedy would force a roll call at the convention – perhaps even for the presidential nomination. As frequently was the case, he complained about the loyalty of his political advisers and White House staff: apart from Bill Moyers and Walter Jenkins, "the rest of them are their people,"

[189] Ben Bradlee, "An Informal Talk with RFK," *Newsweek*, 6 July 1964.

[190] *New York Times*, 5 July 1964; *Washington Star*, 6 July 1964; Jeff Shesol, *Mutual Contempt: Lyndon Johnson, Robert Kennedy, and the Feud That Defined a Decade* (New York: W. W. Norton, 1997), p. 196.

[191] President Johnson and Robert Kennedy, 11:19 A.M., 2 July 1964, Tape WH6407.01, Citation #4117, LBJ Recordings.

[192] President Johnson and John Connally, 11:38 A.M., 3 July 1964, Tape WH6407.03, Citation #4145, LBJ Recordings.

[193] *Washington Post*, 20 May 1964.

[194] *New York Herald Tribune*, 27 Mar. 1964.

who spent their time promoting the attorney general. Connally himself had no doubt that Kennedy wanted to see Johnson defeated in the fall. "He's an arrogant, he's an egotistical, selfish person," the Texas governor fumed, "that feels like he's almost anointed." If Johnson decided to confront Kennedy "in a goddamn fight, let's take him on."[195]

Throughout July, despite regularly issuing the almost comical claim that he was "pretty well removed from the political thing," the president pondered how he could most gracefully remove Kennedy from contention.[196] He first tried the argument that naming Kennedy would produce such an unworkable administrative structure that he would be better off not running at all. Chatting with former Pennsylvania governor David Lawrence, Johnson asserted (in an unintended commentary of the role he envisioned for his vice president) that "the President oughtn't to be required to get in bed and sleep with a woman he doesn't like."[197] Observing this process from the outside, Evans and Novak noted that Johnson's concern with the Kennedy threat – to such an extent that he was worried about the timing of the John Kennedy memorial film at the convention – bespoke of a larger concern, namely, that "Mr. Johnson is more uncertain about his hold over the Democratic Party than he ought to be."[198] The immediate run-up to Johnson's decision to eliminate Kennedy from the ticket confirmed the columnists' hunch.

On July 22 Johnson's longtime associate Cliff Carter urged the president to end the Kennedy candidacy once and for all, so as to avoid the possibility of a convention stampede.[199] Johnson was not sure, however, that he could pull it off: he doubted the loyalty of the key power brokers from the North.[200] Richard Daley was a particular concern. When the president confided that he was considering eliminating the attorney general from the vice-presidential race, the Chicago mayor responded coolly. In politics, Daley maintained, it was perfectly natural for someone who wanted a position to campaign for it. In any case, he had detected no Kennedy movement that could embarrass the president. Johnson tried

[195] President Johnson and John Connally, 5:31 P.M., 23 July 1964, Tape WH6407.13, Citation #4320, LBJ Recordings.

[196] President Johnson and George Brown, 9:10 A.M., 29 July 1964, Tape WH6407.17, Citation #4378, LBJ Recordings.

[197] President Johnson and Dave Lawrence, in President Johnson and Spessard Holland, 12:50 P.M., 17 July 1964, Tape WH6407.09, Citation #4264, LBJ Recordings.

[198] *New York Herald Tribune*, 28 July 1964.

[199] Shesol, *Mutual Contempt*, p. 205.

[200] President Johnson and Cliff Carter, 12:40 P.M., 23 July 1964, Tape WH6407.13, Citation #4319, LBJ Recordings.

another tack, suggesting that Kennedy's continuing his campaign could make the party look weak for the fall campaign.[201] Daley, relenting, said that he would broach the topic with the attorney general. The mayor did as promised, but he returned with unwelcome news: it was clear to him that Kennedy would not trigger a floor fight for the nomination. Therefore, Daley saw no reason for hasty action.[202]

Back at the White House, Johnson asked Clark Clifford to develop a more convincing rationale for denying the attorney general a spot on the ticket. Clifford's national fame came from his role in Harry Truman's presidential triumph, but, like Fortas, his relationship with Johnson dated from the Johnson-Stevenson recount fight of 1948. Now Clifford made the case for eliminating Kennedy: "The Goldwater nomination and the resulting situation in the South and in the Border States makes it clear that the President cannot choose the Attorney General." Such a move did not imply a lack of respect for Kennedy; indeed, Johnson and the Democratic Party had the "greatest need for the Attorney General's help" in continuing the Kennedy-Johnson partnership, fortifying the Democratic tendencies of American Catholics, and tapping Kennedy's "unequaled talent for the management of a campaign." Accordingly, Clifford urged Johnson to designate Kennedy as his campaign chair. Clifford subsequently approached Kennedy about his interest in running the campaign, but Kennedy demurred.[203]

Just after 1 P.M. on July 29, Kennedy arrived to see the president; shortly thereafter, Johnson recounted the conversation to Clifford and McGeorge Bundy. According to the president, he told his attorney general that in many ways he was doing Kennedy a favor: "I don't think that you'd be very happy there – although I'm not in charge of your happiness."[204] Johnson claimed that he had reached his decision because he needed a running mate who could neutralize Goldwater's strength in the Middle West and the border states, mirroring the regional approach used by John Kennedy in 1960. He stressed that Robert Kennedy should not interpret the decision personally. The tone of the exchange pleased

[201] President Johnson and Richard Daley, 3:29 P.M., 21 July 1964, Tape WH6407.11, Citation #4297, LBJ Recordings.

[202] President Johnson and Richard Daley, 10:01 A.M., 25 July 1964, Tape WH6407.14, Citation #4336, LBJ Recordings.

[203] Clark Clifford, "The President's Campaign Objectives," 23 July 1964, Box 26, WHCF-PL, Lyndon B. Johnson Presidential Library.

[204] President Johnson and McGeorge Bundy, 2:30 P.M., 29 July 1964, Tape WH6407.18, Citation #4394, LBJ Recordings.

the president; much to his surprise, Kennedy "wasn't combative," while Johnson himself "leaned over backwards" to avoid arrogance.[205]

Incredibly, Kennedy then told the president that he wanted to talk "about the Bobby Baker thing" – undoubtedly confirming Johnson's long-held suspicions that the Justice Department was using the investigation to harm him politically. "I think," the attorney general continued, that "it might be highly embarrassing." Johnson said he would support whatever action the Justice Department took and reiterated his familiar (and false) claim that he had no contact with Baker after leaving the Senate.[206]

Only one sticking point remained: how to announce the decision. The president offered to handle the matter any way that Kennedy desired, and the attorney general requested time to consider the matter.[207] Johnson's concern then shifted to whether the favorable tone of the conversation would continue after Kennedy consulted with his advisers. On this score, Bundy, who chatted briefly with the attorney general after he left the Oval Office, provided reassurance. The president, Bundy concluded, "handled it just Grade-A." Johnson, typically, worried about acting "before somebody" – perhaps pro-Kennedy columnists Anthony Lewis or Mary McGrory – "writes it up unfairly."[208]

Kennedy did not get back to Johnson during the afternoon; by 8:00 that evening, Johnson started worrying that Kennedy was contacting party operatives around the country to challenge the decision.[209] Calls thus went out to Richard Daley, Pat Brown, Philadelphia party boss Frank Smith, and (oddly) Vermont governor Philip Hoff, pressing them for public statements supporting the president's freedom of action in choosing a running mate.[210] Kennedy, meanwhile, rejected Johnson's request to say

[205] President Johnson and Clark Clifford, 2:17 P.M., 29 July 1964, Tape WH6407.18, Citation #4392, LBJ Recordings.

[206] President Johnson and Clark Clifford, 2:17 P.M., 29 July 1964, Tape WH6407.18, Citation #4392, LBJ Recordings.

[207] President Johnson and Clark Clifford, 2:17 P.M., 29 July 1964, Tape WH6407.18, Citation #4392, LBJ Recordings.

[208] President Johnson and McGeorge Bundy, 2:30 P.M., 29 July 1964, Tape WH6407.18, Citation #4394, LBJ Recordings.

[209] President Johnson and Clark Clifford, 8:21 P.M., 29 July 1964, Tape WH6407.19, Citation #4409, LBJ Recordings.

[210] President Johnson and Richard Daley, 8:30 P.M., 29 July 1964, Tape WH6407.19, Citation #4410, LBJ Recordings; President Johnson and Philip Hoff, 9:08 A.M., 30 July 1964, Tape WH6407.19, Citation #4414, LBJ Recordings; President Johnson and Joseph Barr, 9:16 A.M., 30 July 1964, Tape WH6407.19, Citation #4419, LBJ Recordings; President Johnson and Frank Smith, 9:55 A.M., 30 July 1964, Tape WH6407.19, Citation #4418, LBJ Recordings; President Johnson and Pat Brown, 10:32 A.M., 30 July 1964, Tape WH6407.20, Citation #4422, LBJ Recordings.

that he withdrew from consideration, speciously arguing that his doing so would be unfair to volunteers who had worked on his behalf.[211]

With Kennedy refusing to cooperate, Johnson resolved to make the statement himself. But loath to single out the attorney general, he decided to rule out all members of the Cabinet. Longtime Kennedy confidante Ken O'Donnell's indication that the attorney general would view such a move positively sealed the decision.[212] Johnson subsequently expanded the list to include all figures that regularly met with the Cabinet, thus allowing him to eliminate Adlai Stevenson, whom he never seriously considered, and Sargent Shriver, whose promising chances had vanished as the president had the opportunity to work with him more closely in developing the anti-poverty program.[213] (Shriver, confused as to whether he was covered by the exclusion, asked to remain under consideration. Upon hearing the news, Johnson's special assistant Larry O'Brien remarked that Shriver possessed "the one ingredient, frankly, I've been lacking in my life: gall.")[214] Jack Valenti joked that apart from Hubert Humphrey and Minnesota senator Eugene McCarthy, "you just wiped out the whole list right there." The president, chortling, noted, "I just had to eliminate one."[215]

Though transparent in nature, the decision to exclude the Cabinet served multiple purposes. At several points in the preceding months, Johnson had floated McNamara's name as a running mate, partly out of admiration for the Defense Secretary's performance in trimming Pentagon spending, partly because he liked McNamara's profile as a Republican former business executive. These rumors, however, had encountered strong resistance from Democratic regulars. Reluctantly, Johnson had concluded that "the bosses would just, from what they've said to me, would just – I think they would revolt."[216] Expanding the list to the entire Cabinet offered a way to gracefully end talk of McNamara's vice-presidential prospects.

[211] President Johnson and McGeorge Bundy, 10:01 A.M., 30 July 1964, Tape WH6407.19, Citation #4419, LBJ Recordings.

[212] President Johnson and Ken O'Donnell, no time reported, 30 July 1964, Tape WH6407.20, Citation #4426, LBJ Recordings.

[213] President Johnson and James Rowe, 5:28 P.M., 30 July 1964, Tape WH6407.20, Citation #4427, LBJ Recordings.

[214] President Johnson and Larry O'Brien, 6:10 P.M., 31 July 1964, Tape WH6407.22, Citation #4558, LBJ Recordings.

[215] President Johnson and Jack Valenti, conversation before telephone call between President Johnson and Richard Russell, 6:10 P.M., 30 July 1964, Tape WH6407.20, Citation #4439, LBJ Recordings.

[216] President Johnson and McGeorge Bundy, 10:01 A.M., 30 July 1964, Tape WH6407.19, Citation #4419, LBJ Recordings.

The press greeted Johnson's announcement with a mixture of criticism and ridicule. The *Washington Star* wondered if Johnson would have more smoothly "accomplished the same result by ruling out any man who lives in McLean, Virginia, or who owns a large dog," as Kennedy did. There was, the editors supposed, "no easy, painless way to do a hatchet job of this sort."[217] Kennedy himself, who had retreated to his family compound in Hyannisport with Averell Harriman and Arthur Schlesinger, Jr., pondered humorous responses to the affair, trying out lines such as "It seems to me premature to stop the vice presidential boom for [Secretary of State] Dean Rusk" and "I swear to the best of my knowledge I am not now and never have been a member of the cabinet on the ground that it might tend to eliminate me."[218]

This plethora of "bad stories" soured the president's mood.[219] If he kept reading datelines from Hyannisport, Johnson scowled, "I'm going to sock him right in the puss." To those who criticized his tactics, the president awaited a recommendation on a superior approach. Inventing a history that never existed, he claimed to have been beaten down by pressure from partisans of Rusk (!), Stevenson, and McNamara. Secretary of Agriculture Orville Freeman, he asserted, had "the biggest ambition of any of them to run for Vice President."[220] This pressure threatened to destroy public confidence in the government, as the nation interpreted every Cabinet member's acts as a gambit in the race for the vice presidency. In any case, he was tempted to ask the Cabinet why they wanted the position – the jabs from his period of exile still hurt.

Johnson never could contain his fury well, and in this instance he failed entirely. The day after his conference with Kennedy, the president provided Tom Wicker of the *New York Times,* Edward Folliard of the *Washington Post,* and Douglas Kiker of the *New York Herald Tribune* with a commentary on the previous day's events, with considerable exaggeration. When he gave Kennedy the news, the president claimed, the attorney general gulped, his "Adam's apple going up and down like a yo-yo."[221] Johnson's mockery soon spread around the Capitol. When he returned

[217] *Washington Star*, 1 Aug. 1964.

[218] Arthur Schlesinger, Jr., *Robert Kennedy and His Times* (Boston: Houghton Mifflin, 1978), p. 662.

[219] President Johnson and Robert McNamara, 9:00 A.M., 1 Aug. 1964, Tape WH6408.01, Citation #4601, LBJ Recordings.

[220] President Johnson and Larry O'Brien, 5:42 P.M., 2 Aug. 1964, Tape WH6408.02, Citation #4619, LBJ Recordings.

[221] Shesol, *Mutual Contempt*, p. 210.

to Washington, Kennedy confronted the president. Johnson denied any such discussion; ostentatiously, he checked to see if his appointment book contained a conversation that he might have forgotten. It was not his finest moment.

The awkward handling of the Kennedy exclusion could have festered. But for the first of two occasions in the campaign, a foreign policy crisis deflected attention away from a Johnson political crisis. Four days after the president met with Kennedy, the vice-presidential story was displaced by a confused naval skirmish on seas – the Gulf of Tonkin, of which few Americans had ever heard. For several months Johnson had tried to avoid a public debate about the conflict in Vietnam; indeed, he sought to avoid any discussion of foreign policy at all. The campaign, Johnson's aide Henry Wilson contended, needed "to cut down Goldwater," not spell out a convincing foreign policy rationale.[222]

The events in the Tonkin Gulf paved the way for Johnson to implement Wilson's strategy.[223] As historian Fredrik Logevall has observed, the administration also had a pressing international need to demonstrate its resolve, lest South Vietnamese resistance collapse entirely. On August 2 North Vietnamese vessels fired upon the USS *Maddox,* which was patrolling, as part of a mission for the National Security Agency, waters that North Vietnam claimed as territorial. The operation coincided with South Vietnamese raids of nearby North Vietnamese islands.[224] McNamara admitted that the South Vietnamese raids combined "with this destroyer in that same area undoubtedly led them to connect the two events."[225] Certainly the *Maddox* was not the victim of an unprovoked attack.

The president's initial public statement on the matter was firm but bland. Describing matters to former treasury secretary and longtime confidante Robert Anderson the next morning, "There have been some covert operations that we have been carrying on – blowing up some bridges and things of that kind, roads and so forth – so I imagine they [the North Vietnamese] wanted to put a stop to it." The North Vietnamese attacked, U.S. forces responded with overwhelming firepower, and the

[222] Henry Wilson to McGeorge Bundy, 18 July 1964, Box 1, Henry Wilson Papers, Lyndon B. Johnson Presidential Library.

[223] Lady Bird Johnson, *A White House Diary* (New York: Holt, Rinehart, and Winston, 1970), entry for 11 July 1964, p. 176.

[224] Fredrik Logevall, *Choosing War: The Lost Chance for Peace and the Escalation of War in Vietnam* (Berkeley: University of California Press, 1999), p. 197.

[225] President Johnson and Robert McNamara, 10:20 A.M., 3 Aug. 1964, Tape WH6408.03, Citation #4633, LBJ Recordings.

status quo – with U.S. reinforcements – returned. Reminding Johnson that "you're going to be running against a man who's a wild man on this subject," Anderson recommended a more forceful public response. While, obviously, "you've got to do what's right for the country," the president needed to explain to the American public that "we're not soft." Therefore, Anderson concluded "that if I were there, I'd knock them off the moon."[226]

Anderson's words had their desired effect. Later that morning, the president informed McNamara that he wanted to leave an impression "that we're going to be firm as well without saying something that's dangerous." (Thinking back to his February address at UCLA, where his description of events in Vietnam as a "deeply dangerous game" triggered widespread press criticism, undoubtedly reinforced the desire to avoid this particular adjective.) "All the country," Johnson contended, wanted a firm policy, "because Goldwater is raising so much hell about how he's going to blow them off the moon." Anything less could create a backlash, giving the Arizona senator a new issue.[227]

Two nights later an even more confusing set of events occurred in the Tonkin Gulf. The *Maddox* reported another attack, although the ship's commander, Captain John Herrick, conceded that freak weather and an over-eager sonar man might have accounted for the supposed sightings of North Vietnamese patrol boats. But in Washington such confusion was not apparent, at least not until after the president and McNamara had authorized the key decisions. On the evening of August 4, Johnson invited 16 congressional leaders to the White House for a briefing from Robert McNamara, Dean Rusk, Director of Central Intelligence John McCone, and Joint Chiefs of Staff chairman Earle Wheeler. Of the group, only Senator Mike Mansfield opposed retaliatory raids against North Vietnam.

By this stage the president's concerns were quite clearly political.[228] Since the military could not propose anything to fit Johnson's desire for aggressiveness without the possibility of escalation, the president focused on publicly relaying the news in a way that made it appear as if he had authorized the toughest response possible. He had one principal

[226] President Johnson and Robert Anderson, 9:46 A.M., 3 Aug. 1964, Tape WH6408.03, Citation #4632, LBJ Recordings.

[227] President Johnson and Robert McNamara, 10:20 A.M., 3 Aug. 1964, Tape WH6408.03, Citation #4633, LBJ Recordings.

[228] President Johnson and Robert McNamara, 9:43 A.M., 4 Aug. 1964, Tape WH6408.04, Citation #4658, LBJ Recordings.

requirement: he wanted his statement issued before the conclusion of the 11:00 late local news.[229] Johnson also telephoned Goldwater, then vacationing off the California coast with General Wedemeyer, and obtained the senator's support.[230]

Weather and technical difficulties delayed the launch of some of the U.S. warplanes – those taking off from the USS *Ticonderoga* departed on time, but the last planes did not leave from the USS *Constellation* until 1:15 A.M. Eastern time. But the president went ahead with his announcement nonetheless, addressing the nation at 11:37 P.M.[231] The timing of Johnson's address did not escape the notice of one of his most vituperative critics, Ed Foreman. The freshman Republican congressman from El Paso accused the president of giving "an hour and a half notice to our attack upon the Communists." Could Johnson's television appearance, Foreman wondered, "be termed publicity-happy political irresponsibility?" Or perhaps "shooting from the lip?"[232] Johnson spent the next several days complaining about "that little shit-ass Foreman," whose vulnerable congressional seat suddenly became a particular presidential target.[233]

The difficulties with Foreman constituted Johnson's only political faux pas in handling the North Vietnamese attacks. Since he could not demonstrate his firmness in a military fashion, Johnson did so in another way, using the occasion to ensure congressional support. As early as May 20, the president had stated his desire to "ask Congress to join in a national decision authorizing all necessary action, including military force, to make the Communists stop their subversion."[234] Johnson even ordered the State Department to draw up a draft resolution. But, fearful of triggering public debate on the war, he backed off; at the time only 37 percent of those polled by George Gallup indicated that they were following events in Southeast Asia closely, and Johnson had no desire to see that figure rise.[235] Now the North Vietnamese action had provided an excuse to act. Accordingly, the administration proposed

[229] President Johnson and Robert McNamara, 9:15 P.M., 4 Aug. 1964, Tape WH6408.06, Citation #4706, LBJ Recordings.

[230] President Johnson and Barry Goldwater, 10:06 P.M., 4 Aug. 1964, Tape WH6408.06, Citation #4715, LBJ Recordings.

[231] *New York Times*, 5 Aug. 1964.

[232] 110 *Congressional Record*, 88th Cong., 2nd sess., p. 18547 (7 Aug. 1964).

[233] President Johnson and John McCormack, 3:01 P.M., 7 Aug. 1964, Tape WH6408.11, Citation #4807, LBJ Recordings.

[234] Logevall, *Choosing War*, p. 147.

[235] Gallup, *The Gallup Poll, 1935–1971*, vol. 3, poll for May 27, 1964, p. 1881.

a measure, which came to be known as the Tonkin Gulf Resolution, authorizing the president to "take all necessary measures to repel any armed attack against the forces of the United States and to prevent further aggression."[236]

The bill unanimously passed the House; on the floor of the Senate, two of the president's closest allies, Foreign Relations Committee chairman William Fulbright (D-Arkansas) and Richard Russell, served as co-managers. Apart from Foreman's complaints, conservatives praised the president's actions. Liberals, however, were quite concerned. By August 1964 around a dozen senators, many of whom had been critical of Johnson on other issues (such as the tax bill and the Bobby Baker case), had expressed skepticism about U.S. involvement in Vietnam. Gaylord Nelson, George McGovern, and Frank Church all privately worried about the resolution's open-ended wording. But Fulbright assured them that the resolution's principal purpose was to insulate the president from Goldwater's criticism and asked the three senators to defer their public criticisms until a later time.[237] Persuaded by the argument, Church and McGovern relented; Nelson, however, insisted on a colloquy with Fulbright in which the Foreign Relations Committee chair promised that the president would return to Congress before broadening the U.S. role in Vietnam.[238] The trio's conduct only confirmed *New Yorker* writer Richard Rovere's hunch "that the rise of Goldwater had been one of the factors – and perhaps the most important one – determining the timing and magnitude" of the Tonkin Gulf response.[239]

That left just two members of the upper chamber who refused to go along with the president's plan. Ernest Gruening's career as a dissenter had begun fifty years earlier as a crusading newspaper editor. He thereafter had served as an anti-imperialist journalist, administrator of American colonial possessions, and territorial governor of Alaska before winning election as one of Alaska's first two senators. To the seventy-seven-year-old Democrat, Johnson's "allegation that we are supporting freedom in South Vietnam has a hollow sound." He believed that the United States had intervened in a civil war that grew out of a French colonial war. U.S. policy therefore was blocking, rather than championing, the forces of reform. Given these facts, he contended that "all Vietnam is not worth

[236] *New York Times*, 6 Aug. 1964.
[237] Personal Interview, George McGovern, Washington, DC, 6 Jan. 1994.
[238] Personal Interview, Gaylord Nelson, Washington, DC, 9 Jan. 1994.
[239] Richard Rovere, "Letter from Washington," *The New Yorker*, 22 Aug. 1964.

the life of a single American boy."[240] Only Oregon's Wayne Morse joined Gruening; befitting his status as a former dean of Oregon Law School, Morse attacked the resolution as unconstitutional – a "predated declaration of war."[241] But Gruening and Morse had both been strongly criticizing the U.S. involvement for some time, and at this stage few noticed figures dismissed by Rovere as "chronic dissenters."[242] One who did, however, was Lyndon Johnson: he denounced Gruening as "no good" and termed Morse "just undependable and erratic as he can be."[243]

The Tonkin Gulf Resolution represented a political success beyond Johnson's expectations. It joined the New Hampshire primary, the passage of the farm bill, the Oregon primary, and Robert Kennedy's elimination from the vice-presidential race as a major turning point in the contest. First, as many historians have observed, the measure effectively removed Vietnam as an issue in the campaign – despite predictions at the time that it might have the opposite effect.[244] Support for Johnson's handling of events in Southeast Asia surged from 42 percent to 72 percent.[245] Moreover, public interest in Vietnam soon sharply declined.[246] Since no additional military flare-ups occurred in Vietnam until just before Election Day, Tonkin Gulf came across as a prudent use of U.S. deterrent power that achieved the desired effect.

The political effects of the Tonkin Gulf Resolution extended well beyond Vietnam. Since the outbreak of the Panamanian riots in January, Johnson had seemed out of his league in international affairs. He articulated a simplistic rationale for the U.S. role in the world, appeared indecisive, and worried excessively about the domestic and especially the congressional ramifications of his decisions. In the spring every Republican campaign – including, in its own way most spectacularly, the Draft Lodge effort – planned to use foreign policy against Johnson. Then, with Tonkin Gulf, the president faced his most important crisis to date, and he seemed

[240] 110 *Congressional Record*, 88th Cong., 2nd sess., p. 18449 (6 Aug. 1964); Robert David Johnson, *Ernest Gruening and the American Dissenting Tradition* (Cambridge, MA: Harvard University Press, 1998).

[241] 110 *Congressional Record*, 88th Cong., 2nd sess., p. 18450 (6 Aug. 1964).

[242] Richard Rovere, "Letter from Washington," *The New Yorker*, 22 Aug. 1964.

[243] President Johnson and John McCormack, 3:01 P.M., 7 Aug. 1964, Tape WH6408.11, Citation #4807, LBJ Recordings.

[244] *Washington Star*, 7 Aug. 1964, 10 Aug. 1964, 17 Aug. 1964.

[245] Melvin Small, *Johnson, Nixon, and the Doves* (New Brunswick, NJ: Rutgers University Press, 1988), pp. 47–50.

[246] Kathleen Hall Jamieson, *Dirty Politics: Deception, Distraction, and Democracy* (New York: Oxford University Press, 1992), p. 247.

to respond perfectly. (Obviously history has not been as kind to Johnson in this regard.) The success of the retaliatory attacks and the support generated by the congressional resolution shattered the image of Johnson's incompetence in dealing with international affairs.

Moreover, since he no longer had to remain on the defensive when discussing national security issues, the president could implement Henry Wilson's earlier recommendations about using foreign policy to his advantage. Johnson knew just how to accomplish this task. As he told his press secretary, George Reedy, he needed only to say one word on the issue: "Atom. A-T-O-M."[247] Several weeks later Richard Rovere detected the significance of this development. Normally, the challenger in a presidential race at least had the advantage of selecting the questions on which the campaign would be waged. But "in foreign policy, Johnson had taken the play away from Goldwater and made 'nuclear responsibility' the largest issue."[248]

Johnson thus entered the Democratic convention in a much stronger position politically than a few weeks before when the GOP's national gathering had come to a close. Goldwater's campaign had failed to sustain its momentum from San Francisco, bogged down by internecine rivalry in the GOP and a series of surprisingly sharp denunciations from prominent religious figures. More important, the Tonkin Gulf Resolution altered the contour of the campaign, allowing Johnson to shake the image of a president overmatched on international affairs. The crisis thus set the stage for the biting, effective Democratic attacks on Goldwater's national security positions in the fall.

At no point between the start of May and the end of July did Johnson's lead over his Republican foes narrow to such an extent that the president had to consider what it might be like not to run the 1964 campaign from ahead. But at the very start and very end of this period – for two of only three times during the year – a bona fide threat to Johnson's political security emerged. In early May, before his loss in Oregon, Henry Cabot Lodge seemed to have developed enough momentum for his longshot bid to succeed. As a self-described "progressive Republican" with expertise in foreign affairs, an impeccable record on civil rights and ethical issues, and an educational and regional background that reminded many of John Kennedy's, Lodge could challenge Johnson on both of his

[247] President Johnson and George Reedy, 11:10 A.M., 20 Aug. 1964, Tape WH6408.29, Citation #5407, LBJ Recordings.

[248] Richard Rovere, "A Reporter at Large," *The New Yorker*, 17 Oct. 1964.

vulnerabilities – international affairs and personal ethics – while not losing the base vote of the GOP in the Northern and Eastern states. In late July, immediately following the convention, Barry Goldwater presented a very different type of threat, that of someone eager to cultivate a backlash vote of Southern whites and Northern ethnics. Of the two, as Johnson himself recognized, Goldwater presented the easier target, as the Arizona senator's inability to sustain his post-convention momentum proved. But looming events presented the president with both an opportunity and a threat: would he be able to contain the backlash and come out of his party convention relatively unscathed?

4

The Atlantic City Convention

The Republican convention ensured that the politics of race would be a major theme of the 1964 campaign. Internal Democratic politics, especially over the seating of the Mississippi delegation, intensified the problem for Johnson. Yet the president was convinced that he could use his political skills to overcome the backlash and in the process provide a model for the Democrats to retain their majority status in the post–civil rights era. How to accomplish this goal – and to ensure that he was not saddled with Robert Kennedy as a running mate – dominated his thinking through most of the summer of 1964.

With a host of issues uncertain, the Democrats arrived in Atlantic City for the party's thirty-fourth national convention, which met from August 24 through 27. Johnson remained in Washington but spent "uncounted and uncountable hours on the phone" directing convention affairs.[1] Four days later he was officially the Democratic presidential nominee, but only after a gathering made stale by his micromanaging style, in which the emotion was supplied not by Johnson but by Hubert Humphrey and Robert Kennedy.

Johnson told aides that he wanted a harmonious convention without controversy. Elizabeth Harris, a liaison between the White House and the Democratic National Committee for convention planning, expected

[1] *Time*, 4 Sept. 1964. The president, sensitive to such observations, told Walter Jenkins, "It's *very* important that everybody up there say they're not talking to me." President Johnson and Walter Jenkins, 1:11 P.M., 24 Aug. 1964, Tape WH6408.34, Citation #5152, LBJ Recordings.

a "deadly dull" affair.[2] Johnson aide Bill Moyers opened discussions with Frank Stanton of CBS about ways of heightening drama, such as beginning the convention with the keynote address or arranging a parade to the convention hall after the president arrived in Atlantic City.[3] Acting on Johnson's orders, the DNC "deliberately tied" a planned memorial film for John Kennedy with remembrances of other prominent Democrats who had passed away since the previous election, Eleanor Roosevelt and Sam Rayburn.[4] This scheduling would minimize the possibility of "Bobby's boys" trying to "steamroller" the convention.[5] Johnson wanted a short, bland platform, modeled – yet again – on the approach Franklin Roosevelt used in 1940.[6]

Accepting Moyers's advice, the president also showcased younger Democrats, so as to prove that his Democratic Party could inspire idealism just as John Kennedy's had.[7] And he wanted no controversy with recalcitrant Southern delegations. He told Speaker of the House John McCormack to seat the Mississippi and Alabama delegations "near the nearest exit. If they want to walk out, let them walk out, but not us throw them out."[8] The Speaker did just that. The two states' delegations occupied opposite sides of the convention hall, right next to the exits.[9]

Johnson's involvement with so many convention details attracted notice.[10] Journalist Douglas Kiker, for instance, contended that "the Atlantic City preparations border on a state of chaos" because the president had "insisted on being the final authority on every tiny detail concerning this convention."[11] Johnson dismissed such criticism as the ramblings of the Washington press corps, "this little bunch of pig

[2] Elizabeth Harris to Walter Jenkins, 19 June 1964, Box 34, Office Files of Bill Moyers, Lyndon B. Johnson Presidential Library.

[3] Bill Moyers to President Johnson, 16 July 1964, Box 78, WHCF-PL, Lyndon B. Johnson Presidential Library.

[4] Elizabeth Harris to Walter Jenkins, 19 June 1964, Box 34, Office Files of Bill Moyers, Lyndon B. Johnson Presidential Library.

[5] Elizabeth Harris to Bill Moyers, 19 June 1964, Box 34, Office Files of Bill Moyers, Lyndon B. Johnson Presidential Library.

[6] President Johnson and Richard Daley, 3:29 P.M., 21 July 1964, Tape WH6407.11, Citation #4297, LBJ Recordings.

[7] President Johnson and Richard Daley, 3:29 P.M., 21 July 1964, Tape WH6407.11, Citation #4297, LBJ Recordings.

[8] President Johnson and John McCormack, 9:20 A.M., 14 July 1964, Tape WH6407.08, Citation #4224, LBJ Recordings.

[9] *Christian Science Monitor*, 24 Aug. 1964.

[10] *Washington Post*, 28 July 1964; *Washington Star*, 11 Aug. 1964.

[11] *New York Daily News*, 4 Aug. 1964; *New York Herald Tribune*, 8 Aug. 1964.

punks."[12] But his allies voiced similar concerns: his old friend prominent Washington attorney Jim Rowe reported that everyone in Atlantic City was "justifiably complaining that they cannot get answers out of the White House."[13]

Johnson's hope for an uneventful convention and his preference for micromanaging soon would be tested. In 1964 the Mississippi Democratic Party was the most reactionary state party in the country. The state's senior senator, James Eastland, used his chairmanship of the Judiciary Committee to obstruct civil rights legislation. Eastland's colleague, John Stennis, although best known for his hard-line foreign policy views, also adamantly opposed civil rights. The duo was moderate compared to Governor Paul Johnson and his predecessor, Ross Barnett, whose actions had forced John Kennedy to send the army to integrate Ole Miss. The state's congressmen included the reactionary William Colmer, the second-ranking member of the House Rules Committee and a close ally of Chairman Howard Smith; Tom Abernethy, a figure even Eastland considered an extremist; and John Bell Williams, who in 1965 would be stripped of his seniority by the Democratic caucus for endorsing Goldwater. Relations between the congressional delegation and the Kennedy administration deteriorated to such an extent that the White House took the unprecedented step of denying patronage rights to Mississippi's members of Congress.

In Freedom Summer, Mississippi symbolized the apartheid political system that existed in much of the Deep South. Civil rights organizations such as the Student Non-Violent Coordinating Committee (SNCC) and Martin Luther King's Southern Christian Leadership Council (SCLC) sent scores of volunteers, black and white, many of them college students, to the state. The activists hoped to organize voter registration drives, create "Freedom Schools," and improve the daily life of the state's poor black citizens. Mississippi, however, was also the center of racist violence in the South. In June three of the volunteers – Michael Schwerner, James Chaney, and Andrew Goodman – disappeared; the FBI discovered their bodies several weeks later.[14]

[12] President Johnson and George Reedy, 11:10 A.M., 7 July 1964, Tape WH6407.05, Citation #4169, LBJ Recordings.

[13] Rowe quoted in Toi [no last name] to Bill Moyers and Walter Jenkins, 5 Aug. 1964, Box 78, WHCF-PL, Lyndon B. Johnson Presidential Library.

[14] Taylor Branch, *Pillar of Fire: America in the King Years, 1963–1965* (New York: Simon & Schuster, 1998), pp. 362–400.

The murders focused national attention on the political and social situation in Mississippi. On August 6 the Mississippi Freedom Democratic Party, a predominantly black group sponsored by national civil rights organizations, held its founding convention at Jackson's Masonic Temple. Two thousand people braved threats of terror to select delegates and alternates to the Democratic National Convention. The MFDP, which claimed 63,000 members statewide, termed itself the only true Democratic Party in the state because, unlike the regulars, it was open to all citizens and generally supported the positions of national Democrats.

Before departing Mississippi, Aaron Henry, one of the MFDP's leaders, conceded, "As things stand now, we don't know what the hell we're going to do when we get to Atlantic City."[15] (Neither did the Atlantic City police; the White House advance team found the city's eighty-man force "near panic over the prospect of civil rights demonstrations during the convention.")[16] But its connection to the civil rights movement gave the MPFD an entry point among national liberals. Joseph Rauh, a Washington lawyer and one of the founding members of Americans for Democratic Action, presented the MFDP's case before the convention credentials committee. Rauh adopted a strategy of "11 and 8." First, he needed to find the required eleven votes from the 108-member credentials committee to present a minority report to the convention. Then, delegations from eight states needed to demand a roll call vote. If a roll call vote occurred, Rauh – and Johnson – believed, Northern delegations would find it politically impossible to vote against seating the MFDP.[17]

The creation of the MFDP revealed the differing approaches to politics within the 1960s liberal coalition. Martin Luther King, Jr., hailed the development, arguing, "America needs at least one party which is free of racism."[18] The White House, on the other hand, fretted that the civil rights leadership "simply does not understand the political facts of life." The MFDP's founders were "not sophisticated enough to understand the theory of the backlash."[19] That the Mississippi regulars had followed all procedural guidelines in selecting their delegation compounded the administration's difficulties. No one expected Mississippi Democrats to

[15] Branch, *Pillar of Fire*, p. 439.
[16] Hayes [no first name] to Bill Moyers, 6 Aug. 1964, Box 34, Office Files of Bill Moyers, Lyndon B. Johnson Library.
[17] Branch, *Pillar of Fire*, p. 439.
[18] Branch, *Pillar of Fire*, p. 413.
[19] Hobart Taylor to President Johnson, 17 July 1964, Box 3, White House Executive File-HU4, Lyndon B. Johnson Presidential Library.

support Johnson in the fall; but if the national convention refused to seat a delegation chosen according to its own rules, the party risked alienating additional Southern delegations.[20]

Ironically, Johnson himself had once participated in a convention challenge that superficially resembled the MFDP case. The 1944 Texas Democratic convention featured denunciations of FDR as a usurper and condemned the influence of organized labor over the national Democratic Party.[21] The convention elected a slate of delegates pledged to an uncommitted choice, rather than to renominating Roosevelt. Led by Johnson, around 300 pro-Roosevelt delegates walked out of the convention hall (to the tune of "God Be with You till We Meet Again") and convened a pro-Roosevelt rump gathering. At the Chicago national convention, in something of a victory for Johnson, the Democratic credentials committee split the Texas vote between the regular slate and the pro-Roosevelt forces.[22]

Twenty years later Johnson was much less sympathetic to the idea of a credentials challenge. In late July he typically speculated that the MFDP was part of a Robert Kennedy plot. Reflecting on the issue, the president confided to John Connally that he had trouble sleeping one night. "About 2:30, I waked up, and I tried to figure out what I would do if I were a candidate for Vice President and I was going to be confronted with what he's going to be confronted with, and the boss man would say, 'I can't take you on account of the South.'" In a revealing commentary on his own approach to politics, Johnson said, "The first thing I'd do is try to make the South of no value to him or me."[23]

By the time the problem came to national attention, though, the president was evaluating matters more rationally. He began by trying to cut off the MFDP's national support. He pressured Hubert Humphrey to use his connections to compel the MFDP to accept a compromise. The Minnesota senator's first go-around failed to produce the desired result. The president himself could see "no justification for messing with the Freedom Party," which he considered little more than a "communist group" attempting to oust the legally elected state delegation and

[20] *Congressional Quarterly Weekly Report*, 28 Aug. 1964, p. 1958.

[21] D. B. Hardamen and Donald Bacon, *Rayburn: A Biography* (Austin: Texas Monthly Press, 1987), pp. 296–7.

[22] George Norris Green, *The Establishment in Texas Politics: The Primitive Years, 1938–1957* (Westport, CT: Greenwood Press, 1979), pp. 47–50.

[23] President Johnson and John Connally, 5:31 P.M., 23 July 1964, Tape WH6407.13, Citation #4320, LBJ Recordings.

threatening to "bring the convention down damn quick" in the process.[24] Humphrey was told to try harder.

The practical politician in Johnson could not understand why civil rights activists insisted on pressing the issue. What would the MFDP delegates gain by being seated? Now that he had disarmed the Kennedy threat, the convention probably would not even have a roll call. "If I were the Negro," the president mused, "I'd think the thing that I'd do is I'd just let Mississippi sit up on the platform if they wanted to. I'd stand at attention and salute the son of a bitch. Then I'd nominate Johnson for President and my Vice President, and I'd go out and elect my congressmen, and I'd come back here in the next four years and I'd see the Promised Land."[25] Instead, it seemed as if "this is coming to pieces," threatening to turn Atlantic City into another San Francisco.[26]

The president had only to compare the responses of two of his warmest supporters outside of Washington to realize the damage the MFDP question could cause. To Chicago mayor Richard Daley, anything other than seating the MFDP "would be just disastrous." Daley contended that if "we make a mistake on this one, we erase everything that happened in San Francisco, and we make ourselves look pretty foolish." Johnson clearly was not expecting a statement of high idealism from one of the party's most pragmatic politicians. The matter, the president reiterated, was a "practical question": the Mississippi regulars had followed procedures. Regardless, the real problem was the party's position in other Southern states: Why should the Democrats take "unwise actions" that could "almost shovel over to Goldwater 15 other states"? But Daley had an answer for this argument. Recalling the 1948 election, when "they all thought we were going to lose it" after the party adopted a strong civil rights plank, Harry Truman had said, "'Well, if that's what they want to do, let them do it.'" And Truman had prevailed, showing that Democrats could reconcile idealism and pragmatism – if they had the political will to do so.[27]

A different reaction came from Georgia governor Carl Sanders, the only Southern governor who testified before the platform committee on

[24] President Johnson and Hubert Humphrey, 11:05 A.M., 14 Aug. 1964, Tape WH6408.19, Citation #4917, LBJ Recordings.

[25] President Johnson and Roy Wilkins, 9:50 A.M., 15 Aug. 1964, Tape WH6408.21, Citation #4940, LBJ Recordings.

[26] President Johnson and Walter Reuther, 3:53 P.M., 14 Aug. 1964, Tape WH6408.20, Citation #4926, LBJ Recordings.

[27] President Johnson and Richard Daley, 9:36 A.M., 17 Aug. 1964, Tape WH6408.25, Citation #4978, LBJ Recordings.

behalf of the Civil Rights Act. But on the question at hand, Sanders was no more willing than Daley to see the merits of the other side. He sympathized with Johnson's predicament but had one of his own. Northern Democrats had to offer some concessions to provide their Southern colleagues with "some genuine reasons to stay in there and pitch and fight." As with Daley, local politics limited how far Sanders could – or would – go.[28]

Breaking the logjam required desperate measures. First, Johnson used his personal relationship with Eastland. In private conversations with the Mississippi senator, the president claimed that he wanted to seat the Mississippi regulars but predicted between 15 and 30 votes existed in the credentials committee in favor of the MFDP, more than enough to authorize a minority report. Liberals then could muster the eight state delegations necessary for a roll call. Though these figures were wildly exaggerated, Johnson asked Eastland to recommend that his state's delegation ignore the question of the MFDP. The Mississippi regulars could recognize that no roll call votes would occur and agree to seat both delegations. The president also pressed the senator to get at least some of the delegation to publicly commit to supporting the nominee. Eastland promised nothing but said that he would do his best.[29]

Having bargained with Eastland, Johnson approached United Auto Workers president Walter Reuther. At the president's request, Reuther worked the whole weekend of August 14–17 on "that Mississippi thing," but he had little good news to report. Even the NAACP's Roy Wilkins said that after the Cheney, Goodman, and Schwerner murders he could not consider supporting a compromise short of seating both delegations. To a perturbed Johnson, the political equation was straightforward: "You're going to carry Georgia for Goldwater if you run out the governor of Mississippi." Civil rights advocates would also sacrifice influence with Democrats if their actions cost the party several states. It was about time that liberals started "to figure out what they can do to satisfy their people and not run off my votes." Reuther, a political pragmatist, required no persuasion on this point, but, like Johnson, he realized that such appeals would not sway the most committed civil rights advocates. The president asked Reuther to float the idea of having the credentials

[28] President Johnson and Carl Sanders, 5:52 P.M., 17 Aug. 1964, Tape WH6408.26, Citation #5000, LBJ Recordings.

[29] President Johnson and James Eastland, 12:13 P.M., 17 Aug. 1964, Tape WH6408.26, Citation #4992, LBJ Recordings.

committee debate the matter throughout the entire convention, resulting in the seating of neither delegation.[30]

As the opening of the Atlantic City gathering drew near, the resolution of the MFDP problem remained elusive. Florida senator George Smathers reported that the Tennessee, Louisiana, South Carolina, and some of the Georgia delegations would walk out if the convention unseated the Mississippi regulars.[31] The president, meanwhile, searched for someone to blame for the impending fiasco, and Humphrey offered the most convenient target. It was about time, the president fumed, for the Minnesota senator to realize "that he's got no future in this party at all if this big war comes out here and the South wants out."[32] Johnson instructed his aide Walter Jenkins to tell Humphrey, "If you haven't got any influence with this ADA crowd, tell us who has."[33] Humphrey, desperate to keep his vice-presidential hopes alive, did his best to accommodate, but he could not win over the MFDP.

The two-hour credentials committee hearing on Mississippi could not have gone worse for the administration. The *Washington Post* described a scene dominated by "a hymn-singing group of dedicated men and women who feel as though they had temporarily escaped from a Mississippi prison and who think they may be jailed when they get back home."[34] Rita Schwerner, widow of one of the slain civil rights activists, testified, as did civil rights luminaries Martin Luther King, Jr., James Farmer, and Roy Wilkins. But the most forceful remarks came from Fannie Lou Hamer, who described in gruesome detail the economic and personal suffering she had endured simply for trying to register to vote. To deflect attention, Johnson hastily arranged a press conference announcing a meeting of the Democratic governors at the White House. Television coverage switched to Washington, in the expectation that the president might announce his running mate. The move backfired when all of the networks replayed Hamer's testimony on their evening news broadcasts.[35]

Johnson himself was inching toward a compromise solution, as he revealed when he got back to Eastland two days before the proceedings

[30] President Johnson and Walter Reuther, 6:14 P.M., 17 Aug. 1964, Tape WH6408.27, Citation #5003, LBJ Recordings.

[31] President Johnson and Walter Jenkins, 8:30 P.M., 21 Aug. 1964, Tape WH6408.32, Citation #5107, LBJ Recordings.

[32] President Johnson and Walter Reuther, 6:14 P.M., 17 Aug. 1964, Tape WH6408.27, Citation #5003, LBJ Recordings.

[33] Branch, *Pillar of Fire*, p. 469.

[34] *Washington Post*, 22 Aug. 1964.

[35] Branch, *Pillar of Fire*, pp. 458–60.

in Atlantic City began. The terms: the regular delegates would affirm their intention to support the nominee and promise that when the state convention reconvened on September 9, it would not undo the commitments the delegates made in Atlantic City. Eastland admitted that requirement could be a problem, because some members of the delegation never would support Johnson. The president understood and offered a legalistic way out of the dilemma: the delegates could say that they intended to support the nominee when they went to Atlantic City. If, after having attended the convention, they decided in good conscience that they could not do so, no one could possibly object. Second, the MFDP delegation would receive tickets to the convention hall, although they would not have the right to vote. Third, the national convention would state that, in the future, the question of racial equality would be given predominance when challenges to state delegations occurred. That way, Johnson reasoned, the MFDP delegates could claim a moral victory even though the convention itself refused to seat them.[36]

As Johnson admitted, the MFDP issue exacerbated the administration's already perilous political situation in the South. Chatting with Louisiana senator Russell Long in late July, Johnson maintained, "I'm trying my damndest to walk the tightrope that I've got to walk to try to be fair to all concerned and to be worthy of the confidence they have in me."[37] Despite the president's considerable political talents, however, his effort bore few signs of success: as one Georgia congressman remarked, "It would be poison now to say you'd even heard of Lyndon Johnson in Georgia."[38] Hayden Burns, the Democratic gubernatorial nominee in Florida, announced that he would not campaign for Johnson and predicted that Goldwater would carry the Sunshine State.[39] Governor Orval Faubus issued a similar forecast for Arkansas.[40] When John McKeithen of Louisiana publicly considered endorsing Goldwater, Long called his state's governor a "stupid ass."[41] At the end of July pollster Samuel Lubell predicted that Goldwater would carry not only the Deep South states

[36] President Johnson and James Eastland, 11:00 A.M., 22 Aug. 1964, Tape WH6408.32, Citation #5117, LBJ Recordings.

[37] President Johnson and Russell Long, 5:20 P.M., 20 July 1964, Tape WH6407.10, Citation #4280, LBJ Recordings.

[38] *Washington Star*, 26 July 1964.

[39] *Time*, 7 Aug. 1964.

[40] Cliff Carter to President Johnson, 15 Aug. 1964, Box 83, WHCF-PL, Lyndon B. Johnson Presidential Library.

[41] President Johnson and Russell Long, 5:45 P.M., 13 Aug. 1964, Tape WH6408.19, Citation #4911, LBJ Recordings; *Time*, 7 Aug. 1964.

but also Florida, the Carolinas, and Virginia. Even in Texas, Johnson maintained only an "uneasy" advantage.[42]

Privately, John Connally offered a similar and more detailed appraisal. At Johnson's request, the Texas governor polled his Southern colleagues in mid-July. Like virtually every other observer, Connally knew that Johnson would lose Mississippi or Alabama, but even so, conditions there took him aback: "The backlash," he reported, "is unbelievable." Louisiana also offered bleak news: conditions were "*rough, rough, rough,*" with Johnson trailing even in traditionally Democratic Catholic areas and in New Orleans. South Carolina governor Donald Russell, a moderate, begged the president "*please, please, please*" not to nominate either Kennedy or Humphrey for vice president. Connally accepted conventional wisdom that the ticket probably would lose Arkansas, but he detected some hope in Virginia and Florida. He added, however, one problematic state not previously on the list – New Mexico, where signs of a backlash had appeared in the state's conservative but traditionally Democratic "Little Texas" region.[43]

Kennedy's elimination as a running mate somewhat improved this bleak outlook, and the president even began plotting strategy as to how he might just carry most of the South. Any victory, he understood, would begin with the votes of newly enfranchised Southern blacks, who favored him by a 20-to-1 margin in an early August poll. In Arkansas, Florida, Georgia, North Carolina, South Carolina, Tennessee, Texas, and Virginia, the increase in black registration between 1960 and 1964 exceeded the margin of victory achieved by either Kennedy or Nixon in 1960.[44] (When informed of these numbers, George Smathers rejoiced, but counseled, "Don't print that!")[45] Policy issues could provide some assistance. A few days after the Tonkin Gulf attacks, Johnson noted that "the Vietnam thing helped some," given the South's pro-military posture.[46] The president also wanted Southerners to remember that in the spring he "went to bat for all the boys in Georgia and South Carolina and North Carolina on their cotton bill"; he expected payback now.[47]

[42] *Time*, 7 Aug. 1964.

[43] President Johnson and John Connally, 5:31 P.M., 23 July 1964, Tape WH6407.13, Citation #4320, LBJ Recordings.

[44] *New York Times*, 23 Aug. 1964.

[45] President Johnson and George Smathers, 2:29 P.M., 6 Aug. 1964, Tape WH6408.09, Citation #4782, LBJ Recordings.

[46] President Johnson and Carl Sanders, 10:40 A.M., 13 Aug. 1964, Tape WH6408.18, Citation #4904, LBJ Recordings.

[47] President Johnson and Carl Sanders, 3:53 P.M., 1 Aug. 1964, Tape WH6408.02, Citation #3617, LBJ Recordings.

Beyond issues, Johnson believed that a different psychological outlook could ameliorate his problems in the South. In conversations with key Southern leaders, he outlined a revisionist interpretation of his role in passing the Civil Rights Act. Since he inherited the legislation from Kennedy, he claimed that he had no choice but to go forward with it. In any case, over four-fifths of the Republicans in the Senate voted for the final bill, so the GOP deserved some "blame" for the measure.[48] Southern Democrats, meanwhile, needed to start talking about how their situation was improving, lest liberal calls for abandoning the region become too powerful to resist. At the least, he needed to win Texas, for purposes of pride. "If we don't carry but one state in the Union, it's got to be this one."[49]

While Johnson sought to mitigate the effects of race on his political standing, he also worried about how the backlash might weaken him with traditionally Democratic groups, especially union voters. In a bizarre manifestation of his fascination with polls, he asked Edwin Weisl (counselor for Johnson's Preparedness Subcommittee in the early 1950s) to survey New York City taxi drivers, whom the president considered reliable barometers of community opinion. The results offered no comfort. Ninety percent said they supported Goldwater, which the president interpreted as a "definite backlash." The administration, Johnson feared, had done a poor job explaining the Civil Rights Act, leaving union workers to fear "that under the civil rights bill, the Negro organizations – King and that group – will make a drive on them, and move a Negro in next door to them, where they could lose their home." The press, moreover, was giving the GOP "a victory psychology by talking about backlash." Weisl, more realistically, speculated that when a white, male passenger wearing a suit asked them who they supported for president, taxi drivers automatically said Goldwater, since they assumed that their fare was a Republican.[50]

Race and the MFDP did not represent the only convention-related problem Johnson faced as August 24 drew near. On February 17 the Supreme Court ruled in *Wesberry v. Georgia* that House districts needed to correspond by population. The decision invalidated a practice common in Southern states in which wide variances of population separated

[48] President Johnson and Carl Sanders, 3:53 P.M., 1 Aug. 1964, Tape WH6408.02, Citation #3617, LBJ Recordings.

[49] President Johnson and John Connally, 9:45 A.M., 9 Aug. 1964, Tape WH6408.15, Citation #4844, LBJ Recordings.

[50] President Johnson and Robert Wagner, Jr., 9:22 A.M., 17 Aug. 1964, Tape WH6408.24, Citation #4976, LBJ Recordings.

rural from urban districts, thus giving disproportionate influence to rural voters. In *Reynolds v. Sims,* decided in June, the Court applied the principle to state legislatures as well.

These rulings alarmed those in Congress that benefited from the unequal apportionment structure – Republicans, especially from the Midwest, and Southern Democrats. In response, a host of bills to limit judicial authority over reapportionment cases appeared. In the Senate Majority Leader Mike Mansfield and Minority Leader Everett Dirksen co-sponsored an amendment to stay court orders for population-based reapportionment of state legislatures. Representative William Tuck (D-Virginia) introduced a much stronger measure in the House. The Tuck bill sought to deny to the Supreme Court the right to review state court decisions concerning reapportionment and to block district court jurisdiction over any apportionment question.

For several months the Tuck bill languished in the House Judiciary Committee, where chair Emmanuel Celler (D-New York) and his liberal majority refused to report it. But through an arcane parliamentary maneuver, Southern Democrats managed to report the bill through the Rules Committee, where the committee's six Republicans joined with three Southern Democrats to create a 9–6 majority. In a reversal of the traditional arguments on committee prerogatives, Celler termed the action a "tyrannous abuse of power," while Clarence Brown (R-Ohio), the Rules Committee's ranking Republican, denounced Celler for denying the House an opportunity to vote on a measure of such importance.[51]

The bill generated a short, bitter debate. Democrats and a handful of liberal Republicans considered Tuck's offering an unconstitutional, "vicious attack on the Supreme Court." Congressman Thomas Gill framed the question the most broadly, describing the matter as "perhaps the most important struggle over equal rights in this country."[52] The Hawaii Democrat maintained that Tuck's supporters wanted to disenfranchise millions of urban voters and thus alter the balance of ideological power in the House. Moreover, if an act of Congress could invalidate this Supreme Court decision, might the Court's civil rights or civil liberties decisions be next? As liberalism itself transformed into a rights-related ideology relying on a sympathetic judiciary to implement concepts that the legislature would not approve, the principle behind the Tuck bill posed a mortal threat.[53]

[51] 110 *Congressional Record*, 88th Cong., 2nd sess., p. 20293 (10 Aug. 1964).

[52] 110 *Congressional Record*, 88th Cong., 2nd sess., p. 20294 (10 Aug. 1964).

[53] Hugh Davis Graham, *Civil Rights and the Presidency: Race and Gender in American Politics, 1960–1972* (New York: Oxford University Press, 1992), pp. 50–88.

The opponents of the measure had the better of the arguments, but the bill's supporters had the votes. On August 19, just five days before the start of the Democratic convention, the Tuck bill passed comfortably, 218 to 175. Republicans favored the measure 122 to 35, and 84 of 100 Southern Democrats joined them to provide the margin of victory. Northern Democrats, on the other hand, voted 124 to 12 in opposition.[54]

While the Tuck bill proceeded through the House, the Senate considered the Mansfield-Dirksen amendment. Democratic mayors from around the country lobbied the administration against the amendment, and a small group of liberals engaged in a de facto filibuster. Mansfield accordingly abandoned plans for adjourning the Senate, thus leaving the amendment pending business when the upper chamber would resume activity on August 31.[55]

After this announcement, Senators Joseph Clark and Paul Douglas requested a platform plank upholding *Reynolds v. Sims*. In so doing, they opened the same regional breach in the platform committee then vexing the credentials committee over whether to seat the MFDP.[56]

Johnson long had considered both senators impractical idealists – a belief reinforced by the duo's opposition to shutting down the Bobby Baker inquiry. When the president heard about their call for a reapportionment platform plank, he exploded. As had become customary, Johnson began by assuming that Robert Kennedy was behind the move, so as to "to get this convention disturbed any way he can." And, as had become customary, Humphrey bore the brunt of the initial attack. Like the MFDP question, the Clark-Douglas gambit posed a "practical problem"; if the plank reached the convention floor, Northern delegations would have no choice but to vote for it, thus disrupting the convention. "My own inclination," Johnson maintained, "would be to support the Court," but confrontational tactics played into the hands of the Republicans. Why Clark and Douglas could not see what was perfectly obvious to anyone with any political sense befuddled the president. Evidently, he scoffed, they wanted to uphold their "great moral principles," even if doing so meant "that we are just going to get the living hell beat out of us."[57]

When Bill Moyers reported that Anthony Lewis, the *New York Times* reporter known for his close ties to the attorney general, planned to file

[54] *Congressional Quarterly Weekly Report*, 21 Aug. 1964, p. 1895.

[55] *New York Times*, 16 Aug. 1964, 21 Aug. 1964.

[56] *New York Times*, 23 Aug. 1964.

[57] President Johnson and Hubert Humphrey, 9:20 A.M., 20 Aug. 1964, Tape WH6408.29, Citation #5045, LBJ Recordings.

a story on the reapportionment issue, Johnson had heard enough. He gave Moyers a message to relay to Lewis: liberals could accomplish their goal by filibustering for two weeks, after which Mansfield would set the amendment aside. But by insisting on a platform plank, Clark and Douglas would hamper Democratic efforts in rural areas and the South. One would think, Johnson fumed, that "even a goddamned college professor could understand that," but Douglas (who had taught economics at the University of Chicago before entering the Senate) "has got less sense than any man I know when judgment is required."[58]

Moreover, since Congress had not even adjourned, a good chance existed that the liberals could kill the Tuck bill without going through the hassle of a platform fight. "Does Dr. Douglas," the president hissed, "know that?" If the "liberals want a real plan of attack and Tony Lewis wants something to do," they should "get ten of them out here at a Georgetown house some night with Arthur Schlesinger, and let them all agree that one of them will talk four hours and the other one will talk four hours. That's what they do best: talk." If they pursued that approach for two weeks, the president continued, "the show will be over. The Tuck bill will be dead. The Supreme Court will be riding high. That will be it – period. That's simple. You don't have to be smart to know that. Hell, I knew that before I left Johnson City." (This effort succeeded, and, as Johnson predicted, the Senate refused to impose cloture on the Mansfield-Dirksen amendment, dooming the measure.)[59]

While the credentials and platform fights preoccupied the president's time, politicians and pundits focused on the convention's key unresolved question – the identity of the Democratic vice-presidential nominee. Humphrey remained the frontrunner; the Minnesota senator's advisers alternated between building Humphrey up and identifying the most likely opponent so they could tear him down.[60] Throughout the spring and early summer, they considered Peace Corps director Sargent Shriver their chief competition, but as Shriver's standing declined, the staff saw Humphrey's junior colleague, Eugene McCarthy, as a potential foe. Intelligence from Max Kampelman, one of Humphrey's closest allies, indicated that political tactician Clark Clifford favored McCarthy, and McCarthy (other than

[58] President Johnson and Bill Moyers, 10:00 P.M., 21 Aug. 1964, Tape WH6408.32, Citation #5115, LBJ Recordings.

[59] President Johnson and Bill Moyers, 10:00 P.M., 21 Aug. 1964, Tape WH6408.32, Citation #5115, LBJ Recordings.

[60] Ronald Stinnett to Hubert Humphrey, 1 June 1964, Box 56, Hubert Humphrey Papers, Minnesota State Historical Society.

a personal association with the Kennedys) had many of the same assets enjoyed by Shriver – youth, liberalism, Catholicism.[61]

Indeed, the early summer witnessed something of a McCarthy boom. In a flattering piece, journalist David Broder described Johnson's considering McCarthy "interesting for the light it sheds on the relevance or irrelevance or personal distinction as a criterion for selecting the second man." In political terms, Broder noted, McCarthy had not distinguished himself, but intellectually, the Minnesota senator was "among those who are entranced by the role of the humane intellectual in politics"; one Democratic operative described him as "an Adlai Stevenson with sex appeal." McCarthy did offer some concrete benefits. No Northern liberal, certainly, posed less danger in the South. The Minnesota senator had served so harmoniously with Harry Byrd on the Finance Committee that Byrd held a fundraising dinner for him; McCarthy had been all but invisible during the civil rights bill debate. Moreover, the senator had informed friends he would be content with the traditional scope of vice-presidential duties and had no desire to infringe upon presidential prerogatives.[62]

The Humphrey forces escalated their attack against McCarthy in July. They spread the message that Goldwater's selection of Miller created an image of Republican venality; if Johnson followed suit by similarly selecting someone based largely on religious grounds, the president would have lowered himself to Goldwater's level. McCarthy lacked impressive foreign policy qualifications, and his silence on civil rights would not sit well with liberal activists. Moreover, the junior senator "does not have a reputation for hard, tiring, and tough campaigning."[63] Despite the lobbying, however, McCarthy ranked in the top five candidates in national polls even before the elimination of Kennedy and Stevenson on July 30.

Whatever the strength of Shriver and McCarthy, through the end of July the vice-presidential race seemed to be between Humphrey and Kennedy. Kennedy consistently led in public opinion polls of Democrats (with Humphrey third, behind Stevenson), while the Minnesota senator just as consistently led in polls of Democratic functionaries (with the attorney general almost always second). After the appearance of an

[61] Max Kampelman to Hubert Humphrey, 24 July 1964, Box 76, Hubert Humphrey Papers, Minnesota State Historical Society.

[62] David Broder, "The Able and Willing Eugene McCarthy," *The New Republic*, 20 June 1964.

[63] "McCarthy as the Vice-Presidential Nominee," 23 July 1964, Box 76, Hubert Humphrey Papers, Minnesota State Historical Society.

article by Ben Bradlee in *Newsweek,* Humphrey's forces concluded, in the emphatic words of one of their memoranda, "WE MUST NOT WAIT ANY LONGER. THE TIMING IS PERFECT NOW." And the campaign had a theme that would appeal perfectly to the president – "HHH is the only potential candidate who has the guns to stop RFK."[64]

Johnson's elimination of Kennedy unintentionally derailed the Humphrey strategy, since Johnson no longer needed the one Democrat whose stature rivaled that of the attorney general. Humphrey came to understand the new realities on the evening of July 30, when the president phoned political adviser James Rowe, whom Johnson first had met in the 1930s, when Rowe was a twenty-eight-year-old lawyer for the newly created Securities and Exchange Commission. The president asked Rowe to tell Humphrey that any potential nominee needed to "understand that there ain't going to be nobody running against me for eight years." If Humphrey wanted to be considered, he needed to "make up his mind whether he's ready to go with me all the way on *my* platform, on *my* views, on *my* policies." Johnson would listen respectfully to the Minnesotan. "But when I make up my mind, I don't want to have to kiss the ass of a Vice President."[65]

Johnson then listed a second qualification – Humphrey would need to "try to put a stop to this hell-raising [with the MFDP]." Doing so would allow the president "to see that he's loyal." Johnson needed to "be *sure* that he's for me...be sure he won't be running against me four years from now."[66] Less than an hour later, Humphrey delivered the required message. "I want," the Minnesota senator told the president, "to come right to the point with you. If your judgment leads you to select me, I can assure you – unqualifiedly, personally, and with all the sincerity in my heart – complete loyalty."[67]

Even this personal humiliation and the subsequent harangues over the MFDP and the reapportionment plank did not cinch Humphrey's nomination. As the senator's staff in vain attempted to build a "full *consensus*" behind his bid, they worried about new dark horse threats, such as

[64] Ronald Stinnett to Bill Connell, 6 July 1964, Box 56, Hubert Humphrey Papers, Minnesota State Historical Society.

[65] President Johnson and James Rowe, 5:56 P.M., 30 July 1964, Tape WH6407.20, Citation #4436, LBJ Recordings.

[66] President Johnson and James Rowe, 5:56 P.M., 30 July 1964, Tape WH6407.20, Citation #4436, LBJ Recordings.

[67] President Johnson and Hubert Humphrey, 6:50 P.M., 30 July 1964, Tape WH6407.20, Citation #4441, LBJ Recordings.

Missouri senator Stuart Symington.[68] Press speculation suddenly grew rather frosty about the Minnesota senator: writing in the *Washington Star,* William S. White, arguing that "no realistic politician, in either party, really believes that any running mate can actually assist Mr. Johnson," predicted that the president would choose someone who could do him the least harm – namely, a figure not known for "extreme partisanship" on civil rights.[69]

More alarming, the president started showing signs of impatience with Humphrey – not only because of the MFDP issue but also over Humphrey's well-known tendency to talk freely with the media. After leaks occurred following a Joint Chiefs of Staff briefing with congressional leaders about the Tonkin Gulf attacks, the president fumed to Rowe, "Our friend – Hubert – is just destroying himself with his big mouth." The Minnesotan, Johnson claimed, "blabbed everything that he had heard, just like it was his personal knowledge, and almost wanted to claim credit for it." If Humphrey wanted consideration for a higher post, Johnson implied, "he ought to keep his goddamned big mouth shut on foreign affairs."[70]

Humphrey's staff correctly speculated that Johnson – if for no other reason than maintaining suspense – would not name a nominee before the convention, but they failed to recognize their chief rival for the number-two slot or just how seriously the was president considering him. Mike Mansfield, who subsequently presided over a very different type of Senate, had succeeded Johnson as majority leader. The Montana senator was a professor of East Asian history before entering politics; one of Johnson's first acts as Senate leader had been to secure for Mansfield a slot on the Foreign Relations Committee. Johnson personally liked Mansfield. But he – unfairly – disparaged his successor's skills as a legislative tactician and frequently bypassed him to work through Humphrey. The Montana senator played another important role in the early Johnson administration – that of a quiet but thoughtful critic of the administration's foreign policy. From Vietnam to Panama, Mansfield penned lengthy memoranda, which the president requested and which he always read, worrying that Johnson's foreign policy relied too much on the clichés of the Cold War.

[68] Ted Van Dyk to Bill Connell, 6 Aug. 1964, Box 56, Humphrey Papers; John Horing to Bill Connell, 6 Aug. 1964, Box 76, Hubert Humphrey Papers, Minnesota State Historical Society.

[69] *Washington Star*, 5 Aug. 1964; see also *New York Herald Tribune*, 6 Aug. 1964.

[70] President Johnson and James Rowe, 1:35 P.M., 6 Aug. 1964, Tape WH6408.09, Citation #4777, LBJ Recordings.

To the president's admiration, the majority leader generally confined his comments to private meetings or memos.[71]

Mansfield's name first received press attention from an important source, William S. White, whose July 6 column reported that the majority leader had come under consideration "in the most meaningful of ways" – Johnson himself had mentioned the Montana senator. Upon reflection, White realized, the choice made sense. Mansfield was a Catholic, a Westerner, was not perceived as a civil rights partisan like Humphrey or Kennedy, and had never seemed entirely comfortable as majority leader.[72]

The Montana senator reemerged with an unexpected intensity in the days before the Democratic convention opened. *New York Daily News* reporter Ted Lewis, among others, detected increased discussion of Mansfield in the middle of August; Mansfield even joked about the issue with the president himself – a sharp contrast to the uptight telephone exchanges between Johnson and Humphrey.[73] On the 20th, the president informed Moyers that, in his mind, the "people that are being *very*, very seriously considered" were Humphrey, McCarthy, and Mansfield. Humphrey, Johnson fretted, "hasn't got enough sense"; with his constant talking, "they'll make a full-grown communist with a bastard baby out of him before Monday."[74]

The next morning, the president started "philosophizing a little bit" with his aide Ken O'Donnell. "Hubert," he guessed, "would stir up the liberals more and get more applause from the Negroes, and get a little bigger hand from the liberal columnists, the New Deal and maybe a good deal of the New Frontier than Mansfield. On the other hand, Mansfield has the respect and no one really hates him." In addition, Mansfield was the only candidate that could improve the ticket in the Rocky Mountain states, where Humphrey's affiliation with the ADA would prove a handicap.[75]

Placing Mansfield on the ticket, moreover, could create a win-win situation. The president believed "that Hubert would make the best

[71] Richard A. Baker and Roger Davidson, eds., *First among Equals: Outstanding Senate Leaders of the Twentieth Century* (Washington, DC: Congressional Quarterly, 1991), pp. 144–69.

[72] *Washington Star*, 6 July 1964.

[73] President Johnson and Mike Mansfield, 12:36 P.M., 18 Aug. 1964, Tape WH6408.27, Citation #5014, LBJ Recordings; *New York Daily News*, 14 Aug. 1964.

[74] President Johnson and Bill Moyers, 10:00 P.M., 21 Aug. 1964, Tape WH6408.32, Citation #5115, LBJ Recordings.

[75] President Johnson and Ken O'Donnell, 10:46 A.M., 21 Aug. 1964, Tape WH6408.30, Citation #5063, LBJ Recordings.

[Senate majority] leader that we could possibly have" – a job that he, personally, considered more important than the vice presidency. Viewed from this perspective, the question became not which of the two would make a better vice president but which of the two would make the better majority leader. Johnson reasoned that Humphrey, if majority leader rather than vice president, could still campaign for the party; and while the Minnesotan would lose the opportunity to build up stature, it was unlikely that Mansfield, who would be 69 at the time, would run for president in 1972. From the perspective of bettering the overall campaign effort, the president concluded "that overall you'd get more campaigning out of Mansfield being on the ticket with Humphrey as leader." If he were named Johnson's running mate, Mansfield "might make a pretty good television appearance. He makes a pretty good speech. He's a pretty judicious fellow. He's a pretty careful fellow. He's pretty strong on peace" – of critical importance, since that was an issue "that's showing up in all our polls."[76]

On another delicate matter, "Mansfield would give us an awfully good answer to the Catholic question." Johnson claimed he did not want to make the selection based on religion, but he had to consider practical ramifications. The president certainly did not want Catholic Democrats to say, "Well, we had our man. They wouldn't let him serve but three years, and got him killed. Then, by God, they went in, they picked out a Protestant." Everyone to whom he spoke assured him that his running mate's religious affiliation did not matter, but "saying and really knowing is something else, two months ahead of time."[77] David Broder captured the consensus of the key correspondents in Atlantic City when he wrote, on the eve of the convention, that Johnson had narrowed the vice-presidential field in such a way to increase the likelihood of Mansfield's selection; indeed, the *Star* reported on August 21 that Mansfield's name "has shot to the top of the list."[78]

[76] President Johnson and Ken O'Donnell, 10:46 A.M., 21 Aug. 1964, Tape WH6408.30, Citation #5063, LBJ Recordings.

[77] President Johnson and Ken O'Donnell, 10:46 A.M., 21 Aug. 1964, Tape WH6408.30, Citation #5063, LBJ Recordings.

[78] *Washington Star*, 21 Aug. 1964, 22 Aug. 1964. For contemporary appraisals of the Mansfield candidacy, see Walter Lippmann quoted in McGeorge Bundy to President Johnson, 21 Aug. 1964, Box 4, Bundy NSF, Memos to the President, Lyndon B. Johnson Presidential Library; James Rowe quoted in President Johnson and Walter Jenkins, 8:30 P.M., 21 Aug. 1964, Tape WH6408.32, Citation #5107, LBJ Recordings; *Baltimore Sun*, 21 Aug. 1964; *New York Times*, 23 Aug. 1964.

In the weeks before the convention, then, the president confronted a host of political issues he heretofore had used his nonpolitical posture to avoid. The MFDP and reapportionment planks threatened to revive the traditional distrust the president had faced from liberals, weaken his already perilous political standing in the South, or perhaps both. Johnson's elimination of Robert Kennedy from the vice-presidential race was less than graceful. And the urban riots could only intensify the Northern backlash.

Atlantic City in 1964 was the most improbable – and unsuitable – host of any major-party convention in the twentieth century. Correspondents covering the convention dismissed the city as "the original Bay of Pigs."[79] *The Reporter* acidly commented that "the Democrats will not be able to surpass Atlantic City unless they hold their next convention on a Ferris wheel."[80] Delegates complained about poor accommodations, bad service, and high prices.[81] To the *Times*' food critic Craig Claiborne, "If ever an award is granted to towns with the largest quota of mediocre restaurants, this village is cordially invited to extend its civic hand."[82] Surveying the convention after its conclusion, a Johnson operative detected one area of unanimous agreement: "dislike for everything connected with Atlantic City."[83]

The social center of the convention was Perle Mesta, the self-described "Hostess with the Mostess." The widow of a steel manufacturer, Mesta had been a women's rights activist in the interwar years. She gradually drifted into the political and social milieu of wartime Washington, where she established a permanent residence in 1940 – the same year that she changed her party affiliation to Democrat. She was an early patron of Harry Truman, and after her work for the Democratic finance committee, she handled the social arrangements for the 1948 Inaugural Ball. A stint as ambassador to Luxembourg enhanced her standing, and throughout the 1950s she was the leading hostess in the Capitol – and a favorite of Majority Leader Johnson. In 1960, however, after Mesta endorsed first Johnson and then Richard Nixon, she was left "out in the cold" when

[79] Theodore H. White, *The Making of the President 1964* (New York: Atheneum, 1965), p. 276.

[80] *The Reporter*, 10 Sept. 1964.

[81] *Wall Street Journal*, 26 Aug. 1964.

[82] *New York Times*, 25 Aug. 1964.

[83] Bob Hunter to Douglass Cater, 3 Sept. 1964, Box 83, WHCF-PL, Lyndon B. Johnson Presidential Library.

John Kennedy moved Washington's social life in a different direction. But, as delegates discovered in Atlantic City, "Perle's back on top again."[84]

Mesta rented a mansion two miles from the convention hall, into which she moved her butler, two maids, a party cook, a pair of chauffeurs, and a press secretary. She held one party each evening throughout the convention; her opening night gala cost $150,000 and featured an exclusive guest list of 200.[85] To ensure that her guests would not miss any important events at the convention, Mesta chartered buses designated "Perle's Party Line."[86] To the *Christian Science Monitor,* Mesta's gatherings "might well be the convention hall itself."[87]

Surveying events inside of the convention hall, so massive it had previously hosted high school football games, Charles Bartlett, writing in the *Washington Star,* felt that "for the first time in years, the Democrats will be meeting in an atmosphere of stupefying dullness."[88] The hall featured 87,000 circuit miles of broadcast cable, 19,700 feet of video cable, 3,000 telephones, and 250 Teletype machines. Each state delegation could pick up a telephone and consult party operatives and the convention center. To accommodate television, the majority of the delegates had only a partial view of the platform; 20 percent could not see the speaker at all.[89]

Johnson, meanwhile, was omnipresent. The stage settings, selected by the president, were two 40-foot portraits of Johnson himself. The convention song was Johnson's choice – "Hello, Lyndon," sung to the tune of "Hello, Dolly."[90] (Some critics suggested that "Lola," rather than "Dolly," would have represented a better adaptation – as in "Whatever Lyndon wants, Lyndon gets," parodying a song from the Broadway musical *Damn Yankees.*)[91] Outside of the convention hall, vendors sold Johnson cowboy hats, "LBJ" ashtrays, presidential cuff links, and "LBJ" buttons.[92] Two hundred fifty "Johnson Girls," decked out in red, white, and blue belts and white straw hats with red, white, and blue trim, served as hostesses.[93] *New Yorker* writer Richard Rovere suggested credits for the

[84] *New York Herald-Tribune*, 12 Aug. 1964.
[85] *Washington Post*, 24 Aug. 1964.
[86] *New York Times*, 23 Aug. 1964.
[87] *Christian Science Monitor*, 25 Aug. 1964.
[88] *Washington Star*, 21 Aug. 1964.
[89] *New York Times*, 23 Aug. 1964, 25 Aug. 1964.
[90] *Time*, 4 Sept. 1964.
[91] Leonard Reinsch, *Getting Elected: From Radio and Roosevelt to Television and Reagan* (New York: Hippocrene Books, 1988), p. 204.
[92] *New York Times*, 25 Aug. 1964.
[93] *Christian Science Monitor*, 25 Aug. 1964.

FIGURE 4-1. Images of President Johnson dominate the 1964 Democratic National Convention platform. © Courtesy of the Lyndon Baines Johnson Presidential Library.

gathering: "Idea by Lyndon Johnson, directed by Lyndon Johnson, and starring Lyndon Johnson."[94]

Stray signs of the opposition did appear. Goldwater's campaign purchased a giant billboard hovering over the boardwalk, blazed with the candidate's slogan: "In Your Heart, You Know He's Right." (One enterprising Democrat put a sign reading "Yes, Extreme Right" below the Arizonan's advertisement.)[95] An airplane occasionally flew over the city carrying signs such as "put the Holy Bible back in our schools" or "put a decency plank in the platform." Union boss Jimmy Hoffa ordered a large sign placed on a Teamsters' truck demanding "Investigate the Justice Department."[96]

In only one significant way did Johnson's domination of convention events go astray. Greeting reporters before the opening of the event, Mike Mansfield announced that under no circumstances would he accept the vice-presidential nomination. Perhaps Johnson would have taken the expected route and chosen Humphrey in any case. But the majority leader's action foreclosed the possibility of a surprise choice, something that had seemed increasingly possible in the week before the convention started.[97]

The Mansfield announcement stood out because it clashed with the theme of presidential control throughout the city, as Johnson did everything he could to ensure that things in Atlantic City would remain calm. The MFDP issue remained the most serious problem. Eight Southern senators already had absented themselves from the convention, and the president had no desire to see further walkouts.[98] "Let's just reason this," Johnson said to United Auto Workers chief Walter Reuther as he began his workday on the 24th – but the problem, as Reuther recognized, "is you're dealing with people who are so emotional they can't be rational about these things."[99] And that emotionalism, the president worried, could alienate ethnic Democrats, lest MFDP activists, whose supporters from civil rights groups were holding a sit-in outside of the convention fall, create an image of a Democratic Party controlled by blacks.[100]

[94] Richard Rovere, "Letter from Atlantic City," *The New Yorker*, 5 Sept. 1964.
[95] White, *Making of the President 1964*, p. 277.
[96] *New York Times*, 24 Aug. 1964.
[97] *New York Times*, 25 Aug. 1964.
[98] *Time*, 4 Sept. 1964; see also *Wall Street Journal*, 24 Aug. 1964.
[99] President Johnson and Walter Reuther, 8:46 A.M., 24 Aug. 1964, Tape WH6408.34, Citation #5140, LBJ Recordings.
[100] *New York Times*, 25 Aug. 1964.

Credentials Committee Chairman Dave Lawrence found himself consistently outmaneuvered by Oregon Representative Edith Green, who introduced the MFDP's proposal. The "Green Compromise" called for seating any MFDP delegates and Mississippi regulars who took a loyalty oath to support the party's nominee and then dividing the state delegation's vote between the regular and MFDP contingents. Only three members of the regular delegation seemed likely to sign a loyalty oath, and so this plan was not much of a compromise at all.[101] From Atlantic City, DNC chairman John Bailey sneered, "That Mrs. Green is a *bitch*."[102]

On the morning of the 25th, the president awoke to a string of less than flattering reviews of the convention's first day. In an editorial that particularly infuriated him, the *New York Times* denounced the party's "pallid platform," a document "that blurs the nature of the contest, instead of highlighting the differences in basic philosophy that make this year's presidential campaign so different from any in the last three decades."[103]

The editorial captured the mood of many Democrats in the hall. Erwin Canham, the savvy political editor of the *Christian Science Monitor,* found the Democrats to be "uneasy and uncertain." Democrats sensed that civil rights and Goldwater's nomination had made the fundamental issues in the campaign "not really political" but instead "moral, sociological, and very emotional." Such matters, he understood, "are not questions politicians deal with very well."[104]

As the pressure increased, Johnson showed signs of strain. The chaos surrounding the MFDP fight, fatigue following a grueling battle for the civil rights bill, and the president's own ultra-sensitivity to criticism combined to produce indecision in Johnson's mind about whether he should even go forward with the fight. The First Lady had detected something amiss for some time – on July 6 she had confided to her diary that "Lyndon wants to get out." But, she recognized, "there *is* no way out now."[105]

Faced with the tumult of the convention, and with fatigue exaggerating his customary streak of self-pity, Johnson wrote out a statement of withdrawal. "I have a desire to unite people," the president mused to press secretary George Reedy, but "the South is against me and the

[101] *Washington Star*, 24 Aug. 1964.

[102] President Johnson and John Bailey, 9:22 A.M., 25 Aug. 1964, Tape WH6408.35, Citation #5173, LBJ Recordings.

[103] *New York Times*, 25 Aug. 1964.

[104] *Christian Science Monitor*, 25 Aug. 1964.

[105] Lady Bird Johnson, *A White House Diary* (New York: Holt, Rinehart, Winston, 1970), entry for 6 July 1964, p. 175.

North's against me, and the Negroes are against me, and the press really doesn't have an affection for me."[106] Robert Kennedy (of course) was to blame: "I rather think that this Freedom Party was born in the Justice Department." Johnson complained that people had a "mistaken judgment of him" – he wanted not "great power" but "great solace, and a little love."[107] For a man with such a temperament, he lamented, the barrage of attacks was unbearable.

Whether or not he was ever serious in this plan, Johnson quickly abandoned it, with a decisive intervention from the First Lady. Lady Bird wrote her "beloved" that "to step out now would be wrong for your country, and I can see nothing but a lonely wasteland for your future. Your friends would be frozen in embarrassed silence and your enemies would be jeering."[108]

Thus fortified, the president returned to the issue at hand. As the Credentials Committee showed no hope of resolving the MFDP question, Johnson took more decisive action. He instructed Lawrence to create a special subcommittee to hammer out a compromise. Delegates from Georgia and Texas balanced two partisans of the MFDP. The fifth member of the subcommittee was Minnesota attorney general Walter Mondale, a Humphrey protégé and Humphrey's likely replacement in the Senate should the seat become vacant. Having failed to deliver a compromise thus far, Humphrey would receive one last chance. Mary McGrory in the *Washington Star* described the Minnesota senator as "looking like a presidential errand boy as he scurried around trying to make peace in the vital civil rights strife."[109]

The Majority Whip succeeded. Late in the afternoon of August 25, the subcommittee voted 3–2 on a compromise, with Mondale casting the deciding ballot. First, the convention would seat the regular Mississippi delegates, provided that they agreed to sign a loyalty pledge. Second, all delegations to future Democratic national conventions would have to sign a loyalty oath and assure that voters in the state, "regardless of race, color, creed, or national origin, will have the opportunity to participate fully in party affairs." Third, two MFDP delegates, Aaron Henry

[106] President Johnson and George Reedy, 11:06 A.M., 25 Aug. 1964, Tape WH6408.36, Citation #5176, LBJ Recordings.

[107] President Johnson and Walter Jenkins, 11:23 A.M., 25 Aug. 1964, Tape WH6408.36, Citation #5177, LBJ Recordings.

[108] Jeff Shesol, *Mutual Contempt: Lyndon Johnson, Robert Kennedy, and the Feud That Defined a Decade* (New York: W. W. Norton, 1997), p. 218.

[109] *Washington Star*, 27 Aug. 1964.

and Edward King, would receive slots as delegates-at-large. Finally, the remainder of the MFDP delegation would be welcomed to the convention floor as "honored guests."[110] The full Credentials Committee then adopted the compromise. Rauh and Green agreed not to file a minority report; in exchange, they received the right to insert into the transcript of the convention's proceedings a minority statement. As the convention opened for its evening session, Lawrence presented the plan to the delegates, who passed it without a roll call vote.

Audible nays, however, were detected on the motion.[111] Although Rauh supported the compromise, most in the MFDP did not: Fannie Lou Hamer stated that she had not come to Atlantic City to sit in the back of the bus. (In response, Humphrey scoffed, "The President will not allow that illiterate woman to speak from the floor of the convention.")[112] Meanwhile, the compromise – the minimum possible that liberals found acceptable – still did not eliminate the threat of a Southern walkout, since it would seat some MFDP delegates.

Johnson understood this problem after a discussion with one of the key players in the 1964 political scene, Georgia governor Carl Sanders. The president frequently had spoken in glowing terms about Sanders, a reformer elected governor of the Peach State at age 37. Johnson hoped that figures like Sanders and John Connally would supply the next generation of leadership to the Southern Democratic Party. Sanders, moreover, had attracted national attention when he named to Georgia's convention delegation two black men – Leroy Johnson, the state's first black state legislator in the twentieth century, and A. T. Walden, an Atlanta lawyer. When asked about his decision, he commented, "This is not a social club. This is a political organization and it is right and proper that we have a cross-section of the voters of the state represented."[113]

The question remained, however, whether Sanders – or Connally – could provide leadership for a new generation of Southern Democrats. Connally's feuds with Texas liberals, his hostility to organized labor, and his attack against the public accommodations provision of the Civil Rights Act recalled an earlier generation of Southern Democrats, not a progressive post-Johnson future. Sanders offered more promise. He had, in many ways, staked his own political career on his identification with the national party and with Johnson in particular: it was no coincidence that

[110] *Congressional Quarterly Weekly Report*, 28 Aug. 1964, p. 1960.
[111] *Washington Post*, 26 Aug. 1964.
[112] Branch, *Pillar of Fire*, p. 470.
[113] *Congressional Quarterly Weekly Report*, 31 July 1964, p. 1649.

Lady Bird invited Sanders to sit by her side during Johnson's first speech before Congress. On economic issues, especially education, Sanders compiled a strongly liberal record. Behind the scenes he worked to assemble a "coalition of the reasonable states of the South," led by Connally, South Carolina governor Donald Russell, Florida governor Farris Bryant, and liberals within the Tennessee Democratic Party, to keep part of the region in the Democratic column.[114]

But Sanders displayed much less willingness to embrace the civil rights agenda than Johnson. Even before the MFDP controversy emerged, Sanders argued that the Democrats should consider civil rights questions "more the responsibilities of the local government." He did not want to make civil rights a major issue in the 1964 campaign and urged Johnson to promise that "the federal government is not going to be the one who's going to try to just deliberately cram civil rights down somebody's throat."[115] In Atlantic City, meanwhile, the Georgia governor informed Johnson staffers that a compromise allowing the seating of any MFDP delegates would give him no choice but to depart the convention. "It looks like we're turning the Democratic Party over to the Negroes," Sanders complained to Johnson. "All we've done there is put the Negro – Martin Luther King and a few of them – we've just given in and letting them decide who's going to be the delegates to the Democratic convention."[116]

Johnson greeted Sanders's apostasy with frustration. "The last people" he expected to have objected was "the South, because we're seating Mississippi. We're giving them every vote they've got." After hearing that Bull Connor, chairman of the Alabama delegation, objected to the requirement that all delegates take an oath of loyalty to the party, the president told Sanders, "I'd come up there myself, walk out naked and take [the oath], if it would ease Bull Connor's pressure any." From his perspective in Washington, Mississippi and Alabama had "caused more goddamned trouble and done less for it than any two states I ever heard of in my life to the party that they're supposed to like."[117]

[114] President Johnson and Carl Sanders, 12:30 P.M., 24 July 1964, Tape WH6407.14, Citation #4328, LBJ Recordings.

[115] President Johnson and Carl Sanders, 12:30 P.M., 24 July 1964, Tape WH6407.14, Citation #4328, LBJ Recordings.

[116] President Johnson and Carl Sanders, 4:32 P.M., 25 Aug. 1964, Tape WH6408.37, Citation #5183, LBJ Recordings.

[117] President Johnson and Carl Sanders, 4:32 P.M., 25 Aug. 1964, Tape WH6408.37, Citation #5183, LBJ Recordings.

But Sanders continued to protest, advancing a legalistic argument that the MFDP delegates were not registered Democrats in the state and therefore had no right to a seat at the party's national convention. Johnson had enough. "They're Democrats," he bellowed. "And by God, they tried to attend the convention, and pistols kept them out! These people went in and *begged* to go and participate in the conventions. They've got half the population. They won't let them. They lock them out!" In his opinion a good case existed "to say that the state of Mississippi wouldn't let a Negro come into their damn convention, and therefore they violated the law and wouldn't let them vote," and, "by God, they oughtn't to be seated." But the compromise had explicitly avoided making that case, and therefore Johnson could not see "how they can raise hell – have their cake and eat it too – and just say, 'By God, I'm going to be a dog in the manger. I'm going to have all I got, every vote that the state of Mississippi's got, and then, by God, I'm going to bark if somebody across the hall get a couple.' "[118]

The president pled with Sanders to look to the future. "You and I," he informed the Georgia governor,

> just can't survive our political modern life with these goddamned fellows down there that are eating them for breakfast every morning. They've got to quit that. And they've got to let them vote. And they've got to let them shave. And they've got to let them eat, and things like that. And they don't do it. However much we love [Senators] Jim Eastland and John Stennis, they get a governor like Ross Barnett, and he's messing around there with Wallace, and they won't let one [black] man go in a precinct convention. We've got to put a stop to that, because that's just like the old days, by God, when they wouldn't let them go in and cast a vote of any kind. You've put a stop to it in your state. But we're going to ignore that. We're going to say, "Hell, yes, you did it. You're wrong. You violated the '57 law, and you violated the '60 law, and you violated the '64 law, but we're going to seat you – every damn one of you."

His voice dripping with sarcasm, Johnson concluded his hypothetical statement to the Mississippians: "You lily white babies, we're going to salute you."[119]

With strong doubts coming from Sanders, it was unsurprising that less moderate Southerners reacted with more hostility. One Louisiana Democrat remarked that "Johnson has become the focal point of all the

[118] President Johnson and Carl Sanders, 4:32 P.M., 25 Aug. 1964, Tape WH6408.37, Citation #5183, LBJ Recordings.

[119] President Johnson and Carl Sanders, 4:32 P.M., 25 Aug. 1964, Tape WH6408.37, Citation #5183, LBJ Recordings.

South's animosity toward Washington."[120] Claude Sitton commented that the MFDP controversy had shown that Johnson, "although a Southerner, can expect little more than lukewarm support, if that," in the fall campaign; the *New York Times* reporter presciently anticipated a two-party South that would feature an overwhelmingly white Republican Party and a Democratic coalition of blacks and some white moderates. For the present, on questions dealing with civil rights, many Southerners believed "they have been told, in effect, to accept the national party's position on these matters or get out."[121]

If Johnson could not retain the support of a figure like Sanders, what future existed for the Southern Democratic Party in the post–Civil Rights Act era? The president had ruminated on this problem ever since he signed the bill, but he had not yet confronted its full consequences. Southern resistance to the MFDP compromise forced Johnson to come to grips with just how powerfully the legislation would shake the foundations of the Southern Democratic Party. And as he did so, he began to entertain the possibility of employing a different approach altogether to the Southern question in the campaign.

With leading Southern moderates unwilling or unable to help, Johnson sought to minimize any further convention disruption by turning to an unlikely ally – Jim Eastland. Despite his hostility to civil rights, Eastland had a reputation as, in Bobby Baker's words, "the politician's politician. You could make deals with him."[122] The president now hoped that his former colleague could deliver. Other Mississippi politicians certainly had not. Upon hearing of the MFDP deal, Governor Paul Johnson hinted at a break with the national party, arguing, "Mississippi's debt to the national Democratic Party has now been paid in full." Johnson's predecessor, Ross Barnett, praised the governor for "formally and finally severing relations between Mississippi and the national Democratic Party."[123]

The president pressed Eastland to persuade his fellow state Democrats to recognize that the result was "a victory for our side." More pragmatically, he reminded the Mississippi senator that "this is a long road, and we're going to be here a long time."[124] Just off the phone with Eastland,

[120] *Wall Street Journal*, 24 Aug. 1964.

[121] *New York Times*, 26 Aug. 1964.

[122] Bobby Baker, *Wheeling and Dealing: Confessions of a Capitol Hill Insider* (New York: W. W. Norton, 1978), p. 100.

[123] *New York Times*, 26 Aug. 1964.

[124] President Johnson and James Eastland, later joined by Sidney Livingston, 7:45 P.M., 25 Aug. 1964, Tape WH6408.38, Citation #5193, LBJ Recordings.

Johnson reported on matters with his aide Walter Jenkins, who was coordinating events in Atlantic City. Word soon emerged that four members of the regular Mississippi delegation – Doug Wynn (the president's godson), Judge C. R. Holliday, Fred Berger, and Mrs. Milton McMullan – would sign the loyalty pledge.[125]

MFDP activists did their best to frustrate the president's efforts. After entering the convention hall themselves, some liberal delegates slipped their credentials to MFDP members waiting outside. In an era with far different security requirements than our own, MFDP then used these credentials to reach the convention floor. The president ordered security tightened after reports that Assistant Secretary of State for African Affairs G. Mennen Williams was among those who assisted the MFDP. "That son of a bitch," Johnson fumed. He ordered Bill Moyers "to tell your people – just say that 'you've damn near elected Goldwater.' You ought to call your preachers and tell them. Please tell them to tell [James] Farmer and them to *please* behave, because it's just – the backlash is something awful here."[126]

With the compromise executed, the phony credentials problem resolved, and no signs of a general walkout apparent, Johnson made sure that those in the regular delegation willing to stand up for him would not be forgotten. Press reaction to the compromise was generally favorable: the *Washington Post* hailed Johnson for helping the party to "finally rid itself of the divisive civil rights issue which has plagued every national convention beginning with 1948."[127] William S. White, however, best captured the president's sentiments: "about the best that can be said for the Mississippi 'compromise' is that things might have been worse – worse, that is, from the partisan point of view."[128]

The resolution of the MFDP crisis intensified what struck many observers as the troubled mood in the Democratic convention. To the *Wall Street Journal*'s Al Otten, Northern liberals "seem to be suffering more than their usual portion of torment": while committed to Johnson's election, they did "not particularly trust or like Lyndon," whose pragmatism and compromising approach alarmed them. Otten, for one, considered this suspicion justified. The president "obviously lacks the style that

[125] President Johnson and Walter Jenkins, later joined by John Connally, 8:25 P.M., 25 Aug. 1964, Tape WH6408.38, Citation #5197, LBJ Recordings.

[126] President Johnson and Jack Valenti, later joined by Bill Moyers, 12:50 P.M., 26 Aug. 1964, Tape WH6408.39, Citation #5221, LBJ Recordings.

[127] *Washington Post*, 27 Aug. 1964.

[128] *Washington Star*, 26 Aug. 1964.

appeals to the liberal," since "he is flamboyant, corny, unpolished." On a personal level, Johnson demanded "complete loyalty and subjugation; he is an overwhelming egoist."[129]

In such an environment it was little surprise that the president's chief rival within the party, Robert Kennedy, turned his attention elsewhere. In New York Senator Kenneth Keating, a moderate Republican, was up for re-election in November. The attorney general grew up in the state, New York's nominal residency requirement would allow him to file for the Senate without worrying about a possible legal challenge, and state Democrats had struggled to come up with a viable candidate. Former New York governor Averell Harriman strongly backed a Kennedy bid; New York mayor Robert Wagner, Jr., also did so, albeit much less enthusiastically.[130]

Despite his rival's Senate candidacy, Johnson's concerns about the possibility of Kennedy stampeding the convention continued until virtually the moment the president received the nomination. Ken O'Donnell recalled that Johnson "just lived in mortal fear of what was going to happen to him at that convention"; both O'Donnell and special assistant Larry O'Brien found Johnson's concerns hard to explain.[131] At the president's request, his FBI contact Deke DeLoach and an FBI team arrived in Atlantic City posing as NBC reporters, ostensibly to guard against unrest, but actually to help "in bottling up Robert Kennedy – that is, in reporting on the activities of Bobby Kennedy." Forty-four pages of what DeLoach termed "vital tidbits" of information were eventually passed to Jenkins, reporting on this and other nonexistent threats.[132] Even so, Johnson complained that he was forced to sit around the White House and "let Bobby and them dominate that convention. That's what the stories are today. You know, he's got all these Irish Catholic girls writing for him," generating headlines such as "Bobby Sweeps Atlantic City" and "Kennedy Magic."[133]

Only in Johnson's eyes, however, was Robert Kennedy the central story of the convention. To Evans and Novak, "the Outs of 1960 are

129 *Wall Street Journal*, 26 Aug. 1964; see also *Christian Science Monitor*, 27 Aug. 1964.

130 Shesol, *Mutual Contempt*, p. 213.

131 Ken O'Donnell oral history, Lyndon B. Johnson Presidential Library; Larry O'Brien oral history, Lyndon B. Johnson Presidential Library.

132 Arthur Schlesinger, Jr., *Robert Kennedy and His Times* (Boston: Houghton Mifflin, 1978), pp. 662–4.

133 President Johnson and Richard Nelson, later joined by Bill Moyers, 12:05 P.M., 26 Aug. 1964, Tape WH6408.39, Citation #5216, LBJ Recordings. The president was obviously referring to Mary McGrory.

fast becoming the Ins of 1964."[134] *Wall Street Journal* editor Vermont Royster went back further in time than the Outs of 1960. In his opinion the dominant historical presence in Atlantic City was that of Franklin Roosevelt: "President Johnson's handling of this convention shows the teaching and influence of his first political mentor." The "Roosevelt touch" manifested itself in Johnson's preference for consensus, his pragmatism, his desire to avoid controversial matters on the convention floor.[135] Erwin Canham agreed, but wondered whether Johnson approached the Roosevelt standard – since as far as he could determine, "efforts to smooth over the civil rights issue at this convention have been completely unsuccessful." Johnson's political challenge exceeded that of Roosevelt in 1940, since the president faced a campaign in which "mood seems to be dominant" and in which traditional politics would not work. Johnson needed to discover a "counter-mood," but Canham doubted he could succeed.[136] The *Christian Science Monitor* editor underestimated the president's political ability.

The critical aspect to Johnson's production of a "counter-mood" came in his ability to coin a new word in the political lexicon: "frontlash." Pollster Oliver Quayle actually had first used the term in the spring, to describe Republican voters attracted by Johnson's moderate economic policies.[137] But with Goldwater's nomination, the concept became much more powerful, as moderate Republicans from the Northeast, Northwest, and Midwest, repulsed by their nominee's views on civil rights and nuclear strategy, began to look anew on the Democratic Party as an option. Even when he arrived in Atlantic City, the *Los Angeles Times'* Richard Wilson found Democrats unconcerned about the backlash. "Instead," he observed, "they confidently say they hear what they call the much larger crack of a moderate Republican 'frontlash' against Barry Goldwater."[138] If the MFDP controversy had lasting effects on the president's standing in the South, these frontlash voters suddenly loomed as much more important – and Johnson wanted to be sure that the press knew that he would tailor his campaign to appeal to them. He instructed aides to distribute copies of polls showing one-third of Republicans favoring him "to all the networks. Try to get some of our people like [John] Connally and the others to point out, then, what the

[134] *New York Herald-Tribune*, 26 Aug. 1964.
[135] *Wall Street Journal*, 26 Aug. 1964.
[136] *Christian Science Monitor*, 26 Aug. 1964.
[137] White, *Making of the President 1964*, p. 257.
[138] *Los Angeles Times*, 24 Aug. 1964.

FIGURE 4-2. President Johnson with pollster Oliver Quayle. The president was obsessed with polls: later in the campaign, when he discovered that he had polls from every state except New Mexico and Alaska, he demanded surveys of the two lagging states. © Courtesy of the Lyndon Baines Johnson Presidential Library. Photo by Yoichi Okamoto.

polls show on the frontlash. Use nothing but the word frontlash; quit talking about backlash. Tell him to really stampede that convention with frontlashes."[139]

The frontlash propaganda campaign certainly paid dividends. From Atlantic City, David Broder reported that the "'frontlash' idea" was the talk of political strategists.[140] Richard Wilson termed the Democrats "the political party of stability and responsibility and calm judgment," so much so that "it could almost be imagined that this was the Republican Party of the past." This development, of course, would make "it easier for moderate-minded Republicans to vote for President Johnson."[141]

On the other hand, Johnson critics, on both the left and the right, greeted the new approach skeptically. Journalist Joe Kraft argued that "together, the two parties have moved the axis of American politics not only westwards, southwards, and rightwards, but also about five to ten years backwards." The president's refusal to address key liberal issues – reapportionment, the MFDP, supporting democratic regimes abroad – showed that the "frontlash" movement would transform the Democrats into what earlier could have passed for moderate Republicans.[142]

The frontlash strategy required deemphasizing the link between Johnson and the Democratic Party. Thomas O'Neill expressed amazement at the "eagerness of rough and ready Democrats to accept without a murmur a strategic platform." This development, the *Baltimore Sun* columnist suggested, reflected the party's "electoral uneasiness," despite the favorable polls. Even the campaign's new slogan – "LBJ All the Way" – made an orphan of the party identification. The frontlash approach seemed geared to transform the Democrats into an anti-Goldwater party rather than an organization with positive political principles.[143]

In this sense the president was a political generation ahead of his time. Just as Bill Clinton and Tony Blair, in the 1990s, attempted to craft a "Third Way" between 1930s liberalism and free-market conservatism, Johnson, too, wanted to fashion a Democratic Party that would base its philosophy on stimulating economic growth rather than attacking the corporate elite, while simultaneously focusing more on social issues. Unlike Clinton and Blair, however, Johnson's "Third Way" – or frontlash – was more a

[139] President Johnson and Richard Nelson, later joined by Bill Moyers, 12:05 P.M., 26 Aug. 1964, Tape WH6408.39, Citation #5216, LBJ Recordings.

[140] *Washington Star*, 28 Aug. 1964.

[141] *Los Angeles Times*, 28 Aug. 1964.

[142] *Washington Star*, 28 Aug. 1964; see also *New York Daily News*, 27 Aug. 1964.

[143] *Baltimore Sun*, 26 Aug. 1964.

political strategy than a committed ideological approach, explaining the difficulty in its implementation.

Moreover, Johnson confronted a much more powerful liberal movement than did his reform-minded successors in the 1990s. Given the suspicion with which many national liberals still viewed him, selecting Humphrey as his running mate represented one way for Johnson to reaffirm his faith in traditional Democratic principles. As Ted Lewis observed, by this stage, all of the vice-presidential possibilities had "been pawns in a most cruel political game," which had lasted so long that "even the delegates got bored with trying to figure out whom President Johnson wanted for the second spot."[144]

Johnson decided to end the charade by tipping off the White House media to his selection. He invited reporters for a walk, which turned into quite a hike – 15 laps of the White House, or nearly four miles, lasting 95 minutes in 90-degree heat.[145] Afterwards, journalists accompanied Johnson to his living quarters in the White House, where he undressed in front of them and revealed that he had invited Humphrey and Connecticut senator Thomas Dodd to fly down from Atlantic City to the White House. Since no one considered Dodd a serious contender for the nomination, it was clear Humphrey would be the selection. At 3:25 P.M., the Minnesota senator left Atlantic City for the trip to Washington. In the *Christian Science Monitor,* George Sperling reported that Humphrey "seemed happier than a bouncing beagle" with the news.[146]

The question now became how to handle the announcement to the delegates, as well as Johnson's formal receipt of his own nomination. The president had initially planned to address the convention via a large closed-circuit connection from the White House, which would have created the jarring live image of Johnson, flanked by two 40-foot-tall banners of Johnson overlooking the delegates.[147] As it was, Dean Burch mocked the convention as "old faces presenting old ideas with the baleful eye of Lyndon Johnson looking down disapprovingly over the whole proceedings."[148] Then Richard Daley suggested a departure from tradition, urging the president to make an unannounced visit to Atlantic City

[144] *New York Daily News*, 24 Aug. 1964, 27 Aug. 1964.

[145] *Time*, 4 Sept. 1964.

[146] *Christian Science Monitor*, 28 Aug. 1964.

[147] President Johnson and Pierre Salinger, 9:18 P.M., 25 Aug. 1964, Tape WH6408.38, Citation #5205, LBJ Recordings.

[148] *Washington Post,* 26 Aug. 1964.

to accept the nomination in person.[149] Overruling his advisers, Johnson accepted Daley's recommendation and set out for New Jersey.

At about the same time that the president left Washington on the evening of August 26, the roll call of the state delegations began in Atlantic City. Johnson had meticulously planned the nominating process. Governors John Connally and Pat Brown delivered his principal nomination speeches, with four others seconding the nomination. The president had selected the last delegate to second his nomination earlier that afternoon, telling Bill Moyers he wanted a younger woman to perform the task. Moyers struggled to come up with a name, but Johnson pressed the issue. "Christ, almighty," he complained. "There's bound to be some good-looking woman in one of those delegations up there."[150] Moyers eventually settled on an "attractive" Florida delegate, Mrs. Lloyd Damsey, whose husband was president-elect of the American Medical Association. (The *Washington Post* described Damsey as a "pretty brunette.")[151] As Connally spoke, the president arrived in Atlantic City and confirmed that he would choose Humphrey as his running mate. He then began a slow procession to the convention hall itself. At 11:03 P.M., the convention nominated Johnson by acclamation; 15 minutes later, the president entered the convention hall to say that he had picked Humphrey as "the best qualified man to assume the office of the President."[152] Humphrey was nominated by acclamation at 12:24 A.M.

For the president, the passing of midnight had ushered in his fifty-sixth birthday, which he enjoyed in style. Johnson lingered in the convention hall after his appearance to chat with members of the Texas delegation, causing what the *New York Times* described as a "crushing mob scene" near the speaker's podium; once or twice, the president was nearly carried off his feet. A great fireworks display on the boardwalk culminated in a firework production of a 600-square-foot portrait of Johnson; an event emceed by actor Paul Newman featured performances by singers and Democratic activists Barbra Streisand and Peter, Paul, and Mary.[153]

The final day of the convention was dominated by the three towering figures in the post-assassination Democratic Party – Lyndon Johnson,

[149] President Johnson and Richard Daley, 5:55 P.M., 26 Aug. 1964, Tape WH6408.40, Citation #5231, LBJ Recordings.

[150] President Johnson and Jack Valenti, later including Bill Moyers, 12:50 P.M., 26 Aug. 1964, Tape WH6408.39, Citation #5221, LBJ Recordings.

[151] *Washington Post*, 27 Aug. 1964.

[152] *Congressional Quarterly Weekly Report*, 26 Aug. 1964, p. 2017.

[153] *New York Times*, 28 Aug. 1964.

FIGURE 4-3. President Johnson with Hubert Humphrey at the Democratic National Convention platform, looking out to the delegates, August 27, 1964. © Courtesy of the Lyndon Baines Johnson Presidential Library. Photo by Cecil Stoughton.

Robert Kennedy, and Hubert Humphrey. Kennedy appeared first. He arrived at the podium, just before 9:00 P.M., to introduce the film honoring the late president, triggering the emotional outburst that Johnson so long had feared. For 22 minutes the crowd cheered; Mary McGrory termed the appearance "the most intense emotional communication in four days of heavy-handed rhetorical proceedings."[154] Kennedy's brief address placed President Kennedy as the embodiment of the Democratic Party's long tradition of dedication to progress. He asked those who were dedicated to his brother's program to give a similar effort to electing the Johnson-Humphrey ticket. Still, as Richard Rovere noted, the demonstration suggested that Johnson's "mastery of the party is not quite complete and probably never will be."[155]

The final section of the address was the most emotional. Quoting one of the late president's favorite poets, Robert Frost, Robert Kennedy applied Frost's lines to all Democrats:

> The woods are lovely, dark and deep,
> But I have promises to keep,
> And miles to go before I sleep,
> And miles to go before I sleep.[156]

The attorney general concluded his speech with a quote from *Romeo and Juliet*, supplied by Jacqueline Kennedy. The passage carried an insinuation that Johnson could not have missed:

> When he shall die
> Take him and cut him out in little stars
> And he will make the face of heaven so fine
> That all the world will be in love with night,
> And pay no worship to the garish sun.[157]

The film could not live up to the introduction; at Johnson's explicit instructions, the movie was edited to exclude any shots of the attorney general. As previously arranged, John Kennedy was not the only late figure remembered by the convention; Adlai Stevenson delivered a tribute to Eleanor Roosevelt, while James Farley memorialized Sam Rayburn.

Humphrey then gave his acceptance speech – and the vice-presidential candidate rose to the occasion, as he had sixteen years earlier in Philadelphia. The address praised Johnson, but also amplified on the

[154] *Washington Star*, 28 Aug. 1964.
[155] Richard Rovere, "Letter from Atlantic City," *The New Yorker*, 5 Sept. 1964.
[156] *Washington Post*, 28 Aug. 1964.
[157] *Washington Post*, 28 Aug. 1964.

theme of Goldwater's extremism laid down by Rhode Island senator John Pastore's keynote address. The Minnesota senator turned his rhetorical fire on "the temporary spokesman of the Republican Party," a figure who had failed to learn "that politics should stop at the water's edge." Humphrey then ticked off the programs passed with broad bipartisan support, commenting that most Democrats and Republicans had backed measures like the test-ban treaty, the tax bill, the Civil Rights Act, the establishment of the Arms Control and Disarmament Agency, and education legislation. "But not Senator Goldwater!" The phrase caught the fancy of the crowd, which joined the vice-presidential nominee in bellowing it out.[158]

In this atmosphere Johnson delivered one of his worst speeches of the campaign; the committee-like approach that created the address came through in its delivery. The president argued that the convention and the platform allowed the Democrats to present themselves as "a party for all Americans, an all-American party for all Americans!" Democrats would be the party that agreed with "most Americans" on issues such as medical care for the aged, good farm income, "a decent home in a decent neighborhood," an education for all children to fit their abilities, victory in the war against poverty, and a prosperous and growing economy.[159] The president's discussion of the international scene similarly avoided specifics. After the speech, seeking reassurance, Johnson called Walter Jenkins to ask how long he spoke (42 minutes) and how many instances of applause he received ("practically every sentence").[160] The *New York Times* was less kind – its lead editorial the next day suggested "Death by Boredom" as an appropriate title for the formal events of the convention.[161]

Despite the flat acceptance speech, Atlantic City ended with Johnson fully established as the Democratic political leader. The Democrats reaffirmed the John Kennedy tradition by selecting a powerful vice-presidential nominee, and the national party gave notice to the Southern Democrats that it would no longer tolerate political segregation.[162]

Douglas Kiker used the convention's conclusion to anticipate the coming two months. The *Herald-Tribune* columnist recognized that Johnson's "is perhaps the most completely political world any man has

[158] *New York Times*, 28 Aug. 1964.
[159] *New York Times*, 28 Aug. 1964.
[160] President Johnson and Walter Jenkins, 8:28 A.M., 28 Aug. 1964, Tape WH6408.40, Citation #5244, LBJ Recordings.
[161] *New York Times*, 28 Aug. 1964.
[162] *Baltimore Sun*, 28 Aug. 1964.

ever lived in."[163] Accordingly, there was no doubt that the president would function as his own campaign manager. But Kiker could see three potential problems. Would Johnson's enormous ego interfere with the soundness of his campaign judgment? Would the president, as he embarked on a strategy of running from ahead, generate sufficient enthusiasm from the public and command the loyalty of his campaign staff? And could he successfully articulate concrete views on the policy issues in such a way to fulfill his political agenda? Those questions remained very much in the air as the post-convention segment of the 1964 campaign formally opened.

[163] *New York Herald-Tribune*, 26 Aug. 1964.

5

The Politics of Frontlash

The end of the Atlantic City convention formally opened the 1964 presidential campaign. Reestablishing his commanding lead – the largest at that stage in a presidential contest in American history – gave Johnson the luxury to use the campaign to accomplish more than simply a victory. Liberals pressed the president to run a European-style effort, teaming with the party's congressional candidates to outline a specific agenda for the forthcoming congressional session. Democratic partisans, on the other hand, urged focusing on the South, to prevent the demise of Democratic predominance in the region.

These debates, as events developed, were academic. In his capacity as "the President-Candidate," Johnson opted for a third strategy, one built around cultivating the frontlash.[1] The effort would deemphasize partisanship, wooing moderate and liberal Republicans through attacks on Goldwater's nuclear recklessness, expressions of the president's commitment to social justice, and portrayals of a moderate economic policy. The success of this effort would determine whether 1964 would become a realigning election or merely a strong Democratic triumph.

Implementing this – or any other – strategy proved difficult given the campaign apparatus that Johnson utilized. As journalist Douglas Kiker observed, the Democratic campaign organization was "almost a classic example of confusion, dissension, and chaos"; since Johnson insisted on making all critical decisions, "campaign planning is muscle-bound and bottle-necked." The president's distrust of Kennedy holdovers led Ken O'Donnell to concentrate on Robert Kennedy's Senate race, while Larry

[1] *Washington Star*, 29 Aug. 1964.

O'Brien toiled without any clear definition of his authority. "It is an old rule of politics," Kiker observed, "that no candidate can run and manage his campaign simultaneously." Because Johnson disrespected this dictum, "there is every indication that the confusion will increase in direct proportion to the tension."[2]

A fundamental difference of opinion on the validity of polls compounded the tension between Johnson and most party professionals. Johnson's special consultant Eric Goldman remembered a president with "pockets stuffed with polls, always ready to pull them out for a stentorian reading."[3] (A bit later in the campaign, Johnson complained after discovering that he had figures from 48 states but none from either New Mexico or Alaska; he ordered local Democrats to commence surveys at once.) For Johnson, the polls confirmed what the pundits refused to admit – that his personal popularity, not the Kennedy legacy, explained his large lead over Goldwater.[4] As pollster Lou Harris shrewdly observed, the president was "the truest believer of polls, but only when they tended to support what he was doing."[5]

Most Democrats, on the other hand, considered Johnson's fascination with polls inconsequential at best and counterproductive at worst. Richard Daley, recalling not only the *Literary Digest* fiasco of 1936 (when the magazine's poll predicted that Alf Landon would defeat FDR) but also the more relevant Truman-Dewey contest of 1948, was openly dismissive when the president passed along the latest polling results. In Chicago, the mayor reported, "We don't pay any attention to the polls."[6] Most party operatives seconded Daley's analysis.[7]

Problems of organization, polling, and strategy aside, virtually every Democrat agreed on one tactical issue: his statements about nuclear weapons constituted Goldwater's most vulnerable issue.[8] Chatting with Labor Secretary Willard Wirtz, Johnson noted that polling data suggested that the "anti-Goldwater stuff" about the dangers of nuclear contamination would work particularly well with swing voters in the North. "We

[2] *New York Herald-Tribune*, 30 Sept. 1964.

[3] Eric Goldman, *The Tragedy of Lyndon Johnson* (New York: Knopf, 1969), pp. 195–6.

[4] *Washington Star*, 3 Sept. 1964.

[5] Louis Harris, *The Anguish of Change* (New York: W. W. Norton, 1973), p. 23.

[6] President Johnson and Richard Daley, 12:37 P.M., 29 Aug. 1964, Tape WH6408.41, Citation #5254, LBJ Recordings.

[7] Bob Hunter to Douglass Cater, 3 Sept. 1964, Box 83, WHCF-PL, Lyndon B. Johnson Presidential Library; *U.S. News & World Report*, 28 Sept. 1964; *Baltimore Sun*, 3 Sept. 1964.

[8] *Washington Star*, 12 Sept. 1964.

think," the president noted, "that if we'll just talk about the danger of a woman having a two-headed baby, and men becoming sterile, and drinking contaminated milk, and these things, they'll know who they ought to be scared of without our ever saying so."[9] Goldwater did his best to deflect the issue; David Broder reported in the *Washington Star* that once the Arizona senator could drop "the nuclear-war albatross from his neck, he figures he can start making gains with politically productive promises to restore morality in government."[10]

Goldwater would never achieve his goal, the task made impossible after the most famous campaign advertisement in American history. The spot ran only once, on September 7, during NBC's *Monday Night at the Movies.*[11] The advertisement featured a young girl, picking petals from a daisy, counting from one to ten along the way. Gradually, a technician overpowered the girl's voice, with a countdown from ten to zero, followed by the camera zooming in on the girl's eye, revealing a mushroom cloud and the sound of a blast. Then the president's voice, but not his image: "These are the stakes: to make a world in which all God's children can live, or go into the dark. We must either love each other or we must die."[12]

Privately, Johnson fretted that the advertisement went too far. That night the White House switchboard was swamped with calls complaining about the advertisement's effect, especially on children. The president summoned Bill Moyers to his office. "Holy shit!," Johnson exclaimed. "What in the hell do you mean putting on that ad?" But then he chuckled. "I guess it did what we goddamned set out to do, didn't it?"[13] The next day, Republican National Committee chairman Dean Burch filed a complaint with the Federal Communications Commission charging that "this horror-type commercial implies that Senator Goldwater is a reckless man."[14] Moyers rejoiced: "That's exactly what we wanted to imply. *And we also hoped someone around Goldwater would say it, not us.*"[15]

[9] President Johnson and Willard Wirtz, 10:34 A.M., 9 Sept. 1964, Tape WH6409.08, Citation #5542, LBJ Recordings.

[10] *Washington Star*, 4 Sept. 1964.

[11] Theodore H. White, *The Making of the President 1964* (New York: Atheneum, 1965), p. 327.

[12] William Beloit, *Seeing Spots: A Functional Analysis of Presidential Television Advertisements, 1952–1996* (Westport, CT: Praeger, 1999), p. 39.

[13] Johnson quoted in Rick Perlstein, *Before the Storm: Barry Goldwater and the Unmaking of the American Consensus* (New York: Hill and Wang, 2001), pp. 413–14.

[14] *New York Times*, 9 Sept. 1964.

[15] Bill Moyers to President Johnson, 13 Sept. 1964, WHCF: EX: PL 6–3, Lyndon B. Johnson Presidential Library.

FIGURE 5-1. A screenshot of the "daisy ad." Perhaps the most famous campaign commercial in U.S. history, the commercial ran only once, but cemented the image of Barry Goldwater as reckless on nuclear arms. © Courtesy of the Lyndon Baines Johnson Presidential Library.

As time passed, however, Johnson grew less certain about the wisdom of such an over-the-top strategy. Though he claimed that he was "not being a Dewey," he admitted that he did "really want to play it safe." Harsh attacks on Goldwater could generate accusations that "we're overdoing it," as occurred in what the president described as the ad with "the little girl pulling the petals out on the spot, and the bomb going up."[16] In his own way, Johnson had recognized the dilemma of future political strategists: although voters complained about negative advertising, well-crafted attack ads worked. But in 1964 political professionals recoiled from this fact. "Interestingly enough," Johnson's special assistant Larry O'Brien discovered, at least 90 percent of party operatives criticized the

[16] President Johnson and Willard Wirtz, 10:15 A.M., 5 Oct. 1964, Tape WH6410.03, Citation #5838, LBJ Recordings.

"daisy ad." At the same time, it was O'Brien's "candid opinion that this advertisement did more to crystallize public opinion against Goldwater than any other single tool we are using."[17]

As generally occurred during the campaign, O'Brien's observation hit the mark. From Chicago, Daley reported that "fear of Goldwater is overriding and 'the finger on the trigger' has by far the greatest impact."[18] The message particularly resonated among suburban Republican mothers. The constituency, which a later political generation would come to know as "soccer moms," represented the target of the "frontlash" effort. A September poll showed that even a plurality of Republicans believed that Johnson would do a better job than Goldwater of keeping the peace.[19]

Though the daisy commercial best exemplified the Democrats' vilification of Goldwater, attack ads formed a staple of Johnson's television effort. In percentage terms, the Johnson campaign ran more negative television commercials (42 percent) than any presidential campaign in American history until that time.[20] These advertisements effectively used visuals and humor. In one, to sounds of sawing and water lapping, an announcer intoned, "In a *Saturday Evening Post* article dated August 31, 1963, Barry Goldwater said: 'Sometimes I think this country would be better off if we could just saw off the eastern seaboard and let it float out to sea.' "[21] On screen, a saw cut through a wooden map, and the eastern seaboard floated off into the Atlantic. Other Johnson commercials criticized Goldwater's position on Social Security, suggested the Arizonan lacked the temperament to be president, and alleged that Goldwater had changed his position on matters such as the United Nations, Vietnam, and extremism.[22] The increased cost and frequency of television advertising formed one reason why $34.8 million was spent on the 1964 campaign – a 39 percent increase from 1960, and more than double the $17.2 million from 1956.[23]

[17] Larry O'Brien to President Johnson, 4 Oct. 1964, Box 84, WHCF-PL, Lyndon B. Johnson Presidential Library.

[18] Larry O'Brien to President Johnson, 30 Sept. 1964, Box 3, Office Files of Henry Wilson, Lyndon B. Johnson Presidential Library.

[19] John Kessel, *The Goldwater Coalition: Republican Strategies in 1964* (Indianapolis: Bobbs-Merrill, 1968), p. 199.

[20] Beloit, *Seeing Spots*, p. 44.

[21] Beloit, *Seeing Spots*, p. 41.

[22] Kathleen Hall Jamieson, *Dirty Politics: Deception, Distraction, and Democracy* (New York: Oxford University Press, 1992), p. 221.

[23] Herbert Alexander, *Financing the 1964 Election* (Princeton, NJ: Citizens Research Foundation, 1966), p. 7.

Throughout the fall, it seemed as if the Johnson campaign was willing to attack its foe on any character issue. The president's aide Jack Valenti mapped out the strategy in a memorandum to Johnson in early September. "Our main strength," Valenti contended, "lies not so much in the FOR Johnson but in the AGAINST Goldwater" approach. Valenti understood that Goldwater wanted to link Johnson to the scandals that had dotted his career, such as Bobby Baker and Billy Sol Estes. In response, the Democrats needed to attack the Republicans "before being attacked on specific immorality" and explain how the president amassed his fortune. Johnson himself, meanwhile, needed to stay "above the battle."[24]

The campaign implemented Valenti's plan through an early version of rapid response – the "5:00 club," which prepared immediate responses to statements by the GOP national candidates and planted negative material about Goldwater in the press.[25] (The latter task Johnson considered simple, since reporters were "puppets" who would repeat stories leaked to them.)[26] At times outsiders facilitated the club's efforts – Nelson Rockefeller, for instance, shared his campaign's material on Goldwater.[27] For Valenti, the goal was "to whack at him EVERY day with gags and humor that deny him any right to be called sane or stable."[28]

Demonizing Goldwater represented one component of the frontlash strategy. In this sense, the president did little more than imitate Rockefeller's tactics, only now with the aim of shaking the partisan loyalty of anti-Goldwater Republicans. In Valenti's mind the campaign needed to go no further to ensure victory, and he was right. A Gallup poll in late August indicated that 61 percent of the business and professional community supported Johnson, up from the 43 percent that had voted for Kennedy in 1960.[29] In an early September Harris survey, 45 percent considered Goldwater a radical – as opposed to 3 percent who similarly designated Johnson.[30] For the first time in recent memory, Democrats

[24] Jack Valenti to President Johnson, 7 Sept. 1964, Box 84, WHCF-PL, Lyndon B. Johnson Presidential Library.

[25] Myer Feldman to Bill Moyers, 6 Sept. 1964, Box 84, WHCF-PL, Lyndon B. Johnson Presidential Library.

[26] Robert Dallek, *Flawed Giant: Lyndon Johnson and His Times, 1961–1973* (New York: Oxford University Press, 1998), p. 175.

[27] Myer Feldman to Bill Moyers, 6 Sept. 1964, Box 84, WHCF-PL, Lyndon B. Johnson Presidential Library.

[28] Jack Valenti to Bill Moyers and Myer Feldman, n.d., Box 84, WHCF-PL, Lyndon B. Johnson Presidential Library.

[29] *Congressional Quarterly Weekly Report*, 11 Sept. 1964, p. 2146.

[30] *Newsweek*, 14 Sept. 1964.

were outraising the GOP – as of September 1, the Democrats took in $3.98 million (not counting another $400,000 in expenditures by the AFL-CIO's political arm, the Committee on Political Education) to the Republicans' $3.77 million.[31]

Open rifts among the Republicans contributed to these figures. On September 3 a group of predominantly Republican business and financial leaders, headed by former Eisenhower cabinet member Robert Anderson, formed the National Independent Committee for President Johnson and Senator Humphrey. The group praised the president's ability to reduce taxes and expenditures, thus giving "the free enterprise system an opportunity to do its job." Indeed, the business leaders concluded, "it is the conservative course...to follow a man who is a leader and who is leading well."[32] (Rumors circulated that those who gave a five-figure donation to the committee received a naked dip in the White House pool.)[33] As its title suggested, the organization urged a vote for Johnson as a nonpartisan leader. Privately, Anderson said that he wanted to create "a place where everybody can go for Johnson, who the day after you're elected, will still be a Republican, or can be an independent, or can be what he wants to be.[34]

Although it did not endorse Johnson, another GOP-centered organization offered a similar message. On September 25, Charles Taft, son of William Howard Taft and brother of the late senator, founded the Committee for Forward Looking Republicans. "Republicans who could not in good conscience support the Goldwater-Miller ticket" peopled the new group, which raised funds for GOP moderates in congressional races.[35] The committee, which envisioned a Republican Party defined by "the warm humanitarianism of a Lincoln, the dynamism of a Teddy Roosevelt, the moral dedication of an Eisenhower, the consistent integrity of a Robert Taft, the sound constitutionalism of a Charles Evans Hughes, the progressive independence of a Fiorello LaGuardia," initially contributed to GOP Senate candidates in New York, Pennsylvania, Vermont, and Ohio; by the end of the campaign, 72 Republicans received some sort of assistance.[36] Despite the committee's partisan affiliation, Walter Reuther

[31] *New York Times*, 11 Sept. 1964.
[32] *Newsweek*, 14 Sept. 1964.
[33] Perlstein, *Before the Storm*, p. 436.
[34] President Johnson and Robert Anderson, 10:02 A.M., 3 Aug. 1964, Tape WH6408.03, Citation #4631, LBJ Recordings.
[35] *Washington Star*, 25 Sept. 1964.
[36] *Congressional Quarterly Weekly Report*, 30 Oct. 1964, p. 2579.

provided $10,000 from the coffers of the United Auto Workers, with the president's approval.[37] As Johnson noted, liberal Republicans needed "some useful and healing roles to play while they are driving the kooks over the skyline."[38] In some states the Johnson campaign actually ran commercials instructing voters how to split their tickets.[39]

Although the Anderson and Taft groups were the most significant of the type, James Rowe, who supervised the independent committees for the campaign, oversaw 72 such organizations. (Humorist Art Buchwald uncovered only one surprising organization: "Republicans for Goldwater.")[40] The 50 Johnson-Humphrey state committees existed primarily to skirt federal campaign finance laws, but the 22 thematic committees sought to bring Republican and independent voters into the Johnson fold without abandoning their partisan affiliations.[41] "Not since the 1920s," the *Christian Science Monitor* observed, "has the businessman been so ardently wooed in a presidential election."[42]

In this respect Johnson's 1964 campaign fundamentally differed from Kennedy's in 1960. Both men, of course, did not support a Western European–style, social democratic economic policy. And both envisioned capitalist-fueled economic growth, rather than large-scale income redistribution, as the way to ensure prosperity for all. But Johnson expressly welcomed business support in a way that Kennedy never had. At a press conference, a reporter once opened to Kennedy, "Mr. President, business leaders say they have you just where they want you..." Kennedy responded, to raucous laughter, "I doubt I'm just where they want me." (The clip is still played at the Kennedy Presidential Library.) Johnson, on the other hand, believed that business *did* – or at least *should* – want him in the White House.

Johnson therefore hoped to persuade frontlash Republicans to switch parties permanently, by offering a positive agenda, focused on three principal themes – peace, prosperity, and social justice.[43] On foreign policy matters, his general philosophy of peace and prudence represented a usable, if vague, approach; even before the frontlash emerged as a

[37] President Johnson and Walter Reuther, 10:50 A.M., 5 Oct. 1964, Tape WH6410.03, Citation #5839, LBJ Recordings.

[38] Perlstein, *Before the Storm*, p. 435.

[39] Alexander, *Financing the 1964 Election*, p. 50.

[40] *The Reporter*, 8 Oct. 1964.

[41] James Rowe to Jack Valenti, 14 Sept. 1964, Box 84, WHCF-PL, Lyndon B. Johnson Presidential Library.

[42] *Christian Science Monitor*, 3 Sept. 1964.

[43] *Christian Science Monitor*, 11 Sept. 1964.

definable strategy, the president believed that stressing peace offered a good way of appealing to mothers. On social issues the candidates' contrasting positions on civil rights were a key reason why frontlash voters were attracted to Johnson and the Democrats in the first place. The president might suffer from a backlash in the South and among Northern white ethnics, but Goldwater's civil rights position caused suburban voters in the North to recoil.

First and foremost, though, postwar suburban voters had drifted to the Republican Party because of economic issues, and an economic platform oriented around a social welfare state did not offer much promise for permanently winning over these voters. And although his campaign stressed foreign policy matters and questions of morality, Goldwater did offer traditional Republican fare on economic issues.[44] The Arizona senator promised an across-the-board tax reduction – in contrast to the "politically motivated" Kennedy-Johnson tax cut, which would "drug the economy into an artificial boom that would carry at least past Election Day."[45] Goldwater also argued that "a thriving and compassionate economy," not government handouts, represented the best way to end poverty.[46]

With this background, Johnson looked for a bold economic appeal to the frontlash voters. Since the New Deal, Democratic presidential candidates had formally opened their campaigns with a Labor Day speech in Detroit. Johnson, however, had something very different in mind than the usual offering. When Johnson's special assistant Richard Goodwin showed him a draft address, the president rejected it out of hand, terming it "all political."[47] From Detroit Walter Reuther recommended government health care as the central theme of the speech, but the president parried the idea. "I thought," he stated, "I'd fool them a little bit" by eschewing politics, thus providing "a contrast with Goldwater's speech and harangue and hate."[48]

Reuther seemed less than enthusiastic about this approach. When Goodwin still failed to produce a draft to his own liking, the president took

[44] *Washington Post*, 4 Sept. 1964.

[45] Goldwater quoted in Walter Heller, "Memorandum for the President," 9 Sept. 1964, Box 17, Walter Heller Papers, John F. Kennedy Presidential Library.

[46] *New York Times*, 4 Sept. 1964.

[47] President Johnson and Bill Moyers, 6:20 P.M., 4 Sept. 1964, Tape WH6409.06, Citation #5496, LBJ Recordings.

[48] President Johnson and Walter Reuther, 4:05 P.M., 5 Sept. 1964, Tape WH6409.06, Citation #5505, LBJ Recordings.

matters into his own hands. In a phone call to Bill Moyers, he outlined the sort of speech he desired. In an unintended fashion, though, Johnson revealed the difficulty of articulating a frontlash economic agenda given the more traditional New Deal philosophy to which he adhered.

His aim, the president declared, was a "high level" rather than "a party hack speech." The remarks would lead off with "the basic fundamentals – that Declaration of Independence, Bill of Rights, Constitution thing, wrapped up in one paragraph." As for a policy agenda, Johnson wanted to say that the Democrats favored "a child's mind to be trained. A church to pray in. A home to sleep in. A job to work in." Continuing this bland approach, the president told Moyers to include "education, religion, free speech, free press" that would make clear that the average Democrat was "a well-balanced, tolerant, understanding individual" – "instead of one of these kooks." When Johnson tried his hand at dictating specific lines for the address, he became, if possible, even vaguer, and effectively plagiarized Martin Luther King: "I see a…I have a vision…dash…a vision of a land where a child can…have a home to live in…can read what he wants to, and can *wish* what he wants to, and can *dream* what he wants to…can have training to fit his abilities, a home to protect him from the elements, a church to kneel in." The president instructed Moyers to "put in the words, 'I have a vision,'" as well as including "a little bit of this holy-rolly populist stuff." Finally, he told his aide to "throw at *least* two biblical quotations in, that are very simple, that every one of them have heard – these working [men], these auto mechanics."[49] How this agenda would provide a rationale for frontlash voters to permanently affiliate with the Democrats the president did not say.

Nonetheless, in Detroit, Johnson received what he had requested. The address, though greeted by the crowd in an "apathetic" fashion, provided the campaign's clearest articulation of the frontlash agenda's economic approach.[50] The president called for national unity, based on a common belief in prosperity, justice, and peace. Johnson moved fairly quickly through the first two of these principles, commenting that the economy had expanded for 43 consecutive months and promising that his administration would "seek to give every American, of every race and color, and without regard to how he spells his name, his full constitutional rights under our Constitution and under the law of the land." He went into

[49] President Johnson and Bill Moyers, 4:20 P.M., 5 Sept. 1964, Tape WH6409.06, Citation #5506, LBJ Recordings.

[50] *New York Times*, 8 Sept. 1964.

FIGURE 5-2. President Johnson officially opens the 1964 campaign, in Detroit, September 7, 1964. Johnson's Labor Day address represented his most pronounced attempt to articulate a "frontlash" agenda. © Courtesy of the Lyndon Baines Johnson Presidential Library.

greater detail on peace, championing the 1963 nuclear test ban treaty and criticizing those who failed to recognize that "there is no such thing as a conventional nuclear weapon." As Johnson had commanded, the speech contained a biblical quotation (from Proverbs 16:32): All chief executives needed to remember, "He that is slow to anger is better than the mighty; and he that ruleth the spirit is better than he that taketh a city." The FDR model from 1936 and 1940 had its effect.[51]

The speech's final section also traced its roots to Johnson's call with Moyers. In his youth, the president told the Detroit audience, he would wander out, look at the Texas sky, and wonder what his future would hold. He could now say, "I feel glad in my family, and concern for my children"; his dream "is for the child even now struggling toward birth." That child, Johnson believed, "will find all knowledge open to him. The growing boy will shape his spirit in a house of God, and his ways in the house of his family. The young man will find reward for his work, and feel pride in the product of his skills. The man will find leisure and occasion for the closeness of family, and an opportunity for enrichment of life." His dream was not "the grand vision of a powerful and feared nation. It concerns the simply wants of the people." Standing united, the American people could bequeath for their children "the greatest country that any man has ever known."[52]

Reaction fell along the lines the president desired. *Time* termed the speech "about as partisan as custard pie," filled with words "carefully calculated as an above-party politics plea to Republicans and Democrats alike." The magazine noted that "in taking his leader-of-all stance, Johnson often sounds almost scriptural with his cadenced sentences and their sprinkling of biblical quotations."[53] The *Baltimore Sun*'s Thomas O'Neill astutely noted that two past presidents – Franklin Roosevelt and Harry Truman – offered models for a successful Democratic campaign. Truman's populist, partisan attacks had worked wonders in 1948; Roosevelt, after 1932, had remained above the fray. In O'Neill's mind the Detroit speech confirmed that Johnson would follow the Roosevelt approach.[54] But, of course, this strategy carried risks as well as rewards; as *Time* noted, some Democrats feared that the president's "blandness may get boring," recalling the lessons of Dewey's failure in 1948.[55]

[51] *Congressional Quarterly Weekly Report*, 11 Sept. 1964, pp. 2150–1.
[52] *Congressional Quarterly Weekly Report*, 11 Sept. 1964, p. 2151.
[53] *Time*, 18 Sept. 1964.
[54] *Baltimore Sun*, 8 Sept. 1964; see also *New York Daily News*, 11 Sept. 1964.
[55] *Time*, 18 Sept. 1964.

Johnson's campaign staff provided little assistance in outlining an economic agenda that would simultaneously appeal to frontlash voters and energize the Democratic base. But the president himself consistently returned to the question, mining his own economic advisers, such as Council of Economic Advisers chairman Walter Heller and Treasury Secretary Douglas Dillon, for ideas.[56] In the end Johnson looked to win "with as few divisions as I can. I don't want to be a labor party. I don't want to be a business party. I don't want to be a government party."[57]

Nonetheless, as had occurred before the Detroit address, the president himself had to push for more of the frontlash economic agenda to appear in his campaign speeches. As Moyers informed other aides in late September, Johnson "says that for awhile he wants to talk about prudence, respect, and thrift, subjects which will help keep the frontlash vote."[58] But this goal was never as politically productive or easy to accomplish as the negative aspect of the frontlash strategy – portraying Goldwater as reckless. So in the end the campaign generated an inconsistent economic message. In speeches before traditionally Democratic groups, Johnson touted his support for government-sponsored health insurance for the poor and aged, and championed union-friendly policies.[59]

His dual role as candidate and campaign manager allowed Johnson to generate an unusual amount of attention for what otherwise might have been dismissed as a tactical issue. *Time* noticed how the president "loved to call the anti-Goldwater vote 'frontlash'"; pollster George Gallup, whose mid-September figures showed 27 percent of Republicans intending to vote for Johnson, informed the president of his delight "that you called on the press and the pollsters to bring this out."[60] Meanwhile, Johnson ordered aides to reach out to prominent editors and say, "We don't want this goddamned thing buried. They've been burying the

[56] Walter Heller, "Memorandum for the President," 9 Sept. 1964, Box 17, Walter Heller Papers, John F. Kennedy Presidential Library; Douglas Dillon, "Key Points on Fiscal Responsibility," 23 Sept. 1964, Box 6, Walter Heller Papers, John F. Kennedy Presidential Library.

[57] President Johnson and John Knight, 3:32 P.M., 5 Sept. 1964, Tape WH6409.06, Citation #5502, LBJ Recordings.

[58] Bill Moyers to Walter Heller, 24 Sept. 1964, Box 6, Walter Heller Papers, John F. Kennedy Presidential Library.

[59] *New York Times*, 16 Sept. 1964, 21 Sept. 1964.

[60] George Gallup quoted in President Johnson and Richard Nelson, 11:50 A.M., 3 Sept. 1964; *Time*, 28 Aug. 1964.

frontlash." "I'm really trying," he admitted to one aide, "to get the frontlash out there."[61]

Copious evidence existed of Republicans supporting Johnson. One observer in Illinois commented, "The Republican crossover to Johnson is to be seen, heard, and sensed everywhere in the state." In places like DuPage County, Goldwater had become "a 'controversial' figure among Republicans in the upper-income and upper-cultural reaches" – an amazing development, considering that the Chicagoland suburbs had remained faithful to the GOP even at the height of the New Deal.[62] In Wisconsin one poll showed more than a quarter of Republican farmers planning to vote for Johnson.[63] In New York State an early September survey indicated that almost half those who backed Nixon in 1960 planned to defect to Johnson. Traditionally Republican upstate New York favored the president by a 2-to-1 margin; the figures in suburban Maryland were similarly impressive.[64]

Well-known Republicans were not immune from the effect. Rumors circulated throughout the fall that Henry Cabot Lodge would formally back the Democratic ticket, perhaps in exchange for Johnson naming him secretary of state.[65] (Dean Rusk originally had said he planned to serve only one term.) After blasting Goldwater's "sordid" appeal to white "revulsion against the civil rights movement," New Jersey senator Clifford Case joined Lodge and New York's Kenneth Keating in refusing to endorse his party's nominee.[66] The GOP keynote speaker, Oregon governor Mark Hatfield, and Ohio governor James Rhodes endorsed but did not campaign for Goldwater.[67] Political historians had to reach back to 1912 and Theodore Roosevelt's Bull Moose bolt to see comparable Republican dissension.

Along these lines, Johnson rejoiced, "a good many papers that were normally moderate and conservative are supporting us."[68] Here, too, the president's frontlash strategy reaped rewards. From 1940 through 1960, the nation's top 100 newspapers endorsed the GOP presidential nominee

[61] President Johnson and Richard Nelson, 11:50 A.M., 3 Sept. 1964, Tape WH6409.03, Citation #5452, LBJ Recordings.
[62] Robert Bendiner, "Illinois: Bellwether State?" *The Reporter*, 22 Oct. 1964.
[63] *U.S. News& World Report*, 28 Sept. 1964.
[64] *U.S. News& World Report*, 7 Sept. 1964.
[65] *U.S. News& World Report*, 24 Aug. 1964; *Washington Star*, 3 Sept. 1964.
[66] Meg Greenfield, "Senator Goldwater and the Negro," *Reporter*, 8 Oct. 1964.
[67] *Christian Science Monitor*, 8 Sept. 1964.
[68] President Johnson and Edwin Weisl, Sr., 11:35 A.M., 5 Sept. 1964, Tape WH6409.06, Citation #5499, LBJ Recordings.

77 percent of the time; in 1952 Adlai Stevenson even complained of a "one-party press" distorting American democracy.[69] But in 1964 Johnson received the nod from almost 60 of the top 100 papers, along with a host of lesser-known but traditionally Republican dailies. The *Binghamton Sun-Bulletin,* New York's oldest morning daily newspaper, broke its tradition of having endorsed every Republican nominee since the founding of the party.[70] Three papers – the *Brattleboro Reformer,* the *Rutland Herald,* and the *Barre-Montpelier Times-Argus* – urged their readers to move Vermont into the Democratic column for the first time since before the Civil War. The *St. Louis Globe-Democrat* and the *Wisconsin State Journal,* both of which had backed the GOP nominee in each previous election in their histories, could not do so in 1964: the papers made no endorsement at all.[71]

Among more prominent Republican journals, the eight-paper Hearst newspaper chain endorsed Johnson on September 19.[72] The *Philadelphia Inquirer,* for the first time in its history, recommended a Democrat for president.[73] The *New York Herald Tribune,* the newspaper Horace Greeley founded and whose history was identified with the Republican cause, crossed party lines to back Johnson. Like many Republican papers, it flavored its decision in anti-Goldwater tones, noting that the Arizona senator "has no grasp of the infinite complexities of a dangerous, volatile, and frustrating world."[74] Perhaps the least enthusiastic such endorsement came from the *Saturday Evening Post,* which devoted almost a full page to explaining why Goldwater, "a wildman, a stray, an unprincipled and ruthless political jujitsu artist like Joe McCarthy," was so unfit for the presidency that his very nomination "seriously endangered" the two-party system.[75] In the end Johnson received the backing of 445 newspapers, with a combined circulation of 61.5 percent of all U.S. readers. Even Alf Landon, in 1936, had fared better than Goldwater's total of 368 newspaper endorsements, representing 22 percent of the nation's readers.[76]

Throughout September the long-term implications of these endorsements remained unclear. George Gallup, for one, detected the possibility

[69] Perlstein, *Before the Storm*, p. 426.
[70] *Binghamton Sun-Bulletin*, 17 Aug. 1964.
[71] *Congressional Quarterly Weekly Report*, 25 Sept. 1964, p. 2218.
[72] *New York Journal-American*, 19 Sept. 1964.
[73] *Philadelphia Inquirer*, 11 Sept. 1964.
[74] *New York Herald-Tribune*, 29 Sept. 1964.
[75] *Saturday Evening Post*, 8 Oct. 1964.
[76] Robert Goldberg, *Barry Goldwater* (New Haven, CT: Yale University Press, 1995), p. 223.

of a "major realignment" of the parties, since "the strategy of both candidates calls for an appeal to voters in a mood to shift allegiance."[77] As Gallup suggested, Goldwater no less than Johnson looked to use the 1964 contest as a realigning election. On September 3 the Arizona senator opened his campaign in Prescott, Arizona, as he had done for his two Senate efforts. Goldwater based his effort on achieving "peace through preparedness, progress through freedom, purpose through constitutional order."[78] But the address focused mostly on what the GOP candidate viewed as his strongest issues – morality in government and the civil rights backlash.

The senator developed these themes at length over the following several weeks. On civil rights Goldwater approached the issue as Dwight Eisenhower had done at the GOP convention – through the framework of "law and order." The Arizona senator remarked, "Crime grows faster than population, and those who break the law are accorded more consideration than those who try to enforce the law...Lawbreakers are defended. Our wives, our women, feel unsafe in the streets." Given his federalist beliefs, Goldwater denied advocating federal enforcement of local laws. But the White House, he maintained, did have a responsibility to "make sure that it, and its spokesmen and its supporters, do not *discourage* the enforcement or incite the breaching of these laws." Those critical of the civil rights demonstrators could not have asked for a more favorable statement.[79]

Goldwater's major campaign address on civil rights, co-authored by future Supreme Court Chief Justice William Rehnquist, cited the ideal of a color-blind Constitution to maintain that "it is just as wrong to compel children to attend certain schools for the sake of so-called integration as for the sake of segregation...Our aim, as I understand it, is neither to establish a segregated society nor to establish an integrated society. It is to preserve a *free* society." Accordingly, busing to achieve racial balance in the public schools was "morally wrong," because it "re-introduces through the back door the very principle of allocation by race that makes compulsory segregation morally wrong and offensive to freedom."[80]

The Arizona senator tortuously reconciled the emphasis on morality with his anti-government principles. He contended that "nothing is more clear from history than that moral decay of a people begins at the

[77] *U.S. News&World Report*, 28 Sept. 1964.
[78] *Washington Post*, 4 Sept. 1964.
[79] *New York Times*, 4 Sept. 1964.
[80] Perlstein, *Before the Storm*, pp. 461–2.

top." And what, the senator asked, tweaking Johnson's earlier promise to reduce federal expenditures by decreasing the White House light bill, "do we see today in those unlighted highest offices? We see the shadow of scandal cast across the White House itself."[81] In Goldwater's mind, Johnson's immorality extended to the governing process itself, manifested in the president's "twisting arms and banging heads together...buying and bludgeoning votes...turning people into numbers and manipulating them with computers in the White House."[82]

The 1964 campaign began with the death of a symbol of another major ethical scandal: on September 7, "Checkers" – the subject of Richard Nixon's famous 1952 apologia and the only canine ever to attend the Gridiron dinner – passed away, at age 13.[83] But new symbols of political immorality would soon emerge. In early September Goldwater received one of his biggest breaks of the campaign when the Bobby Baker case, presumed over, suddenly resurfaced.

Throughout the spring, rumors existed that "Delaware's one-man FBI" had withheld nuggets of damaging testimony from the Rules Committee, as insurance that North Carolina senator Everett Jordan and his fellow Democrats would not whitewash the investigation.[84] If that were John Williams's intent, obviously, it failed. But on September 1, Williams exacted his revenge. Speaking before the Senate, the Delaware Republican charged that Matt McCloskey, former Democratic National Committee treasurer and President Kennedy's ambassador to Ireland, had used Baker to illegally funnel $25,000 to the Kennedy-Johnson campaign in 1960. The conduit for these funds was Williams's chief source, insurance agent Don Reynolds, who said that McCloskey had written him a check for $25,000 more than his fee for writing the performance bond for the D.C. Stadium. (Williams displayed a copy of the canceled check to his colleagues.) According to the Delaware senator, the financier instructed Reynolds to give the money to Baker. Williams admitted that he did not know whether Baker passed the money onto the campaign. But, if Reynolds's allegations were true, McCloskey's action violated federal law, which limited individual campaign donations to $5,000.[85]

As journalist Richard Strout recognized, the revelations "couldn't have come at a more embarrassing time" for a president desperate to shelve the

[81] *Boston Globe*, 25 Sept. 1964.
[82] *Washington Post*, 30 Sept. 1964.
[83] *Washington Star*, 8 Sept. 1964.
[84] *Newsweek*, 21 Sept. 1964.
[85] 110 *Congressional Record*, 88th Cong., 2nd sess., p. 21561 (1 Sept. 1964).

ethics issue.[86] Armed with this new information, Williams demanded that the Senate reopen the Baker inquiry, to "let the American people know that we as senators do not consider anyone above the law, no matter how high he may be in the administration." This material, the Delaware senator continued, proved "why someone in the high command ordered these [Jordan committee] hearings closed."[87]

Johnson always had feared that the Baker investigation might expand from business improprieties, where the evidence against him was weak and indirect, to campaign finance, an issue on which he had flouted the law throughout his career. Indeed, the previous December he had urged McCloskey to intensify his activities for the 1964 campaign, after former Pennsylvania governor David Lawrence had termed the financier "just indispensable" to the Democratic fundraising effort.[88] Mary Lasker, one of the party's biggest donors, joked to McCloskey about how "it is terrible for you to have so much money to collect – but you do it so well!"[89]

As soon as the McCloskey story broke, the president urged Majority Leader Mike Mansfield to turn the case over not to the Rules Committee but to the FBI. If this appeal fell short, then Mansfield could play political hardball and promise his Republican counterpart Everett Dirksen that any inquiry would "get very messy," because it would also explore Goldwater's tenure as chair of the Republican Senate Campaign Committee. Anticipating a likely objection from the ultra-partisan Rules Committee Republican Carl Curtis, the president threatened to look into rumors of natural gas lobbyists making payoffs to the Nebraska senator.[90]

To a panicked Everett Jordan, the president made his partisan intentions perfectly clear. He urged the North Carolina senator to summon as his first witness the only Republican implicated in the first round of Baker hearings, Wisconsin congressman John Byrnes.[91] Privately, Johnson was even more direct. He instructed Larry O'Brien to "make this your personal business – this McCloskey thing." The administration had to ensure that "we don't let Jordan loose again"; if the senator examined campaign

[86] *Christian Science Monitor*, 5 Sept. 1964.

[87] 110 *Congressional Record*, 88th Cong., 2nd sess., pp. 21561–2 (1 Sept. 1964).

[88] President Johnson and Dave Lawrence, 10:15 A.M., 19 Dec. 1963, Tape K6312.10, PNO #16, LBJ Recordings.

[89] Mary Lasker to Matthew McCloskey, 25 Oct. 1961, Box 155, Mary Lasker Papers, Columbia University.

[90] President Johnson and Mike Mansfield, 10:58 A.M., 2 Sept. 1964, Tape WH6409.01, Citation #5416, LBJ Recordings.

[91] President Johnson and B. Everett Jordan, 5:36 P.M., 2 Sept. 1964, Tape WH6409.02, Citation #5430, LBJ Recordings.

finance in the 1960 election, "it looks to me like there might be a lot of things involved." The ideal would be to persuade the FBI to "investigate this Don Reynolds." Failing that, Johnson told O'Brien to remind Republicans of the dangers of a "bipartisan, objective investigation."[92]

The president then turned to Abe Fortas for legal and political counsel, as he had throughout the Baker case. The duo developed a response that inched Johnson ever closer to obstruction of justice. First, Johnson and Fortas sought to coordinate the recollections of Baker and McCloskey, assuming that if both men denied Reynolds's allegations, the resulting confusion would ensure that the story would have no long-term political effect. The president harbored no illusions about the guilt of either man. He admitted that "Bobby has got some bad marks on him," and as to McCloskey – "when a man buys a bond that costs $70,000 and pays $110,000, it's not very good."[93]

Johnson's concern, however, was not the law but the potential political threat. Bowing to White House pressure, McCloskey retained Tom McBride, a "very good friend" of Fortas, to handle his legal representation. McBride in turn agreed to work with Edward Bennett Williams, Baker's lawyer. Though Williams reported that Baker thrice had denied receiving campaign kickbacks from Reynolds, Fortas noted, "Ed is worried about it." Johnson got the message. He told Fortas, "The key to the thing is McBride and Williams ought to spend a good deal of time talking to each other, and you ought to direct them." And if McCloskey still "takes the position that he did make a political contribution, why, he's had it." McCloskey went along.[94]

Beyond orchestrating the versions of events supplied by Baker and McCloskey, Johnson used the instruments of governmental power to frustrate the inquiry. Certainly, he mused, if the case ever got to court, Baker and McCloskey could subpoena Reynolds's Air Force records "and make them see what kind of guy he is...Is he just a good clean citizen or is he a fellow that's been abducting little 13-year-old girls?" But the president himself had options before reaching that stage. Johnson wondered whether the time had come to order an IRS audit on Reynolds, to establish "that what he's trying to do is, he didn't report this income, and he's

[92] President Johnson and Larry O'Brien, 11:05 A.M., 2 Sept. 1964, Tape WH6409.02, Citation #5441, LBJ Recordings.

[93] President Johnson and Edwin Weisl, Sr., 11:35 A.M., 5 Sept. 1964, Tape WH6409.06, Citation #5499, LBJ Recordings.

[94] President Johnson and Abe Fortas, 11:45 A.M., 2 Sept. 1964, Tape WH6409.02, Citation #5422, LBJ Recordings.

trying to conceal it." If, of course, Reynolds wound up with an unfair tax case, "he's a questionable character anyway."[95]

Meanwhile, Fortas told Acting Attorney General Nicholas Katzenbach that he should not "go to the mat for awhile."[96] Katzenbach, who was serving at the president's pleasure for the duration of the campaign, agreed. Johnson himself pressed Katzenbach to target Republicans if the Senate undertook an aggressive inquiry: "The best defense," the president later maintained, "is an offense."[97] The first case, of course, would be "this son of a bitch Byrnes." If the Republicans really wanted to go down this path, Johnson railed, the administration should "maybe call [former Eisenhower chief of staff] Sherman Adams back in here. I think if they want to play with this thing, we're going to have to play. That's the only way we're going to stop them."[98] Dirksen, as the president well understood, was particularly vulnerable in this regard. In 1962, the minority leader, in the midst of an unexpectedly difficult reelection contest against reform congressman Sidney Yates, had accepted fifty $100 bills from Baker as a campaign contribution. Fortas supplied this information to McCloskey's attorney, who reported back that "Dirksen said he'd play along with Mike Mansfield on anything we wanted."[99]

The president also wanted to turn the tables on John Williams by making it appear as if the Delaware senator, and not the White House, had handled the case in a political fashion. (Both sides, of course, had done so.) Johnson pressed Edward Bennett Williams to argue that the case was "cheap politics, and it's dirty politics, and it's smearing politics." The fact that Reynolds waited "until two months before the election" to reveal a spectacular charge unmentioned in previous testimony certainly cast doubt on his motives. In a best-case scenario, the McCloskey charge could benefit the White House, by putting "the attack right on him [Williams], what kind of a guy he is."[100]

[95] President Johnson and Abe Fortas, 11:45 A.M., 2 Sept. 1964, Tape WH6409.02, Citation #5422, LBJ Recordings.

[96] President Johnson and Abe Fortas, 11:45 A.M., 2 Sept. 1964, Tape WH6409.02, Citation #5422, LBJ Recordings.

[97] President Johnson and Abe Fortas, 12:06 P.M., 10 Sept. 1964, Tape WH6409.09, Citation #5569, LBJ Recordings.

[98] President Johnson and Abe Fortas, 6:55 P.M., 3 Sept. 1964, Tape WH6409.05, Citation #5472, LBJ Recordings.

[99] President Johnson and Abe Fortas, 8:25 P.M., 2 Sept. 1964, Tape WH6409.02, Citation #5440, LBJ Recordings.

[100] President Johnson and Abe Fortas, 11:45 A.M., 2 Sept. 1964, Tape WH6409.02, Citation #5422, LBJ Recordings.

Johnson recognized the risks in this approach. But he also understood the high stakes: "They can't run it on all three networks all night and all morning without it blowing up." Therefore, the matter was a simple "question of who's going to survive." The issue was not whether Williams proving the charges against McCloskey would cause grave political damage – it clearly would. The only question would be "whether the party's had it now, because he has been the *national* finance chairman." Johnson detected the potential for getting "back into the Insull deal, or Teapot Dome," interwar scandals that had tarnished the Hoover and Harding administrations. "It's a question," the president contended, "of who's going to destroy whom."[101] Both he and Williams would not survive the confrontation.

Unfortunately for the president, Williams proved a wily foe. On September 10 the Delaware senator offered a resolution empowering John McClellan's Permanent Investigations Subcommittee to investigate any financial or business activities by present or former senators, officers, or employees of the Senate involving "violations of law, conflicts of interest, or improprieties of any kind," or any action at all that reflected "unfavorably on the integrity of the Senate." Since the conservative McClellan had a well-earned reputation as a dogged investigator, any hearings that he oversaw promised to be thorough. Returning the inquiry to the incompetent Jordan, Williams claimed, was "merely mixing another batch of whitewash to be applied."[102]

"The hell of it is," Johnson fretted, "we have no control over anything."[103] Williams "is just going to stir them up and raise hell."[104] An open investigation would "just throw them the goddamned election," since "we'll have nothing but headlines every week now, every day, from now until the election."[105] The administration would lose regardless of the Senate outcome. Either "it will be in McClellan's hands after a very vicious, mean debate," or "it will go to the Rules Committee, and they'll say, 'I told you so. It's a whitewash.' "[106]

[101] President Johnson and Abe Fortas, 11:45 A.M., 2 Sept. 1964, Tape WH6409.02, Citation #5422, LBJ Recordings.

[102] 110 *Congressional Record*, 88th Cong., 2nd sess., pp. 21911–14 (10 Sept. 1964).

[103] President Johnson, Abe Fortas, and Ken O'Donnell, 11:26 A.M., 10 Sept. 1964, Tape WH6409.09, Citation #5565, LBJ Recordings.

[104] President Johnson and Abe Fortas, 6:55 P.M., 3 Sept. 1964, Tape WH6409.05, Citation #5472, LBJ Recordings.

[105] President Johnson, Abe Fortas, and Ken O'Donnell, 11:26 A.M., 10 Sept. 1964, Tape WH6409.09, Citation #5565, LBJ Recordings.

[106] President Johnson and Abe Fortas, 6:55 P.M., 3 Sept. 1964, Tape WH6409.05, Citation #5472, LBJ Recordings.

The president then caught a break: McClellan, though no friend of the administration, publicly opposed the Williams amendment, saying that he did not wish to investigate the Baker matter. This statement doomed the amendment and thus returned the investigation to the Rules Committee, though with an instruction to "give particular emphasis" to the McCloskey allegations.[107] But since the Senate narrowly rejected an amendment offered by Carl Curtis to allow any three members of the committee to call witnesses (thus empowering the committee's minority to act without the chairman's consent), Jordan could continue his inert approach.

The North Carolina senator, who dismissed Williams's revelations as mere Republican "shouting," performed as expected.[108] He began by informing Williams that he had to delay hearings because he needed time to gather relevant documents. The Delaware senator tartly responded that "practically all" of the documents "have been incorporated into the *Congressional Record* and many of them are already in your committee files."[109] Jordan then announced that, in the midst of the campaign season, he was struggling to find a convenient meeting date for all nine committee members. This revelation prompted even some conservative Democrats to complain. A. Willis Robertson (D-Virginia) blasted his colleague for not promptly calling Reynolds, Baker, and McCloskey to testify. "You are such a fine man and such a good friend of mine," Robertson warned, "that I hate to see you headed for what could be the end of your political career."[110] Another conservative Democrat, Frank Lausche of Ohio, told a GOP colleague, "If you fellows had the sense to nominate John Williams, I would go out and campaign for him."[111] (Ironically, both Robertson and Lausche would fail to win renomination the next time they faced their state's Democratic voters.) But Jordan, though confessing that he did not "care to be in any more controversy about this mess," held firm.[112] On October 13 he announced that hearings on the McCloskey issue would not begin until 1965.

[107] 110 *Congressional Record*, 88th Cong., 2nd sess., pp. 21906–9 (10 Sept. 1964).

[108] B. Everett Jordan to Fred Kienel, 16 Sept. 1964, Box 37, B. Everett Jordan Papers, Duke University.

[109] John Williams to B. Everett Jordan, 24 Sept. 1964, Box 32, John Williams Papers, University of Delaware.

[110] A. Willis Robertson to B. Everett Jordan, 15 Sept. 1964, Box 36, B. Everett Jordan Papers, Duke University Library.

[111] Lausche quoted in Goldwater state campaign report, Box 3, Barry Goldwater Papers, Hayden Library, Arizona State University.

[112] B. Everett Jordan to L.P. McLendon, 17 Sept. 1964, Box 36, B. Everett Jordan Papers, Duke University Library.

Despite having avoided public hearings, Johnson suffered from the new charges. From the field Larry O'Brien reported that the Baker case, in combination with questions about how the president obtained his wealth, was the GOP's most powerful issue.[113] The Goldwater staff concluded similarly.[114] The president himself, prone to overreaction, had come to view the ethics issue as a time bomb that could cost him the election. "Somebody," Johnson lamented, "has got to take this. This is a Teapot Dome." He complained that the Justice Department, the IRS, and the FBI all acted as if they wanted to assist Williams instead of protecting the president. And all of it, in the end, came back to his nemesis: "I think it was that Bobby Kennedy felt that [Baker] was a symbol of Johnson, and he'd tie him to him."[115]

Ironically, one of the president's most vituperative critics helped deflect attention from his ethical difficulties. Dubbed by *Newsweek* "his party's unofficial hatchet man," William Miller's performance on the stump confirmed people's worst expectations of the selection.[116] (His low point came when he charged that Johnson had authorized the State Department to burn files before a Goldwater-Miller administration could gain access to them.)[117] Critiquing the judicial system, the nominee complained that "the Communists and Communist sympathizers and the hoodlums in this country have hardly lost a case in the Supreme Court in years." He defended the GOP ticket against the charge of extremism by asserting, "I am just not concerned about it."[118] Miller spent most of September campaigning in out-of-the-way places to small crowds; in Bangor, Maine, for example, the congressman attracted only three dozen people, half of whom were children.[119] Moreover, when people did come hear him speak, he received at best a lukewarm reception; according to Larry O'Brien's reports, the congressman was a "complete zero."[120]

[113] Larry O'Brien to President Johnson, 4 Oct. 1964, Box 84, WHCF-PL, Lyndon B. Johnson Presidential Library.
[114] "Oct. 5 Campaign Survey," Box 8, Barry Goldwater Papers, Arizona State University.
[115] President Johnson, Abe Fortas, and Ken O'Donnell, 11:26 A.M., 10 Sept. 1964, Tape WH6409.09, Citation #5565, LBJ Recordings.
[116] *Newsweek*, 21 Sept. 1964.
[117] Harold Faber, ed., *Road to the White House: The Story of the 1964 Election* (New York: McGraw-Hill, 1965), p. 189.
[118] *New York Times*, 12 Sept. 1964.
[119] *Newsweek*, 21 Sept. 1964.
[120] Larry O'Brien to President Johnson, 8 Oct. 1964, Box 3, Office Files of Henry Wilson, Lyndon B. Johnson Presidential Library.

At nearly every campaign stop, Miller framed the contest as a battle between "character and corruption" and recited a litany of misdeeds that demonstrated the president's unethical behavior.[121] But as events developed, the congressman himself had a less than pristine ethical record. As an example of Johnson's "intellectual dishonesty" and "hypocrisy" regarding civil rights, Miller (correctly) pointed to seven lots sold in 1945 by the president on the outskirts of Austin.[122] When Johnson had purchased the properties in 1938, they contained no restrictive covenant; when he sold them in 1945, the deeds prevented the new owners from selling the property to blacks. Press Secretary George Reedy, less than convincingly, termed it unrealistic to expect the president to remember real estate transactions from two decades before. Then, on September 18, *Newsday* revealed that Miller's own home, in Bethesda, Maryland, contained a restrictive racial covenant. The congressman attempted to explain how his covenant differed from Johnson's, but his talk about the president's intellectual dishonesty on civil rights ceased.[123]

The day after the *Newsday* story appeared, former Mississippi congressman Frank Smith charged that when the two had served together in Congress, Miller had offered him a monthly stipend in exchange for nonexistent publicity work for a New York felt company. The bribe offer came at a time when Smith sat on a House subcommittee with jurisdiction over legislation, supported by Miller, to allow New York state utilities to develop hydroelectric power at Niagara Falls. Miller denied the charge and said that Smith had misunderstood him. But when Smith refused to vote for the bill, the offer for public relations work was withdrawn.[124]

Then the press started looking into Miller's financial disclosure form, which he had filed on September 6. Unfortunately for the congressman, the statement contradicted similar forms already on record with the House of Representatives. First, the forms revealed that Miller, while in Congress, also served as an officer of the Lockport Felt Company, for which he received $7,500 annually. Miller had failed to notify his colleagues of a conflict of interest when he spoke against 1956 and 1958 legislation that affected the company's financial well-being.[125] Miller also admitted that he had put John Stenger, a partner of his former law firm, on his congressional payroll at a $13,742 salary for part-time work. Stenger

[121] *New York Times*, 27 Sept. 1964.
[122] Faber, *Road to the White House*, p. 180.
[123] *Newsday*, 18 Sept. 1964.
[124] *Newsweek*, 28 Sept. 1964.
[125] *New York Herald-Tribune*, 20 Sept. 1964.

never reported to Washington, and the congressman struggled to describe exactly what services he had performed. Instead, Miller denounced the reports as "sleazy, unsubstantiated smears."[126]

Privately, the president could not restrain his glee. He urged Humphrey to have his House allies demand that "Miller tell them why he got his $200,000 in retainers for 10 years." (The next day, California's Don Edwards introduced a resolution calling for a select House committee to investigate Miller's finances.) "Are we," Johnson sarcastically quipped, "going to turn the vice presidency over to the Lockport Felt Company?" Regardless of the seriousness of the allegations, the president wanted to "keep that going a little bit," because "that takes the heat off us."[127] After a few days to reflect on the matter, Johnson was even more excited – he told Georgia governor Carl Sanders that the reports could provide "the answer to the Bobby Baker stuff."[128] Johnson always had wanted to go on the offensive regarding the morality issue, and now he could do so.

The Miller revelations certainly slowed the Republicans' morality drive, even if they did not, as some predicted when the news broke, nullify ethics as a campaign issue.[129] The Republicans were subsequently forced to find more creative ways to raise the question. Iowa congressman H. R. Gross, whose speeches urging a more aggressive investigation of the Bobby Baker matter dated from the previous December, now called for reopening the "call girls" issue, preposterously suggesting a possible plot between Baker and the deported East German Ellen Rometsch in which "our missile secrets have been fed behind the Iron Curtain via the call-girl apparatus."[130]

Gross, however, seemed more interested in getting scandalous charges in play than in safeguarding U.S. national security. He described rumors that Rometsch was "a visitor at the lavender-colored townhouse" from which Baker based his illicit activities; the Iowa congressman passed along reports of a party that culminated in "a nude champagne bath."[131] His colleagues ignored Gross's pleas. Goldwater, meanwhile, announced that he would celebrate October 7 as "Bobby Baker Day," to mark the

[126] 110 *Congressional Record*, 88th Cong., 2nd sess., p. 23360 (1 Oct. 1964).

[127] President Johnson and Hubert Humphrey, 9:46 P.M., 1 Oct. 1964, Tape WH6410.01, Citation #5802, LBJ Recordings.

[128] President Johnson and Carl Sanders, 1:01 P.M., 6 Oct. 1964, Tape WH6410.03, Citation #5840, LBJ Recordings.

[129] *Washington Star*, 4 Oct. 1964.

[130] *Washington Post*, 1 Oct. 1964.

[131] *Washington Post*, 1 Oct. 1964.

one-year anniversary of the former aide's resignation from his Senate position; the RNC would, perhaps, reveal its new nursery rhyme: "The Butcher, the Baker, and the Stereo-Taker."[132] Dwight Eisenhower, asked about such remarks, admitted, "The campaign is getting to be a confused state of affairs...I don't know – something's wrong."[133]

As occurred with the morality question, Goldwater struggled to maximize the political benefit from the backlash. As the conventions closed, a Gallup poll gave Goldwater a narrow lead throughout the 11 states of the Old Confederacy, with a realistic chance to sweep the region. In two states – Mississippi and Alabama – Goldwater was comfortably safe. In Louisiana, though Governor John McKeithen retreated from earlier hints that he might endorse the GOP ticket (he remained neutral instead), Lieutenant Governor C. C. Aycock and Secretary of State Wade Martin backed Goldwater, as did most of the state's major newspapers.[134]

In other Southern states Goldwater's advantage was more tenuous. Virginia had voted Republican in 1952, 1956, and 1960, but the president's cultivation of Harry Byrd kept the "Byrd machine" from mobilizing on the GOP's behalf in 1964.[135] In North Carolina Goldwater needed to carry traditionally Democratic voters from the eastern part of the state – who in future years would be labeled "Jessecrats," due to their support for Republican senator Jesse Helms – that had supplied Dan Moore his margin of victory in the Democratic gubernatorial primary. (In that contest, Moore had denounced his opponent, Richardson Preyer, for representing "the bloc Negro vote.")[136] A divided state Democratic Party likewise enhanced Goldwater's chances in South Carolina. The state's senior senator, Olin Johnston, one of the region's few liberals (on issues other than civil rights), strongly backed the president; junior senator Strom Thurmond, the Dixiecrat nominee from 1948, showed no sympathy for the national ticket. The Palmetto State promised to test the president's hope that the farm bill would help his standing in the South; both sides agreed that whoever carried the textile workers would win the state.[137]

[132] *New York Times*, 22 Sept. 1964.
[133] *Congressional Quarterly Weekly Report*, 9 Oct. 1964, p. 2396.
[134] *Congressional Quarterly Weekly Report*, 9 Oct. 1964, p. 2355.
[135] Goldwater campaign state updates, Box 3, Barry Goldwater Papers, Arizona State University; *New York Times*, 4 Oct. 1964.
[136] *Congressional Quarterly Weekly Report*, 3 July 1964, p. 1353.
[137] *Washington Post*, 7 Oct. 1964.

Several other states were more difficult to predict. In Florida both campaigns struggled to gain sure footing. Jacksonville mayor Hayden Burns, the Democratic nominee for governor, reluctantly endorsed Johnson's reelection bid, but framed his campaign around such issues as removing the "pinks and Commies" that populated the University of Florida's faculty.[138] Arkansas, with its segregationist governor, Orval Faubus, appeared fertile ground for the Goldwater message – except that the state GOP had nominated as its gubernatorial candidate none other than Nelson Rockefeller's brother, Winston, who attacked Faubus for his position on civil rights. (The Goldwater campaign commented on the "curious paradox" of "Johnson moderates" in Arkansas voting Republican for governor.)[139] Georgia long had sported a powerful state Democratic Party, but Senator Richard Russell absented himself from the national campaign, and Governor Carl Sanders's opponents saw a Goldwater victory in the state as an opportunity to weaken Sanders before an expected 1966 Senate primary against Russell.[140]

Georgia's primary, held on September 12, further discouraged the president's chances. In the newly created 3rd District, a three-way Democratic primary eliminated the only candidate who supported Johnson's reelection, producing a runoff between a Democrat who endorsed Goldwater and one who expressed neutrality in the presidential race. In the Atlanta-based 5th District, Charles Weltner, the sole Georgia congressman to vote for the Civil Rights Act, managed only 60 percent of the vote against a weak challenger and faced stiff Republican opposition in the fall.[141] Meanwhile, in the 9th District, Representative Phil Landrum, who sponsored the administration's anti-poverty bill, won renomination with only 52 percent of the vote. Though Landrum's opponent, a young state senator, began the campaign by attacking the congressman from the left, by September he was espousing a militantly conservative position.[142] A future generation of Georgians would witness a similar ideological transformation when Landrum's 1964 challenger, Zell Miller, concluded his public career: after two terms as a populist governor in the 1990s, Miller served in the Senate from 2000 to 2005 as an ultra-conservative.

[138] *Congressional Quarterly Weekly Report*, 9 Oct. 1964, p. 2351.

[139] "State by State Analysis Newspapers/Polls," 19 Oct. 1964, Box 8, Barry Goldwater Papers, Arizona State University.

[140] Ralph McGill to President Johnson, 30 Sept. 1964, Box 84, WHCF-PL, Lyndon B. Johnson Presidential Library.

[141] *U.S. News&World Report*, 21 Sept. 1964.

[142] *Congressional Quarterly Weekly Report*, 9 Oct. 1964, p. 2354.

Tennessee had voted for Eisenhower in 1952 and 1956 (both times by less than 6,000 votes) and had given Nixon a slightly larger margin in 1960. At the same time, it also elected the two most liberal Southern senators, Estes Kefauver and Albert Gore. Since Gore's seat came up in 1964, Kefauver's death in 1963 meant that the 1964 election saw races for both of the state's Senate seats. In the race to fill out the two years remaining on Kefauver's term, the Democratic frontrunner, Governor Frank Clement – a protégé of the president's chief Tennessee ally, former governor Buford Ellington – lost in the primary to Representative Ross Bass, a liberal who had voted for the Civil Rights Act. Thereafter, as the *New York Times* noted, the "state Democratic Party virtually came apart," and the backlash was strong, especially around Memphis.[143] Republicans had their own problems, since Goldwater's oft-stated call for selling off the Tennessee Valley Authority badly hurt his chances in the state. Though the only published poll, from late August, showed Goldwater with a 20-point lead, both sides viewed the race as much closer by September.[144]

The final wild card was the president's own state, Texas – the only Southern state where Johnson consistently led in all autumn polling. Seven months earlier, Joe Kilgore had warned that the president's intervention on behalf of Ralph Yarborough could prove costly, and now Kilgore's prediction was bearing fruit. Surveying the Senate race in early August, Johnson scowled, "This damn [George H. W.] Bush is just as mean as he can be."[145] Indeed, the future president had launched a furious challenge against Yarborough, whom Bush charged "more nearly represents Michigan labor bosses than Texas." The Republican nominee, who termed himself 100 percent for Goldwater, campaigned on what he called the "Freedom Package" – a firm foreign policy, a balanced budget, blocking Medicare, backing state right-to-work laws, and opposing the Civil Rights Act. Yarborough, meanwhile, ridiculed his foe as a "carpetbagger" and "foreign oil importer" who had joined "hands with the John Birch Society." He urged Texans to "show the world that old Senator [Prescott] Bush can't send little Georgie down here to buy a Senate seat."[146] Polls showed Yarborough faltering in the face of a well-organized attack by the Bush

[143] *New York Times*, 4 Oct. 1964. As Orville Freeman conceded after visiting the state, "much work needed to be done." Orville Freeman diary, 3 Sept. 1964, Box 14, Orville Freeman Papers, Minnesota State Historical Society.

[144] *Wall Street Journal*, 22 Aug. 1964.

[145] President Johnson and George Reedy, 8:27 A.M., 9 Aug. 1964, Tape WH6408.14, Citation #4837, LBJ Recordings.

[146] *Time*, 16 Oct. 1964.

forces. With Johnson running only around five points ahead of Yarborough, the senator's weakness threatened to drag down the entire ticket, except Governor John Connally, who was coasting to reelection.[147]

Into this environment Goldwater plunged with an eight-day, nine-state Southern tour. Two hundred thousand welcomed him to Atlanta; young business students greeted the candidate with their right arms in slings, holding signs, "We'd Give Our Right Arm for Barry."[148] In Memphis Goldwater spoke to more than 30,000; a police officer stated, "I have never witnessed such a crowd for an event here."[149] In Montgomery the candidate attracted more than 24,000; in South Carolina, one local newspaper crowed, "These seem like Goldwater days in the South."[150] In Tampa Goldwater's crowd exceeded that of Kennedy in 1960 – and of Eisenhower in 1956.[151] In New Orleans Goldwater drew more people than The Beatles in what the *New Orleans Times-Picayune* described as a "real cheer-the-hero, hiss-the-villain" appearance.[152]

Though avoiding specific references to civil rights, Goldwater left little doubt about his intentions: "The more the Federal Government has attempted to legislative morality, the more it actually has incited hatreds and violence."[153] The senator denounced Johnson as "the wildest spender of them all," a "scheming wire puller" who should rename the White House "the Whitewash House."[154] The *Greensboro Daily News* observed that "from the intensity of the applause, it was hard to tell whether the crowd was angriest with Bobby Baker, Johnson, the Supreme Court, communism, South Vietnam, or centralized government."[155] But for Goldwater it did not matter – as long as the crowd was angry, its members likely would pull a Republican lever. And those who attended the Goldwater rallies were receptive to such a message. Journalist Richard Strout, who followed the Arizona senator throughout the tour, commented that "a

[147] Patrick Cox, *Ralph W. Yarborough* (Austin: University of Texas Press, 2001), p. 215.

[148] *Atlanta Journal* clipping, Box 3, Barry Goldwater Papers, Arizona State University.

[149] *Memphis Commercial Appeal*, clipping, Box 3, Barry Goldwater Papers, Arizona State University.

[150] *Charleston News and Courier*, Box 3, Barry Goldwater Papers, Arizona State University.

[151] *Tampa Tribune* clipping, Box 3, Barry Goldwater Papers, Arizona State University.

[152] *New Orleans Times-Picayune* clipping, Box 3, Barry Goldwater Papers, Arizona State University.

[153] *Time*, 18 Sept. 1964.

[154] *Time*, 25 Sept. 1964.

[155] *Greensboro Daily News* clipping, Box 3, Barry Goldwater Papers, Arizona State University.

foreigner traveling with Barry Goldwater in the South wouldn't know there were any Negroes in it."[156]

Unfortunately for the candidate, beyond the crowd reception, the news was less positive; it seemed, according to *Charlotte Observer* columnist Edwin Lahey, as if the Southern trip was "under the control of men who did graduate work at college in the arts of ineptitude."[157] Goldwater's style played poorly in a region used to fiery political rhetoric. Strout detected a "dreamlike quality to the campaign," as the candidate "makes electrifying assertions and then wafts away."[158] Even the campaign staff's own post-mortem conceded, "Often, with the audience keyed to a fever pitch, the Senator's remarks took the steam out."[159]

A dull delivery was not Goldwater's only difficulty. Erwin Canham, writing in the *Christian Science Monitor*, puzzled at why the senator would issue "bluntly challenging statements in localities where they would seem to be least welcome."[160] The *St. Petersburg Times* entitled its headline "Right City, Wrong Speech" after the senator delivered an address about law and order in a city with a low crime rate but a high population of elderly citizens concerned about Social Security.[161] In Knoxville Goldwater reiterated his support for privatizing the Tennessee Valley Authority; in Atlanta he decried the *Wesberry v. Sanders* decision, which had given the city another House district.[162] The senator's disappointed Louisiana backers wondered if Goldwater would have better served the campaign by not coming to the state.[163]

The one tangible benefit Goldwater derived from the tour came on September 16, when Strom Thurmond declared himself a "Goldwater Republican." The Democratic Party, he charged, "is leading the evolution of our nation to a socialistic dictatorship."[164] Initial reaction expressed doubts about the political importance of the party switch. The *Washington Star*, noting that one Washington magazine poll had rated Thurmond the least effective member of the Senate (Russell and Humphrey had ranked

[156] *The New Republic*, 26 Sept. 1964.
[157] *Charlotte Observer* clipping, Box 3, Barry Goldwater Papers, Arizona State University.
[158] *The New Republic*, 26 Sept. 1964.
[159] Dick Thompson to Pam Rymer, "The Goldwater Tour of the South," n.d., Box 3, Barry Goldwater Papers, Arizona State University.
[160] *Christian Science Monitor*, 22 Sept. 1964.
[161] *St. Petersburg Times* clipping, Box 3, Barry Goldwater Papers, Arizona State University.
[162] *Time*, 25 Sept. 1964.
[163] Dick Thompson to Pam Rymer, "The Goldwater Tour of the South," n.d., Box 3, Barry Goldwater Papers, Arizona State University.
[164] *U.S. News&World Report*, 28 Sept. 1964.

first and second), doubted that the Democrats would miss the South Carolina apostate.[165] Joe Clark invited his Pennsylvania colleague, Hugh Scott, who was in the midst of a rough reelection bid, to ask Thurmond to campaign for him in Pennsylvania; Scott demurred.[166] Richard Russell saw little in the Thurmond defection to worry the president.[167]

Russell rarely misjudged Southern politics, but in this case he did: Thurmond would capture six elections as a Republican and retire as the longest-serving senator in U.S. history. In 1964 Thurmond played an active and effective role for the remainder of the campaign. He accompanied Goldwater throughout the South, frequently introducing the senator – and arousing the crowd much more effectively than did his Arizona colleague.[168] Thurmond also followed national Democrats who campaigned in the South, appearing at the same location the next day to serve as a "truth squad."[169] The senator certainly tilted his home state toward the GOP. Republican staffers noted that "all South Carolina papers" were "so strong for Goldwater that it is difficult to tell which ones are considered outright endorsements."[170]

As with Thurmond, the other stimulation of the backlash came from a source outside the campaign's direct control. In his travels around the country, Larry O'Brien expressed amazement at the impact of right-wing hate literature, especially *A Texan Looks at Lyndon*. In Missouri, Oklahoma, and Arkansas, the book – written by J. Evetts Haley, a self-styled "cowman and historian" – was "distributed by the carload."[171] In Richmond Haley's work was the hottest-selling book in the city.[172] In Kansas the Democratic state coordinator heard "Haley's book quoted more than anything else in the campaign."[173] In Nevada Democratic

[165] *Washington Star*, 16 Sept. 1964; see also *Baltimore Sun*, 17 Sept. 1964.
[166] *Baltimore Sun*, 21 Sept. 1964.
[167] President Johnson and Richard Russell, 7:54 P.M., 18 Sept. 1964, Tape WH6409.11, Citation #5606, LBJ Recordings.
[168] Dick Thompson to Pam Rymer, "The Goldwater Tour of the South," n.d., Box 3, Barry Goldwater Papers, Arizona State University.
[169] Ralph McGill to President Johnson, 30 Sept. 1964, Box 84, WHCF-PL, Lyndon B. Johnson Presidential Library.
[170] Dick Thompson to Pam Rymer, "The Goldwater Tour of the South," n.d., Box 3, Barry Goldwater Papers, Arizona State University.
[171] Larry O'Brien to President Johnson, 1 Oct. 1964, Box 3, Office Files of Henry Wilson, Lyndon B. Johnson Presidential Library.
[172] Larry O'Brien to President Johnson, 4 Oct. 1964, Box 84, WHCF-PL, Lyndon B. Johnson Presidential Library.
[173] Larry O'Brien to President Johnson, 2 Oct. 1964, Box 3, Office Files of Henry Wilson, Lyndon B. Johnson Presidential Library.

governor Grant Sawyer was "inundated" with Haley's screed. On the Mexican border reports reached the Johnson campaign about Spanish translations of the book.[174]

Haley, Illinois activist Phyllis Schlafly (*A Choice, Not an Echo*), and Missouri anticommunist John Stormer (*None Dare Call It Treason*) collectively had more than 16,000,000 copies of their books in print. In highly demagogic fashion, the volumes portrayed Johnson as someone whose views clashed with the American political tradition. Ironically, Goldwater's own efforts in this regard were consistently poor.[175] Reflecting the overly ideological tone of its staff, the Goldwater campaign believed that highlighting the arcane issue of Hubert Humphrey's ties to the Americans for Democratic Action could show the Democrats' dangerous ideological tendencies.[176] Since few Americans listed ADA membership as a high-profile issue, this strategy made little sense.

While Goldwater and Miller railed against the ADA, they spent much less time on foreign policy than anyone would have guessed six months before: the nuclear issue and the Tonkin Gulf Resolution had transformed the nature of the campaign. Johnson was no more eager to discuss the specifics of international affairs than previously, although just after the Democratic convention his aide McGeorge Bundy gingerly suggested that he do so.[177] Those more politically attuned than Bundy, such as Moyers, "discouraged" such a move. Any general debate – or even a morale-boosting trip to Southeast Asia by Dean Rusk or Robert McNamara – would only "increase public attention and concern about the situation out there," contradicting the campaign's hope "that public discussion of Vietnam could be kept to a minimum."[178]

Goldwater struggled against such a strategy. Desperate to find some way to shake free of the recklessness charge, Goldwater opened his national advertising campaign, on September 18, with an ineffective 30-minute address on the topic.[179] The Arizonan's highest profile effort to neutralize his negative image occurred in a 30-minute campaign film with Eisenhower, filmed at the general's Gettysburg farm. The commercial was

[174] Larry O'Brien to President Johnson, 6 Oct. 1964, Box 3, Office Files of Henry Wilson, Lyndon B. Johnson Presidential Library.

[175] Faber, *Road to the White House*, p. 215.

[176] "Repudiation Book," Box 2, Barry Goldwater Papers, Arizona State University.

[177] McGeorge Bundy, "Memorandum for the President," Box 2, Bundy NSF File, Lyndon B. Johnson Presidential Library.

[178] Bill Moyers to President Johnson, 3 Oct. 1964, Box 33, Bill Moyers Office Files, Lyndon B. Johnson Presidential Library.

[179] *Newsweek*, 5 Oct. 1964.

unscripted, although Goldwater's staff gave Eisenhower the topics they wanted to cover. Eisenhower delivered the desired line: when Goldwater asked the former president about the charge that the Republicans were warmongers, Eisenhower responded, "Well, Barry, in this mind, this is actual tommyrot." But the closest the former president came to actually urging a vote for Goldwater was his comment, "Now, you know about war. You've been through one. Any man who knows anything about war is not going to be reckless about this." As Rick Perlstein has observed, such an endorsement could have applied to any veteran watching the commercial.[180]

Johnson chortled when the Goldwater-Eisenhower half-hour had attracted an 8.6 rating, swamped by *Petticoat Junction* at 27.4 and *Peyton Place* with 25.0.[181] (By early October, fewer than one in five voters had seen even one Goldwater 30-minute campaign advertisement, negating the GOP's spending edge in television advertising.)[182] Indeed, by early October Johnson was so confident that foreign policy would not hurt him that he could joke over the matter. After a GOP attack on his handling of the Southeast Asian conflict, the president teased Secretary of Defense Robert McNamara that Goldwater had "transferred this from 'McNamara's War' to 'Johnson's War.'"[183]

By the middle of September, meanwhile, the GOP staff conceded the obvious: "Generally speaking, Goldwater is slipping all over the country."[184] Public opinion surveys confirmed the pessimism: a September 18 Gallup poll showed Goldwater's 11-point August lead in the South had evaporated. The president's advantage outside of the South had reached overwhelming proportions: he led by 52 percent in the East, 36 percent in the West, and 44 percent in the Midwest, a 15-point gain since the selection of Humphrey.[185] A hastily planned Goldwater whistle-stop tour through Illinois, Indiana, and Ohio did little to help. *Newsweek* observed that the senator delivered serious charges in "the same passionless, reasonable voice he uses for wholly innocuous statements," blunting the effect of his attacks.[186]

[180] Perlstein, *Before the Storm*, p. 264.
[181] White, *Making of the President 1964*, p. 330.
[182] "Oct. 5 Campaign Survey," Box 8, Barry Goldwater Papers, Arizona State University.
[183] President Johnson and Robert McNamara, 8:39 P.M., 24 Sept. 1964, Tape WH6409.15, Citation #5686, LBJ Recordings.
[184] Jody Baldwin to Pam Ryner, 20 Sept. 1964, Box 8, Barry Goldwater Papers, Arizona State University.
[185] *New York Herald-Tribune*, 19 Sept. 1964.
[186] *Newsweek*, 12 Oct. 1964.

With Goldwater unable to find any issue beyond Johnson's alleged immorality and the president struggling to articulate a positive agenda to accompany the negative attacks of his frontlash strategy, the campaign, as Richard Strout noted, disappointed those "who like a strong dash of unpredictability in their politics."[187] What might have been a debate between two sharply contrasting political philosophies instead developed into a campaign that featured attacks on the other candidate's personality. Goldwater was perceived as reckless, Johnson as lacking ethics.

In the president's mind, however, polls vindicated his performance as both a candidate and a political tactician. In early September published surveys showed him with leads of nearly 20 points in battleground states of Indiana and Wisconsin; margins approaching 40 points in Maryland, New York, and Hawaii; and an advantage of almost 60 points in a state that had previously voted Democratic for president only once – Maine.[188] Campaign surveys taken later in the month showed all of these leads holding steady, coupled by a phenomenal showing in traditionally Republican Ohio, where the president was outpacing Goldwater by 46 points.[189]

Word from another state especially excited the president. In a mid-September phone call, newspaper magnate Eugene Pulliam expressed his belief that the president could carry Arizona. The publisher added that the Democrats even had a chance in the race for Goldwater's Senate seat, where Senator Carl Hayden's administrative assistant, Roy Elson, was challenging Governor Paul Fannin, a Goldwater protégé.[190] Much to Johnson's surprise, the normally cautious O'Brien confirmed the judgment two weeks later, reporting that not only did the president lead in Arizona polls by five points, but also that his margin was increasing. Elson, meanwhile, claimed that he was in a "real horse race" with Fannin.[191] Neutral observers were more skeptical, but Elson said he could score a surprise, largely due to strong backing from Hayden – provided that Johnson appeared in the state.

[187] *The New Republic*, 3 Oct. 1964; see also *New York Daily News*, 25 Sept. 1964.

[188] *U.S. News&World Report*, 7 Sept. 1964.

[189] Oliver Quayle poll, 3 Oct. 1964, Box 175, Office Files of Fred Panzer, Lyndon B. Johnson Presidential Library; Larry O'Brien to President Johnson, 1 Oct. 1964, Box 3, Office Files of Henry Wilson, Lyndon B. Johnson Presidential Library; Larry O'Brien to President Johnson, 4 Oct. 1964, Box 84, WHCF-PL, Lyndon B. Johnson Presidential Library.

[190] President Johnson and Eugene Pulliam, 12:06 P.M., 23 Sept. 1964, Tape WH6409.13, Citation #5641, LBJ Recordings.

[191] Larry O'Brien to President Johnson, 6 Oct. 1964, Box 3, Office Files of Henry Wilson, Lyndon B. Johnson Presidential Library; *Christian Science Monitor*, 13 Oct. 1964.

The Johnson campaign had not scheduled a swing through Arizona, which had only five electoral votes. But these reports were too tempting for the president to resist. In early October Johnson asked Elson to coordinate a visit to the state. Initially, the president decided that he would refuel in Phoenix, "say hello to my friends there, and tell them that I was mighty happy to see Roy Elson." An excited Elson, who "very, very, very much" wanted a visit, urged the president to spend a little more time; since the scheduled stop would occur on a Sunday morning, maybe Johnson could accompany the Senate candidate to church. When Elson passed along up-to-the-minute polling data that showed Johnson having boosted his lead in Maricopa County, the state's population center, the decision was sealed – Johnson would come to Arizona, stay for church, and perhaps even deliver a "nonpolitical" talk.[192]

Just as Johnson was turning his attention to state contests, so too were other political observers. In a year that featured an unusually large number of close elections, especially for the Senate, local races featured starker ideological contests than did the presidential battle. Moreover, the fate of several moderate Republicans – Hiram Fong in Hawaii, Kenneth Keating in New York, and Hugh Scott in Pennsylvania – would test whether the frontlash strategy would produce a Democratic realignment.

At the start of the fall campaign, Larry O'Brien considered five Republican Senate seats – Maryland, New York, New Mexico, Hawaii, and Delaware – potentially vulnerable, balanced by three seats the Democrats were likely to lose (Utah, Ohio, and Oklahoma) and three potentially close races with Democratic incumbents – North Dakota, Wisconsin, and Wyoming.[193] The development of the presidential race added four more seats to this list. Johnson's overpowering strength in the Northeast put Hugh Scott's Pennsylvania seat in jeopardy, and the president's surprising standing in Arizona gave Roy Elson a chance; Goldwater's appeal in the South gave Republicans opportunities at both Tennessee seats. Finally, a combination of unexpectedly strong GOP candidates and Democratic incumbents with glaring weaknesses placed the Republicans within striking distance in Texas, Nevada, and California.

As Johnson aide Henry Wilson had recognized several months earlier, no guarantee existed for impressive Democratic gains in the year's down-the-ticket races. Democrat Joseph Tydings seemed certain to oust J. Glenn

[192] President Johnson and Roy Elson, 8:35 P.M., 8 Oct. 1964, Tape WH6410.04, Citation #5848, LBJ Recordings.

[193] Larry O'Brien to President Johnson, 22 Aug. 1964, Box 83, WHCF-PL, Lyndon B. Johnson Presidential Library.

Beall in Maryland, but that contest was offset by the situation in Ohio, where few in either party expected Democratic senator Stephen Young to survive Robert Taft's challenge, and Oklahoma, where former Oklahoma University football coach Bud Wilkinson, running as a Republican, comfortably led the upset winner of the Democratic primary, State Senator Fred Harris.[194] Many of the other close Senate contests occurred in either Southern or predominantly rural states in which Goldwater enjoyed disproportionate strength.

Local factors wound up shaping most of these races.[195] Six Senate elections, however, involved themes of relevance to political culture after 1964. The Texas race between Ralph Yarborough and George H. W. Bush promised to test the survival skills of a Southern liberal in the newly two-party South. In Nevada first-term senator Howard Cannon began the year as an overwhelming favorite: he had compiled a moderate record in his first term and, through his position on the Armed Services Committee, steered federal funds toward Nevada. But in a year in which political ethics was a major issue, Cannon's liabilities outweighed his assets. In 1962 Bobby Baker had organized a fundraiser on Cannon's behalf, and the Nevada senator, who had served three terms as Las Vegas city attorney before winning election to the upper chamber, had repaid the Senate aide by facilitating contacts between Baker and Las Vegas gambling interests. Cannon then declined to recuse himself from the Rules Committee investigation of Baker's financial dealings, leaving his votes to terminate the inquiry difficult to defend. In the primary three little-known Democrats tied him to Baker and illicit gaming interests. Despite the incumbent's dismissal of such "smears, innuendoes, and character assassination," the challengers held him below 60 percent of the vote.[196]

In the fall contest Cannon confronted Nevada's only Republican statewide officeholder, Lieutenant Governor Paul Laxalt. (Ironically, Laxalt had won in 1962 with Cannon's tacit support; the senator doubted that Democratic governor Grant Sawyer would challenge him if Sawyer knew that a Republican would succeed to the governorship.)[197] Only 41 years old, Laxalt was a natural campaigner – an asset against an incumbent that the *New York Times* later described as "a rather colorless man, who has

[194] *New York Times*, Oct. 4, 1964.

[195] Larry O'Brien to President Johnson, 2 Oct. 1964, Box 3, Office Files of Henry Wilson, Lyndon B. Johnson Presidential Library; *Christian Science Monitor*, 3 Oct. 1964.

[196] *Congressional Quarterly Weekly Report*, 21 Aug. 1964, p. 1927; 4 Sept. 1964, p. 2035.

[197] *Time*, 16 Oct. 1964.

never cut a swath through Washington."[198] Cannon offered an ingenious excuse for refusing to debate Laxalt: "I am not sure that my opponent, who is only halfway through his first four-year term, would know the issues unless he studied very hard."[199] With the incumbent already softened up by the primary challenge, Laxalt focused more on national matters, especially the senator's decision to break from his senior Democratic colleague, Alan Bible, in supporting cloture for the Civil Rights Act. Johnson, meanwhile, offered what help he could, joking with Cannon, "I'll come on out there and campaign either for you or against you. Whichever you think will do you the most good."[200] A presidential visit thus was scheduled for the same trip that would take Johnson to Arizona. With Cannon under 50 percent even in Democratic polls, he needed all the help he could get.[201]

In Pennsylvania Secretary of Internal Affairs Genevieve Blatt sought to become the first woman in U.S. history elected to the Senate without having succeeded her late husband in Congress. Incumbent Hugh Scott enjoyed strong support from organized labor, had delayed endorsing the Goldwater-Miller ticket after the San Francisco convention, and was the largest recipient of funds from Charles Taft's Committee for Forward Looking Republicans. Moreover, his warm personal relationship with his senior colleague, Democrat Joe Clark, prompted speculation that Clark secretly preferred Scott's reelection. Though Scott had fortified his partisan credentials by playing up his work in the Baker inquiry, he eagerly reminded voters of occasions when he had sided with Democratic administrations, such as on civil rights and the test-ban treaty.[202] (Despite the bold rhetoric, Scott had discussed his strategy with the Goldwater campaign, which, recognizing political reality, voiced no objection.)[203] The Philadelphia dailies endorsed Johnson for president, but all sided with Scott for the Senate.[204]

Blatt, the first woman elected to statewide office in the Keystone State, was associated with the reform faction of the state party, having worked

[198] *New York Times*, quoted in K. J. Evans, "Howard Cannon: Quiet Clout," in *The First 100: Portraits of Men and Women Who Shaped Las Vegas*, ed. K. J. Evans and A. D. Hopkins (Las Vegas, NV: Donrey Media Group, 1999), p. 27.

[199] *Las Vegas Review-Journal*, 5 Oct. 1964.

[200] Johnson quoted in Evans, "Howard Cannon: Quiet Clout," p. 30.

[201] Larry O'Brien to President Johnson, 6 Oct. 1964, Box 3, Office Files of Henry Wilson, Lyndon B. Johnson Presidential Library.

[202] *Congressional Quarterly Weekly Report*, 2 Oct. 1964, p. 2288.

[203] *Wall Street Journal*, 13 July 1964.

[204] *New York Times*, 25 Oct. 1964.

for Adlai Stevenson in 1960. She confirmed her electoral strength in 1962, when she was the only statewide Democrat to survive the Scranton sweep.[205] Blatt entered the general election, however, crippled from a divisive primary. The Philadelphia and Pittsburgh machines had backed state Supreme Court Justice Michael Musmanno, a 67-year-old who had not faced the voters since 1951. Blatt led on primary night by a narrow margin, but then Frank Smith's machine went to work. In precinct after precinct in Philadelphia, Musmanno received 10 or 12 more votes than the initial total had showed, with Blatt's return reduced by an identical number. Then Philadelphia election officials added several thousand more votes to Musmanno by counting as votes for the justice ballots punched in the blank space below Musmanno's name. Election lawyers had a field day with the ensuing dispute. Challenges by Blatt to every absentee ballot in Philadelphia substantially narrowed Musmanno's margin; at one point in the recount, Blatt and Musmanno were tied. In the end, the key question became the validity of the blank-line ballots. By a 4–3 margin, the Pennsylvania Supreme Court invalidated them, giving Blatt the victory by 491 votes out of 921,731 cast.[206]

In the fall campaign, Blatt targeted women voters through a series of "coffee and questions" sessions.[207] But otherwise she struggled to articulate a positive agenda, listing accepting "change in the world" as the campaign's fundamental issue; when asked by Philadelphia's NBC affiliate for something more specific, she could not come up with an answer. But she gambled that going negative and linking her fate to Johnson's would pull her through.[208] Scott feared the same result: the senator complained, "I have to treat her like a lady, but she fights like a man."[209]

Another unexpectedly close contest occurred in California, which featured what the *Christian Science Monitor* termed "the clearest choice" ideologically ever in a Golden State Senate race.[210] Most observers had assumed that Pierre Salinger would easily retain the seat once he defeated Alan Cranston in the primary. Appointed to the Senate in June following Clair Engle's death, Salinger ran as the incumbent, an enormous asset given the lack of personal contact in California statewide elections.[211] But

[205] *Congressional Quarterly Weekly Report*, 2 Oct. 1964, p. 2298.
[206] *Christian Science Monitor*, 21 Aug. 1964.
[207] *Wall Street Journal*, 15 Oct. 1964.
[208] *Washington Star*, 10 Oct. 1964.
[209] *Wall Street Journal*, 15 Oct. 1964.
[210] *Christian Science Monitor*, 8 Sept. 1964.
[211] *Christian Science Monitor*, 11 Sept. 1964.

the GOP nominee, former movie actor George Murphy, turned Salinger's main advantage – his ties to the Kennedys – on its head. Described by the *New York Times* as "a soft-spoken, well tailored smiling man with a leisurely story for anyone who is willing to listen," Murphy termed his opponent a "synthetic" candidate "trading on the reflected glory of others."[212] Pointing to another Democrat grappling with the carpetbagger issue (Robert Kennedy in New York), the Republican promised, "I am part of no national conspiracy to serve the personal interests and ambitions of others."[213]

On the key issue of the campaign, Salinger opposed Proposition 14 (which called for repealing the state's open housing measure) and repeatedly said that he would rather lose than remain silent on the proposal. Murphy, on the other hand, declined to state his position, thus satisfying both factions in the state GOP. Moreover, Murphy's support for the Civil Rights Act and his opposition to making Social Security voluntary appealed to moderate Republicans.[214] Salinger countered by relentlessly linking Murphy to Goldwater. He termed the Republican "Goldwater's California echo," an "actor who wouldn't know what to say next if Barry Goldwater didn't keep shoving scripts into his hand."[215] Salinger's line of attack was aided by the refusal of the state's senior Republican, Thomas Kuchel, to endorse the GOP nominee. (Kuchel cited Murphy's backing from right-wing extremists.)[216] Nonetheless, by mid-September, Salinger's 20-point margin had dipped to single digits in one poll and 12 points in another.[217] Undecided voters were breaking for Murphy by a 2-to-1 margin.

The reasons for Salinger's decline very much troubled the president, who worried about the backlash in states like California.[218] Thinking back to George Wallace's showing in the Wisconsin primary, Johnson fretted that "we are getting a lot of static from workers in Milwaukee and Chicago and New York and Los Angeles and Seattle that Bobby Kennedy and me are going to bring out the Negroes to take their jobs the day after the election."[219] He pressed Attorney General Katzenbach to grant

[212] *New York Times*, 2 Oct. 1964.
[213] *New York World Telegram*, 29 Aug. 1964.
[214] *Christian Science Monitor*, 8 Sept. 1964.
[215] *Christian Science Monitor*, 29 Sept. 1964.
[216] *Los Angeles Times*, 18 Oct. 1964.
[217] *New York Times*, 2 Oct. 1964.
[218] *U.S. News&World Report*, 31 Aug. 1964.
[219] President Johnson and Larry O'Brien, 5:52 P.M., 19 Sept. 1964, Tape WH6409.12, Citation #5620, LBJ Recordings.

more television interviews indicating that the Civil Rights Act would not threaten whites' jobs.[220] But it was not so easy to counteract rumors such as one circulated by border state Republicans that the administration would force companies to replace 10 percent of their white workforce with blacks.[221] Even AFL-CIO President George Meany conceded that opposition to civil rights legislation among the white working class would "affect the campaign to some extent."[222]

Johnson tried to overcome the backlash with what the Goldwater campaign termed his "victory psychology" – touting poll numbers indicating that less than 10 percent of non-Southern Democrats were planning to vote Republican.[223] But to many observers the fact that the polls did not register a large backlash total suggested flaws in the polls, not the lack of a backlash. In the words of a Pennsylvania GOP official, "If it weren't for the possibility of a white backlash, the contest could be considered over." But as matters stood, race remained "an undercover issue" throughout the Middle Atlantic and Midwest.[224] Even President Kennedy's aide Ted Sorensen, observing the campaign in mid-September from a self-imposed political exile, predicted a Johnson victory with at least 400 electoral votes, with one caveat: "The only possible, but not present, danger to such a margin is the 'violence in the streets – race mobs – Negro crime – white backlash' issue."[225]

Some concrete signs existed, however, that the backlash in Northern states would lack the potency that national Democrats feared. In early 1964 Michigan legislators, seeking to create a black-majority district in Detroit, had combined the districts of two Democratic representatives, John Dingell and John Lesinski. The two sported remarkably similar political pedigrees: Army veterans, sons of congressmen, strong supporters of organized labor. Despite these similarities, Dingell and Lesinski differed radically on civil rights. Lesinski was the only Northern Democrat in the House to vote against the civil rights bill; Dingell supported the measure. During the campaign Lesinski overtly appealed to backlash sentiment, claiming a media conspiracy to cover up murders of whites by

[220] President Johnson and Nicholas Katzenbach, 2:27 P.M., 19 Sept. 1964, Tape WH6409.12, Citation #5613, LBJ Recordings.

[221] Ralph McGill to President Johnson, 30 Sept. 1964, Box 84, WHCF-PL, Lyndon B. Johnson Presidential Library.

[222] *Newsweek*, 17 Aug. 1964.

[223] "Oct. 5 Campaign Survey," Box 8, Barry Goldwater Papers, Arizona State University.

[224] *U.S. News&World Report*, 21 Sept. 1964.

[225] Ted Sorensen to Jack Valenti and Bill Moyers, 14 Sept. 1964, Box 84, WHCF-PL, Lyndon B. Johnson Presidential Library.

Detroit blacks. Since the new district was 90 percent white and contained 80 percent of Lesinski's old territory, Lesinski began the race as the favorite. But contrary to predictions, Dingell triumphed comfortably, 57 to 43 percent. After the vote the victor had a simple explanation for the result: "I can make an understandable and intelligent speech, where my opponent, frankly, cannot."[226]

Like Dingell, Johnson hoped that enthusiastic, effective campaigning would neutralize the Northern backlash. Since Congress remained in session until early October, Johnson restricted his September campaigning to relatively narrow time windows. Mimicking the strategy pursued by FDR in 1936 and 1940, the president used the power of his office as a campaign tool.[227] In El Paso, Johnson celebrated the signing of the Chamizal Treaty with Mexico in a speech proclaiming the benefits of diplomacy. "It's easy," he said, "to become impatient and impulsive. It's easy to tell the other fellow, 'Here is our ultimatum and you do as we say or else.' "[228] On another occasion, Johnson invited 25 newsmen and cameramen to accompany him as he toured the damage caused by Hurricane Cleo.[229] A few days earlier, the president had traveled to Cape Kennedy to mingle with astronauts – and to defend the space program, which Goldwater had deemed too expensive.[230] That these trips took Johnson to battleground states – Florida, Georgia, and Texas – went unmentioned. Johnson also originated the tactic of appearing before the cameras and microphones in the White House driveway, previously used for interviews with White House visitors, to make brief statements, in what was the first campaign photo-op.[231]

While maximizing political gain through nonpolitical activities, the president also obtained the greatest possible benefit from the occasions he did go out on the hustings, as in his 30-hour tour through New England. On September 28 and 29, he added 24 unscheduled stops, slept for under three hours, and attracted over 300,000 people.[232] To huge crowds in Burlington, Vermont, a state that had voted Republican for president in every election since 1856, Johnson charged that "one of our great parties has been captured by a faction of men who stood outside

[226] *Time*, 11 Sept. 1964.
[227] *Christian Science Monitor*, 22 Sept. 1964.
[228] *Baltimore Sun*, 26 Sept. 1964.
[229] *Baltimore Sun*, 19 Sept. 1964.
[230] *Baltimore Sun*, 16 Sept. 1964.
[231] *Baltimore Sun*, 19 Sept. 1964.
[232] *Christian Science Monitor*, 30 Sept. 1964.

FIGURE 5-3. President Johnson campaigning in New Hampshire, September 1964. © Courtesy of the Lyndon Baines Johnson Presidential Library. Photo by Cecil Stoughton.

the whole range of common agreement and common principles which have brought us to the summit of success."[233] A little later, in Manchester, New Hampshire, the crowd chanted "We want Johnson!" The president joyfully responded, "All right, wait a minute and you'll get him."[234] It was as if, Richard Rovere observed, Johnson "is eager to demonstrate to others, and perhaps to himself, that he has with the masses of the American people what he has lately taken to calling 'rapport.'"[235]

Of course, the president harbored such concerns because of widespread anecdotal evidence that voter enthusiasm for him was weak. The *New York Post*'s Milton Viorst described the "strange" condition of a campaign with "no dearth of volunteers," but who became active because they feared the opposition party's candidate. "The absence of spirit," Viorst declared, "is the most disquieting sign in the Johnson camp."[236]

Increasingly, many Democrats speculated that this lack of enthusiasm directly resulted from the frontlash strategy itself. The campaign certainly had succeeded – with, admittedly, a lot of help from the media and Goldwater himself – in demonizing the Arizona senator. But Johnson had struggled to articulate a positive agenda, to give moderate Republicans and independents a reason to affiliate with the Democrats beyond a fear that Goldwater, if elected, might trigger a nuclear war. With his advisers unable to develop speeches that fit his need, the president increasingly offered statements so bland as to be meaningless. In Providence, Rhode Island: "We're in favor of a lot of things and we're against mighty few."[237] In Harrisburg, Pennsylvania: "We're a nation of lovers and not a nation of haters."[238]

By the end of September, two alternatives to the frontlash strategy had emerged within the campaign apparatus. The first urged refocusing on the South. The president already had authorized the First Lady to make a Southern whistle-stop tour, but most of his advisers doubted that this effort alone would keep the region Democratic. In late September Henry Fowler, the future Treasury Secretary, proposed a "Project South," to target the Old Confederacy (excluding Alabama and Mississippi) and the border states. Fowler contended that the national Democrats had

[233] *Washington Post*, 29 Sept. 1964.
[234] *New York Times*, 29 Sept. 1964.
[235] Richard Rovere, "A Reporter at Large," *The New Yorker*, 17 Oct. 1964.
[236] Milton Viorst, "Johnson's Campaign Machinery," *The New Republic*, 5 Sept. 1964; see also *Baltimore Sun*, 21 Sept. 1964.
[237] *Boston Globe*, 30 Sept. 1964.
[238] *Christian Science Monitor*, 12 Sept. 1964.

allowed civil rights to blind them to the basic assumption that, as in other regions, "the winning issue in the South from our point of view is economics." In particular, Fowler urged appealing to business officials, on the grounds that the region needed "the leadership and initiative of far-sighted businessmen." Intrigued, the president authorized Fowler to proceed with his plan.[239]

Liz Carpenter, the First Lady's press secretary, independently reached the same conclusion. Carpenter contended that, despite polling figures, the Democrats could carry every state on the Atlantic Seaboard from Virginia through Florida, with the possible exception of North Carolina, where Democratic gubernatorial nominee Dan Moore remained hostile. After speaking with 30 newspaper editors and publishers, she contended that the chief problem was that the local campaigns lacked encouragement and guidance. With Johnson apparently devoting all of his resources to other regions, the "victory psychology" that helped the Democrats elsewhere was absent in the South. Like Fowler, Carpenter urged concentrating on winning back disaffected Southern voters.[240]

From the other side of the party came a different appeal. Throughout the Midwest and Far West, Larry O'Brien heard one straightforward request – that "the time is ripe for greater emphasis on the Lyndon B. Johnson positive program."[241] John Bartlow Martin, the former ambassador to the Dominican Republic whom Johnson used as a freelance speechwriter, likewise concluded that the president enjoyed "very broad but rather shallow support." Ironically, Johnson's consistent efforts to appear nonpolitical and above the fray had (correctly) been interpreted as a political tactic, thus failing to counter his image as a politician who would do or say anything to be elected. Accordingly, "the big landslide trend to the President seems to be more an anti-Goldwater trend than a pro-Johnson trend."[242]

Martin returned to the issue more ambitiously a few days later, just after Fowler proposed "Project South." The former ambassador argued that while Goldwater had reached a low point in the election, "we are

[239] Henry Fowler to President Johnson, 29 Sept. 1964, Box 84, WHCF-PL, Lyndon B. Johnson Presidential Library.

[240] Liz Carpenter to President Johnson, 28 Sept. 1964, Box 84, WHCF-PL, Lyndon B. Johnson Presidential Library.

[241] Larry O'Brien to President Johnson, 29 Sept. 1964, Box 3, Office Files of Henry Wilson, Lyndon B. Johnson Presidential Library.

[242] John Bartlow Martin to Bill Moyers, 22 Sept. 1964, Box 84, WHCF-PL, Lyndon B. Johnson Presidential Library.

stalled," with both polls and the press "breeding overconfidence and indifference among Democrats." From what Martin could detect, "the campaign has aroused little interest or enthusiasm, considerable disappointment, and some disgust" – to such an extent that some state races, notably Robert Kennedy's New York Senate bid, were overshadowing the presidential contest. As an alternative, Martin contended that the president needed to deliver some "programmatic" speeches; the strategy of attacking Goldwater without any positive content would simply "play into Goldwater's hands, cut the president down to Goldwater's level." The nuclear issue had run its course; the Democrats' constantly portraying Goldwater as reckless could create a sympathy vote for the Arizona senator. Johnson, Martin pleaded, "needs to *say something*" during the final weeks of the campaign.[243] Victory for victory's sake would not suffice.

From the campaign trail, Hubert Humphrey had reached a similar conclusion. Since the convention the vice-presidential candidate's staff worried about press portrayals of the Democratic effort as simply anti-Goldwater.[244] Humphrey himself wanted to deliver a "thoughtful and substantive speech, without too much shouting and a great deal of quiet but persuasive performance" – the Johnson effort had all but ignored topics such as the Alliance for Progress or an agenda for world peace. "I just feel," the Minnesota senator maintained, "that we have to develop some substantive matter, to proclaim this administration, to show that we know what we are doing."[245]

While relatively few Democrats wanted Johnson to use the remainder of the campaign to articulate a liberal agenda under which he could govern, many agreed with Humphrey and Martin that the president had allowed his "nonpolitical" approach to go too far. At the start of the campaign, Johnson declined to make sound or film clips for Democratic senators standing for re-election, lest he appear excessively partisan.[246] Given that the president had gone so far as to authorize Reuther's donation to the Taft committee, it came as little surprise that local candidates started grumbling about Johnson's insufficient interest in their problems.[247] From

[243] John Bartlow Martin to Bill Moyers, 1 Oct. 1964, Box 84, WHCF-PL, Lyndon B. Johnson Presidential Library.

[244] Ted Van Dyk to Bill Connell, 21 Sept. 1964, Box 75, Hubert Humphrey Papers, Minnesota State Historical Society.

[245] Hubert Humphrey to Gene Foley, 16 Sept. 1964, Box 74, Hubert Humphrey Papers, Minnesota State Historical Society.

[246] Jack Valenti to President Johnson, 25 Aug. 1964, Box 83, WHCF-PL, Lyndon B. Johnson Presidential Library.

[247] *New York Herald-Tribune*, 30 Sept. 1964.

the president's own staff, Larry O'Brien now recommended increased coordination between the presidential and congressional campaigns and urged Johnson – to no avail – that "immediate cash assistance," perhaps on the order of $200,000, "to congressional candidates in several close races might well be the impetus to victory."[248]

In early October the president started floating a third option – an approach that would maximize his personal margin of victory. Johnson wanted more attention paid to his record of "legislative results," a theme that resonated powerfully. (He received higher marks in the category than in any other polling area.) The president also believed that the time had come for a 15-minute television advertisement on the possibility of nuclear war – "that's the only thing that really makes them pee in their britches." He had a general script in mind: "Now, I'm not going to say anything about my opponent. I want you to know that he's served as a senator from a great state. I'm not going to recommend him or not recommend him – you can be your own judge. Who do you want to answer that phone and who do you want to have that thumb there on that table close to that button? That's a question for you to decide: you decide on your own judgment, and you decide without emotion. You decide without fear." From a more positive angle, he ordered 30-minute television ads featuring prominent lawyers, scientists, and women – "because we need that dignity that goes with the scientists, with the head of the American Bar, with some of these top women." In each of these programs, he wanted the panelists to emphasize his carrying on the program of President Kennedy. "I think," Johnson reasoned, "we can pull a lot of people – hold them – that way."[249]

Ken O'Donnell once recalled that Johnson ran a campaign as if he were standing for the House of Representatives.[250] Johnson now expressed concern that local offices lacked sufficient quantities of literature and bumper stickers, all while "there are Goldwater stickers all over the country." If the president had one order for his nominal campaign manager, Larry O'Brien, it was to "see that they get out stickers." Johnson also wondered why Jim Rowe (busy coordinating his 72 citizen committees) had not done more to position quality billboards around the country. "I'm convinced," he theorized, that billboards "can do a lot of good

[248] Larry O'Brien to President Johnson, 4 Oct. 1964, Box 84, WHCF-PL, Lyndon B. Johnson Presidential Library.

[249] President Johnson, Walter Jenkins, and Bill Moyers, 10:38 A.M., 10 Oct. 1964, Tape WH6410.05, Citation #5851, LBJ Recordings.

[250] Ken O'Donnell oral history, Lyndon B. Johnson Presidential Library.

quick, and I think we need them." Moreover, all advertisements needed to read "Vote Democratic," not "Vote Democrat," since "Democrat is a Republican way of saying it."[251] Johnson was also taken with homemade signs. After spotting one such sign (reading "Twenty Percent Less Cavities with Johnson," a tweak on the far right's suspicion of fluoridating public water supplies), the president instructed an aide, "Get a lot more of those handmade signs made."[252]

While any good campaign needed bumper stickers, billboards, and literature, Johnson considered newspaper advertisements of little value. "The trouble is when you get an advertisement, some son of a bitch just puts a scoop full of dictionary in it," making the print unreadable. The president urged shifting the resources previously allocated to newspapers to television spots. On that issue Johnson wanted to pressure some of his oldest benefactors – Texans Gus Wortham and George Brown – recalling that both had promised at the start of the year that they would produce $1 million for the campaign.[253] He wanted that amount in increased media expenditures before Election Day alone.[254]

The president also critiqued the performance of the other half of his ticket. Someone had to tell Humphrey not to call him "Lyndon or Lyndon Johnson. Refer to him as the President." The Minnesota senator, Johnson fumed, "is just like a gigolo." He ought to say, "'They're hitting our dear President.' Or, 'Our great President.'" Moreover, Humphrey's speeches lacked punch – "he's just talking about stuff that nobody understands." And the campaign needed to do some hitting of its own, perhaps by spreading the rumor that Goldwater was "psychotic."[255]

With all state polls now in – except for Alaska and New Mexico – the campaign needed its "best propagandist" to start publicizing the favorable numbers, "something that I've been carrying on psychologically up to now almost alone with my polls." Johnson particularly worried about surveys suggesting that a presidential landslide would not affect House and Senate contests. "We've got," he maintained, "to scare the congressmen, we've got to scare the senators that if they get tied in with

[251] President Johnson, Walter Jenkins, and Bill Moyers, 10:38 A.M., 10 Oct. 1964, Tape WH6410.05, Citation #5851, LBJ Recordings.

[252] Richard Rovere, "A Reporter at Large," *The New Yorker*, 17 Oct. 1964.

[253] President Johnson, Walter Jenkins, and Bill Moyers, 10:38 A.M., 10 Oct. 1964, Tape WH6410.05, Citation #5851, LBJ Recordings.

[254] Alexander, *Financing the 1964 Election*, p. 46.

[255] President Johnson, Walter Jenkins, and Bill Moyers, 10:38 A.M., 10 Oct. 1964, Tape WH6410.05, Citation #5851, LBJ Recordings.

Goldwater, it's going to be a clean sweep, and it's going to be worse than '36" – yet another reference to Franklin Roosevelt's greatest triumph, when the Democrat carried 46 states against Alf Landon. The president knew that many of his political advisers opposed going after Goldwater so hard, concerned that the campaign had become too negative, "but I don't give a damn. I've been winning these elections, and I haven't been winning them listening to other people."[256]

Johnson had one initiative of personal import: he ordered the Democratic National Committee "to put a little money in Maine and Vermont" – at least $20,000 – "right away." He rationalized the move on the grounds of building up the New England Democratic Party. Since the last poll from Maine had shown the president with a 58-point lead and Larry O'Brien considered Vermont a sure victory, the states hardly seemed to need additional campaign cash.[257] But Maine and Vermont had one common element: they were the only two states that Roosevelt failed to carry in the 1936 election. In 1964, at least in this respect, Johnson would outperform his mentor.

Johnson once described O'Brien's political reports as "the best I've seen."[258] And it was O'Brien, at the end of his national campaign inspection, who informed the president once and for all that the frontlash strategy had failed. On October 11 O'Brien indicated that he had no reason to believe "that these 'Johnson Republicans' are likely to become Democratic converts." Indeed, he doubted that they would even vote a straight Democratic ticket in 1964 – many would vote for the president, but then would "swing right back to the big R for the other state contests."[259] For 1966 and beyond, the administration should not expect to find them in the Democratic column.

A few days later the *Christian Science Monitor*'s shrewd political editor, Erwin Canham, reached the same conclusion. He predicted that November 3 would feature ticket-splitting to a degree unprecedented in American history. On the surface, such a development raised the possibility that the 1964 campaign would be a realigning election. But, at best,

[256] President Johnson, Walter Jenkins, and Bill Moyers, 10:38 A.M., 10 Oct. 1964, Tape WH6410.05, Citation #5851, LBJ Recordings.

[257] Larry O'Brien to President Johnson, 9 Oct. 1964, Box 84, WHCF-PL, Lyndon B. Johnson Presidential Library.

[258] President Johnson, Walter Jenkins, and Bill Moyers, 10:38 A.M., 10 Oct. 1964, Tape WH6410.05, Citation #5851, LBJ Recordings.

[259] Larry O'Brien to President Johnson, 11 Oct. 1964, Box 3, Office Files of Henry Wilson, Lyndon B. Johnson Presidential Library.

he foresaw a "temporary realignment." On the central question of the frontlash strategy – "Will the so-called moderate Republicans who are jumping from the Goldwater ticket remain on the Democratic side?" – Canham offered an unequivocal response: "There is no indication that they will, or want to."[260]

As the campaign entered its final weeks, Johnson returned to the issue he first had faced in the aftermath of the convention: what exactly did he hope to accomplish with his victory? His lead now seemed insurmountable, with the Goldwater campaign disintegrating. If he could not permanently win over the frontlash voters, should he attempt to save the Southern Democratic Party? Use the rest of the campaign to gain a popular mandate for his 1965 legislative program? Seek to bolster his historical legacy? Assist Democratic congressional candidates?

The six weeks between the end of the Democratic convention and early October represented one of the most unusual periods in any twentieth-century presidential campaign. Barry Goldwater and his running mate traveled the country, delivered speeches, ran television ads, and devised political strategy. But, for all practical purposes, the Republican national campaign had no effect. In this sense Johnson was not only running from ahead; he was running against himself. His overwhelming lead provided the luxury to campaign for purposes other than achieving victory. The central debate of this period came not between Johnson and Goldwater but within the Democratic effort itself, over the campaign's purpose. Because Johnson functioned as the "President-Candidate," his preferred approach – the frontlash strategy – prevailed. But this strategy proved remarkably difficult to implement beyond the savagely negative campaign against Goldwater on which all Democrats agreed. By early October, when widespread evidence existed that the frontlash approach would not realize its goal of permanently winning over moderate Republicans, the more traditional strategic alternatives floated after the Atlantic City convention resurfaced.

Then, for a stunning 24-hour period, a political scandal threatened to render all these debates moot.

[260] *Christian Science Monitor*, 15 Oct. 1964.

6

Beyond 1936

Lyndon Johnson trusted relatively few people in his life. But Walter Jenkins, who had worked for him in one capacity or another for nearly three decades, did earn the president's faith. *Time* described Jenkins as "the mysterious, slightly out-of-focus fellow who seldom had his picture taken or got in the papers but who knew everything that was going on."[1] After being implicated in the Bobby Baker investigation, Jenkins lowered his profile even further, but the quality of his service for Johnson remained high.

Jenkins advised Johnson on virtually all legislative and political matters. And if Johnson served as his own campaign manager, Jenkins functioned as deputy, performing the campaign tasks for which the president lacked either the time or the patience. Johnson's going full time on the campaign trail increased Jenkins's importance. The president telephoned Washington to discuss matters with his aide at least once a day; sometimes the two talked for over an hour, covering everything from broad campaign strategy to the size of LBJ bumper stickers. In one of these conversations, the president left Jenkins with a list of 45 people that he wanted called.[2]

On October 7, with Johnson on the campaign trail, Jenkins and his wife attended a party to celebrate the opening of the *Newsweek* building. Jenkins drank heavily, and, after his wife went home, he went to the nearby Washington YMCA, a well-known spot for illicit homosexual

[1] *Time*, 23 Oct. 1964.

[2] President Johnson and Walter Jenkins, 8:21 P.M., 10 Oct. 1964, Tape WH6410.07, Citation #5868, LBJ Recordings.

rendezvous. (The evening that the arrest became known, Kenneth Crawford of *Newsweek* termed the Y "a stinkhole for years," noting, "Every time I look out of the window at it, I am afraid of what I will see.")[3] There Jenkins was arrested. At his booking, he listed himself a "clerk," forfeited a $50 fine, and returned to work late that evening at the White House.

Jenkins was hardly the first prominent policymaker embroiled in such a scandal. In 1943 Undersecretary of State Sumner Welles was forced to resign after Maine senator Owen Brewster threatened a congressional investigation into reports that Welles had solicited a black, male railroad porter. Ten years later Arthur Vandenberg, Jr., withdrew his nomination as Eisenhower's appointments secretary after an FBI background check discovered possible homosexual behavior. Beyond its perceived immorality, homosexuality was considered a security risk: Soviet agents could – it was argued – use a gay liaison as material for blackmail. For these reasons Eisenhower issued an executive order prohibiting not only the federal government but also all companies with federal contracts from employing gay people. The order remained in place under Kennedy and Johnson.

By October 13 sources within the Goldwater campaign had learned of the Jenkins incident; one contacted John Williams to promise "a lot of information on Walter Jenkins."[4] The next morning word leaked to the Washington newspapers, which called the White House requesting comment. Jenkins immediately confessed all to Abe Fortas, who found the aide "well off his rocker."[5] Fortas, joined by Washington power broker Clark Clifford, met with the publishers of the *Washington Post,* the *Washington Star,* and the *Washington News,* pleading, in the name of common decency, not to run the story. At each stop they received assurances that the papers themselves would not break news of the affair. In the event, Republican National Committee chairman Dean Burch forced the issue. Just after 6:00 P.M., Burch issued a public statement alleging, "There is a report sweeping Washington that the White House is desperately trying to suppress news strongly affecting national security."[6] At 8:09 P.M., the UPI news service issued the first bulletin on the story.

[3] Crawford quoted in Katie Louchheim journal, 15 Oct. 1964, Box 79, Katie Louchheim Papers, Library of Congress.

[4] John Williams memorandum, 13 Oct. 1964, Box 32, John Williams Papers, University of Delaware.

[5] President Johnson and Abe Fortas, 1:13 A.M., 15 Oct. 1964, Tape WH6410.10, Citation #5888, LBJ Recordings.

[6] *Washington Post*, 15 Oct. 1964.

As word of the arrest spread, the president was in New York, to serve as the main speaker for the evening's Al Smith Memorial Dinner. Johnson biographer Robert Dallek has speculated that, given their relationship, Jenkins must have told Johnson about the arrest immediately after it occurred, and that the president ordered his aide to keep the matter confidential.[7] Although Dallek's theory is plausible, no evidence to confirm it exists in the lengthy (recorded) conversations between Jenkins and Johnson from October 9 and 10. Moreover, when Fortas and Clifford informed the president of events, Johnson's reaction was one of palpable shock, so intense that this master of phone conversations could not disguise his feelings.[8]

Johnson immediately cancelled all of his engagements except his Smith dinner speech. For several tense hours, well into the wee hours of the morning, the president engaged in a series of increasingly frantic conversations with Fortas, Clifford, and other trusted advisers, such as John Connally and New York lawyer Edwin Weisl. With the story out "in all its gruesome details," Johnson understood that Jenkins had to resign at once. "What the goddamned hell confidence are [people] going to have in the presidency," the president hissed, if he responded to knowledge of the arrest by "pussyfooting and procrastinating and so forth."[9]

The more he considered matters, the more panicked Johnson became. The revelation "could mean the ballgame," the president fretted to Fortas. He imagined that "every farmer in the country is upset about it." ("City folks not so much," the president speculated; "they're upset, too, but not anything like it.") Johnson expected the Republicans to demand an immediate congressional inquiry into possible compromises of national security – perhaps, he speculated, he should preempt them by appointing a special commission, modeled on the Warren Commission, to look into the matter.[10] Attempts by Fortas and Clifford to soothe the president were undermined by an over-the-top reaction from Connally, who told Johnson that the arrest "will obviously be harmful, because...they'll be

[7] Robert Dallek, *Flawed Giant: Lyndon Johnson and His Times, 1961–1973* (New York: Oxford University Press, 1998), pp. 179–81.

[8] President Johnson and Abe Fortas, later including Clark Clifford, 3:56 P.M., 14 Oct. 1964, Tape WH6410.08, Citation #5876, LBJ Recordings.

[9] President Johnson and Clark Clifford, later joined by Abe Fortas, 8:02 P.M., 14 Oct. 1964, Tape WH6410.09, Citation #5880, LBJ Recordings; President Johnson and Abe Fortas, later joined by George Reedy, 8:32 P.M., 14 Oct. 1964, Tape WH6410.09, Citation #5881, LBJ Recordings.

[10] President Johnson and Abe Fortas, 1:13 A.M., 15 Oct. 1964, Tape WH6410.10, Citation #5888, LBJ Recordings.

digging up the Sumner Welles thing, at least in their private conversations, you know." Moreover, Connally fretted, the Republicans would surely start "talking about communists and homos and everything else that infiltrated the government, and all that sort of thing, and tie it into the morals business – although they've been talking about morals in a completely different light."[11]

The president searched in vain for a way to place a positive spin on the story. Perhaps, he mused to Clifford, the administration could find a way to say something "that's good," such as telling journalists, "off the record, if none of you have never had anything like this in your family, why, you wouldn't understand it, but nearly every family's had some problem." (Clifford torpedoed the idea, since "of course, every family has problems, but they don't happen to have this kind.")[12] Then Johnson reflected on the fact that Jenkins, like many in the Washington elite, had served in the Army Reserve unit commanded by none other than Goldwater – and therefore "Goldwater was his commanding officer just like me."[13] The absurd claim that he and Goldwater were Jenkins's "two bosses" recalled the president's legalistic approach to the Baker affair, when he implausibly compared the kicked back hi-fi set to Goldwater's office staff having bought the senator a miniature television set as a Christmas gift.

As he had done following the Baker/McCloskey revelations, Johnson next turned to the FBI. Since coming to office, his relationship with the agency had repeatedly blurred the line between professional and political. Johnson had asked Hoover to track down White House leaks to the press. He had encouraged Deke DeLoach, the FBI's White House liaison, to be sure that damaging information about Don Reynolds found its way to the press. And, most brazenly, he had used the FBI to monitor Kennedy forces at the Atlantic City convention. So it came as little surprise that, in the minutes before his Smith dinner speech, the president telephoned DeLoach to order a full FBI investigation, hoping to trade on the FBI's public image as impartial arbiters of the law to produce an investigation that would neutralize any political harm. He added that the

[11] President Johnson and John Connally, 8:45 P.M., 14 Oct. 1964, Tape WH6410.09, Citation #5882, LBJ Recordings.

[12] President Johnson and Mildred Steagall, later including Abe Fortas, Clark Clifford, and Edwin Weisl, 9:36 P.M., 14 Oct. 1964, Tape WH6410.10, Citation #5885, LBJ Recordings.

[13] President Johnson and Abe Fortas, 12:02 A.M., 15 Oct. 1964, Tape WH6410.10, Citation #5887, LBJ Recordings.

inquiry should begin immediately, with a report ready for release within a week.[14]

Jenkins's arrest and its revelation could not have come at a worse time for Johnson. The president was out of Washington, with a politically important speech to deliver, dependent upon updates from Clifford and Fortas for the latest information. The situation required immediate decisions before Johnson and his key advisers could meet and think things through. And Jenkins was at the nerve center of the campaign, magnifying the effect of his abrupt departure.

As word of Jenkins's resignation reached Texas, Don Cook, a longtime Johnson associate and public utilities executive, returned from the telephone shaking, telling friends, "There is something fishy."[15] Cook guessed that documents had surfaced proving that Jenkins had lied in the Baker scandal. The situation was actually far worse. The president had ordered an immediate FBI inquiry into all issues relating to Jenkins, but the safe in the disgraced aide's White House office – which federal agents would be examining the following morning – contained documents suggesting financial improprieties by the Johnson campaign.

In the weeks before his arrest, Jenkins had been working closely with New York philanthropist Mary Lasker. Lasker's longstanding relationship with both the president and the First Lady was only one element of a remarkably diverse career. A Radcliffe graduate, she was best known for her work with the Albert and Mary Lasker Foundation, which awarded grants to further medical research on cancer, heart, stroke, and blindness. Active in the New York cultural scene, Lasker also teamed with New York urban planner Robert Moses to support beautification projects in New York. To Moses she possessed "the irresistible combination Madison Avenue dreams of – the blend of many essences in the beautiful package."[16]

Lasker's advocacy for increased public funding for medical research brought her into the world of politics, and after the late 1940s she became a key player in Democratic politics. By 1964 she was a member of the President's Club, the exclusive organization – whose membership was not

[14] President Johnson and Cartha (Deke) DeLoach, 9:00 P.M., 14 Oct. 1964, Tape WH6410.09, Citation #5884, LBJ Recordings.

[15] Cook quoted in Katie Louchheim journal, 15 Oct. 1964, Box 79, Katie Louchheim Papers, Library of Congress.

[16] Moses quoted in "About Albert and Mary Lasker," www.laskerfoundation.org/about/albertmary.html, last accessed 10 Nov. 2007.

publicly revealed – consisting of the party's biggest donors.[17] Democratic National Committee Treasurer Richard Maguire once told her that she deserved the title "Mrs. Democrat" for all that she did for the party.[18]

Partly because of her friendship with the First Lady, Lasker enjoyed unusually close connections with Johnson. In 1960 she lobbied New York liberals in her circle, such as Eleanor Roosevelt and *New York Post* publisher Dorothy Schiff, to view Johnson more generously. "It was very hard," she recalled, "to convince people that he was a genuine liberal, as I was sure he was." Had Johnson more aggressively courted liberals like Roosevelt and Schiff, Lasker believed that "he could have convinced them. But he was too busy as majority leader, and the convincing couldn't be done secondhand."[19]

After Johnson assumed the presidency, Lasker regularly traveled to the White House and offered loans from her extensive art collection. (The First Lady, in turn, commented on Lasker's "rare quality of making suggestions in a way that, somehow or other, winds up by getting them done.")[20] The president, meanwhile, wanted to name her ambassador to Finland, but she demurred on the grounds that she would feel as if she were "being exiled."[21] Instead, Johnson brought her in as a campaign fundraiser and appointed her a trustee for the newly created John F. Kennedy Center for the Performing Arts.

It was in this context that the Jenkins-Lasker discussions took place. On October 10 Jenkins informed the president that Lasker was "very anxious" to swear in the new trustees as soon as possible; she thought "that if you could swear them in a 10-minute ceremony, that she could then hit some of them up." After Johnson gained Jenkins's assurance that Lasker had "done everything she said she'd do," he approved the list and promised to move ahead with the ceremony.[22] The aide then placed into his office safe the documentation about the names and specific amounts

[17] John Bailey to Mary Lasker, 3 Feb. 1964, Box 155, Mary Lasker Papers, Columbia University.

[18] Richard Maguire to Mary Lasker, 3 June 1965, Box 155, Mary Lasker Papers, Columbia University.

[19] Robert Mann, *The Walls of Jericho: Lyndon Johnson, Hubert Humphrey, Richard Russell, and the Struggle for Human Rights* (New York, Harcourt, Brace, 1996), p. 270.

[20] Lady Bird Johnson, *A White House Diary* (New York: Holt, Rinehart, and Winston, 1970), entry for 25 May 1964, p. 146.

[21] President Johnson and Mary Lasker, 7:50 P.M., 20 Jan. 1964, Tape WH6401.17, Citation #1440, LBJ Recordings.

[22] President Johnson and Walter Jenkins, 8:21 P.M., 10 Oct. 1964, Tape WH6410.07, Citation #5868, LBJ Recordings.

promised. One of the few people to have seen the safe's contents was Edwin Weisl, whom Johnson had installed as New York state party chair and who was with the president when word of Jenkins's arrest broke. Weisl immediately told Johnson that there were "lots of names involved, and lots of other things."[23]

Given the difficulties that the president had already experienced with the McCloskey revelations, even a hint that he had traded federal positions for campaign contributions would be, as Johnson himself stated, a "bombshell."[24] He quickly realized that the documents needed to be removed before the FBI gained access to them. Such an act, however, would constitute obstruction of justice.

Johnson already had veered close to this line in September, when he ordered Fortas to work with the attorneys for Bobby Baker and Matt McCloskey to coordinate their (false) responses to Don Reynolds's claim that McCloskey had illegally funneled funds to the 1960 Kennedy-Johnson campaign. Now Johnson crossed the line. The president bluntly told Fortas that as he was "fearful that as Deke's [FBI] boys go to following through, that they might be coming over there for certain, looking for confidential papers and other things," he needed to "be sure that you'd got in there and got all of that material...and took it to your office."[25] Three times during the evening of October 14th Johnson ordered Fortas to remove the compromising files; on the third occasion, he reached Fortas at Jenkins's office, in the process of going through the safe. (Johnson previously had instructed Jenkins's secretary, Mildred Steagall, to remain at her post and admit no one until Fortas arrived.) The FBI never gained access to the material, and no mention of the Lasker connection appeared in the campaign or any time thereafter.

With the threat posed by the Lasker documents neutralized, Johnson went to bed, just before 4:00 A.M. He awoke to the morning papers of October 15, which portrayed the Jenkins affair as a serious threat to the president's reelection. In the *New York Times,* Scotty Reston argued that the case could only "be detrimental" for Johnson, with the sole question just how much it would hurt. Reston reasoned that the particulars

[23] President Johnson and Abe Fortas, later including George Reedy, 8:32 P.M., 14 Oct. 1964, Tape WH6410.07, Citation #5868, LBJ Recordings.

[24] President Johnson and John Connally, 8:45 P.M., 14 Oct. 1964, Tape WH6410.09, Citation #5882, LBJ Recordings.

[25] President Johnson and Mildred Steagall, later including Abe Fortas, Clark Clifford, and Edwin Weisl, 9:36 P.M., 14 Oct. 1964, Tape WH6410.10, Citation #5885, LBJ Recordings.

of the arrest might not have harmed another president. But, all along, Johnson's "major handicap" came in his identification "with the frontier politics of his native state." Goldwater had successfully articulated a "more general moral case in the election, namely, that the easy ethics of political Washington have contributed to a general decline of morals in the nation." Reston now heard a number of people predicting that the Jenkins arrest might just "blow the lid" off other Johnson scandals, paving the way for a Goldwater victory on November 3.[26] After reading the column, Eugene McCarthy scowled that as Reston was a "round-headed Presbyterian, he thinks like every other Presbyterian."[27] But this Presbyterian captured the consensus of the political classes.

Facing reactions such as Reston's, and convinced that the arrest would provide another excuse for "these historians writing about the Hardings, and so forth" – figures who wanted to portray his administration as a scandal-plagued failure – the president responded more aggressively. Just before 8:00 A.M., Johnson phoned Attorney General Nicholas Katzenbach for a 50-minute off-the-cuff discussion of how the administration could use – and abuse – the powers of government to, in his words, "fuzz" up the morals issue sufficiently that he could survive unscathed until Election Day. Maybe, he mused, the whole thing was "a frame-up," since RNC staffers were "tipping everybody in town" about the arrest. Or, perhaps, Katzenbach could "get somebody looking into this [Lockport] Felt Company outfit," to see if Miller's law partner "had any contacts with the Federal Trade Commission in connection with their immediate problems." And Johnson was "damn tired" of the IRS "messing around"; the time had come to get the agency "turned loose" on Don Reynolds's finances. "I want them working nights," the president told his chief law enforcement officer. "Pull any people in there that they can." It seemed to him that "because of [John] Williams, they've been scared to touch" Reynolds. If the Jenkins affair promised to intensify attacks on his ethics, Johnson wanted to create renewed allegations against the ethics of his opponents.[28]

Katzenbach smartly parried these requests, although Johnson would press the issue for the rest of the campaign. The other aspect of the morning-after offensive, the president expected, would be easier. The night

[26] *New York Times*, 15 Oct. 1964.

[27] McCarthy quoted in Katie Louchheim journal, 15 Oct. 1964, Box 79, Katie Louchheim Papers, Library of Congress.

[28] President Johnson and Nicholas Katzenbach, 7:56 A.M., 15 Oct. 1964, Tape WH6410.11, Citation #5891, LBJ Recordings.

before, John Connally spoke bluntly to Johnson: "The only place you're vulnerable at all is on the morals thing, the character thing." Therefore, the Texas governor urged, the president had to carefully craft his personal image, chiefly by drawing "your family as close to you as you can." Johnson needed to remind voters – "particularly in the light of what's happened" with Jenkins – that "you're a husband, and your wife and your two daughters. You are an American family."[29]

The First Lady, however, had other ideas. With Johnson headed to Buffalo for a morning campaign appearance, Lady Bird, who had plotted out her own response to the Jenkins resignation, delayed the president on his way to his plane. She argued that, in this case, personal sympathy represented not only the humane thing to do but also the appropriate political response. Johnson was unconvinced. "The average farmer," he told his wife, "just can't understand your knowing it and approving it, or condoning it – any more than he can [Dean] Acheson not turning his back" on Alger Hiss. (As with his fear of becoming another Harding, the president regularly interpreted contemporary political crises through the lens of history; in this case, he was referring to the ill-considered statement of Harry Truman's secretary of state that he would not "turn his back" on his old friend, Hiss, when the alleged communist spy went on trial for perjury.) But the First Lady had called to inform, not to ask permission: she already had decided her course of action. And she was the one figure in Johnson's entourage who had the power to act independently. She would promise only to "*try* to be discrete," but reiterated her "*strong* feeling that a gesture of support to Walter on our part is best."[30]

As she made clear to her husband, the First Lady had every intention of issuing a statement of support on Jenkins's behalf. "My heart," she told the American public later that day, "is aching for someone who has reached the end point of exhaustion in dedicated service to his country." Two thousand miles away, campaigning in Denver, Barry Goldwater was asked for his response. He initially remarked, "I don't know what the hell this is about," and later refused comment altogether.[31] Ironically, earlier in the day, in Harlingen, Texas, the GOP candidate had delivered remarks that would prefigure the dilemma to face Johnson: "The people," Goldwater declared, "have looked at the White House and found it

[29] President Johnson and John Connally, 8:45 P.M., 14 Oct. 1964, Tape WH6410.09, Citation #5882, LBJ Recordings.

[30] President Johnson and Lady Bird Johnson, 9:12 A.M., Tape WH6410.11, Citation #5895, LBJ Recordings.

[31] *Time*, 23 Oct. 1964.

dark with scandal. The people have looked at the man who now occupies the White House and have found him shadowed by suspicions which no amount of handshaking and hurrah can chase away."[32]

Henry Gemmill of the *Wall Street Journal* spent October 15 on the telephone with his sources in both parties and the next day offered an even more troubling interpretation for the president. Gemmill noted that the arrest "strikes politicians as the one thing that just might snatch a Democratic presidential defeat from the jaws of victory." One Republican senator privately compared the arrest to the Profumo affair – "except here it's boys instead of girls." (In 1963 British defense minister John Profumo resigned after revelations that his mistress also had slept with a Soviet naval attaché; the scandal ultimately led to the collapse of the Conservative government.) Meanwhile, at Democratic headquarters, "there's a pall of gloom"; one Johnson staffer conceded that the arrest "coincides with the one point on which the Goldwater campaign seems to be making any headway." Asked how the administration should respond, one top labor activist admitted, "You just pray, I guess."[33]

Despite Goldwater's restrained initial reaction, the issue quickly seeped into GOP campaign oratory. Arguing that the case "raises very, very serious questions" of security, William Miller reasoned that Johnson needed to explain "how a man of such convictions could be appointed to the highest councils of government."[34] Goldwater, meanwhile, charged that Johnson had used "every power of his great office, right now – yesterday and tomorrow – to cover up one of the sorriest rumors we have ever had in the nation's capital." In response, Republican headquarters announced the formation of a new committee – Mothers for a Moral America – designed to "restore moral leadership in the nation."[35]

In the hours after the resignation, editorialists and columnists weighed in on the turn of events. The *Baltimore Sun* gave the story an eight-column headline; the resignation received five columns in the *New York Herald Tribune*.[36] Expressing the most partisan view, the *Chicago Tribune* asked, "How does Lyndon Johnson collect these characters?" The litany of figures with ethical problems – first Billy Sol Estes, then Bobby Baker, and now Walter Jenkins – suggested either the "blindness of misguided loyalty"

[32] *U.S. News & World Report*, 26 Oct. 1964.

[33] *Wall Street Journal*, 17 Oct. 1964.

[34] *Christian Science Monitor*, 17 Oct. 1964.

[35] *The Times* (London), 16 Oct. 1964.

[36] John Kessel, *The Goldwater Coalition: Republican Strategies in 1964* (Indianapolis: Bobbs-Merrill, 1968), p. 211.

or "moral obtusity" on Johnson's part.[37] The *Christian Science Monitor,* which endorsed neither candidate, reasoned that the resignation gave the morality issue "a far deeper cutting edge" by adding to the "highly controversial and unclarified issues" in Johnson's public background.[38]

Commentators, in general, took an even more apocalyptic view. Erwin Canham of the *Christian Science Monitor* argued that "unless new and clearly mitigating facts come to light, it seems to me that the Jenkins case will hurt President Johnson seriously," by reinforcing voters' preexisting suspicions of Johnson's personal integrity.[39] Samuel Lubell predicted in the *Los Angeles Times* that the arrest would decrease Republican support for Johnson and increase voter disgust with the campaign, especially in the South, thus depressing turnout. Both outcomes would benefit Goldwater.[40] *The Times* of London termed the resignation "a severe setback" to the president, as it violated the "postwar political primer for beginners: perversion is synonymous with treason." The paper's Washington correspondent dryly noted that given Johnson's management style, "between the errand running and relaxation over a whisky and soda, [Jenkins] must have been privy to many of the presidential decisions and national secrets."[41]

Throughout the year, as the attacks on his public morality and allegations of personal corruption had intensified, Johnson had grown increasingly willing to do whatever was necessary to defend himself. During the initial stage of the Bobby Baker affair, he tried to discredit Don Reynolds and squelch the Senate inquiry from behind the scenes. When John Williams used the McCloskey allegations to revive the Baker issue, the president approved efforts by Fortas to have the principals coordinate their stories – fully aware that in doing so, it was unlikely that Baker and McCloskey would tell the truth. Now, with the ultimate threat to his political survival, Johnson went even further, instructing Fortas to remove evidence that could torpedo his reelection.

In the short term Johnson paid no penalty for his dubious actions. A week after the arrest, John Williams was left to chide the national media for "closing its eyes on the recent exposures."[42] To the Delaware

[37] *Chicago Tribune*, 16 Oct. 1964.
[38] *Christian Science Monitor*, 17 Oct. 1964.
[39] *Christian Science Monitor*, 17 Oct. 1964.
[40] *Los Angeles Times*, 17 Oct. 1964.
[41] *The Times* (London) 16 Oct. 1964.
[42] John Williams to T. C. Link, 21 Oct. 1964, Box 32, John Williams Papers, University of Delaware.

senator's chagrin and the surprise of most political observers, international events crowded the Jenkins scandal off the front pages. Just as the Tonkin Gulf attacks shifted attention from the awkward elimination of Robert Kennedy as a running mate, now international instability turned the nation's focus from Jenkins. And so, in one of the ironies of the campaign, foreign policy, the president's one-time weakness, yet again helped him politically. On October 15 an announcement came from Moscow that Nikita Khrushchev had fallen from power. The same day Harold Wilson captured the closest election in British history, becoming prime minister with a five-seat Labour majority. Within 24 hours, the People's Republic of China successfully tested its first atomic bomb.[43]

Johnson immediately cancelled all campaign events and returned to the White House for two days of high-profile consultations. He delivered a nationally televised address promising that the administration would guard against international turbulence threatening national security. In another example of the way in which the presidency's institutional powers could control the campaign agenda, a hastily assembled panel of consultants came to the White House to join Johnson in discussing events.[44] At the gathering the president announced that he was doing everything possible to bring U.S. foreign policy up to speed with the changed international environment. (As soon as the television cameras were turned off, he left the meeting.) The reaction played the turbulence for all it was worth: as Scotty Reston observed, "the world has not been kind" to Barry Goldwater.[45]

The Chinese nuclear test and change of Soviet leadership blunted the momentum of the Jenkins story. Meanwhile, the First Lady's expression of personal sympathy – delivered despite the president's opposition – paid political dividends, showing that on this issue at least, her political instincts were keener than her husband's. In some respects, ironically, Johnson also benefited from mid-1960s attitudes toward homosexuality. In an era before Stonewall, the U.S. public had not passed through what the British novelist E. M. Forster described as "the change from ignorance and terror to familiarity and contempt," revealing that "what the public really loathes in homosexuality is not the thing itself but having to think

[43] *New York Times*, 16 Oct. 1964, 17 Oct. 1964.

[44] "The President's Panel of Consultants on International Affairs (9:00 A.M., Wednesday, Oct. 21, 1964)," Box 1, NSF, Bromley Smith Files, Lyndon B. Johnson Presidential Library.

[45] *New York Times*, 18 Oct. 1964.

about it."[46] As a result, Goldwater and leading Republicans struggled to find a comfortable way to speak about the scandal. Instead, they resorted to oblique hints about Johnson's "curious crew" without describing the specifics of the allegations against Jenkins.

Even though the Jenkins affair gradually receded from the headlines, Johnson remained convinced that the GOP would revive it. At his business adviser Don Cook's suggestion, the president arranged for Jenkins to check himself in for psychiatric treatment, at least until after the election.[47] Meanwhile, Johnson privately relayed to selected media contacts what he termed "very strong circumstantial evidence" that GOP operatives, led by RNC executive director John Grenier, had entrapped Jenkins. (This claim was untrue.) The president cast doubt on an earlier Jenkins arrest on a morals charge in 1959, on the grounds that the arresting officer's report had been "doctored" to add the word "pervert."[48] (This claim was untrue too.) He also informed a host of the nation's publishers that J. Edgar Hoover shared his suspicions.[49] (This claim was also untrue.)

More substantively, Johnson pressed the FBI to quickly release its report into the affair.[50] As agents discretely looked into whether any Goldwater aides had exhibited homosexual tendencies, they unsuccessfully pressured doctors to diagnose Jenkins as suffering from a "mysterious disease which causes disintegration of the brain" – which, conveniently, would absolve Johnson of any responsibility for not discerning Jenkins's so-called deviant tendencies.[51]

The president got most of what he wanted when the report appeared on October 22, a week after he had ordered it. In what it absurdly termed an "extensive investigation," the FBI announced that no evidence existed that Jenkins had compromised national security or government secrets. "Extensive interviews" by FBI agents determined that "gross fatigue and overwork" prompted the aide's breakdown.[52] Goldwater

[46] E. M. Forster, *Maurice: A Novel* (New York: W. W. Norton, 1971), terminal note, Sept. 1960.

[47] President Johnson and Don Cook, 2:35 P.M.., 17 Oct. 1964, Tape WH6410.12, Citation #5902, LBJ Recordings.

[48] President Johnson and John Knight, 12:55 P.M., 20 Oct. 1964, Tape WH6410.13, Citation #5922, LBJ Recordings.

[49] President Johnson and Joseph Keenan, 11:55 A.M.., 20 Oct. 1964, Tape WH6410.12, Citation #5920, LBJ Recordings.

[50] President Johnson and Deke DeLoach, 9:08 P.M., 20 Oct. 1964, Tape WH6410.13, Citation #5933, LBJ Recordings.

[51] Curt Gentry, *J. Edgar Hoover: The Man and His Secrets* (New York: W. W. Norton, 1991), pp. 580–1.

[52] *Washington Post*, 24 Oct. 1964.

not unreasonably dismissed the report as incomplete. He also claimed, McCarthy-style, to possess a list of 150 State Department employees who lacked security clearances. J. Edgar Hoover publicly denied the allegation.[53]

Sensing which way the political winds were blowing, the FBI director worked in other ways to bolster the president's political standing, in the process intensifying the already unhealthy relationship between Johnson and the FBI. In a scare to the administration, a *New York Herald Tribune* reporter managed to reach Jenkins's hospital room by telephone and spoke to the aide's distraught wife. (The president did not want Marge Jenkins talking to the media: the day after the arrest, she told the First Lady, "You've ruined my life, and you've ruined my husband's life, and what am I going to tell my children?")[54] In response, Hoover had a "long talk" with Fortas to "get orders issued to the switchboard so that no incoming calls should be taken." The FBI director also recommended institutionalizing Jenkins at a location such as Walter Reed Memorial Hospital, where "they would have better control over people going in to see him" – lest "some of these newspaper people get into him and talk to him."[55]

Johnson worked in other ways to inoculate himself against further charges of immorality. Working through Bill Moyers, himself a former seminary student, he pressed the Reverend Billy Graham for a formal endorsement. Graham told the president that in sleepless nights after the arrest he had gotten "on my knees and prayed for you that the Lord would just give you strength," but he demurred on the endorsement request. The religious leader did, however, accept an invitation to conduct a Sunday service at the White House. Graham praised Johnson for having responded "tenderly," as "Jesus dealt with people with moral problems like dear Walter had." The president replied in kind. Johnson informed Graham that he too had been asking for strength: "*Please*, dear Lord," he had prayed, "I need you more than I ever did in my life. I've got the Russians on one side of me taking after the Chinese, [who] are dropping bombs around contaminating the atmosphere. And the best man I ever knew had a stroke and a disease hit him." The two men discussed matters both spiritual and temporal: Graham assured

[53] *Christian Science Monitor*, 24 Oct. 1964.

[54] President Johnson and Lady Bird Johnson, 9:12 A.M., Tape WH6410.11, Citation #5895, LBJ Recordings.

[55] President Johnson and J. Edgar Hoover, 6:00 P.M., 23 Oct. 1964, Tape WH6410.14, Citation #5948, LBJ Recordings.

the president, "You've got this election wrapped up and, in my opinion, you've got it wrapped up big."[56]

Graham's political intelligence was correct: a Harris survey released shortly thereafter showed that the international events had obscured the Jenkins scandal to such an extent that the president's lead had actually increased by two points.[57] In detailed interviews with 70 people around the country, the *Christian Science Monitor* found no Democrats or independents previously committed to Johnson who had abandoned the president. For some Republicans previously leaning to the incumbent, such as a Westchester County housewife, "This Jenkins affair changes my mind. I don't like Goldwater, but he now is the lesser of two evils." Most of these pro-Johnson Republicans, however, agreed with a Pennsylvania partisan who commented, "Jenkins might have had some influence on me, but then Khrushchev and China made it a sort of two-against-one consideration."[58] He would stay with the president.

Goldwater did all that he could to transform the morality charge into his "go-for-broke weapon."[59] In a seven-page document entitled "Operation Home Stretch," the campaign focused on a claim that "a shocking decline in political morality" had produced "moral decay" and resulted in "a national disgrace." Republicans had to push to "get rid of the wheeler-dealers and put conscience back in government."[60] In a subtle change of approach, the Arizona senator increasingly framed his attacks on Johnson's ethical shortcomings as a way to stimulate the smaller-than-expected backlash vote.[61] Campaigning in downstate Illinois, Goldwater peppered his speeches with frequent references to Johnson's "curious crew," in the hopes that emphasizing a cultural divide between middle America and the president would have the same effect that many had anticipated from the backlash.[62] One GOP television ad pointedly noted that Jenkins was "Johnson's *closest* friend."[63]

[56] President Johnson and Billy Graham, 5:00 P.M., 20 Oct. 1964, Tape WH6410.13, Citation #5926, LBJ Recordings.

[57] *Christian Science Monitor*, 24 Oct. 1964.

[58] *Christian Science Monitor*, 23 Oct. 1964.

[59] *Los Angeles Times*, 15 Oct. 1964.

[60] Kessel, *The Goldwater Coalition*, p. 204.

[61] Larry O'Brien to President Johnson, 6 Oct. 1964, Box 3, Henry Wilson Papers, Lyndon B. Johnson Presidential Library.

[62] Richard Cooper, "Goldwater in Illinois," *The New Republic*, 31 Oct. 1964.

[63] Kathleen Hall Jamieson, *Dirty Politics: Deception, Distraction, and Democracy* (New York: Oxford University Press, 1992), p. 249.

The campaign also looked to use crime to link ethics and the backlash; the issue combined the senator's "trickle-down" view of morality with a covert appeal to race.[64] Goldwater struggled, however, to gain traction on the question. An October 14 Gallup poll revealed that a healthy plurality (41 percent) listed parents and home life as the chief causes of crime; only 6 percent pointed to the moral deterioration of society, the same percentage that blamed crime on spoiled youth.[65]

Samuel Lubell argued that Johnson was, in fact, "hurt politically by suspicions of his personal honesty and by how the Bobby Baker case has been handled." But, the pollster noted, questions of morality could not compensate for Goldwater's more general weaknesses. Instead, doubts about presidential integrity caused "considerable wavering among Mr. Johnson's supporters," explaining their lack of enthusiasm.[66] Anecdotal evidence confirmed Lubell's hypothesis: Republican crowds consistently responded the most enthusiastically to Goldwater's attacks on the president's morality, as spontaneous cries of "thief" and "steal away" greeted the Arizonan's discussion of Bobby Baker and KTBC.[67] Richard Strout, author of *The New Republic*'s liberal "TRB" column, worried that "the cynicism and the arrogance with which the [Baker] inquiry has been soft-pedaled is not a happy augury for the future."[68]

Johnson aide Ken O'Donnell repeatedly cautioned him to avoid responding to the allegations of corruption and immorality in government, and the president generally followed this advice – with one major exception.[69] Campaigning in San Diego in late October, Johnson termed unfair GOP treatment of the Jenkins affair, since Eisenhower "had the same type of problem with one of the men in his retinue." (Johnson was recalling the case of Arthur Vandenberg, Jr.) "The only difference is," the president continued, "we Democrats felt sorry for him and thought it was a case of sickness and disease and didn't capitalize on a man's misfortune."[70] Journalist Mary McGrory termed the comment "the lowest note" of the campaign, a "totally gratuitous blunder."[71]

[64] Richard Rovere, "Letter from San Francisco," *The New Yorker*, 25 July 1964.
[65] George Gallup, *The Gallup Poll, 1935–1971*, vol. 3, poll for Oct. 14, 1964, p. 1905.
[66] *Philadelphia Bulletin*, 8 Oct. 1964.
[67] *Los Angeles Times*, 14 Oct. 1964.
[68] *The New Republic*, 24 Oct. 1964.
[69] Ken O'Donnell to President Johnson, 21 Oct. 1964, Box 85, WHCF-PL, Lyndon B. Johnson Presidential Library.
[70] *New York Herald-Tribune*, 27 Oct. 1964.
[71] *Washington Star*, 29 Oct. 1964.

But the opposition made its own descent into tastelessness. In a campaign appearance in the Philadelphia suburbs, Goldwater charged that "minority groups run this country," and "Americans are getting sick and tired of it."[72] Republican commercials in the South featured what the president himself described as a "fine-looking, honest, clean, pink-cheeked boy that got fired" as a result of the Civil Rights Act, his job taken by an "arrogant-looking Negro boy."[73] The senator still had some hope for a hidden vote: as the *Saturday Evening Post* commented, "The chief characteristic of the backlash is its wavering uncertainty." One steelworker in Gary, ground zero of the Northern backlash, told a reporter, "When you get back to Washington, tell Johnson to come up here and have his wife and kids walk the street with niggers. Then maybe I'll vote for him."[74]

Meanwhile, the 1964 campaign featured a first in American political history: a campaign commercial that failed to clear network censors. Mothers for a Moral America debuted with an advertisement entitled "Choice," which illustrated the American decline into immorality by interspersing photos of Bobby Baker and Billy Sol Estes with clips of blacks rioting in the streets, women in topless bathing suits, a montage of pornographic magazine covers, and scenes from strip-tease joints. A speeding Lincoln Continental whose driver tossed beer cans out of his window (a reference to the story about Johnson) provided the spine to the story. The commercial's narrator lamented that "honest, hard-working America" was vanishing now that the nation's "young, inspiring leader is gone."[75] Russell Watson, public relations director of Citizens for Goldwater, candidly remarked that the film would play to the "prejudice" of "people who were brought up in small towns and on the farms, especially in the Midwest."[76]

Unfortunately for the campaign, the candidate repudiated what he termed "nothing but a racist film."[77] Goldwater still absorbed criticism, however: Robert Kintner, president of NBC, denounced "Choice" as "an appallingly tasteless production," while Ralph McGill of the *Atlanta Constitution* argued that the "luridly sensational" screening

[72] *New York Herald-Tribune*, 7 Oct. 1964.

[73] President Johnson and McGeorge Bundy, 7:00 P.M., 24 Oct. 1964, Tape WH6410.14, Citation #5962, LBJ Recordings.

[74] Ben Bagdihian, "How Strong Is the Hate Vote?" *Saturday Evening Post*, 8 Oct. 1964.

[75] *Washington Star*, 20 Oct. 1964.

[76] *The New Republic*, 31 Oct. 1964.

[77] *Washington Star*, 23 Oct. 1964.

showed Republicans practicing "politics at its lowest level."[78] Observing events from afar, George Hinman, Rockefeller's chief political adviser, commented, "The chickens are all coming home to roost as far as our national ticket is concerned, but they can't ever say we didn't give them an alternative."[79]

The "Choice" fiasco demonstrated what the *New York Post* termed "one of the remarkable facts about the current campaign – the failure of the big Goldwater campaign 'break' [the Jenkins arrest] to break as it should have."[80] (Things got so bad that a group of Dallas GOP leaders demanded an investigation to discover "the inside saboteurs who are misdirecting the campaign.")[81] The Jenkins affair might have made a difference had Goldwater stood within striking distance of the president, or had international events not intervened. But the campaign could not get beyond the negative image of Goldwater created in the primary season, which Johnson's attacks only strengthened. The Republicans stopped polling in mid-October, considering the expenditure needless; when journalists asked for private time with the candidate, Goldwater's press secretary responded, "What good would it do us?"[82]

In this atmosphere the most effective exposition of the Republican effort came from two politicians who would emerge as key players in the post-Goldwater GOP. In the South, Strom Thurmond reveled in welcoming his audiences with the cry, "My fellow extremists!"[83] The South Carolinian concluded his campaign with a one-hour Halloween rally televised in 13 Southern and border states. Thurmond argued that electing Johnson would "be pushing the button for new street riots and looting in the South as well as the North."[84]

In the West the most impressive Republican spokesman was Ronald Reagan, the former movie actor who dazzled audiences in Southern California. A Reagan speech used as a 30-minute television advertisement

[78] *Washington Star*, 31 Oct. 1964; Dallek, *Flawed Giant*, p. 179.

[79] George Hinman to William Wahl, 15 Oct. 1964, Box 82, George Hinman Papers, Rockefeller Archives.

[80] *New York Post*, 21 Oct. 1964.

[81] Rick Perlstein, *Before the Storm: Barry Goldwater and the Unmaking of the American Consensus* (New York: Hill and Wang, 2001), p. 458.

[82] Roger Kahn, "Goldwater's Desperate Battle," *Saturday Evening Post*, 15 Oct. 1964; Theodore White, *Making of the President 1960* (New York: Atheneum, 1961), p. 333.

[83] Roger Kahn, "Goldwater's Desperate Battle," *Saturday Evening Post*, 15 Oct. 1964.

[84] Harry Dent to Robert Manuel, 10 Oct. 1964; Strom Thurmond press release, 28 Oct. 1964; both in Box 13, Strom Thurmond Papers, Campaign Series, Strom Thurmond Institute, Clemson University.

was the most effective commercial of the entire Republican campaign.[85] It also typified a striking change in the GOP fundraising effort: only 28 percent of Goldwater's total budget came from contributions of more than $500. To compensate, Goldwater attracted donations from 650,000 people – as compared to the 40,000 who gave money to Eisenhower's campaign in 1956 and the 44,000 who had contributed to Nixon's 1960 effort.[86]

Some in the campaign continued to hold out the promise of victory. In mid-October Goldwater's longtime confidante attorney Dennis Kitchel told a friend, "Having been on the campaign trial with Barry ever since he started this activity, I can assure you that the campaign is going very well and that, contrary to the indications in the polls, we have something really going on which is going to produce a victory on November 3rd." Goldwater partisans tried to downplay the unfavorable poll numbers through bumper stickers reading "Gallup Never Asked Me." RNC chairman Dean Burch tried another approach: he fired the organization's pollsters, who showed Johnson with a healthy lead, and proclaimed, "I know we're on the verge of victory."[87]

Goldwater was more realistic, setting a schedule that suggested he had all but conceded defeat weeks before the election. His final campaign swing took him to places like Dover, Delaware; Cheyenne, Wyoming; Salisbury, Maryland; Bristol, Tennessee; London, Kentucky; Oshkosh, Wisconsin; Cedar Rapids, Iowa; and Altoona, Pennsylvania – almost all areas of little electoral significance.[88] Goldwater held three rallies in Arizona in the final four days of the campaign, confirming a (legitimate) fear of losing his home state.[89]

The president, on the other hand, intensified his effort, seeking an overwhelming triumph. In the *Saturday Evening Post* Stewart Alsop noted that "given the kind of man he is, it is no wonder that Lyndon Johnson so much wants to win big."[90] Gradually, the president's goal for the campaign was shifting. By early October he had conceded that the frontlash strategy would not succeed; moderate Republicans might cast

85 Perlstein, *Before the Storm*, pp. 499–510.

86 Herbert Alexander, *Financing the 1964 Election* (Princeton, NJ: Citizens Research Council, 1966), pp. 11, 84.

87 Perlstein, *Before the Storm*, pp. 462–3, 474.

88 Kessel, *The Goldwater Coalition*, p. 215.

89 *Wall Street Journal*, 2 Nov. 1964.

90 Stewart Alsop, "The Meaning of the Margin," *Saturday Evening Post*, 29 Oct. 1964.

their ballots for him on November 3, but they would not ultimately join the Democratic Party. So, even before the Jenkins scandal broke, Johnson began to embrace a new strategy. Bypassing the options presented by members of his campaign staff, he aimed to make the 1964 election his equivalent of Roosevelt's victory in 1936 – an overwhelming personal triumph. Such an outcome, he noted gleefully, would make Kennedy's 1960 victory "look like a pathetic peep."[91]

The political correspondent for the London *Times,* who spent a day on the hustings with the president, relayed his experience to a British audience accustomed to a more genteel campaign style. It seemed as if Johnson's "intense energy can be generated only by a mysterious compulsion" – traveling 10,000 miles through 14 states, Johnson had been "bouncing jovially and effervescently in and out of his aircraft, and mixing freely, to the despair of his secret service guards, with enthusiastic crowds, the very picture of a square peg in a square hole." This "natural campaigner" clearly wanted to "win in every state, even in Arizona." In the planned visit on behalf of Roy Elson, the president never made it to church. Instead, Johnson joined the Democratic Senate nominee in riding past four churches – coincidentally arriving at all four just as services were concluding – as part of a whirlwind tour that included 17 impromptu stops.[92] (The only negative event of the day came when a 17-year-old accidentally hit Johnson over the head with a Goldwater/Miller campaign sign.)[93] The *Times* correspondent noted that Johnson's "humor is earthy and his sentiments often too sentimental, but his knowledge of local politics and requirements is encyclopedic and his sense of timing superb." That timing was increasingly oriented less around the traditional Johnson themes – "peace and prosperity" – than on attacks against Goldwater. Johnson went after his opponent "with all the intensity of a Texan cowhand separating a calf from the herd."[94]

These criticisms were, indeed, biting. In Texas Johnson declared, "The west will not be won by a man on a horse who thinks he can settle every argument with a quick draw and a shot from the hip."[95] In Los Angeles

[91] Lee Edwards, *Goldwater: The Man Who Made a Revolution* (Washington, DC: Regnery, 1995), p. 305.

[92] In response, Goldwater issued a statement criticizing Johnson for making "a political travesty of the Lord's day." *Washington Star*, 14 Oct. 1964.

[93] *New York Times*, 14 Oct. 1964.

[94] *The Times* (London), 14 Oct. 1964.

[95] *The Times* (London), 14 Oct. 1964.

FIGURE 6-1. President Johnson campaigning with Arizona gubernatorial candidate Roy Elson, October 11, 1964. © Courtesy of the Lyndon Baines Johnson Presidential Library. Photo by Don Stoderl.

Johnson charged that the campaign had shown that "some people have more guts than brains."[96] To a group of schoolchildren, the president announced that only an overwhelming GOP defeat would "restore moderation in that once great party of Abraham Lincoln and the leadership would then unite and present a solid front to the world."[97]

[96] *Los Angeles Times*, 29 Oct. 1964.
[97] Perlstein, *Before the Storm*, p. 498.

Privately, the president sought to stimulate even harder-hitting criticism. He told the New York Liberal Party's Alex Rose that he had a job for him, one that had to be more effective "than the Nixon telecast was on his dog." Unfortunately, Johnson complained, the press did not "seem to follow through on anything that really we get started on these folks that hurts them." Therefore, he declared, Rose needed to start spreading the (false) rumor that Goldwater belonged to the John Birch Society, "the outfit that was saying that Eisenhower was a stooge of the communists." The society was a "secret organization," and "no President ought to be tied in with anything like that." Once the rumor was established, then the campaign could hammer Goldwater about his nonexistent ties to secret organizations like the KKK. Johnson instructed Rose to urge his contacts in the journalistic community to ask "how he can be a member of the Klan or the Birch Society and be a member of the Senate at the same time."[98]

His own campaign, Johnson complained, had failed to make the case – "Humphrey is speaking all the time, and he charges him with this and that, but they're too damn scholarly, and it's not getting us votes." "The thing that gets you votes," the president asserted, "is when they get scared about a man that's going to be a Klansmen." Therefore, the press needed "to just hound him to death every day – 'Is he resigning? Will he quit it? Will he denounce it? Is it not true that he's on it? Did he intend it to be against Eisenhower? What kind of a secret thing? Has he ever had any connections with the Klan?'" Rose himself, the president speculated, could go public with the charge, while working on "your literary people and some of your groups up there to get upset about the Birch thing, and make them go to asking him questions." "Get a rabbi here, and a professor there, and a scientist over here, and an author here" – by the time the election came around, everyone would accept the charge as true. Rose promised to work on the matter instantly.[99] The New York political leader failed to get quoted by either the *Times* or the (then) liberal *New York Post,* but Johnson continued his attempt to smear Goldwater with charges of a KKK link.

This embrace of an even more negative approach came over the express opposition of many in the president's campaign machinery. Ken O'Donnell pleaded for concluding the campaign with "a strong, issue-oriented, high-level program, discussing the future programs and

[98] President Johnson and Alex Rose, 2:22 P.M., 10 Oct. 1964, Tape WH6410.06, Citation #5860, LBJ Recordings.

[99] President Johnson and Alex Rose, 2:22 P.M., 10 Oct. 1964, Tape WH6410.06, Citation #5860, LBJ Recordings.

activities of President Johnson in 1965."[100] Typifying press commentary, the *Washington Star*'s Max Freedman faulted the president for waging "one of the emptiest campaigns in history." Johnson, Freedman predicted, would discover that "once lost, this opportunity for public enlightenment cannot be regained." Freedman was not naïve. But he wondered why Johnson had failed to realize that "even from the narrow political viewpoint, he stands to gain" from an issue-oriented campaign, because otherwise his triumph would not produce a mandate.[101]

The president also showed little inclination for boosting most down-the-ticket Democrats. In the Nevada visit requested by Howard Cannon, one observer was stunned to find that Johnson "seemed to practically forget about Cannon," plugging only his own election.[102] The appearance created the impression that the Nevada senator was a presidential rubber stamp – thus strengthening a central charge made by Cannon's foe, Republican Paul Laxalt. Johnson took a similar approach in Arizona, when he touted his own prospects but failed to mention Roy Elson by name, reinforcing the accusation leveled by Elson's opponent, Paul Fannin, that Elson was better qualified to be an administrative assistant than a U.S. senator.[103]

Johnson defended this strategy by citing polling data that claimed a relationship between congressional gains and the percentage of the popular vote received by the party nominee.[104] But, of course, in an election that had stimulated unprecedented talk of ticket-splitting, some of it encouraged by the Democratic campaign itself, such statistics meant little. Johnson's Nevada and Arizona appearances contributed to what Stewart Alsop termed a perception of hubris.[105] This evolution paralleled Johnson's performance as Senate majority leader, where he abandoned any semblance of humility as his accomplishments increased.

As part of his goal of outperforming his political mentor, Johnson first looked to amass a higher percentage of the popular vote than FDR's 60.8 percent in 1936. Demonizing Goldwater, rather than articulating a positive program that might alienate some of the anti-Goldwater constituency,

[100] Ken O'Donnell to President Johnson, 20 Oct. 1964, Box 85, WHCF-PL, Lyndon B. Johnson Presidential Library.

[101] *Washington Star*, 14 Oct. 1964.

[102] "State by State Analysis, Newspapers/Polls," 19 Oct. 1964, Box 8, Barry Goldwater Papers, Arizona State University.

[103] *The Times* (London), 14 Oct. 1964.

[104] President Johnson, Walter Jenkins, and Bill Moyers, 10:38 A.M., 10 Oct. 1964, Tape WH6410.05, Citation #5851, LBJ Recordings.

[105] Stewart Alsop, "The One Weakness of LBJ," *Saturday Evening Post,* 22 Oct. 1964.

thus made sense. Second, the president wanted to approach FDR's total number of states won – and hence the sudden interest in Maine and Vermont, as well as the revived attention to Southern states like Florida and Georgia, whose electoral votes would be critical not for victory but for his historical legacy. When Johnson started to speak openly of his goal of a landslide triumph, Lou Harris warned that such remarks could generate complacency within the Democratic base. The president dismissed such advice as "crazy as hell."[106]

A campaign strategy built around achieving the maximum tally in both the popular vote and the Electoral College had to reckon with the president's comparatively weak position in the South. Johnson was blunt: "I want to carry the South; I'm going to carry 40 states." By early October, a few Southern states remained very much in play, with Georgia first on the list. The president believed that with Richard Russell sitting the election out, the national ticket needed strong support from the state's junior senator, Herman Talmadge, to appeal to conservatives reluctant to affiliate with Carl Sanders. Talmadge had thus far maintained his neutrality and now needed to know that the president "wants you to help him in Georgia. And while he may not be able to help you much in Georgia now, he thinks that in another two or three years, the way things are developing, he *will* be able to help you in Georgia." The message to fence sitters would stress the dangers for the Peach State's "future to be wound up with Strom [Thurmond]." Still, Johnson admitted, "I'm awfully worried."[107]

What journalist William S. White termed the "long expected Democratic counterattack" in the South began with another path-breaking event from the 1964 campaign: a whistlestop tour not by the candidate but by his wife.[108] For the First Lady's chief of staff Liz Carpenter, the event looked "to woo with real courthouse politics on that train."[109] And the First Lady wanted to "bear down" on the states that seemed the most doubtful – especially Georgia.[110]

Mary McGrory described the *Lady Bird Special* as no less than an "assault on the heart and mind of the South."[111] For four days and over

[106] President Johnson, Walter Jenkins, and Bill Moyers, 10:38 A.M., 10 Oct. 1964, Tape WH6410.05, Citation #5851, LBJ Recordings.
[107] President Johnson, Walter Jenkins, and Bill Moyers, 10:38 A.M., 10 Oct. 1964, Tape WH6410.05, Citation #5851, LBJ Recordings.
[108] *Washington Star*, 13 Oct. 1964.
[109] Liz Carpenter oral history, Lyndon B. Johnson Presidential Library.
[110] Lady Bird Johnson, *White House Diary*, entry for 4 Sept. 1964, p. 194.
[111] *Washington Star*, 11 Oct. 1964.

1,628 miles, the First Lady and her supporters traveled by a 19-car train through eight states of the Old Confederacy. (A minesweeper train preceded the First Lady's cars to check for explosives on the tracks.) Bess Abell, the First Lady's social secretary, stocked the train with a variety of souvenirs: 160 cases of saltwater taffy whose wrappers were imprinted with the words "Choose LYNDON," 6,000 ladies' straw hats with "LBJ" in red, white, and blue stitched in, and 100,000 postcards. To feed those

FIGURE 6-2. Aboard the "Lady Bird Special." Lady Bird's swing through the South featured the unprecedented development of the First Lady making major campaign appearances on her own. © Courtesy of the Lyndon Baines Johnson Presidential Library.

traveling with her, the First Lady chose specialties of the state through which the train then was passing.[112]

Traditional Southern values dictated a polite response to a woman, but even here racial politics often prevailed: when the First Lady asked Virginia senator Harry Byrd to appear with her, she recalled that "an invisible silken curtain fell across his face." A. Willis Robertson, Byrd's colleague, scheduled a hunting trip to Montana. North Carolina gubernatorial nominee Dan Moore, continuing his dispute with the national party, did not return the First Lady's phone calls; neither did Hayden Burns, the party's gubernatorial candidate in Florida. Louisiana governor John McKeithen unsurprisingly declined to appear with her. And even Lady Bird's personal appeals could not get Richard Russell to campaign for the Johnson-Humphrey ticket.[113] Among prominent Southern politicians only Majority Whip Hale Boggs (D-Louisiana) offered wholehearted support, accompanying the train on its entire journey.[114] Anticipating a campaign three decades hence, the First Lady asked listeners to "vote for both Johnsons."[115] She urged her listeners not to believe reports that her husband had written off the South,[116] and she proved steely in the face of heckling, especially in South Carolina and Georgia.[117]

The swing concluded in New Orleans, and, as he had at its start, the president joined his wife. In the process he delivered the most memorable speech of the 1964 campaign. Two thousand of Louisiana's top Democrats attended the event, which was broadcast live in Louisiana and Mississippi. After paying tribute to populist Huey Long, Louisiana's former governor and senator, the president offered a full-out defense of the Civil Rights Act. "Whatever your views are," Johnson declared, "we have a Constitution and a Bill of Rights, and we have the law of the land. And two-thirds of the Democrats in the Senate voted for it, and three-fourths of the Republicans. I signed it, and I am going to enforce it, and I am going to observe it." Then the president relayed a story. He spoke of an old Southern senator, on his deathbed, who told Sam Rayburn that he yearned for the strength to make one more speech to his home state. "'I feel like I have one in me!'," Johnson quoted the senator. "'The poor

[112] Jan Jarboe Russell, *Lady Bird: A Biography of Mrs. Johnson* (New York: Scribner, 1999), pp. 250–2.

[113] Lady Bird Johnson, *White House Diary*, entry for 11 Sept. 1964, pp. 195–6.

[114] Russell, *Lady Bird*, pp. 252–5.

[115] *Washington Star*, 7 Oct. 1964.

[116] *New York Times*, 7 Oct. 1964.

[117] *New York Times*, 8 Oct. 1964.

old state, they haven't heard a Democratic speech in thirty years. All they ever hear at election time is, Nigger! Nigger! Nigger!' "[118]

Johnson press secretary George Reedy commented shortly afterwards that the address left everybody "gasping."[119] Katherine Graham and Mary McGrory separately termed it the best speech they had ever heard.[120] An eyewitness described the audience reaction as "a physical thing – surprise, awe – ears heard what they plainly could not hear."[121]

If the speech earned the president new admiration among the press corps, it failed to improve his standing in Louisiana, where the central obstacle remained Governor McKeithen. As Russell Long noted, with McKeithen everything "must be an on-the-barrel head trade." The governor wanted Johnson's backing on the tidelands dispute, a decade-long feud between the federal government and Louisiana, Texas, and California over whether Washington or state governments controlled offshore oil fields. (The issue was critical to oil companies, since the federal royalty was more than double that levied by the states.) In exchange, McKeithen implied, he would endorse the Democratic ticket. Local Democrats, led by Long, persuaded the president not to give in, and so McKeithen maintained his pro-Goldwater neutrality. Louisiana would go Republican.[122]

With Mississippi and Alabama already lost, Johnson could not concede any other state if he wanted to exceed FDR's 1936 tally of 46 total states carried. And here the *Lady Bird Special* promised to be of some assistance. Max Freedman correctly termed the tour a "serious political enterprise, carefully planned and gallantly undertaken," since a victory would "lose some of its savor for Mr. Johnson if he does not do very well in the Southern states." In Freedman's view, the First Lady's swing enabled the Southern Democratic Party to mobilize its entire apparatus in whatever locale she passed through, something that had not happened heretofore in the campaign.[123]

[118] Taylor Branch, *Pillar of Fire: America in the King Years* (New York: Simon and Schuster, 1998), p. 514.

[119] President Johnson and George Reedy, 12:25 P.M., 10 Oct. 1964, Tape WH6410.06, Citation #5857, LBJ Recordings.

[120] *Washington Star*, 11 Oct. 1964.

[121] Branch, *Pillar of Fire*, p. 515. Press reports the next day toned down the president's remarks, stating that the address had concluded with the words "Negro! Negro! Negro!"; the *New York Times* did not even include the passage in its coverage.

[122] Henry Wilson to Larry O'Brien, 24 Oct. 1964, Box 1, Henry Wilson Papers, Lyndon B. Johnson Presidential Library.

[123] *Washington Star*, 12 Oct. 1964.

The First Lady's activities did not fall on entirely fallow ground. Johnson staffers in late October confirmed what pollster Lou Harris had intimated earlier in the month: the black vote gave the president a chance at a string of narrow victories in the region. Johnson aide Larry O'Brien believed that a Democratic triumph in anywhere from four to six Southern states hinged on the black vote – the Carolinas, Georgia, and Florida, and possibly so in Tennessee and Virginia. Mining this vote, of course, represented a "new experience" for Southern Democratic leaders. The Democratic National Committee filled the void in an operation conducted independently of state party structures. Totals around the region suggested that despite the continuing threat of violence, 2.1 million Southern blacks were registered to vote, with 625,000 newly on the rolls in the previous 12 months. If the black vote coalesced, O'Brien speculated, the Democrats could carry every Southern state but Alabama and Mississippi.[124]

Johnson had two other advantages in the region. First, in an economy that remained heavily dependent upon agriculture, the political muscle the president had employed on behalf of the farm bill was now paying dividends.[125] Second, as occurred nationwide, the Southern wing of the Goldwater campaign collapsed in the closing weeks; even in Mississippi, Governor Paul Johnson detected a trend away from the Republican nominee.[126] This movement, in turn, brought into the South the "victory psychology" on which Johnson had relied elsewhere; as one Florida Democrat noted in mid-October, "Mr. Johnson put the squeeze on Florida officials to see that he had solid support from the state."[127] But he also imitated some of the more generous appeal of the *Lady Bird Special:* in Augusta, Georgia, Johnson promised to keep in mind "the ordeals that have tried the South all these years."[128]

With his renewed attention to the South, Johnson assumed comfortable leads in polls taken in Texas, Oklahoma, Kentucky, Tennessee, and Arkansas, with smaller leads in Virginia, North Carolina, and Florida. South Carolina and Georgia were considered too close to call, but even

[124] Larry O'Brien to President Johnson, 23 Oct. 1964, Box 3, Henry Wilson Papers, Lyndon B. Johnson Presidential Library.

[125] "State by State Analysis Newspapers/Polls," 19 Oct. 1964, Box 8, Goldwater Papers, Arizona State University; *U.S. News&World Report*, 19 Oct. 1964; *Time*, 30 Oct. 1964.

[126] *Washington Post*, 20 Oct. 1964.

[127] *U.S. News&World Report*, 19 Oct. 1964; see also *Washington Star*, 29 Oct. 1964.

[128] *Congressional Quarterly Weekly Report*, 30 Oct. 1964, p. 2586.

here signs for optimism existed.[129] When coupled with Roy Elson's latest poll from Arizona – which showed Johnson's lead over Goldwater expanding to 10 points, 51 to 41 percent – the president had a realistic chance of winning 47 states.[130] That total would exceed Roosevelt's margin by one state (since Alaska and Hawaii had not yet joined the Union in 1936) and would also give Johnson the two states that FDR had failed to carry, Maine and Vermont.

Developments outside of the South offered nothing but good news for the president. In California a voter registration drive netting seven new Democrats for every three new Republicans contributed to an enormous Johnson lead.[131] In Colorado things were so bad for the Goldwater effort that the GOP state coordinator described himself as "very much encouraged" by a poll showing Johnson ahead by 34 percent.[132] In the Upper Midwest the Goldwater campaign itself termed its effort "futile"; Johnson forces celebrated polls showing the Democrat leading by almost 50 points in Minnesota, Illinois, and Michigan.[133] In traditionally Republican Iowa, Johnson assumed a 36-point advantage, with the local Goldwater forces just "going through the motions."[134] In Pennsylvania and New Jersey, Republicans' hope of a backlash showed no signs of materializing.[135] Nationally, a late October Gallup poll showed Johnson ahead 64 to 29 percent, while a Harris survey from about the same time positioned the president's lead at 60 to 36 percent.[136]

This master politician increasingly sought to use his expected landslide to exact political retribution. As Election Day grew near, Johnson focused on congressional races, although not in the way that many national Democrats had hoped. Instead, the president targeted his most vituperative congressional critics. Both he and the First Lady scheduled visits to El Paso, center of the congressional district that elected Republican Ed

[129] Larry O'Brien to President Johnson, 20 Oct. 1964, Box 3, Henry Wilson Papers, Lyndon B. Johnson Presidential Library.

[130] Averell Harriman to President Johnson, 23 Oct. 1964, Box 84, Lyndon B. Johnson Presidential Library.

[131] *Time*, 30 Oct. 1964.

[132] State by State Analysis Newspapers/Polls, 19 Oct. 1964, Box 8, Barry Goldwater Papers, Arizona State University.

[133] Gifford Philips to Jack Valenti, 30 Oct. 1964, Box 85, WHCF-PL, Lyndon B. Johnson Presidential Library; State by State Analysis Newspapers/Polls, 19 Oct. 1964, Box 8, Barry Goldwater Papers, Arizona State University.

[134] State by State Analysis Newspapers/Polls, 19 Oct. 1964, Box 8, Barry Goldwater Papers, Arizona State University; *U.S. News & World Report*, 19 Oct. 1964.

[135] *U.S. News & World Report*, 19 Oct. 1964.

[136] *Christian Science Monitor*, 30 Oct. 1964.

Foreman – the "damn fool" who had criticized the timing of Johnson's Tonkin Gulf address.[137] (Foreman, who had narrowly won in 1962, faced a strong challenge from Richard White, a conservative state representative.) Privately, Johnson placed Foreman "high up on our list."[138]

The president did not confine himself to rhetorical attacks. In a conversation with Charles Guy, editor of the *Lubbock Avalanche Journal,* Johnson "confidentially" revealed that El Paso's Biggs Air Force Base likely would be closed after the election. Unfortunately, he slyly noted, "their own man can't help a damn bit," since "he's telling the generals every day that they sent off the planes in Vietnam and endangered the lives." El Paso residents needed to understand the rules of the political game: "If you want to have a Republican congressman, why, they're going to get what the Republicans get." If, on the other hand, the district sent White to Congress, perhaps Biggs would be spared. Guy got the message.[139]

Johnson's distaste for Foreman paled in comparison to his feelings for John Williams. By late October Johnson was more interested in the Delaware Senate race than in any contest in the country other than his own. On paper Williams was not particularly vulnerable. In 1958 his 53 percent of the vote made him the first Delaware senator ever popularly elected to a third term – and he did so confronting a national Democratic tide. For 1964 the Democrats nominated the same candidate that had lost to Williams in 1958, Elbert Carvel, who was concluding his second nonconsecutive term as the First State's governor. Carvel was in a weaker position in 1964 than in 1958; his support for civil rights, including a statewide open housing law, had alienated the traditional Democratic base in southern Delaware, while the national attention that Williams derived from his role in the Baker inquiry had played well at home.[140]

Beyond criticizing Williams's negativity, Carvel struggled to articulate a reason why he should be elected. As the campaign got underway, he repeatedly attacked Williams's vote against the tax bill, taking out newspaper ads listing all of the major legislation that the state's senior senator

[137] President Johnson and Charles Guy, 6:50 A.M., 11 Oct. 1964, Tape WH6410.08, Citation #5874, LBJ Recordings.

[138] President Johnson and Walter Jenkins, 8:21 P.M., 10 Oct. 1964, Tape WH6410.07, Citation #5868, LBJ Recordings.

[139] President Johnson and Charles Guy, 6:50 A.M., 11 Oct. 1964, Tape WH6410.08, Citation #5874, LBJ Recordings.

[140] Roger Martin, *Elbert N. Carvel* (Wilmington: Delaware Heritage Commission, 1997), pp. 99–102.

had opposed since first arriving in the Senate in 1946.[141] But when pressed for a positive agenda, the governor could do no better than to promise to be "for the people."[142] In response, Johnson sent in national Democrats to prop up Carvel's effort. Secretary of Agriculture Orville Freeman spent the day in the state in early October, denouncing Williams for "unadulterated political deception and chicanery."[143]

Williams had little difficulty parrying such attacks. Armed with campaign posters hyperbolically describing himself as "the man who blew the lid off the most widespread political scandals within memory," he dismissed Carvel as a rubber stamp for the White House.[144] He turned the governor's attack on his tax bill vote on its head by claiming that Johnson nationally, like Carvel in Dover, lacked fiscal responsibility.[145] And the senator attracted his own national support; a few days after Freeman's trip, Richard Nixon arrived in Wilmington to laud Williams as the "single most valuable" member of the Senate.[146] When Larry O'Brien canvassed the state at about the same time, he reported that it was "very doubtful" that Carvel could prevail; private polls gave the senator a 10-point lead, and the governor's weaknesses as a candidate made overcoming such a margin unlikely.[147]

Johnson, however, had no intention of conceding the race to Williams. Instead, armed with O'Brien's report, the president outlined a five-pronged program to rejuvenate Carvel's effort. Successful Senate campaigns, as always, began with money. Recalling tactics from his time as Majority Leader, Johnson pressed national labor groups to give Carvel from $10,000 to $15,000 – which, in a race where Williams's official budget was $6,360, promised to have substantial effect.[148] DNC Treasurer Dick Maguire also spoke with Carvel about ways the national party could surreptitiously funnel campaign cash into the state.[149]

[141] *Wilmington Evening Journal*, 5 Oct. 1964.
[142] *Wilmington Evening Journal*, 1 Oct. 1964.
[143] *Wilmington Evening Journal*, 5 Oct. 1964.
[144] Williams campaign poster, Box 131, John Williams Papers, University of Delaware.
[145] *Wilmington News*, 1 Oct. 1964.
[146] *Wilmington News*, 9 Oct. 1964.
[147] Larry O'Brien to President Johnson, 8 Oct. 1964, Box 84, WHCF-PL, Lyndon B. Johnson Presidential Library.
[148] Carol Hoffecker, *Honest John Williams* (Newark: University of Delaware Press, 2000), p. 201.
[149] President Johnson and Walter Jenkins, 8:21 P.M., 10 Oct. 1964, Tape WH6410.07, Citation #5868, LBJ Recordings.

FIGURE 6-3. President Johnson hits the hustings with John Williams's challenger, Governor Elbert Carvel, on a Delaware campaign stop, October 31, 1964. © Courtesy of the Lyndon Baines Johnson Presidential Library. Photo by O. J. Rapp.

Second, the president championed voter registration. Johnson's first move regarding Delaware had occurred in the summer, when he asked labor and civil rights groups to sponsor a voter registration drive in the state. That successful undertaking boosted the Democratic registration edge to more than 30 points.[150] Now, he wanted to focus more on blacks. The president passed word to the NAACP's Roy Wilkins that Delaware was "the one state I want him to really spend some time working on. See that his people get registered."[151]

[150] Larry O'Brien to President Johnson, 8 Oct. 1964, Box 84, WHCF-PL, Lyndon B. Johnson Presidential Library.

[151] President Johnson, Walter Jenkins, and Bill Moyers, 10:38 A.M., 10 Oct. 1964, Tape WH6410.05, Citation #5851, LBJ Recordings.

Third, Johnson sought to influence the state's business and financial elite – which, in Delaware, meant the DuPont family. Before World War II the DuPonts had participated actively in both parties, but after 1945 their allegiance shifted overwhelmingly to the GOP. Now, however, they received a message from the president: Clark Clifford visited family headquarters to say, "By God, we're going to be President, and *we want their help*. And we want their paper," the *Wilmington Journal*.[152]

Fourth, the president instructed organized labor's political arm, the Committee on Public Information (COPE), to send activists to Delaware, "and have them really turning things upside down in that state."[153] "Don't wait," Johnson cautioned, "until it's too late"; labor needed to "get some women up there on telephones" and "put some extra money in it."[154] The president ordered campaign aides to inform COPE director Al Barkan that "we want you to get your best regional men into Delaware."[155] He reserved for himself the task of telling AFL-CIO president George Meany "to personally take over the job of getting every laborer they can in Delaware *really* to fighting."[156] If Carvel could not generate a grassroots campaign, the president would create one for him.

Finally, Johnson promised to supply his own coattails by committing to a late October campaign trip to Delaware, despite his overwhelming lead in polls for the state's three electoral votes. He envisioned "the biggest rally for me that they can *possibly* organize in Wilmington." Despite all of this effort, he still doubted that Carvel could win. "But I sure want him to make a good showing. And *I* want to carry it, over Williams, for a lot of other reasons."[157] When, on October 12, a *Wilmington News* poll showed the Senate race a statistical dead heat, the president wondered, "Maybe we can do something there."[158]

[152] President Johnson, Walter Jenkins, and Bill Moyers, 10:38 A.M., 10 Oct. 1964, Tape WH6410.05, Citation #5851, LBJ Recordings.

[153] President Johnson and Walter Jenkins, 8:21 P.M., 10 Oct. 1964, Tape WH6410.07, Citation #5868, LBJ Recordings.

[154] President Johnson and Joseph Keenan, 11:55 A.M., 20 Oct. 1964, Tape WH6410.12, Citation #5920, LBJ Recordings.

[155] President Johnson and Walter Jenkins, 8:21 P.M., 10 Oct. 1964, Tape WH6410.07, Citation #5868, LBJ Recordings.

[156] President Johnson, Walter Jenkins, and Bill Moyers, 10:38 A.M., 10 Oct. 1964, Tape WH6410.05, Citation #5851, LBJ Recordings.

[157] President Johnson, Walter Jenkins, and Bill Moyers, 10:38 A.M., 10 Oct. 1964, Tape WH6410.05, Citation #5851, LBJ Recordings.

[158] President Johnson and Walter Jenkins, 8:21 P.M., 10 Oct. 1964, Tape WH6410.05, Citation #5851, LBJ Recordings; *Wilmington News*, 12 Oct. 1964.

If Johnson were going to do something, however, he would have to do it without much assistance from Carvel, whose campaign sputtered along ineffectively. In a state where Democrats had captured only two Senate contests in the previous 22 years, Williams relentlessly linked Carvel to controversial aspects of the national Democratic agenda – labor policy, civil rights, and liberalism. Carvel responded weakly. On the incredible grounds that "civil rights is not an issue in our state," he announced that he would not discuss the question in the campaign.[159] Before a labor group, Carvel advocated repealing the Taft-Hartley Act, but when Williams attacked him on the matter, the governor claimed to have been misquoted.[160] And Carvel refused to divulge his opinion of Americans for Democratic Action, only stating that he was "proud" of Hubert Humphrey, thereby allowing Williams to contend that the governor was "deliberately evading" the question of whether or not he endorsed a liberal agenda.[161]

Searching for an issue, Carvel tried to turn Williams's reputation against him, charging that the senior senator "has been seeking publicity by trying to tear down other people's houses for the last 18 years."[162] What the First State, said the governor, "wants in the Senate is not a policeman but a statesman."[163] But Delaware was one state where the Jenkins arrest had a major effect, helping Williams to deflect Carvel's attacks. Indeed, the senator suggested the morning after Jenkins's arrest was revealed, the president should "display his vaunted leadership abilities" by reopening the Baker investigation. Johnson's continued silence could only be construed as "an endorsement of the Baker type of influence-peddling."[164] With Carvel on record as saying he would "represent the White House, not the people of Delaware," Williams wondered exactly where "Lyndon Johnson's rubber-stamp candidate for the Senate" really stood on the "question of morals and corruption."[165]

[159] *Wilmington News*, 14 Oct. 1964.

[160] *Wilmington Evening Journal*, 20 Oct. 1964.

[161] Williams press release, 23 Oct. 1964, Box 131, John Williams Papers, University of Delaware; *Wilmington Evening Journal*, 23 Oct. 1964.

[162] *Wilmington News*, 14 Oct. 1964; *Wilmington Evening Journal*, 20 Oct. 1964.

[163] President Johnson and Everett Dirksen, 11:22 A.M., 4 Nov. 1964, Tape WH6411.03, Citation #6164, Recordings of Telephone Conversations – White House Series, Recordings and Transcripts of Conversations and Meetings, Lyndon B. Johnson Library.

[164] Williams press release, 15 Oct. 1964, Box 131, John Williams Papers, University of Delaware.

[165] Williams press release, 12 Oct. 1964, Box 131, John Williams Papers, University of Delaware; Williams press release, 14 Oct. 1964, Box 131, John Williams Papers,

Checked on the Baker question, Carvel tried to raise the negativity charge in another fashion. In the campaign's only debate, on October 21, he promised to do a better job than Williams in securing Delaware's fair share of federal largesse, asserting that Williams had alienated too many people in Washington. But the incumbent ridiculed this line of attack as well, contending that Carvel wanted to serve as the First State's "bag man"; the framers envisioned a senator's job as more than simply bringing back federal funds to his home state.[166]

In this atmosphere it came as little surprise that newspaper after newspaper endorsed Williams's reelection bid. For the *Delmarva News,* recommending Williams was the editors' "easiest choice" of the election season.[167] The *Newark Weekly* noted "there is only one Senator Williams in the world."[168] The *Delaware State News* agreed with Williams that Carvel would be a "rubber stamp" for Johnson; the *Wilmington Journal* considered it "unthinkable" that Delaware voters not return Williams to the Senate.[169] And the *Wilmington News,* describing Williams's tenure as "the most illustrious political career to emerge from this state in decades," argued that his contribution to the cause of good government made him a figure of "national distinction."[170]

The president still refused to give up. A week before Election Day, he confided to Robert Kennedy that he was going all out to oust Williams, since "that son of a bitch is going to give us hell for four years if he's still there."[171] Before his trip to the First State, Johnson telephoned a Carvel rally in Wilmington, describing Delaware's Senate vote as "the most important decision that you'll make in your lifetime." When the microphone in the hall went dead, Carvel and the president were left to discuss details. Already committed to stops in Wilmington and Dover, Johnson expressed his willingness to go anyplace else in the state that Carvel desired. The governor (incredibly) declined the offer. Assuming his role as campaign manager, Johnson chided Carvel for not promptly getting back to Hugh Carcella, an official of the United Steelworkers who had the labor money – $10,000 – for Delaware that Johnson had requested,

University of Delaware; Williams press release, 16 Oct. 1964, Box 131, John Williams Papers, University of Delaware.

[166] *Wilmington News*, 22 Oct. 1964.

[167] *Delmarva News*, 11 Oct. 1964.

[168] *Newark Weekly*, 14 Oct. 1964.

[169] *Delaware State News*, 20 Oct. 1964; *Wilmington Evening Journal*, 22 Oct. 1964.

[170] *Wilmington News*, 21 Oct. 1964.

[171] President Johnson and Robert Kennedy, 11:45 P.M., 26 Oct. 1964, Tape WH6410.15, Citation #5968, LBJ Recordings.

supplied by the steelworkers and Walter Reuther's United Auto Workers. The president passed on Carcella's home phone number and the name of the Atlantic City hotel where the union official would be staying the following day. Three times in less than ten minutes he instructed Carvel to get in touch with Carcella immediately, expressing amazement that the governor had not already done so.[172]

Raising the question of which man actually was the candidate in the race, Johnson pressed further for suggestions: "How can additional things help you? Can you get additional spots?" He urged Carvel to intensify his television advertising, and instructed the governor "to get plenty of people for Election Day to get on phones." Johnson also expressed his pleasure that the NAACP had sent "some people in there to help you." Confirming the other aspect of the president's effort, Carvel commented that while the Wilmington papers had not endorsed him, they were "giving us a damned good break." Carvel, indeed, seemed remarkably unworried, pointing to the publication of a poll of schoolchildren showing him 16 points ahead. The president, prudently, found this margin hard to believe.[173]

On October 31 Johnson traveled to Delaware; in Dover, with a population of 15,000, he attracted a crowd of 8,000 people. Joking that he had just dropped by "to say howdy," the president urged his listeners to get out to vote – one reason, he said, why "I am going to spend more time in Dover than in New York City."[174] Ironically, Johnson's visit seemed to work to Williams's advantage, allowing national Republicans to portray the senator as a David against the president's Goliath.[175] Williams himself stated that being the Democrats' "Number 1 target" was the "highest compliment they can pay me." He promised Delaware voters that White House "immorality" would remain his number one target.[176] Privately, though, the senator expressed concern in facing "the nastiest campaign which I have ever experienced."[177]

[172] President Johnson and Elbert Carvel, 9:50 P.M., 29 Oct. 1964, Tape WH6410.16, Citation #5984, LBJ Recordings.

[173] President Johnson and Elbert Carvel, 9:50 P.M., 29 Oct. 1964, Tape WH6410.16, Citation #5984, LBJ Recordings.

[174] *New York Times*, 1 Nov. 1964.

[175] John Williams press release, 29 Oct. 1964, Box 131, John Williams Papers, University of Delaware; *Washington Star*, 30 Oct. 1964.

[176] *Harrington Morning News*, 30 Oct. 1964.

[177] John Williams to Edward Keily, 9 Nov. 1964, Box 131, John Williams Papers, University of Delaware.

The outcome of what amounted to a race between Johnson and Williams remained uncertain when November began. The president himself left Delaware for New York, where Robert Kennedy had struggled mightily in what the *Congressional Quarterly* termed "the crucial Senate contest of 1964."[178] In the weeks after the Democratic convention, Kennedy ran a surprisingly passive campaign, while Keating proved to be a resilient foe.[179]

The incumbent also profited from the relentless hostility of the state's most influential paper, the *New York Times,* to "Bobby-come-lately," a figure for whom the Senate was a stepping stone to higher office.[180] The unfavorable coverage culminated in a mid-October endorsement in which the *Times* described Keating as an "enlightened, industrious liberal" but focused on vitriolic personal opposition to Kennedy: the former attorney general, the editors claimed, "is now attempting to use New York and the senatorial office in a relentless quest for greater political power."[181] Other liberals joined the crusade. Gore Vidal organized a "Democrats for Keating" committee that included I. F. Stone, Carey McWilliams, James Baldwin, Richard Hofstadter, Paul Newman, and Barbara Tuchman.[182]

By early October a Kraft poll showed Keating with the slimmest of advantages; the pollster reported to the administration that Kennedy was "destroying himself every day by milking his brother."[183] That problem was reinforced by what columnist Marguerite Higgins termed a "not-so-subtle whispering campaign" that the president would be "secretly delighted" to see Kennedy lose.[184] In Brooklyn political circles the joke circulated, "I'm for Keating because he's for Johnson but you don't know who Kennedy's for."[185]

[178] *Congressional Quarterly Weekly Report*, 2 Oct. 1964, p. 2282.

[179] "Memo: To All Advance Men," n.d., Box 24, Robert Kennedy Senate Papers, John F. Kennedy Presidential Library; *New York Times*, 27 Sept. 1964; *The New Republic*, 16 Sept. 1964.

[180] Jeff Shesol, *Mutual Contempt: Lyndon Johnson, Robert Kennedy, and the Feud That Defined a Decade* (New York: W. W. Norton, 1998), p. 181.

[181] *New York Times*, 18 Oct. 1964.

[182] Arthur Schlesinger, Jr., *Robert Kennedy and His Times* (Boston: Houghton Mifflin, 1978), p. 669.

[183] President Johnson, Walter Jenkins, and Bill Moyers, 10:38 A.M., 10 Oct. 1964, Tape WH6410.05, Citation #5851, LBJ Recordings; see also *Los Angeles Times*, 9 Oct. 1964.

[184] *Newsday*, 14 Oct. 1964.

[185] Bill Haddad to Robert Kennedy, 11 Oct. 1964, Box 37, Robert Kennedy Senate Papers, John F. Kennedy Presidential Library.

Richard Starnes, a political columnist for the *New York World-Telegram,* observed that for Kennedy "a defeat is a coattail victory."[186] But by October the candidate tentatively reached out to Washington, putting Johnson in a bind. There was, obviously, no love lost between the two men: when Kennedy had submitted his formal resignation, the president was reluctant to even pose for a picture with him, commenting that "it would be kind of hypocritical for both of us."[187] Now, as Kennedy requested quiet assistance, Johnson initially did little to help. To fortify his standing with Jewish voters, Kennedy solicited aid from White House counsel Mike Feldman, but the president vetoed the idea. When word arrived that Kennedy's brother-in-law and campaign manager, Steve Smith, wanted to talk to Johnson about a presidential visit to the Empire State, the president demurred: "If the man, the dictator, the man himself can't do it..." Any approach, Johnson maintained, had to result from having "the Attorney General deal with me."[188] Kennedy swallowed his pride. The president obliged and campaigned enthusiastically for Kennedy when he was in New York for the Alfred Smith Memorial Dinner – the day, ironically, that Johnson received the news about Jenkins's arrest.[189]

Kennedy also retooled his effort, taking advice to heighten criticism of his Republican opponent's liberal credentials.[190] He started appearing on the campaign trail more often with other prominent New York Democrats, notably Robert Wagner and Averell Harriman, and touted endorsements from national figures such as Harry Truman, Robert McNamara, and Treasury Secretary Douglas Dillon. He asked influential intellectuals, such as Arthur Schlesinger, Jr., and John Kenneth Galbraith, to speak before New York City reform groups to firm up his support from this normally reliable Democratic constituency.[191] He changed his campaign slogan to "Get on the Johnson-Humphrey-Kennedy Team" to encourage a coattail effect. Finally, Kennedy, who had husbanded

[186] *New York World-Telegram*, 23 Sept. 1964.

[187] President Johnson and George Reedy, 11:39 A.M., 3 Sept. 1964, Tape WH6409.03, Citation #5450, LBJ Recordings.

[188] President Johnson, Walter Jenkins, and Bill Moyers, 10:38 A.M., 10 Oct. 1964, Tape WH6410.05, Citation #5851, LBJ Recordings.

[189] *Los Angeles Times*, 18 Oct. 1964.

[190] John Douglas to Robert Kennedy, 5 Oct. 1964, Box 37, Robert Kennedy Senate Papers, John F. Kennedy Presidential Library; see also *New York Journal-American*, 14 Oct. 1964.

[191] Bill Haddad memorandum, 20 Oct. 1964, Box 37, Robert Kennedy Senate Papers, John F. Kennedy Presidential Library.

his financial resources, began his television campaign three weeks from Election Day.[192] These changes produced an almost immediate effect. When Larry O'Brien visited the state on October 17, he found the campaign "in better shape that I thought it would be from the reports I had received prior to my arrival."[193]

The strategic shake-up proved more than sufficient to change the campaign's momentum. Keating countered with extreme arguments – such as his claim that the Soviet Central Communist Committee had issued a directive to "purge" him from the Senate.[194] A few days later, the incumbent contended that Egyptian president Nasser had also targeted his reelection.[195] A Keating aide blamed the senator's slide on the fact that the voters were "not intelligent and sophisticated enough to see through the fact that Kennedy is picking up only certain votes and blowing them up out of proportion."[196] But Kennedy, worried about overconfidence, again turned to Johnson for assistance. In the final week of October, he asked the president for another brief campaign swing before the scheduled Madison Square Garden address. Johnson demurred, citing a tight schedule, but Kennedy pleaded, noting that "it would really be a big help."[197] The president demanded one condition – he wanted the former attorney general to ask civil rights leaders to maximize their efforts against John Williams.

While Kennedy's election looked increasingly likely, other key Senate races did not provide similarly encouraging news for the Democrats. In mid-October Lou Harris reported that Pierre Salinger was fading, "and it doesn't look good."[198] In Nevada Republican Paul Laxalt unveiled a brutally effective television commercial linking Howard Cannon to Bobby Baker, implying that the incumbent was ethically unfit to serve in the Senate.[199] (Even Cannon conceded that Laxalt "used the Bobby Baker

[192] *New York Times*, 14 Oct. 1964.

[193] Larry O'Brien to Steve Smith and Robert Kennedy, 17 Oct. 1964, Box 37, Robert Kennedy Senate Papers, John F. Kennedy Presidential Library.

[194] *New York Post*, 22 Oct. 1964.

[195] Bill Haddad memorandum, 29 Oct. 1964, Box 37, Robert Kennedy Senate Papers, John F. Kennedy Presidential Library.

[196] Dave Stratton, quoted in Bill Haddad memorandum, 24 Oct. 1964, Box 37, Robert Kennedy Senate Papers, John F. Kennedy Presidential Library.

[197] President Johnson and Robert Kennedy, 11:45 P.M., 26 Oct. 1964, Tape WH6410.15, Citation #5968, LBJ Recordings.

[198] President Johnson, Walter Jenkins, and Bill Moyers, 10:38 A.M., 10 Oct. 1964, Tape WH6410.05, Citation #5851, LBJ Recordings.

[199] *Las Vegas Review-Journal*, 27 Oct. 1964.

FIGURE 6-4. President Johnson campaigning in New York City with Robert Kennedy, October 1964. As he fell behind incumbent Kenneth Keating in the polls, Kennedy tied himself to Johnson's coattails, asking voters to join the "Johnson-Humphrey-Kennedy Team." © Courtesy of the Lyndon Baines Johnson Presidential Library. Photo by Cecil Stoughton.

issue on me quite badly.")[200] The Texas contest between George Bush and Ralph Yarborough showed signs of a tight finish, although, since Bush had linked his campaign so closely to Goldwater, the Arizonan's late collapse improved Yarborough's chances. And in Pennsylvania, lingering tension from the primary hurt Genevieve Blatt; in Philadelphia's ethnic wards, Frank Smith's Democratic machine openly urged a Johnson-Scott ticket.[201]

[200] President Johnson and Howard Cannon, later including Hubert Humphrey, 9:29 P.M., 4 Nov. 1964, Tape WH6411.05, Citation #6181, LBJ Recordings.

[201] *Philadelphia Inquirer*, 25 Oct. 1964.

With the outcome of the presidential campaign all but decided, more attention turned to such congressional contests. The National Committee for an Effective Congress, a liberal advocacy group, cautioned in late October against a surge of "Goldwaterism" in Congress and contended – in words that must have made Johnson cringe – that "the 1964 election is unique in that one will have to study the congressional returns in order to interpret the meaning of the presidential outcome."[202] The *Washington Star*'s Gould Lincoln seconded the NCEC's prediction, commenting that Goldwater's candidacy could harm the Republican moderates one last time: the Arizona senator's weakness in states where GOP moderates faced tough election contests – such as Ohio, New York, Pennsylvania, Hawaii, and Maryland – might be impossible for them to overcome. On the other hand, Goldwater figured to run better in states like Arizona, California, Oklahoma, Wyoming, and Utah, where the Republicans had nominated right-wing Senate candidates.[203]

House races, typically more susceptible to presidential coattails, were even harder to forecast; a generation had passed since a top-of-the-ticket candidate whose lead resembled Johnson's. At the start of the year, both parties thought the GOP had a chance of recapturing control of the House.[204] That prediction was no longer tenable by the autumn, but few foresaw large-scale Democratic gains; of the 81 seats decided in 1962 by 55 percent or less of the vote, 41 were held by Democrats, 40 by Republicans.[205] As late as mid-October, optimistic Democrats were hoping for a 10-seat pickup; at the same time, Johnson aide Henry Wilson, fearful of a weak Democratic performance in the South, speculated "we could wind up *losing* seats."[206] Larry O'Brien, on the other hand, discerned the possibility for a stronger showing. On October 13 he listed 13 Republican House seats as likely to fall to the Democrats, with 17 more GOP seats considered toss-ups – all while the Democrats were sure to lose only one seat they possessed going into the election.[207] O'Brien, like nearly all political observers, underestimated the effects of the Alabama Democratic Party's collapse, and he also misjudged the weakness of

[202] *Washington Star*, 28 Oct. 1964.

[203] *Washington Star*, 20 Oct. 1964.

[204] *Time*, 9 Oct. 1964.

[205] Harold Faber, ed., *The Road to the White House: The Story of the 1964 Election by the Staff of the New York Times* (New York: McGraw-Hill, 1965), p. 223.

[206] Henry Wilson to Larry O'Brien, 12 Oct. 1964, Box 2, Office Files of Henry Wilson, Lyndon B. Johnson Presidential Library; *U.S. News & World Report*, 19 Oct. 1964.

[207] Larry O'Brien to President Johnson, 13 Oct. 1964, Box 85, WHCF-PL, Lyndon B. Johnson Presidential Library.

incumbent Democrat Ralph Harding of Idaho. Otherwise, his predictions came close to the mark.

As the campaign neared its conclusion, commentators anticipated its legacy, and few had anything positive to say. Stewart Alsop announced that "this has been, by common consent, a dreadful campaign," which tarnished the reputation of every participant.[208] To the editors at *Time*, "the 1964 presidential campaign has been one of the most disappointing ever" – the fault of the president, who "had a ready-made opportunity to set forth national policies and win a mandate for them," but instead spoke "only in generalities."[209] Scotty Reston lamented in the *New York Times*, "The campaign has disillusioned and divided the people, revived their ancient feelings that politics is a dirty business, raised doubts about the integrity of the press, and even cast a shadow on the White House."[210]

A few challenged the conventional wisdom. In the *New Republic* Richard Strout called the election "boring past endurance, but historically fascinating too." Its result would give the president a good deal of freedom of action, since Johnson would emerge from the contest without having "had to define his positions."[211] The *Christian Science Monitor*'s Erwin Canham likewise guessed the campaign had bored most Americans – it lacked suspense, generated strident political advertising, and ignored important policy questions. But Canham also speculated that future historians would look back on the contest and see that "the whole political spectrum has moved to the right," with the American people "increasingly cautious" about liberal social and economic legislation.[212] Perhaps, in that sense, Johnson's strategy of avoiding detailed discussions of the issues was politically shrewder than even the president realized.

In a whirlwind final 100 hours of the campaign, Johnson himself was not considering his historical legacy. Terrified by rumors that the Republicans would "drop a big bombshell" on Halloween – allegedly that a member of the Cabinet was a closeted homosexual – he turned, yet again, to J. Edgar Hoover for reassurance.[213] The night before, the FBI

[208] Stewart Alsop, "The Campaign: What Does It Add Up To?" *Saturday Evening Post*, 3 Nov. 1964.
[209] *Time*, 30 Oct. 1964; see also *The Reporter*, 5 Nov. 1964.
[210] *New York Times*, 29 Oct. 1964.
[211] *The New Republic*, 31 Oct. 1964.
[212] *Christian Science Monitor*, 29 Oct. 1964.
[213] President Johnson and Dean Rusk, 6:25 P.M., 30 Oct. 1964, Tape WH6410.16, Citation #5986, LBJ Recordings.

director lent Johnson raw FBI files on a host of prominent Republicans.[214] Now, in a conversation replete with double entendre (Johnson told Hoover, whose sexual orientation generated speculation both then and now, "I guess you're going to have to teach me something" about how to identify gay behavior, since "I don't know anything about it"; Hoover responded that with the typical homosexual, "It was just the suspicion that his mannerisms and so forth were such that they were suspicious"), the FBI director correctly expressed confidence that a GOP October surprise would fizzle.[215]

Thus assured that no final crisis would derail his effort, Johnson hit the hustings as aggressively as he had at any point in the campaign. His last formal address – at an event billed as "USA for LBJ" – came at Madison Square Garden.[216] The president charged that Goldwater and his followers would tear apart the country's social fabric. "Extremism," he declared, "in the pursuit of the presidency is an unpardonable vice. Moderation in the affairs of the nation is the highest virtue."[217] The president then returned home to Texas, addressing huge rallies in Houston and Austin. Making his final television appearance of the campaign, from Austin on Election Eve, Johnson told Republicans that "only a massive defeat" would drive Goldwater followers "from their place of power."[218]

On the ground, meanwhile, Democratic operatives busied the get-out-the-vote effort, lest what the DNC termed "Dewey-itis" cloud the president's election prospects. The regular Democratic Party operation, Rowe's citizen committees, AFL-CIO political staffers, and "LBJ volunteers" coordinated their activity. Roughly 300,000 campaign workers were ready to go into the field on Election Day, centered on the major industrial states of the Middle Atlantic and Midwest. These workers used traditional tactics – car pools, radio announcements, supplying baby-sitters, sound trucks, and last-minute telegrams – to get voters to the polls.[219] The DNC's final advertisement stressed the president's newest campaign theme, arguing that "a huge landslide vote will really show where our nation stands on the great issues of modern times."[220] Democrats also planned to monitor Republican "poll watchers," who, under the guise

[214] Shesol, *Mutual Contempt*, p. 228.

[215] President Johnson and J. Edgar Hoover, 10:35 A.M., 31 Oct. 1964, Tape WH6410.16, Citation #5989, LBJ Recordings.

[216] Jerry Finkelstein to Mary Lasker, 13 Oct. 1964, Box 155, Mary Lasker Papers, Columbia University.

[217] *New York Times*, 1 Nov. 1964.

[218] *New York Times*, 3 Nov. 1964.

[219] *Christian Science Monitor*, 31 Oct. 1964.

[220] Perlstein, *Before the Storm*, p. 468.

FIGURE 6-5. President Johnson, in Austin, Texas, Election Eve, November 2, 1964. © Courtesy of the Lyndon Baines Johnson Presidential Library. Photo by Cecil Stoughton.

of guarding against voter fraud, could intimidate minorities and lower-income whites into not voting.[221]

After his Election Eve rally, Johnson confided to some neighbors from the Texas hill country, "I have spent my life getting ready for this moment."[222] He rose at 6:30 the next morning and drove the First Lady to their polling place in Johnson City, Precinct 4 of Blanco County. The Johnsons voted at 8:07 A.M., the third and fourth voters to cast their ballots.[223] He spent most of the day in bed, with pains in his back, head, and hips. As he told McGeorge Bundy, "I didn't know how much I'd been doing, and how high up on the mountain I'd been. I've been keyed too high." The president amused himself by making side bets with aides about whether John Williams would be defeated.[224]

Several hundred miles to the west of Johnson, Barry Goldwater and his wife arrived at the polls at 8:30 A.M. and waited in line for over an hour to cast their ballots. When Goldwater emerged from the voting booth, a reporter teasingly asked him if he had split his ticket. The GOP nominee cryptically responded, "I always split it."[225] (He provided no further explanation.) The senator then returned home, where he spent part of his day transplanting cactus plants. He seemed relieved that the contest had ended; Goldwater told reporters that the United States should imitate Britain and shorten its election campaigns: "If you can't get your point across in four weeks," he believed, "you ought to give it up."[226] He did receive a bit of good news – eight voters in Dixville Notch, New Hampshire all voted, per custom, just after polls opened at 12:01 A.M., and all eight cast their ballots for him.[227]

Just before 7:00 Eastern time, the president learned that polling by Oliver Quayle projected a Johnson victory with 63 percent, and that by Harris with 66 percent – figures that would prove overly optimistic.[228] With allegations of vote fraud delaying the South Carolina count, Indiana and Kentucky, whose polls closed at 6:00 P.M., became the first two states

[221] *Christian Science Monitor*, 31 Oct. 1964.
[222] *New York Times*, 3 Nov. 1964.
[223] *Baltimore Sun*, 4 Nov. 1964.
[224] President Johnson and McGeorge Bundy, later including Bill Moyers, Paul Poppel, and Dean Rusk, 5:11 P.M., 3 Nov. 1964, Tape WH6411.01, Citation #6108, LBJ Recordings.
[225] *New York Times*, 4 Nov. 1964.
[226] *Baltimore Sun*, 4 Nov. 1964.
[227] *Baltimore Sun*, 3 Nov. 1964.
[228] President Johnson and Bill Moyers, 5:52 P.M., 3 Nov. 1964, Tape WH6411.01, Citation #6118, LBJ Recordings.

to provide vote tallies. Republicans had carried Indiana in every election since 1936; Kentucky had been in the GOP column in 1956 and 1960. This night, both went to Johnson – with 64 percent in Kentucky and an impressive 56 percent in Indiana.

In addition, returns from the two states offered the first glimpse that the presidential landslide would affect House races more than many had expected. In Indiana Democrat Andrew Jacobs captured an open Indianapolis seat; more startling, Lee Hamilton, later chair of the House Foreign Affairs Committee, stunned Representative Earl Wilson in a traditionally Republican district. Five other incumbent Republicans, including Minority Leader Charles Halleck, prevailed with less than 55 percent of the vote. (This was a far cry from the situation just before the San Francisco convention, when one Indiana Republican congressman stated that because Goldwater was "immensely popular" in his home state, "I'm going to be right with him every chance I get.")[229] Across the Ohio River in Kentucky, Gene Snyder, a conservative, strongly partisan Republican, was ousted by more than 16,000 votes. Johnson rejoiced that "we beat that son of a bitch."[230]

Final returns from New England showed that John Kennedy's stronghold had emerged as the strongest Johnson region in the country. For only the second time in its 145-year history, Maine voted Democratic, giving Johnson 68.8 percent of the vote; Democrat William Hathaway captured the previously Republican 2nd District. In neighboring New Hampshire, the president tallied 63.9 percent of the vote; the Granite State reelected Democratic governor John King, ousted one Republican congressman, and came within 237 votes of sending a Democrat from the 2nd District for the first time since 1912. In Vermont, which had last voted Democratic for president in the 1820s, Johnson captured 66.3 percent. In Massachusetts the president received more votes than had Ted Kennedy in his successful reelection to the Senate. Rhode Island, meanwhile, was Johnson's best state, with 80.9 percent of the vote. And Connecticut, home state of DNC chairman John Bailey, gave 67.8 percent of its votes to the Johnson-Humphrey ticket while retiring its sole Republican congressman.

Throughout the evening Johnson closely followed returns from Delaware's Senate race – "God, I pray on that one," he told Moyers.[231]

[229] *Wall Street Journal*, 13 July 1964.

[230] President Johnson and Bill Moyers, 6:23 P.M., 3 Nov. 1964, Tape WH6411.01, Citation #6128, LBJ Recordings.

[231] President Johnson and Bill Moyers, 9:01 P.M., 3 Nov. 1964, Tape WH6411.02, Citation #6137, LBJ Recordings.

With polls closed for just over two hours and all precincts from Wilmington and Dover having reported, Elbert Carvel had seized a narrow advantage over John Williams. But as the traditionally Democratic – but conservative – rural counties reported in, Carvel's lead evaporated. Just after midnight, the last votes were counted. The final tally showed Williams prevailing with 51.7 percent of the vote, even as Johnson carried the state with 61 percent and Democrat Harris McDowell took the at-large House race with 59 percent of the vote. "God damn it, we could have won the Delaware one," the president told Robert Kennedy. "We ought to have won."[232]

With Carvel's loss in Delaware dashing the president's hopes in the Senate race he considered the year's most important, attention turned to New York, whose polls closed at 9:00 P.M. Kennedy prevailed with 56 percent of the vote, as part of a Democratic sweep that saw the party seize six House seats and win control of both houses of the state legislature. The key, of course, was the performance of the president, who topped the ticket by 2.56 million votes. As Kennedy delivered his victory statement, Johnson fumed at what he considered Kennedy's insufficient gratitude. "Very frankly," he reasoned, it took Kennedy "a long time to admit that the President had anything to do with it. There's 1,000 people in the room, and they kept thanking about – he's got county judge so-and-so, and county surrogate so-and-so, and county so-and-so, but the guy that campaigned up there through 33 miles of Brooklyn, and all the places, and carried it over 2 million, he just never could find it, while I was out bragging on his brother. And I just guess he can't bring himself to it." Instead, it seemed as if Kennedy wanted to pretend that "Averell Harriman was the hero of the deal."[233]

During his final campaign swing through Pennsylvania, Johnson promised Frank Smith, the Democratic city chairman in Philadelphia, a White House dinner if his vote in Philadelphia exceeded that of Kennedy in 1960. Smith had no trouble delivering. But while Smith and the party organization went all out for the president, they did little for Genevieve Blatt, who suffered massive defections in the city's Italian-American wards. Early reports showed Blatt with a sizeable lead, but in the end the difference between Blatt's Philadelphia total and that of the president more than provided the margin of victory for incumbent Hugh Scott,

[232] President Johnson and Robert Kennedy, 11:55 P.M., 3 Nov. 1964, Tape WH6411.02, Citation #6142, LBJ Recordings.

[233] President Johnson, Bill Moyers, and McGeorge Bundy, 10:34 A.M., 4 Nov. 1964, Tape WH6411.03, Citation #6158, LBJ Recordings.

who ran more than 15 points ahead of Goldwater and secured a second term with just over 50 percent of the vote.[234] It would be another fourteen years before the first woman who had not followed her late husband in Congress won a Senate election – Nancy Landon Kassebaum, from Kansas, in 1978.

Returns from the first Midwestern states provided more evidence than had Pennsylvania of Johnson's coattails. In Michigan Johnson swept in a trio of Democratic House challengers and helped Senator Phil Hart win easily. Ticket splitting, however, saved the incumbent governor, liberal Republican George Romney, who ran 24 points ahead of Goldwater to win with 56 percent of the vote. In Minnesota Johnson sailed to victory, with almost 65 percent of the vote; in Illinois the president's 881,000-vote margin rescued Democratic governor Otto Kerner, who had trailed his GOP challenger, Charles Percy, throughout the campaign. And Ohio, despite its Republican leanings, never was in doubt: Johnson secured 63 percent of the vote, helping the Democrats to pick up four House seats and, most remarkably, embattled incumbent senator Stephen Young to win reelection. Only in Wisconsin, where the unpopularity of Governor John Reynolds had weakened the Democratic ticket, were the results mixed: Reynolds lost to the state's Republican lieutenant governor, Warren Knowles, and Senator William Proxmire barely prevailed. But Johnson nevertheless captured the state with 62 percent of the vote, helping Democrats Lynn Stalbaum and John Race score upset victories in House contests.

In an act that many viewed as petulant, Goldwater refused to deliver a concession speech, depriving Johnson of the traditional Election Night victory address. Instead, the senator stopped watching the returns at 8:00 P.M. Arizona time, retired to answer mail, and then went to bed. The following morning, the Arizona senator released a cold statement, congratulating Johnson on his victory, and adding, "There is much to be done in Vietnam, Cuba, and the problem of law and order in this country, and a productive economy. Communism remains our No. 1 obstacle to peace and I know that all Americans will join with you in honest solutions to these problems."[235] For good measure, Goldwater leveled strong – and, in many cases, justified – criticism of political commentators for their exaggerated attacks against his positions.[236]

[234] *Baltimore Sun*, 4 Nov. 1964.
[235] *New York Times*, 5 Nov. 1964.
[236] *Baltimore Sun*, 5 Nov. 1964.

While Goldwater went to bed, the president was still glued to the televised returns. With South Carolina having joined Mississippi, Alabama, and Louisiana in the Republican column, any chance that Johnson would have at matching FDR's 1936 total number of victorious states depended on his carrying traditionally Republican states such as Nebraska and South Dakota, winning Goldwater's home state of Arizona, which remained too close to call well into the night, and not losing any more Southern states. The traditionally Republican plains states would cross over in the presidential contest, but the president's bid in Arizona came up just short: Goldwater carried his home state 50.5 percent to 49.5 percent, a margin of less than 5,000 votes.

Early in the evening, Georgia governor Carl Sanders assured Moyers that the president would carry his state, and pollster Quayle predicted a Johnson victory with 52 percent of the vote. But, as occurred throughout the evening, pollsters' projections consistently ran between 2 and 5 percent above Johnson's actual vote. In the Peach State, Goldwater's total exceeded even that margin of error; the GOP nominee swept to victory with over 54 percent. The president admitted that he was "sorry" about the result: "I didn't care about the other Southern states. Louisiana is a bunch of crooks, and Mississippi's too ignorant to know any better, and Alabama's the same way, but Georgia knows better."[237]

In Alabama Goldwater's win produced a stunning GOP sweep – Republicans seized five House seats and probably would have taken the other two had they filed candidates. In Georgia, however, local Democrats remained strong: Republicans gained only one seat, in the newly created 3rd District (suburban Atlanta), where the Democratic nominee had refused to endorse the president. In metropolitan Atlanta, Charles Weltner survived despite his vote for the Civil Rights Act, and in the rural 9th District, Phil Landrum sailed to victory, unharmed by his having sponsored the administration's anti-poverty legislation.

Reports of various improprieties marred voting throughout the South. In South Carolina initial returns from predominantly minority precincts were inexplicably delayed.[238] In Alabama and Louisiana Goldwater volunteers passed out fliers from the "Negro Protective League," informing first-time black voters to report to the sheriff's office to address unresolved traffic tickets, tax disputes, or job performance complaints before

[237] President Johnson, Bill Moyers, and McGeorge Bundy, 9:56 A.M., 4 Nov. 1964, Tape WH6411.03, Citation #6158, LBJ Recordings.

[238] President Johnson and Bill Moyers, 6:23 P.M., 3 Nov. 1964, Tape WH6411.01, Citation #6128, LBJ Recordings.

they could vote.[239] Johnson denounced such "ballot security" measures in minority precincts throughout the South as "the most fascist operation that I've ever seen."[240]

The president did rally for narrow victories in Florida and Tennessee – in the latter state helping two liberal Senate candidates, Albert Gore and Ross Bass, eke out victories. (Both Gore and Bass would lose the next time they faced the voters.) He also scored a mild surprise in North Carolina and a more expected triumph in Virginia. But the only truly positive Southern news for Johnson came from Texas. Although he ran behind John Connally's total, the president crushed Goldwater in his home state, taking 63.3 percent and winning by more than 700,000 votes. This margin helped Ralph Yarborough beat back George Bush in the Senate race and overwhelmed the House delegation's two Republicans, Bruce Alger and Ed Foreman.

After realizing that Goldwater would not deliver a concession speech, the president decided to address his supporters in Austin. Appearing before a cheering throng at 1:40 A.M., Johnson stated simply, "I doubt if there has ever been so many people saying so many things alike on decision day." The results, he claimed, provided "a mandate for unity, for a government that serves no special interest."[241] Even in victory, Johnson struggled to articulate a concrete agenda.

After concluding his address, the president turned his attention to Senate contests from the West Coast. Roy Elson's bid in Arizona came up short, though by an exceedingly narrow margin: Elson ran only one percentage point behind the president's total in the state, a performance better than all but six other Democratic Senate candidates. In neighboring Nevada, it took more than a day to count the final ballots, with Howard Cannon edging Republican challenger Paul Laxalt by a margin of 67,303 to 67,138 votes. And in Hawaii racial and union politics allowed Republican incumbent Hiram Fong to hold off Thomas Gill, a result that many political insiders considered the biggest upset of the evening.

But the major Western news came from California. Johnson carried the state with 59.8 percent of the vote, but he was outperformed by the "yes" vote on Proposition 14, to nullify the state's open housing

[239] President Johnson and Hubert Humphrey, 5:57 P.M., 3 Nov. 1964, Tape WH6411.01, Citation #6121, LBJ Recordings.

[240] President Johnson and Richard Daley, 11:42 A.M., 4 Nov. 1964, Tape WH6411.04, Citation #6167, LBJ Recordings.

[241] *Baltimore Sun*, 5 Nov. 1964.

law. Those figures played a key role in the Senate outcome: Republican George Murphy began the evening with a small lead and retained it throughout the night, eventually winning with 51 percent of the vote. As one prominent state Democrat observed, backlash voters cast their ballots for the president but voted Republican for Senate.[242] California thus became the only state in 1964 in which a Democratic Senate seat fell into Republican hands. The *Christian Science Monitor* called Murphy's triumph "one of the most amazing come-from-behind victories in California political history."[243]

From late-reporting Iowa, Johnson learned of the scope of the Democrats' House triumphs: initial reports suggested that what the president called "that damn Republican, *mean,* delegation that was up there in the House of Representatives that harasses me all the time" would switch to a 7–0 Democratic majority for the 89th Congress.[244] John Culver, Ted Kennedy's law school roommate and one of the most highly touted Democratic challengers in the country, bested Representative James Bromwell to launch a career that would culminate in his election to the Senate. The seat of retiring Representative Clifford Hoeven fell to the Democrats, while Republicans John Kyl and Ben Jensen, a hard-line conservative who served as ranking Republican on the House Appropriations Committee, both badly lost. In the 1st District, John Schmidhauser, a political science professor at the University of Iowa, barely defeated incumbent Fred Schwengel. Schmidhauser, a first-time candidate whose family relied on cash donations from friends and a large vegetable garden to make ends meet during his campaign, logged 30,000 miles crisscrossing the southeastern Iowa district. Without funds to advertise on television until just before Election Day, he relied on personal appearances, always wary, as Joseph Matthewson of the *Wall Street Journal* noted, of lapsing "into an academic style that appears to befuddle many of his hearers."[245] Meanwhile, in the south-central 3rd District, an unknown 29-year-old Democrat, Stephen Peterson, led H. R. Gross, the president's most acerbic critic in the House, when Johnson went to bed just after 4:00 A.M. As events would develop, the congressman the president called "that damn

[242] *New York Times*, 5 Nov. 1964.

[243] *Christian Science Monitor*, 5 Nov. 1964.

[244] President Johnson and Harold Hughes, 3:15 A.M., 4 Nov. 1964, Tape WH6411.03, Citation #6156, LBJ Recordings.

[245] *Wall Street Journal*, 12 Oct. 1964.

Gross that gives us hell every day" rallied to win by less than 500 votes.[246] Surely Johnson wished that he had devoted a share of the resources allocated to ousting John Williams to Gross's Iowa district.

After a few hours of sleep for Johnson, the full scope of his triumph became clear. The Johnson-Humphrey ticket had prevailed by 15,522,995 votes, carrying every state outside of the Old Confederacy except for Arizona. A two-seat Democratic gain in the Senate gave the party a 68–32 majority, its largest since Franklin Roosevelt's presidency. In the House the conservative coalition that had first formed in 1938 had been shattered. The Democrats seized a 295 to 140 majority that came primarily at the expense of conservative Republicans in the Northeast and Midwest. ("Some of those fellows can thank you for the rest of their lives," Larry O'Brien informed the president.)[247] Not since the congressional session following FDR's 1936 triumph had the Democrats possessed such a margin in the House. In 1937 the House had 333 Democratic members and 89 Republicans; one of those Democrats was Lyndon Baines Johnson.

Was such an overwhelming victory inevitable? Probably not: at the very least, a politician more skillful than Goldwater might have successfully exploited the Jenkins arrest. Certainly Lodge, who had planned to base his campaign on the twin themes of personal ethics and foreign policy expertise, would have been perfectly suited to take advantage of the ethics issues around the Jenkins arrest – followed quickly by the twin foreign policy crises of Khrushchev's fall from power and the Chinese nuclear bomb.

Even Lodge, however, would have confronted a president so intent on victory that he instructed his longtime counselor to remove from a White House safe, just before FBI agents arrived on the scene, potentially incriminating documents about campaign finance irregularities. No action over the course of the campaign more clearly demonstrated the description by Rev. Francis Sayre, dean of Washington's Episcopal Cathedral, of Johnson as "a man whose public house is splendid in its every appearance, but whose private lack of ethic must inevitably introduce termites at the very foundation."[248]

[246] President Johnson and Harold Hughes, 3:15 A.M., 4 Nov. 1964, Tape WH6411.03, Citation #6156, LBJ Recordings.

[247] President Johnson and Larry O'Brien, later including Mildred O'Brien, 2:24 A.M., 4 Nov. 1964, Tape WH6411.02, Citation #6150, LBJ Recordings.

[248] *Time*, 25 Sept. 1964.

In the end Johnson's desire for a massive personal triumph – chiefly by bettering FDR's 1936 totals and ousting his most intense congressional critics, such as John Williams and Ed Foreman – dominated his campaign strategy. Despite the overwhelming victory, the election outcome would not trigger a realignment. Long-term Democratic strength would depend on Johnson's continuing popularity – and as the president came under criticism for his Vietnam policies, urban unrest, and signs of economic difficulties, other Democratic officeholders would suffer.

Epilogue

Virtually every contemporary political commentator remarked on the impressive size of Johnson's triumph. But beyond that point, the president's performance received mixed reviews. The *New York Times* considered it a "tragedy" that the contest featured "no meaningful discussion of the real issues that confront the United States."[1] In the *Washington Post,* Walter Lippmann rejoiced that the election proved the "fallacy" of a silent conservative majority; he considered the outcome a mandate for both parties "to seek their strength and define their issues within, not against, the prevailing consensus."[2] The *Christian Science Monitor* agreed that Johnson's "mandate is that the American people wish to continue in the path of moderation in their domestic and foreign policies."[3]

Al Otten of the *Wall Street Journal* offered a more pessimistic interpretation. He termed the Johnson victory "a triumph for conservatism," with the voters asking the president "not so much to charge forward boldly as to maintain current comforts." Since the president failed to campaign on a positive agenda, Otten felt that Johnson could expect little tangible long-term benefits from his victory.[4] A few days later, the savvy Washington bureau chief wondered whether the size of the triumph could even have negative effects, by intensifying Johnson's "driving ambitions [and] towering ego." Already Johnson had "pushed presidential power in some rather dubious directions," as in his use of the FBI in the Jenkins case or his role in the leak of Don Reynolds's personnel file.

[1] *New York Times*, 4 Nov. 1964.

[2] *Washington Post*, 5 Nov. 1964.

[3] *Christian Science Monitor*, 5 Nov. 1964.

[4] *Wall Street Journal*, 3 Nov. 1964.

Now this "abnormally egotistic man" would face fewer intragovernmental restraints, even as he encountered heightened skepticism from a press corps that no longer worried about a Goldwater election.[5]

The president desperately sought to counter such sentiments. He complained that the press – especially "the little Kennedy folks around" – were intent on writing "that nobody loves Johnson. They're going to have it built up by January that I didn't get any mandate at all, that I was just the lesser of two evils, and the people didn't care, and so on and so forth." Commentators, he fretted, ignored all the evidence from his campaign appearances that he received from voters "the greatest *affection* that had ever been demonstrated before, and the greatest loyalty." Instead, "they write, 'Well, the lesser of two evils. Corn pone. Southern.' "[6]

But, of course, Johnson's own campaign tactics exposed him to such attacks. According to a Gallup poll taken eight days after the greatest Democratic popular triumph in history, a mere 51 percent of Americans believed that liberals had better policies, as opposed to 49 percent who responded that conservatives did. And on the question of which party voters would prefer if the United States featured a "liberal" party and a "conservative" party, 37 percent indicated they would affiliate with the liberals, 34 percent with the conservatives, and 29 percent were unsure.[7] These numbers did not imply a convincing ideological mandate for Johnson.

It would take some time, however, for the full effects of Johnson's failure to achieve a realigning victory to manifest themselves. In the short term, Johnson presided over one of the most productive legislative sessions in American history. In the two years after the election, Congress established the hallmarks of the Great Society – passing the Voting Rights Act, setting up Medicare and Medicaid, and pushing through legislation addressing issues such as consumer rights, environmental protection, and federal government support for the arts and humanities.

In the long term, however, the president could not maintain his 1964 coalition. The Americanization of the war in Vietnam, white voters' increasing concern with urban unrest, and the early signs of an inflationary spiral resulting from the president's "guns and butter" economic policies set the stage for a Republican surge in the 1966 elections. Democrats lost three seats in the Senate and 47 in the House; liberal freshmen in states like Iowa, Wisconsin, Michigan, and Ohio proved particularly vulnerable.

[5] *Wall Street Journal*, 6 Nov. 1964.

[6] President Johnson and Edwin Weisl, 12:46 P.M., 4 Nov. 1964, Tape WH6411.04, Citation #6174, LBJ Recordings.

[7] George Gallup, *The Gallup Poll, 1935–1971*, vol. 3, poll for 11 Nov. 1964, p. 1908.

Two years later, Democratic presidential nominee Hubert Humphrey ran more than 18 points behind Johnson's 1964 percentage of the popular vote and lost the election to Republican Richard Nixon. In the ten presidential elections following Johnson's triumph, the Democratic nominee only once received more than half the popular vote, and then barely so (Jimmy Carter's 50.1 percent in 1976). Twice (in 1972 and 1984), the party's presidential candidate managed to carry only one state. Not only, it seemed, did the frontlash fail to sustain itself beyond 1964, but reaction to Johnson's policies, combined with broader changes in the political culture, created a new, Republican-friendly political map.

What, then, is the legacy of the 1964 campaign, and the political culture that surrounded it? First, and most obvious, was the fusion of politics and policy. Never before had an administration's chief political adviser resided in the Oval Office itself – even FDR delegated substantial components of political strategy. For Johnson, no demarcation existed between politics and policy. At times the two needs were in perfect harmony, as with the tax bill and the budget. Presenting the Senate with a budget plan that reduced Kennedy's proposed spending represented the only way that the tax bill could clear the Senate. That this move allowed Johnson to reaffirm his reputation as a fiscally responsible Democrat and rob the Republicans of a line of criticism offered an enormous political bonus.

On other occasions, however, the president had to choose between what would serve him best politically and what seemed like the soundest policy decision. In such cases, without exception, he followed the course that maximized his political benefits. The farm bill exemplified this pattern, but so too did early international initiatives, such as the hard-line responses to Panama and Cuba. Any analysis of Johnson's presidency thus needs to begin with an assumption that the president would not act in a way he believed would cause him political harm.

That said, the manner in which Johnson fused politics and policy differed from more recent practitioners of the art – figures such as the Clintons, Mark Penn, and James Carville among the Democrats, or George W. Bush and Karl Rove among the Republicans. Johnson rarely saw policy initiatives as an opportunity to generate a wedge issue, or to triangulate himself between congressional Democrats and the opposition party, or to diminish popular faith in government. Nor did his campaign rely on scarcely credible spin as a way to woo public opinion. And Johnson never extended a demand for political benefit from policy initiatives throughout the executive branch to the extent seen in either the Clinton or Bush administrations.

Of course, Johnson frequently misinterpreted the political effects of his actions, and no more spectacularly so in his handling of government ethics. From Credit Mobilier to Teapot Dome to "Korea, Communism, and Corruption" in 1952, ethics long had played a prominent role in presidential campaigns. But despite his conviction that his opponents were out to "ruin us and make a Harding out of us," it was the president's own actions that most caused him harm.[8] First, Johnson's tendency to act according to his political instincts caused him to see no problem in using, and abusing, the levers of government to cover up even minor ethical misdeeds. Future chief executives, such as Richard Nixon and Bill Clinton, would share this unfortunate habit. But while Watergate and the Lewinsky affair produced resignation or impeachment, Johnson got away with obstructing administrative and legislative inquiries. He lived in an era with a less suspicious press, and the media's almost unrelenting hostility to Goldwater caused journalists to overlook what seemed like minor indiscretions by the president.

The 1964 election also previewed events to come in the prominence that "morality" would play in political discourse. In attacking the president's ethical improprieties, Barry Goldwater adopted what one commentator described as a "trickle-down" approach to morality, making the argument that the chief executive's personal and political ethics would shape the moral attitude of the nation as a whole. This strategy did not result in Goldwater's election, but for the next four Republican victors in presidential contests – Richard Nixon, Ronald Reagan, George H. W. Bush, and George W. Bush – a promise to restore morality to public life would play a critical element in their appeal.

That these four men even entered the White House testified to another important effect of the 1964 campaign – its failure to emerge as a realigning election. It certainly could have done so. Henry Cabot Lodge's vision of a Republican Party celebrating civil rights, championing a Marshall Plan for the cities, and espousing the foreign policy Establishment's approach to the Cold War represented a very different type of GOP from that which emerged after 1964. At the very least, a Lodge nomination would have delayed the development of the Southern Republican Party; at most, it would have moved the GOP in an entirely different direction ideologically.

The next attempt at realignment came in late August and September, with Johnson's frontlash strategy. The president understood that the Civil

[8] President Johnson and Edwin Weisl, 12:46 P.M., 4 Nov. 1964, Tape WH6411.04, Citation #6174, LBJ Recordings.

Rights Act would permanently alter American political culture – but, unlike virtually every other prominent Democrat, he saw this development as not only a threat but also an opportunity for the party. Perhaps the majority of Southerners would abandon the Democrats, at least in Deep South states like Alabama, Mississippi, Louisiana, and even Georgia. But as figures like Strom Thurmond and John Tower became more the national face of the GOP, a chance existed that moderate Republicans would offset the Southerners' defection by switching from the GOP to the Democrats. To accomplish this goal, however, Johnson needed to achieve his greatest political triumph, practicing historical revisionism to suggest that the Democrats did not threaten the economic interests of the frontlash constituency.

In the end this task proved too much even for a politician as skilled as Lyndon Johnson. As a result, his electoral triumph produced a false sense of party change. Political commentators in early November 1964 wondered if the Republican Party could survive as a political entity. But because Johnson had concluded his campaign not by articulating his postelection agenda but merely by attempting to obtain the greatest possible vote total, his margin of victory served him little long-term good.

That said, the prospect of either a Lodge nomination or the success of Johnson's frontlash strategy should remind historians and political observers that the 1960s-1970s political transformation was not a linear process, with grassroots and demographic shifts inexorably moving the nation to the right. Either a Lodge victory in 1964 or a permanent affiliation by frontlash voters with the Democratic Party – outcomes that were possible, if not likely – would have fundamentally altered subsequent political history. Moreover, while the "Southern Strategy" eventually would work to the Republicans' benefit, in 1964 the backlash vote remained very much confined to a handful of states. The outcome in 1964, in short, suggests that issues of race and racism did not make inevitable a national GOP majority. Outside of the South and (to a lesser extent) California and Idaho, the 1964 pollsters were largely correct: the backlash never emerged as a significant threat to either Johnson or to the Democratic Party as a whole.

The 1964 campaign also represented a moment of transition in American political culture. In some ways it looked backward. It was, for instance, the last presidential election in which the New Deal Coalition of blacks, white ethics, intellectuals, and Southern whites held together. It also was the last contest in which at least one candidate (Goldwater, in this instance) devoted the bulk of his advertising resources to 5- or

30-minute commercials. And it was the final time that a presidential candidate essentially managed his own campaign.

The contest also previewed presidential campaigns to come. As Johnson discovered, a candidate's personal ethics and most aspects of his personal life no longer fell beyond the scope of either media or public interest. The backlash against civil rights divided Democrats, while also providing new openings for the party to upscale social liberals. And spin, tailored messages, negative ads, and opposition research became far more sophisticated campaign practices.

Finally, the campaign revolved around the personality, political abilities, and presidential power of Johnson himself. He produced high drama, as in his October address in New Orleans. He demonstrated remarkable skills of legislative management, as in his manipulation of the farm bill. He showed passion, as when he rebuked Carl Sanders for opposing the MFDP compromise. He displayed a remarkable tin ear to public sentiment, as in his legalistic responses to the Bobby Baker investigation. He was blinded by personal hostility, as when confronting Robert Kennedy or John Williams. He provided keen political insights, as when he recognized the realigning potential of the frontlash vote. And he set aside ethics when politically necessary, as when he ordered Abe Fortas to retrieve the campaign finance documents from Walter Jenkins's safe before FBI agents arrived on the scene.

Through it all, however, Lyndon Johnson was, as Alex Rose recognized at the time, the contest's "star performer."[9]

[9] President Johnson and Alex Rose, 2:22 P.M., 10 Oct. 1964, Tape WH6410.06, Citation #5860, LBJ Recordings.

Index